lonely planet

Chicago

Ryan Ver Berkmoes

LONELY PLANET PUBLICATIONS
Melbourne • Oakland • London • Paris

Chicago
2nd edition – September 2001
First published – May 1998

Published by
Lonely Planet Publications Pty Ltd ABN 36 005 607 983
90 Maribyrnong St, Footscray, Victoria 3011, Australia

Lonely Planet Offices
Australia Locked Bag 1, Footscray, Victoria 3011
USA 150 Linden St, Oakland, CA 94607
UK 10a Spring Place, London NW5 3BH
France 1 rue du Dahomey, 75011 Paris

Photographs
Many of the images in this guide are available for licensing from
Lonely Planet Images.
email: lpi@lonelyplanet.com.au

Front cover photograph
N Michigan Ave, Chicago (Richard Cummins)

Map section photograph
Richard I'Anson

ISBN 1 86450 210 X

text & maps © Lonely Planet 2001
photos © photographers as indicated 2001

Printed by Printed by The Bookmaker International Ltd
Printed in China

Contents

Andy's Jazz Club
Hubbard St. (near
Shaw's Crab House)

The Author

Ryan Ver Berkmoes

Ryan grew up in Santa Cruz, California, but he left at age 17 for college in the Midwest, where he discovered snow. All the joy of this novelty soon wore off. His first job was in Chicago at a small muckraking publication where he had the impressive title of Managing Editor because he was second on a two-person editorial staff and the first person was called Editor. After a year of 60-hour weeks, Ryan took his first European trip, which lasted for seven months and confirmed his long-suspected wanderlust. Since then his byline has appeared in scores of publications, and he has covered everything from wars to bars. He definitely prefers the latter.

With this edition of *Chicago*, Ryan's life with Lonely Planet comes full circle. His first gig for LP was the first edition of this book in 1997. Since then he's written *Moscow*, cowritten *Texas*, *Canada* and *Western Europe* and acted as coordinating author for *Russia, Ukraine & Belarus*; *Great Lakes*; *Out to Eat London*; *Netherlands*; *Britain* and *England*. He and his journalist wife Sara Marley fondly recall their London flat, which was their home for 2½ fun-filled years and was near the point of inspiration for noted musician Nigel Tufnel. Their next stop is likely to mean that Ryan's life will have come full circle in another way, as they plan to live in San Francisco, just up the coast from Santa Cruz.

FROM THE AUTHOR

I'd like to thank my many friends in Chicago, a town that will always have a deep place in my heart. In particular, Kate Campion, Ted Allen and John Holden are always there for me, even if it requires drinking a beer. Or three. My other pals from the old Gridiron days are also just that, pals. It's great seeing them all for a beer. Or three.

Patricia Sullivan with the Chicago Office of Tourism is one reason that office rocks. I owe her a beer. Or…oh, enough of this running joke. Countless other people helped me with all aspects of this edition, although Samuel L Bronkowitz was especially inspirational. Thanks to all of you.

At LP, Mariah Bear, Kate Hoffman, Michele Posner, Valerie Sinzdak and the rest of the Oakland office are joys to work with. In Melbourne, Jenny Blake is a true demi-goddess for her last-moment outbox skills.

Finally, thanks to my parents, who always enjoy my manic visits while in the middle of an LP book with grace and good humor. And a kiss to Sara Marley, who is my favorite Chicago memory in a town with great memories.

This Book

FROM THE PUBLISHER

Lonely Planet's Oakland office produced this 2nd edition of *Chicago*. Valerie Sinzdak edited the book, with ample guidance from senior editor Michele Posner and managing editor Kate Hoffman. Gabi Knight proofread the book. Cartographer Stephanie Sims drew the maps and made changes in record time, with assistance from Mary Hagemann, John Spelman (who will forever go down in history as the researcher of the 'tree symbol'), Bart Wright, Tim Lohnes and Ivy Feibelman. Senior cartographers Annette Olson and Monica Lepe and cartography manager Alex Guilbert oversaw the whole process. Ruth Askevold designed the book and made those photographs go a long, long way, with the help of design manager Susan Rimerman. Ruth and Jenn Steffey produced the fetching cover. Margaret Livingston created the index. Beca Lafore coordinated the illustration team, which included Hugh D'Andrade, Hayden Foell, Justin Marler and Jenn Steffey. Special thanks to Jenn and Justin for working out last-minute arrangements with the folks at the Art Institute of Chicago. And thanks to Ryan for making this such an easy and enjoyable experience.

ACKNOWLEDGMENTS

Several images in this book have been reproduced with permission from the Art Institute of Chicago: Gustave Caillebotte's *Paris Street; Rainy Day* (1877), from the Charles H and Mary FS Worcester Collection (catalog #1964.336); Edward Hopper's *Nighthawks* (1942), from the Friends of American Art Collection (catalog #1942.51); Georges Seurat's *A Sunday on La Grande Jatte – 1884* (1884–86), from the Helen Birch Bartlett Memorial Collection (catalog #1926.224); and Grant Wood's *American Gothic* (1930), from the Friends of American Art Collection (catalog #1930.934).

An image of the 1893 World's Columbian Exposition was reproduced from the Library of Congress panoramic photographic collection.

Foreword

ABOUT LONELY PLANET GUIDEBOOKS

The story begins with a classic travel adventure: Tony and Maureen Wheeler's 1972 journey across Europe and Asia to Australia. Useful information about the overland trail did not exist at that time, so Tony and Maureen published the first Lonely Planet guidebook to meet a growing need.

From a kitchen table, then from a tiny office in Melbourne (Australia), Lonely Planet has become the largest independent travel publisher in the world, an international company with offices in Melbourne, Oakland (USA), London (UK) and Paris (France).

Today Lonely Planet guidebooks cover the globe. There is an ever-growing list of books, and there's information in a variety of forms and media. Some things haven't changed. The main aim is still to help make it possible for adventurous travelers to get out there – to explore and better understand the world.

At Lonely Planet we believe travelers can make a positive contribution to the countries they visit – if they respect their host communities and spend their money wisely. Since 1986 a percentage of the income from each book has been donated to aid projects and human-rights campaigns.

Updates Lonely Planet thoroughly updates each guidebook as often as possible. This usually means there are around two years between editions, although for more unusual or more stable destinations the gap can be longer. Check the imprint page (usually following the color map at the beginning of the book) for publication dates.

Between editions up-to-date information is available in two free newsletters – the paper *Planet Talk* and email *Comet* (to subscribe, contact any Lonely Planet office) – and on our Web site at www.lonelyplanet.com. The *Upgrades* section of the Web site covers a number of important and volatile destinations and is regularly updated by Lonely Planet authors. *Scoop* covers news and current affairs relevant to travelers. And, lastly, the *Thorn Tree* bulletin board and *Postcards* section of the site carry unverified, but fascinating, reports from travelers.

Correspondence The process of creating new editions begins with the letters, postcards and emails received from travelers. This correspondence often includes suggestions, criticisms and comments about the current editions. Interesting excerpts are immediately passed on via newsletters and the Web site, and everything goes to our authors to be verified when they're researching on the road. We're keen to get more feedback from organizations or individuals who represent communities visited by travelers.

> Lonely Planet gathers information for everyone who's curious about the planet – and especially for those who explore it first-hand. Through guidebooks, phrasebooks, activity guides, maps, literature, newsletters, image library, TV series and Web site we act as an information exchange for a worldwide community of travelers.

Research Authors aim to gather sufficient practical information to enable travelers to make informed choices and to make the mechanics of a journey run smoothly. They also research historical and cultural background to help enrich the travel experience and allow travelers to understand and respond appropriately to cultural and environmental issues.

Authors don't stay in every hotel because that would mean spending a couple of months in each medium-size city and, no, they don't eat at every restaurant because that would mean stretching belts beyond capacity. They do visit hotels and restaurants to check standards and prices, but feedback based on readers' direct experiences can be very helpful.

Many of our authors work undercover; others aren't so secretive. None of them accept freebies in exchange for positive write-ups. And none of our guidebooks contain any advertising.

Production Authors submit their raw manuscripts and maps to offices in Australia, the USA, UK or France. Editors and cartographers – all experienced travelers themselves – then begin the process of assembling the pieces. When the book finally hits the shops, some things are already out of date, we start getting feedback from readers and the process begins again…

WARNING & REQUEST

Things change – prices go up, schedules change, good places go bad and bad places go bankrupt – nothing stays the same. So, if you find things better or worse, recently opened or long since closed, please tell us and help make the next edition even more accurate and useful. We genuinely value all the feedback we receive. A well-traveled team reads and acknowledges every letter, postcard and email and ensures that every morsel of information finds its way to the appropriate authors, editors and cartographers for verification.

Everyone who writes to us will find their name in the next edition of the appropriate guidebook. They will also receive the latest issue of *Planet Talk*, our quarterly printed newsletter, or *Comet*, our monthly email newsletter. Subscriptions to both newsletters are free. The very best contributions will be rewarded with a free guidebook.

Excerpts from your correspondence may appear in new editions of Lonely Planet guidebooks, the Lonely Planet Web site, *Planet Talk* or *Comet*, so please let us know if you *don't* want your letter published or your name acknowledged.

Send all correspondence to the Lonely Planet office closest to you:

Australia: Locked Bag 1, Footscray, Victoria 3011
USA: 150 Linden St, Oakland, CA 94607
UK: 10a Spring Place, London NW5 3BH
France: 1 rue du Dahomey, 75011 Paris

Or email us at: talk2us@lonelyplanet.com.au

For news, views and updates, see our Web site: www.lonelyplanet.com

HOW TO USE A LONELY PLANET GUIDEBOOK

The best way to use a Lonely Planet guidebook is any way you choose. At Lonely Planet, we believe the most memorable travel experiences are often those that are unexpected, and the finest discoveries are those you make yourself. Guidebooks are not intended to be used as if they provided a detailed set of infallible instructions!

Contents All Lonely Planet guidebooks follow roughly the same format. The Facts about the Destination chapters or sections give background information ranging from history to weather. Facts for the Visitor gives practical information on issues like visas and health. Getting There & Away gives a brief starting point for researching travel to and from the destination. Getting Around gives an overview of the transport options when you arrive.

The peculiar demands of each destination determine how subsequent chapters are broken up, but some things remain constant. We always start with background, then proceed to sights, places to stay, places to eat, entertainment, getting there and away, and getting around information – in that order.

Heading Hierarchy Lonely Planet headings are used in a strict hierarchical structure that can be visualized as a set of Russian dolls. Each heading (and its following text) is encompassed by any preceding heading that is higher on the hierarchical ladder.

Entry Points We do not assume guidebooks will be read from beginning to end, but that people will dip into them. The traditional entry points are the list of contents and the index. In addition, however, some books have a complete list of maps and an index map illustrating map coverage.

There may also be a color map that shows highlights. These highlights are dealt with in greater detail in the Facts for the Visitor chapter, along with planning questions and suggested itineraries. Each chapter covering a geographical region usually begins with a locator map and another list of highlights. Once you find something of interest in a list of highlights, turn to the index.

Maps Maps play a crucial role in Lonely Planet guidebooks and include a huge amount of information. A legend is printed on the back page. We seek to have complete consistency between maps and text and to have every important place in the text captured on a map. Map key numbers usually start in the top left corner.

Although inclusion in a guidebook usually implies a recommendation, we cannot list every good place. Exclusion does not necessarily imply criticism. In fact there are a number of reasons why we might exclude a place – sometimes it is simply inappropriate to encourage an influx of travelers.

Introduction

Chicago should be the first stop on any visitor's itinerary to the US. And any American who hasn't been here by now (changing planes at O'Hare doesn't count) should make tracks immediately.

Why? Simply because this is the most American of cities. Sure, New York is the biggest and most famous, but it's really another country. Washington, DC? An anomaly most taxpayers would rather give back to the British. New Orleans? A carnival. San Francisco? A beautiful freak show. Los Angeles? Well, there's probably some reason for it, but who knows? As for loudmouth self-boosters such as Dallas or Denver, get back to me in 100 years.

But you can't generalize about Chicago, other than to say that it's flat, it's on the lake and the Cubs suck. The diversity of commentary on the city – good and bad – is altogether fitting, because it is such a diverse place.

Chicago combines a wealth of delights in one very visitor-friendly package. Great music? Ya got it! Good food? Order more!

Beautiful lakefront? Yeah, but pick up your trash! Great summer festivals? Party on! Brutal winter storms? Well, yeah, but they put hair on ya!

The Magnificent Mile is famous for its shops, the Art Institute boasts a world-class collection and the Loop is bustling. These are some of the reasons why Chicagoans are proud of their town and why, for the first time in years, the city's population is growing. Crime is down, the schools are looking up, the parks have never been greener, and there's a sense that Chicago is a place that people don't just want to visit but where they also want to live. The significant problems of racial discrimination and poverty continue, but now the locals seem optimistic about confronting these explosive issues.

It's been said that you can go around the world in 80 hours without leaving the city. (You can, and you'll miss only a few countries.) Chicago is a kaleidoscope of neighborhoods encompassing every ethnic, racial and religious background. Itinerant artists ponder

RICK GERHARTER

their navels in Wicker Park, old Polish women scrub their stoops on Milwaukee Ave, a Vietnamese woman works 18-hour days in her new Argyle St restaurant, yuppies spoil their perfect child in Lincoln Park, an African American mother organizes her block on the West Side, blue-collar guys in Bridgeport bad-mouth whoever is playing the Bears, an old-as-the-hills musician sings the blues in a South Side tavern. These portraits and a million more – make that 2.7 million more – can be seen at any time.

There is a downside to this diversity: the neighborhoods and their residents can be wary of outsiders, showing a kind of fear grounded in prejudice and ignorance. (But then, Chicago is the most American of cities, right?)

What unites Chicagoans is their no-nonsense attitude. Problems are not meant to be pondered; they are meant to be tackled. Look at two of the most popular Chicago Bears of all time: Mike Singleterry and Dick Butkus. They were loved not for their on-field finesse but because they took the heads off opposing players.

Add to this attitude a confident self-reliance: when the city's downtown was destroyed by the great fire of 1871, Chicago invented the skyscraper and filled the Loop with remarkable towers a mere 15 years after the disaster; when Prohibition dried up alcohol, Al Capone supplied it; when actors need to create comedy, they don't wait for a script, they improvise.

Underneath this confidence, however, lies a deep insecurity. Chicagoans' once-proud moniker for their home, 'the Second City,' stemmed from their urge to remind people that although their city wasn't number one in population, it still was right up there. Now Los Angeles is number two in population and nobody seems to be in a hurry to adopt 'the Third City' as a motto.

Chicago's cultural institutions benefit from this insecurity. Corporate and individual donors regularly open their wallets when the museums or orchestras come calling. The folks at the top are just as happy to boast about the Art Institute as the regular folks are to brag about their favorite hot dog stand. And the regular folks take pride in the Art Institute, too, even if they might not know the difference between a Monet and a Miró.

Those who take time to see some of the city will benefit from the locals' uncertainty about their standing in the world, an uncertainty that only makes them more receptive to the flattering attentions of their guests. 'Wow, you really like us?' Chicagoans seem to gush. And whether you're quaffing a beer in a friendly tavern, buying a frock in a designer's boutique, soaking up the blues in a smoky bar or having the best meal of your life in a rollicking restaurant, you'll find out Chicago is a delightful and fascinating place to explore.

If you miss this town, you'll have missed the heart of America.

Facts about Chicago

HISTORY

Chicago emerged as a world-class city in the late 1800s because of the skills of its population in processing the inherent wealth of America's Midwest. Lumber from the vast virgin forests, grains from the rich soil and livestock from the farms were bought, sold and processed here. The city's capitalists developed financial means such as the futures markets to make this commerce possible. The railroads grew to accommodate the resulting freight, and soon it was barely possible to cross the nation without changing trains in Chicago.

Constant immigration from abroad and the US itself swelled the population with people who were willing to risk it all to move to Chicago. These adventurers provided a can-do spirit that drove the city to further heights.

After WWII, the national move to the suburbs decreased the size of the city's vital middle class, and in Chicago this move was hastened by racial fears and the death of manufacturing industries. Though Mayor Richard J Daley boasted that Chicago was 'the city that worked,' the social unrest of the 1960s showed just how hollow his words were.

The late 1980s and 1990s have been good for the city. A new generation of professionals has been discovering the joys of urban living, including Chicago's vibrant cultural and social scene. Billions of dollars in private investment have flowed to neighborhoods, and the city's diversified economic base enabled it to weather the recession of the early 1990s better than others in the US. Chicago cheerfully rode the wave of the US economic boom for the balance of the decade.

A Swamp

No one is sure when Native Americans first lived in the Chicago region, but evidence can be traced back to about 10,000 years ago. By the late 1600s, many tribes made their home in the region, the dominant one being the Potawatomi.

In 1673 Indians directed French explorer Louis Jolliet and missionary Jacques Marquette to Lake Michigan via the Chicago River. The two, who had been exploring the Mississippi River, learned that the Indians of the region called the area around the mouth of the river 'Checaugou,' after the wild garlic (some say onions) growing there.

Various explorers and traders traveled through the area over the next 100 years. In 1779 Quebec trader Jean Baptiste Point du Sable established a fur-trading store on the north bank of the river. Of mixed African and Caribbean descent, Point du Sable was the area's first non-Native American settler and was possibly the first settler period, given that the Indians dismissed this part of the riverbank as a feverish swamp.

After the Revolutionary War, the United States increasingly focused its attention on the immense western frontier. Because of Chicago's position on Lake Michigan, the government wanted a permanent presence in the area and in 1803 built Fort Dearborn on the south bank of the river, on marshy ground under what is today's Michigan Ave Bridge.

Nine years later, the Potawatomi Indians, in cahoots with the British (their allies in the War of 1812), slaughtered 52 settlers fleeing the fort. During this war such massacres had been a strategy employed throughout the frontier: the British bought the allegiance of various Indian tribes through trade and other deals, and the Indians paid them back by being hostile to American settlers. The settlers killed in Chicago had simply waited too long to flee the rising tension and thus found themselves caught.

After the war ended, bygones were quickly forgotten, as Americans, French, British and Indians turned their energies to profiting from the fur trade. In 1816 Fort Dearborn was rebuilt. Two years later Illinois became a state, although much of its small population lived in the south near the Mississippi River.

During the 1820s Chicago developed as a small town with a population of fewer than 200, most of whom made their living from

Chicago Firsts

Not every Chicago invention has been as significant as steel-framed skyscrapers (1885) or hospital trauma rooms (1966). But many others have had far-reaching social impact, if only on the palate or wallet.

1893: Cracker Jack The candy-coated popcorn, peanuts and a prize are still a popular snack.

1893: Zipper People have been groping for them ever since.

1920s: One-Way Ride Gangster Hymie Weiss receives credit for deducing the role cars could play in dispatching rivals. Some historians give this credit to 'Dingbat' Obierta.

1930: Hostess Twinkie Rumors that the very first one is still as fresh as the day it was extruded are thought to be apocryphal.

1930: Pinball Bally is still a large local concern.

1947: Spray Paint Municipalities have been cleaning this stuff off official surfaces ever since. Chicago even banned the sale of spray paint within city limits a few years ago.

1955: McDonald's Chicagoan Ray Kroc opened the first one in nearby Des Plaines. More than 21,000 branches have turned up in 103 countries since then, but there's no word on which one coined 'Would you like fries with that?'

1968: 'Police Riot' This term was used in a government report on police behavior at the Democratic National Convention.

trade. Records show that the total taxable value of Chicago's land was $8000.

Indian relations took a dramatic turn for the worse in 1832, when Chief Black Hawk of the Sauk Indians led a band of Sauk, Fox and Kickapoo from what is now Iowa to reclaim land swiped by settlers in western Illinois. The US reacted strongly, sending in hundreds of troops who traveled through Chicago, fueling its nascent economy. The army routed the Indians, and the US government requisitioned the rest of the Indian lands throughout Illinois, including those of the Potawatomi in Chicago. The Indians were forced to sign treaties by which they relinquished their land at a fraction of its worth, and all were moved west, ending any significant Native American presence in the city or region.

Chicago was incorporated as a town in 1833, with a population of 340. Within three years land speculation had rocked the local real estate market; lots that had sold for $33 in 1829 went for $100,000. The boom was fueled by the start of construction on the Illinois & Michigan Canal, a state project to create an inland waterway linking the Great Lakes to the Illinois River and thus to the Mississippi River and New Orleans.

The swarms of laborers drawn by the canal construction swelled the population to more than 4100 by 1837, when Chicago incorporated as a city. But the bullish city boosters quickly turned bearish that same year, after a national economic depression brought the unstable real estate market crashing down. On paper, Illinois was bankrupt; canal construction stopped for four years.

By 1847 the economy had recovered and the canal was being pushed forward at full pace. More than 20,000 people lived in what had become the region's dominant city. The rich Illinois soil supported thousands of farmers, and industrialist Cyrus Hall McCormick moved his reaper factory to the city to serve them. He would soon control one of the Midwest's major fortunes.

In 1848 the canal opened, and shipping began flowing through the Chicago River from the Caribbean to New York via the Great Lakes and the Saint Lawrence

Seaway. It had a marked economic effect on the city. One of its great financial institutions, the Chicago Board of Trade, opened to handle the sale of grain by Illinois farmers, who had greatly improved access to Eastern markets thanks to the canal.

Railroad construction absorbed workers freed from canal construction. By 1850 a line had been completed to serve grain farmers between Chicago and Galena, in western Illinois. A year later the city gave the Illinois Central Railroad land for its tracks south of the city. It was the first land-grant railroad and was joined by many others, whose tracks eventually would radiate out from Chicago. The city quickly became the hub of America's freight and passenger trains, a status it would hold for the next hundred years.

Rapid Growth

In the 1850s Chicago grew quickly. State St south of the river became the commercial center, as banks and other institutions flourished with the growing economy. The city's first steel mill opened in 1857, the forerunner of the city's economic and industrial diversification. By the end of the decade, Chicago supported at least seven daily newspapers. Immigrants poured in, drawn by jobs at the railroads that served the expanding agricultural trade. Twenty million bushels of produce were shipped through the city that year. The population topped 100,000.

By then Chicago was no longer a frontier town. Its central position in the US made it a favorite meeting spot, a legacy that continues to this day. In 1860 the Republican Party held its national political convention in Chicago and selected Abraham Lincoln, a lawyer from Springfield, Illinois, as its presidential candidate.

Like other northern cities, Chicago profited from the Civil War, which boosted business in its burgeoning steel and tool-making industries and provided plenty of freight for the railroads and canal. In 1865, the year the war ended, an event took place that would profoundly affect the city for the next hundred years: the Union Stockyards opened on the South Side, unifying disparate meat operations scattered about the city. Chicago's rail network and the development of the iced refrigerator car meant that meat could be shipped east to New York, spurring the industry's consolidation.

The stockyards become the major supplier of meat to the entire nation. But besides bringing great wealth to a few and jobs to many, the yards were also a source of many problems, including water pollution (see the boxed text 'Pig Problems').

The stockyard effluvia polluted not only the Chicago River but also Lake Michigan. Flowing into the lake, the fouled waters spoiled the city's source of fresh water and caused cholera and other epidemics that killed thousands. In 1869 the Water Tower and Pumping Station began bringing water into the city through a two-mile tunnel that had been built into Lake Michigan in an attempt to draw drinking water unpolluted

PRISCILLA EASTMAN

The Water Tower dates from the 1860s.

by the Chicago River. But this solution proved resoundingly inadequate, and outbreaks of illness continued.

Two years later, the Illinois & Michigan Canal was deepened so that the Chicago River would reverse its course and start flowing south, away from the city. Sending waste and sewage down the reversed river provided relief for Chicago residents and helped ease lake pollution, but it was not a welcome change for those living near what had become the city's drainpipe. A resident of Morris, about 60 miles downstream from Chicago, wrote, 'What right has Chicago to pour its filth down into what was before a sweet and clean river, pollute its waters, and materially reduce the value of property on both sides of the river and canal, and bring sickness and death to the citizens?'

The river still occasionally flowed into the lake after heavy rains; it wasn't permanently reversed until 1900, when the huge Chicago Sanitary Canal opened.

The Chicago Fire

On October 8, 1871, the Chicago fire started just southwest of downtown. Although the cause is now debated (see the boxed text 'Don't Look at Me – It Was the Cow'), the results were devastating. The fire burned for three days, killing 300 people, destroying 18,000 buildings and leaving 90,000 people homeless. 'By morning 100,000 people will be without food and shelter. Can you help us?' was the message sent east by Mayor Roswell B Mason as Chicago and City Hall literally burned down around him.

The dry conditions set the stage for a runaway conflagration, as a hot wind carried flaming embers to unburned areas, which quickly caught fire. The primitive, horse-drawn fire-fighting equipment did little to keep up with the spreading blaze. Almost every structure was destroyed or gutted in the area bounded by the river on the west, what's now Roosevelt Rd to the south and Fullerton Ave to the north.

Mayor Mason earned kudos for his skillful handling of Chicago's recovery. His best move was to prevent the aldermen on the city council from getting their hands on the millions of dollars in relief funds that Easterners had donated after the mayor's fireside plea, thus ensuring that the money

Don't Look at Me – It Was the Cow

For more than 125 years, legend has had it that a cow owned by a certain Mrs O'Leary kicked over a lantern, which ignited some hay, which ignited some lumber, which ignited the whole town. The image of the hapless heifer has endured despite official skepticism from the start. Now that story may have been milked for the last time.

Richard Bales, a lawyer and amateur historian, has spent years examining the case from every angle. His conclusion is that Bessie was a victim of circumstances. It seems that Mrs O'Leary's barn was shared by a neighboring family. Each day Daniel 'Peg Leg' Sullivan dropped by to feed his mom's cow. Bales' evidence, gathered from thousands of pages of post-inferno investigations, indicates that Peg Leg accidentally started the fire himself and then tried to blame it on the bovine. After all, if you had just burned down what was then the fourth-largest city in the US, who would *you* blame?

The Chicago City Council has accepted Bales' version of the story; in 1997 the cream of Chicago politics passed a resolution officially absolving the O'Leary family of blame. Of course, for proponents of the cow story, this revision is udder nonsense.

actually reached the rabble living in the rubble.

The Chicago Historical Society later collected quotes from survivors of the inferno. Bessie Bradwell, then 13, described her mother's quick evacuation from their home: 'With her birdcage tightly clasped in her arms and the poor little bird gasping for breath in the smoke, she went down to the lake....'

A young Clarence Augustus Burley, who was later the president of the historical society, described the scene in his evacuated neighborhood:

At the corner of Randolph Street was a fire engine standing idly without hose or any appliances for fire fighting, and as I passed, a huge plank about six feet long, all on fire, whirled over and dropped beside it. Huge cinders of like kind were dropping all about, and I did not consider it wise to wait.

Chicago Tribune writers James T Sheahan and George T Upton explored the city as the ashes cooled and later published a detailed and highly imaginative account of what they found. An excerpt:

Yonder, burnt and bruised and blackened, stands the church, its pealing organ stilled forever. Through its gaping portals no more wedding parties shall pass....The young men who, in the intoxication of first love, followed their sweethearts there, and who endured the sermon for the sake of being near the beloved, have outlived the passionate ardor...and will not regret the ruined sanctuary, which, to them, was the temple of Cupid, and not Jehovah.

Chicago Reborn

Despite the human tragedy, the fire's effect on Chicago was much the same as that of a forest fire: within a few years there was rapid new growth, a wealth of new life. The best architects in the world poured in to snare the thousands of rebuilding contracts, giving Chicago an architectural legacy of innovation that endures today. (See the special section 'Chicago Architecture: A Study in Innovation' for details.) Rebuilding efforts added to the city's economy, which had been scarcely slowed by the conflagration, and by 10 years after the fire, the population of Chicago had tripled.

The later decades of the 19th century saw Chicago on a boom-and-bust economic cycle. While in general the economy grew, it often fell prey to short-lived recessions. During one of these in 1873, thousands of men thrown out of work marched on City Hall, demanding food. The police, who were always on call for governmental and economic interests, beat the protesters, who had dispersed after they were promised free bread. It was the beginning of a history of clashes between labor and police that would stretch over the next 50 years.

In 1876 strikes began in the railroad yards as workers demanded an eight-hour workday. Traffic was paralyzed, and the unrest spread to the McCormick Reaper Works, which was then Chicago's largest factory. The police and federal troops broke up the strikes, killing 18 civilians and injuring hundreds more.

By then, May 1 had become the official day of protest for Chicago labor groups. On that day in 1886, 60,000 workers in the city

RICHARD I'ANSON

Brick buildings sprung up after the fire.

went on strike, demanding an eight-hour workday. As was usual, police attacked the strikers at locations throughout the city. Three days later, self-described 'anarchists' staged a protest in Haymarket Square where a bomb exploded, killing seven police officers. The government reacted strongly to what became known as 'the Haymarket Riot.' Eight anarchists were convicted of 'general conspiracy to murder' and four were hanged, although only two had been present at the incident and the actual bomber was never identified.

While the city's workers agitated for better working conditions, other progressive social movements were also at play in Chicago. Immigrants were pouring into the city at a rate of 10,000 a week, and they lived in squalid conditions, enjoying few if any government services. In 1889 two young women from middle-class families, Jane Addams and Ellen Gates Starr, founded Hull House on the city's West Side. The two women opened soup kitchens, set up schools for immigrant children, established English classes for adults and offered other services, such as medical care, to ease the immigrants' hardships.

Meanwhile, the city went on a big annexation campaign, nabbing the independent townships of Lake View, Hyde Park and others to gain their tax revenues. Also, civic leaders hoped that Chicago's larger population would give it prominence on the world stage.

In 1892 society legend Bertha Palmer followed the lead of other Chicago elite by touring Paris. A prescient art collector, she nabbed a score of Monets, Renoirs and other impressionist works before they had achieved universal acclaim. Her collection would later form the core of the Art Institute.

The 1893 World's Columbian Exposition marked Chicago's showy debut on the international stage. Centered on a grand complex of specially built structures on the lakeshore south of Hyde Park, the exposition became known as 'the White City' for its magnificent white-painted buildings, which were brilliantly lit by electric searchlights. Designed by architectural luminaries such as Daniel Burnham, Louis Sullivan and Frederick Law Olmsted, the fairgrounds were meant to show how parks, streets and buildings could be designed in a harmonious manner that would enrich the chaotic urban environment.

Open only five months, the exposition attracted 27 million visitors, many of whom rode the newly built El to and from the Loop. The fair's attractions were divided between the high-minded and the lowbrow. In the former category, the Electricity Building, the Women's Building, and other structures offered exhibits showing the fine inventions made possible by the modern age. Catering to more popular tastes, the world's first Ferris wheel spun on the midway and the 'Street of Cairo' exhibit proved itself little more than a thinly veiled excuse to show thinly veiled women dancing the 'hootchy-kootchy,' an erotic belly dance.

The spectacular buildings surrounded ponds plied by Venetian gondolas. The entire assemblage made a huge impact not

The World's Columbian Exposition transformed the lakeshore in 1893.

just in Chicago but around the world, as the fair's architects were deluged with huge commissions to redesign cities. The buildings themselves, despite their grandeur, were short lived, having been built out of a rough equivalent of plaster of Paris that barely lasted through the fair. The only survivor was the Fine Arts Building, which was really rebuilt from scratch to become the Museum of Science and Industry.

Chicago's labor troubles reached another critical point in 1894, when a recession caused the Pullman Palace Car Company to cut wages. Worker unrest spread from the huge South Side factory complex, which built railroad cars, to the railroads themselves, and more than 50,000 workers walked off their jobs, paralyzing interstate commerce. Federal troops were called in to Chicago and gradually broke the strike through a series of battles that left scores of workers injured.

At the turn of the century, Chicago's population had reached 1.7 million, and the city had become a far bigger place than anyone could have imagined just seven decades before. Despite this growth, though, Chicago still had its wild and woolly elements, many of which could be found in the notorious Levee District, a one-stop Sodom and Gomorrah south of the Loop run not by gangsters but by the top cops and politicians in the city.

Meanwhile, Chicago's industries continued to prosper at the expense of the environment and worker health. In 1906 Upton Sinclair's fictional account of the stockyards, *The Jungle*, was published. Although Sinclair hoped it would arouse sympathy for exploited workers living in squalid conditions, it ignited public fury with its lurid portrayal of conditions in the factories where the public's food was prepared.

Pig Problems

In *The Jungle*, Upton Sinclair described the Chicago stockyards this way: 'One could not stand and watch very long without becoming philosophical, without beginning to deal in symbols and similes, and to hear the hog-squeal of the universe.'

These were slaughterhouses beyond compare. By the early 1870s they processed more than one million hogs a year and almost as many cattle, plus scores of unlucky sheep, horses and other critters. It was a coldly efficient operation. The pigs themselves became little more than a way to turn corn into a denser, more easily transportable substance that was thus more valuable.

The old saw – that once the animals were in the packing houses, everything was used but the squeal – was almost true. Some bits of pig debris for which no other use could be found were fed to scavenger pigs, who turned the waste into valuable meat. But vast amounts of waste were simply flushed into the south branch of the Chicago River, and it then flowed into the lake. Beyond the aesthetic and health problems that ensued, the packers had to contend with other consequences of their pollution.

Meat processed in Chicago was shipped in ice-packed railroad cars to the huge markets in the East. The ice was harvested from lakes and rivers each winter and then stored for use all year long. But ice that was taken from the Chicago River returned to its stinky liquid state as it thawed over the meat on the journey east, thus rendering the carcasses unpalatable. The packers finally had to resort to harvesting their ice in huge operations in unpolluted Wisconsin.

For a look at the packing houses' squalid legacy, see the Bridgeport section of the Things to See & Do chapter.

Though working conditions were bad, they didn't stop the continual flow of immigrants to Chicago. People from Midwestern farms and impoverished nations in Europe continued to pour in, followed, in the early 20th century, by poor blacks from the South.

The Great Migration
In 1910 eight out of 10 blacks still lived in the southern states of the old Confederacy. Over the next decade a variety of factors combined to change that, as more than two million African Americans moved north in what came to be known as the Great Migration.

Chicago played a pivotal role in this massive shift of population, both as an impetus and as a destination. Articles in the black-owned and nationally circulated *Chicago Defender* proclaimed the city a worker's paradise and a place free from the horrors of Southern racism. Ads from Chicago employers promised jobs to anyone willing to work.

These lures, coupled with glitzy images of thriving neighborhoods like Bronzeville, inspired thousands to take the bait. Chicago's black population zoomed from 44,103 in 1910 to 109,458 in 1920 and continued growing. The migrants, often poorly educated sharecroppers with big dreams, found a reality not as rosy as promised. Chicago did not welcome blacks with open arms. In 1919 white gangs from Bridgeport led days of rioting that killed dozens. Employers were ready with the promised jobs, but many hoped to rid their factories of white unionized workers by replacing them with blacks, which further exacerbated racial tensions. Blacks also found that they were promoted and advanced only so far before reaching an unofficial ceiling.

Blacks were also restricted to living in South Side ghettos by openly prejudicial real estate practices that kept them from buying or renting homes elsewhere in the city.

Prohibition
Efforts to make the United States 'dry' had never found favor in Chicago; the city's vast numbers of German and Irish immigrants were not about to forsake their favored libations. During the first two decades of the 20th century, the political party that could portray itself as the 'wettest' would win the local elections. Thus, the nationwide enactment in 1920 of Prohibition, the federal constitutional amendment making alcohol consumption illegal, was destined to meet resistance in Chicago, where voters had gone six to one against the law in an advisory referendum. However, few could have predicted how the efforts to flout Prohibition would forever mark Chicago's image worldwide (see the boxed text 'Capone's Chicago').

An important year for the city, 1933 saw Prohibition repealed and a thirsty populace return openly to the local bars in droves. Another world's fair, this time called the Century of Progress, opened on the lakefront south of Grant Park and promised a bright future filled with modern conveniences, despite the ongoing grimness of the Great Depression. And in 1933 Ed Kelly became mayor. With the help of party boss Pat Nash, he strengthened the Democratic Party in the city, creating the legendary 'machine' that would control local politics for the next 50 years. Politicians doled out thousands of city jobs to people who worked hard to make sure their patrons were reelected. The same was true for city vendors and contractors, whose continued prosperity was tied to their donations and other efforts to preserve the status quo.

Mayor Richard J Daley
The zenith of the machine's power began with the election of Richard J Daley in 1955. Initially thought to be a mere party functionary, Daley was reelected mayor five times before dying in office in 1976. With an uncanny understanding of machine politics and how to use it to squelch dissent, he dominated the city in a way no mayor had before or has since. His word was law, and a docile city council routinely approved all his actions, lest a dissenter find his or her ward deprived of vital city services.

But Daley and those in the entrenched political structure were oblivious – both by intent and accident – to many of the changes and challenges that Chicago faced in the

1950s and later. After suffering through the Depression, the city experienced sudden affluence during WWII. Factories ran at full tilt, and once again people flocked to Chicago for jobs during the war years. In 1950 the population peaked at 3.6 million. But the postwar economic boom also made it possible for many Chicagoans to realize the dream of buying their own homes. Farms and wetlands surrounding the city were quickly turned into suburbs that attracted scores of middle-class people fleeing the crowded city.

The tax base diminished and racial tensions grew. Blacks moved from the ghettos on the South Side to other areas of the city, while whites, succumbing to racism fueled by fears of crime, grew terrified at the prospect of ethnically integrated neighborhoods (see the boxed text 'White Flight').

A 1957 *Life* magazine report that called Chicago's cops the most corrupt in the nation didn't make Chicagoans feel more secure. Although Daley and the machine howled with indignation over the article, further exposés by the press revealed that some cops and politicians were in cahoots with various crime rings. None of this was news to the average Chicagoan.

Chicago's voting practices were also highly suspect, never more so than in 1960, when John F Kennedy ran for president of the US against Richard Nixon, then vice president. The night of the election, the results were so close nationwide that the outcome hinged on the vote in Illinois.

White Flight

From the late 1950s through the '70s, Chicago's ethnic neighborhoods in the southern, western and southwestern neighborhoods of the city underwent rapid change. Whole neighborhoods that had been filled with Irish, Lithuanian and other immigrant residents became populated entirely by black residents in a matter of months.

The causes were both simple and complex. White residents, raised with racist assumptions about the dangers of having blacks as neighbors, engaged in panic selling at the first appearance of an African American on the block. 'For Sale' signs sprouted like weeds throughout the neighborhoods. People who had worked two or more jobs to afford their dream home sold at below-market prices and fled with their families to the suburbs.

The blacks who could afford to do so fled the slums and snapped up the homes but soon found they had a new set of problems: insurance companies and mortgage lenders engaged in 'redlining,' the practice of refusing to write policies and grant loans in areas that had 'gone black.' The new homeowners were often forced to purchase mortgages and insurance from unscrupulous businesses – many of them owned by African Americans – that charged far more than market rates. Soon some families were forced to default on their loans, and their once-tidy homes became derelict, blighting otherwise healthy blocks.

Discrimination also took the form of 'housing covenants,' unwritten agreements in the real estate industry whereby houses in certain neighborhoods were not sold to people deemed 'unsuitable.'

Government agencies attempted to alleviate these problems by outlawing 'For Sale' signs, punishing firms that engaged in redlining and requiring banks to open branches in African American communities and to grant mortgages under the same conditions that applied to white communities. These new policies slowed the destabilizing turnover of neighborhoods, and in the few places where true integration has occurred, neighboring black and white homeowners find that they share many of the same concerns: good schools, low crime rates, affordable taxes, timely trash removal, instant eradication of snow and a melancholy wish for the return of Michael Jordan and Mike Ditka.

Capone's Chicago

Chicagoans traveling the world often experience an unusual phenomenon when others ask where they're from. When they answer 'Chicago,' the local drops into a crouch and yells something along the lines of 'Rat-a-tat-a-tat, Al Capone!' Although civic boosters bemoan Chicago's long association with a scar-faced hoodlum, it's an image that has been burned into the public consciousness by television shows such as *The Untouchables*, movies and other aspects of pop culture.

Capone was the mob boss in Chicago from 1924 to 1931, when he was brought down on tax evasion charges by Elliot Ness, the federal agent whose task force earned the name 'The Untouchables' because its members were supposedly impervious to bribes. (This wasn't a small claim, given that thousands of Chicago police and other officials were on the take, some of them taking in more than $1000 a week.)

Capone came to Chicago from New York in 1919. He quickly moved up the ranks to take control of the city's South Side in 1924. He expanded his empire by making 'hits' on his rivals. These acts, which usually involved thousands of bullets shot out of submachine guns (also called 'Tommy guns'), were carried out by Capone's lieutenants. Incidentally, Capone earned the nickname 'Scarface' not because he ended up on the wrong side of a bullet but because a dance-hall fight left him with a large scar on his left cheek.

The success of the Chicago mob was fueled by Prohibition. Not surprisingly, the citizens' thirst for booze wasn't eliminated by government mandate, and gangs made fortunes dealing in illegal beer, gin and other intoxicants. Clubs called 'speakeasies' were highly popular and were only marginally hidden from the law, an unnecessary precaution given that crooked cops usually were the ones working the doors. Commenting on the hypocrisy of a society that would ban booze and then pay him a fortune to sell it, Capone said: 'When I sell liquor, they call it bootlegging. When my patrons serve it on silver trays on Lake Shore Drive, they call it hospitality.'

It's a challenge to find traces of the Capone era in Chicago. The city and the Chicago Historical Society take dim views of Chicago's gangland past, with nary a brochure or exhibit on Capone or his cronies (though the CHS bookstore does have a good selection of books). Many of the actual sites have been torn down; what follows are some of the more notable survivors.

Capone's Chicago Home This South Side home (7244 S Prairie Ave) was built by Capone and mostly used by his wife, Mae, son 'Sonny' and other relatives. Al preferred to stay where his vices were. The house looks almost the same today.

Mayor Daley called up Kennedy and assured him, 'With a little bit of luck and the help of a few close friends, you're going to carry Illinois.' Kennedy did win Illinois, by 10,000 votes, which gave him the presidency. For many, that was the perfect embodiment of electoral politics in Chicago, a city where the slogan has long been 'Vote early and vote often' and voters have been known to rise from the grave and cast ballots.

In 1964 the Civil Rights movement came to Chicago. Martin Luther King Jr spoke at

Capone's Chicago

Maxwell St Police Station This station (943 W Maxwell St, two blocks west of Halsted St; Map 10) exemplified the corruption rife in the Chicago Police Department in the 1920s. At one time, five captains and about 400 uniformed police were on the take here.

City Hall This building (121 N La Salle St; Map 3) was the workplace of some of Capone's best pals. During William 'Big Bill' Thompson's successful campaign for mayor in 1927, Al donated well over $100,000.

Holy Name Cathedral Two gangland murders took place near this church (735 N State St; Map 3). In 1924, North Side boss Dion O'Banion was gunned down in his floral shop (738 N State St) after he crossed Capone. In 1926 his successor, Hymie Weiss, died en route to church in a hail of Capone-ordered bullets emanating from a window at 740 N State. These bullets also damaged the cathedral's facade; look for the pock marks.

St Valentine's Day Massacre Site In perhaps the most infamous event of the Capone era, seven members of the Bugs Moran gang were lined up against a garage wall and gunned down by mobsters dressed as cops. After that, Moran cut his losses and Capone gained control of Chicago's North Side vice. The garage (2122 N Clark St) was torn down in 1967 to make way for a retirement home. The building just to the south remains. A house used as a lookout by the killers stands across the street (2119 N Clark St).

Green Mill This tavern (4802 N Broadway St; Map 8) was one of Capone's favorite nightspots. During the mid-1920s the cover for the speakeasy in the basement was $10. You can still listen to jazz in its swank setting today. See the Jazz & Blues section of the Entertainment chapter for details.

Mt Carmel Cemetery Capone is now buried in this cemetery (Roosevelt Rd at Wolf Rd) in Hillside, west of Chicago. He and his relatives were moved here in 1950. Al's simple gray gravestone, which has been stolen and replaced twice, is concealed by a hedge; it reads 'Alphonse Capone, 1899-1947, My Jesus Mercy.' Capone's neighbors include old rivals Dion O'Banion and Hymie Weiss. Both tried to rub out Capone, who returned the favor in a far more effective manner.

For a guided tour of many of these sights, along with enthusiastic amateur theatrics, try **Untouchable Gangster Tours** (☎ 773-881-1195). Using an old school bus, two actors lead the tour, taking people for a $20 ride that's part show, part history.

But be careful about getting too caught up in the romance of the Capone era – remember that gangs continue to peddle vice throughout the city today. But their toll on society is much worse: whole neighborhoods have been devastated by the drug trade and its inherent criminality. The murder rate in Chicago for contemporary gang members is often more than 10 times that of 1926, when 75 mobsters were killed.

rallies, demanding better conditions for blacks and an end to segregation. He led marches through all-white neighborhoods where some racist residents attacked the marchers with rocks and bottles. In one march, King was hit in the head by a brick, foreshadowing events for which Daley and the machine would be ill prepared.

The year 1968 proved an explosive one for Chicago. When King was assassinated in Memphis, Tennessee, the West Side exploded in riots and went up in smoke. Whole stretches of the city were laid to waste, and Daley and the many black politicians in the machine were helpless to stop the violence. Worse yet, the city's hosting of the Democratic National Convention in August degenerated into a fiasco of such proportions that its legacy dogged Chicago for decades (see the boxed text 'When Cops Riot').

Meanwhile, the city's economic structure was changing. In 1971 financial pressures caused the last of the Chicago stockyards to close, marking the end of one of the city's most infamous enterprises (see the boxed text 'Pig Problems'). Elsewhere in the city, factories and steel mills shut down as companies moved to the suburbs or the southern US, where taxes and wages were lower.

A decade of economic upheaval saw much of Chicago's industrial base erode. Many companies simply went out of business during the recession of the late 1970s. Chicago and much of the Midwest earned the moniker 'Rust Belt,' which described the area's shrunken economies and their rusting factories. The human costs in the city were high; thousands of blue-collar workers lost their high-paying union jobs with virtually no hope of finding replacement work.

But two events happened in the 1970s that were harbingers of the city's more promising future. The world's tallest building (at the time), the Sears Tower, opened in the Loop in 1974, beginning a development trend that

When Cops Riot

With the war in Vietnam rapidly escalating and general unrest spreading through the US, the 1968 Democratic National Convention became a focal point for protest groups of all stripes. Even though then-president Lyndon Johnson announced he was washing his hands of the mess and not running for reelection, the mass gathering of the politicians who ran the US government was an irresistible draw for anyone with a beef – which in the late 1960s seemed like just about everybody.

Regardless, conservative old Mayor Daley – the personification of a 'square' if there ever was one – was planning a grand convention. Word that protesters would converge on Chicago sparked plans to crack the head of anybody who got in the way of Daley's show. Local officials shot down all of the protesters' requests for parade permits, despite calls by the press and other politicians to uphold the civil right of free assembly.

Enter Abbie Hoffman, Jerry Rubin, Rennie Davis, Tom Hayden, Bobby Seale and David Dellinger. They called for a mobilization of 500,000 protesters to converge on Chicago, and their plans steadily escalated in the face of city intransigence. As the odds of confrontation became high, many moderate protesters decided not to attend.

When the convention opened, there were just a few thousand young protesters in the city. But Daley and his cronies spread rumors to the media to bolster the case for their warlike preparations. Some of these whoppers included claims that hippie girls would pose as prostitutes to give the delegates venereal disease and that LSD would be dumped into the city's water supply. Serious questions – such as what these tales unwittingly implied about the morals of the delegates and exactly how much LSD would be required to have an appreciable effect on the city's water supply – went unaddressed.

The first few nights of the August 25–30 convention saw police staging midnight raids on hippies and protesters attempting to camp in Lincoln Park. The cops went on massive beating sprees, singling some out for savage attacks. Teenage girls were assaulted by cops who shouted, 'You want free love? Try this!' Journalists, ministers and federal Justice Department officials were appalled.

The action then shifted to Grant Park, across from the Conrad Hilton (now the Chicago Hilton & Towers), where the main presidential candidates were staying. A few thousand protesters held a

would spur the creation of thousands of high-paying jobs in finance, law and other white-collar areas. And in 1975 the Water Tower Place shopping mall brought new life to N Michigan Ave. It proved a surprising lure for suburbanites, despite the presence of the very same stores in their own malls. Developers began to realize that the urban environment was an attraction in itself.

Daley's death from a heart attack in 1976 began a process of political upheaval and reform that continued through the 1980s. Chicago's normally docile voters were enraged in 1978, when the city council cheerfully voted itself a 60% pay hike at the height of a recession amid record unemployment. Then, in January 1979, 4 feet of snow

hit Chicago. Daley's 'city that works' didn't, and voters gave Mayor Michael Bilandic a permanent Florida vacation (see the boxed text 'White Blight'), electing outsider Jane Byrne.

The colorful Byrne opened up Chicago to filmmakers, allowing the producers of *The Blues Brothers* to demolish part of Daley Center. She appointed her husband, a gregarious old journalist, as her press secretary, and he soon was answering questions at press conferences with amusing lines like 'The mayor told me in bed this morning...' As a symbolic overture to her minority constituents, Byrne moved into Cabrini-Green, the deeply troubled Near North housing project, but she also showed deep

When Cops Riot

rally, which was met by an overwhelming force of 16,000 Chicago police officers, 4000 state police officers, and 4000 members of the National Guard armed with tear-gas grenades, nightsticks and machine guns.

When some protesters attacked a few officers, the assembled law enforcers staged what investigators later termed a police riot. Among the low-lights: cops shoved bystanders through plate-glass windows and then beat them as they lay bleeding amid the shards; police on motorcycles ran over protesters; police chanting 'Kill, kill, kill!' swarmed journalists and attempted to do just that; and when wounded conventioneers were taken to the hotel suite of presidential candidate Gene McCarthy, cops burst through the door and beat everybody in sight.

The next night Daley went on national TV and attempted to defend the mayhem with an outright lie: he said he knew of plans to assassinate all the presidential candidates. In reality, what Daley and the police did was play right into the hands of the most extreme of the protesters, who had hoped to provoke just such a sorry spectacle.

The long-term effects of the riots were far greater that anyone could have guessed. The Democratic candidate for president, Hubert Humphrey, was left without liberal backing after his tacit support of Daley's tactics, and as a result Republican Richard Nixon was elected president. Chicago was left with a huge black eye for decades. Once the most popular host to the hugely lucrative political conventions, it saw none return for almost 30 years, until 1996. The stories of police brutality, coupled with reports of rampant corruption in the department, led to decade-long changes that made the Chicago police force more racially balanced than it had ever been; it emerged as one of the most professional departments in the country.

Lyndon Johnson's attorney general refused to prosecute any of the protesters for conspiring to riot in Chicago. But in 1969 President Nixon ordered just such prosecutions, even though the actions of those charged may well have helped elect him. The 'Chicago Seven' trial became a total farce; the accused used it as a platform for protest, and aging judge Julius Hoffman showed a Daley-like tolerance for their antics by sentencing them to prison for contempt of court. However, on the central charges of inciting riots, all seven were acquitted.

insensitivity to blacks on several issues, stoking deep-seated anger.

The People's Mayor

In the fall of 1982, a Who's Who of black Chicago gathered in activist Lu Palmer's basement on the South Side. The mood was tense. Newspaper columnist Vernon Jarrett was so angry he was ready to punch Harold Washington. So were a lot of other people who had spent months working their butts off to build the incredible movement that was ready to propel Chicago's first African American mayor – and a reformist to boot – into office. His election would present an obvious change in terms of race, but it was a far bigger challenge to the entrenched interests that had dominated city politics for decades. And now the candidate was dithering about whether he wanted to make the huge commitment to run.

Then-congressman Washington was making it clear that he didn't want to be the sacrificial lamb to a reelection juggernaut by Mayor Jane Byrne. But months earlier, in another meeting in Palmer's basement, he had told Jarrett and the rest that he would consider running if they registered 50,000 new voters. They registered 150,000. The movement to elect Washington was bigger than anybody could have hoped.

Eventually, an irate Washington stormed out of the meeting at midnight, but he couldn't stop the phenomenon he'd tacitly allowed to take root. He did run, and he won the Democratic primary when Byrne and Richard M Daley split the white vote; he then went on to win the general election.

Washington's first term was best described by the *Wall Street Journal*, which called Chicago 'Beirut on the Lake': the entrenched political machine reacted to him with all the hostility you'd expect from people who saw their cozy system under full attack. Much of the political and social chaos that marked city politics from 1983 to 1987 had ugly racial overtones, but at the heart of the conflict was the old guard refusing to cede any power or patronage to the reform-minded mayor. In retrospect, the chaos benefited the city, because it opened up the political process.

The irony is that when Washington died seven months after he was reelected in 1987, he and his allies were just beginning to enjoy the same spoils of the machine they had once battled. Washington had amassed a solid majority of allies on the city council and was poised to begin pushing his own ambitious programs.

A lasting legacy of the Washington years has been the political success of the African American politicians who followed him. Democrat Carol Moseley-Braun's election to the US senate in 1992 can be credited in part to Washington's political trailblazing. And John Stroger, the first black president of the Cook County Board of Commissioners, was elected in 1994.

Overall, the 1980s meant good times for the city. The mid-decade economic boom in the US was especially strong in Chicago. Scores of young urban professionals – the oft-reviled 'yuppies' – found jobs in the fast-growing service and professional sectors and helped spark extensive real estate development that left large portions of the aging North Side renovated and beautified. As these yuppies aged and started families, many of them stayed in the city rather than following their parents to the suburbs. As a result, gentrification keeps on going and going and going, for two decades and counting. As values in some neighborhoods soar, adjoining areas begin to benefit; the comparatively low prices attract new residents and investors. Development has now spread to portions of the city west and south of the Loop.

Daley Redux

In 1989 Chicago elected Richard M Daley, the son of Richard J Daley, as the new mayor. Like his father, Daley owns an uncanny instinct for city politics. Unlike his father, though, he has shown much political savvy in uniting disparate political forces. He has shrewdly kept African Americans within his political power structure, thus forestalling the kind of movement that propelled Washington to the mayor's office.

After Daley's election the city enjoyed two years of cooperation between City Hall and then-governor Jim Thompson, who lived in and loved Chicago. Until then, the squabbles in city government had prevented the city from working effectively with the state. These newly friendly relations meant that state legislators freed up hundreds of millions of public dollars for the city's use, instead of letting the funds languish in state coffers (as they did throughout the '80s). Among the projects that have now borne fruit are an O'Hare airport expansion, the construction of a new South Building and hotel at McCormick Place, and the complete reconstruction of Navy Pier, which turned the pier into a meeting site and tourist attraction.

Daley has moved to solidify his control of the city in a way his father would have applauded but in a much more enlightened manner. Old semi-independent bureaucracies such as the Park District and Department of Education have been restructured under Daley protégés. The parks look better than ever, and the schools – recently the very worst in the nation – are showing definite signs of progress. And the new mayor entertains the city as well. To the delight of residents and commentators, Daley is prone to amusing verbal blabber, such as this classic, his explanation for why city health inspectors had closed down so many local restaurants: 'Whadda ya want? A rat in yer sandwich or a mouse in yer salad?'

But many challenges still face him. The Chicago Transit Authority is underfunded and has been cutting service, the Chicago Housing Authority needs to find scarce funds to transform its horrific and violent housing projects, and many parts of the South and West Sides of the city still suffer from serious disrepair.

Nevertheless, Chicagoans' rising confidence in their city allowed a potentially traumatic 1990 event to pass almost unnoticed. Long called the 'Second City' because of its number-two spot on the population roster of US cities (New York is first), Chicago fell to third place when the 1990 census showed a population of 2.78 million, behind Los Angeles (3.49 million) and New York (7.32 million). Any lingering sadness was dispelled a year later, when the Chicago Bulls won the first of six national basketball championships. And the 1994 World Cup opening ceremony focused international attention on the city.

In 1996 a 28-year-old demon was exorcised when the Democratic National Convention returned to Chicago. City officials spent millions of dollars spiffing up the town, and thousands of cops underwent sensitivity training on how to deal with protests. The convention went off like a dream and left Chicagoans with a distinct sense that they were on a roll.

In 1999 Mayor Daley won his third term as mayor when he handily beat popular black congressman Bobby Rush in the primary election. Normally the primary winnows the field of candidates down to two for the general election but in this case Daley won with 73% of the vote, a virtual landslide. That he got as much as 40% of the vote in many African American wards is a sign that Daley's strategy of spreading the city's largesse evenly through town is working.

GEOGRAPHY

Once flat and swampy, Chicago now is merely flat. The Chicago River used to be a slow, limpid stream that barely provided drainage for its twin branches, whose Y-shape adorns the city's official symbol. But extensive canal and channel digging over

STEPHEN SAKS

Boat traffic thrives on the Chicago River.

the years has transformed the river into a major waterway.

The city, in the northeastern part of Illinois, covers 228 sq miles. It's 25 miles long and 15 miles wide at its widest point on the far North Side. The lakefront within the city limits stretches for 29 miles.

CLIMATE

The nickname 'Windy City' actually has nonmeteorological origins: it was coined by newspaper reporters in the late 1800s in reaction to the oft-blustery boastfulness of Chicago's politicians. Nevertheless, Chicago

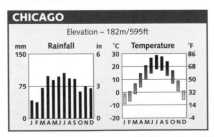

is windy, with everything from cool, God-sent lake breezes at the height of summer to skirt-raising gusts in the spring to spine-chilling, nose-chiseling blasts of icy air in the winter.

You'll experience all four seasons here, with late spring and early fall being generally warm, clear and dry times. Winter and summer behave as expected (see climate chart), but early spring and late fall can freely mix nice days with wretched ones.

Chicago has no true rainy season; its 34 inches of average annual precipitation are spread throughout the year. In winter the precipitation can be wadded into snowballs if some city worker doesn't clear it away first. In spring and fall the storms tend to last for several hours, but they come with plenty of warning from the sky and from forecasters. In summer, as in much of the central US, thunderstorms build in the afternoons and can appear with sudden violence for 10 minutes, then disappear. This happens on the clearest of days and often catches people unawares. Lightning usually accompanies the thunderstorms but rarely strikes people in the city.

Unlike stormy days, cloudy ones are not spread so evenly throughout the year. Although the number of annual gray days averages a not-so-sunny 46%, most of them fall from November to March. (You may not realize just how heavily they're grouped together until the sun breaks through one day and you can't remember when it last appeared.)

On the score card of summer enjoyment, Chicago gets high marks on one (mosquitoes) and not-so-high marks on another (humidity). All that pavement and development means that mosquito counts are very low, and many people never suffer a bite all season, but in July and August the humidity can be uncomfortably high.

ECOLOGY & ENVIRONMENT

Few square inches of Chicago have not been subject to massive development and change in the past 150 years.

The period when Chicago was a blighted industrial landscape is over, but its lingering effects remain. Heavy metals and other toxic substances from the stockyards and steel mills still lace the mud that covers much of the lake bottom. Although the water itself is clean enough for swimming, large, bottom-feeding lake fish such as trout and coho salmon are considered unsafe to eat if they're caught from the southern end of Lake Michigan.

The water quality of the Chicago River, which was reversed to send pollution out of town, is gradually improving. It too has problems with toxic sediment, and during heavy storms the sewers still pour polluted overflow into the river. But the dream of Loop workers being able to fish in the river at lunchtime is no longer unthinkable. Still, the water is not safe for swimming.

Air quality is like that in other urban areas: not very good due to heavy traffic.

FLORA & FAUNA

Chicago was once a huge swamp and wetland, with dunes in the areas on the lake north and south of the river. No trace of this

ANDRE JENNY

Clouds loom: a not-infrequent sight.

past remains, except for a slight rise in Lincoln Park, which was built on a sand dune. Native vegetation, such as the delicate wild onion that gave the city its name, is long gone. To see some of the wildflowers that used to cover much of the inland area, visit the Wildflower Works at the north end of Grant Park (see the Things to See & Do chapter).

The trees lining the streets are mostly hardy varieties such as locust and ash, which can weather the road salt and other forms of urban abuse. The city is becoming increasingly green thanks to Mayor Richard M Daley's love of trees. Even as other city programs have been slashed, the tree-planting program gets more money each year for tens of thousands of new trees on the streets and in the parks.

After decades when the only wildlife in the city consisted of unruly residents and rats, various native species are beginning to return in numbers that are sparking scientific study. Such woodsy creatures as skunks

Wildflowers brighten up Lincoln Park.

and opossums have found that temperate garages off alleys make wonderful winter homes. Deer have been found in Lincoln Park, which is remarkable because the nearest woods they could have come from are more than 5 tough urban miles away.

One of the most amazing occurrences is the increasing number of coyotes moving into the city. After generations of shunning people, this extremely shy species seems to be evolving into an urban predator. For several months one notable coyote gained fame for prowling Gold Coast alleys at night, feasting on rats and other vermin. Its welcome only came to an end after it took out a poodle. (Privately, many neighbors preferred the coyote.)

GOVERNMENT & POLITICS

Chicago politics is a popular spectator sport. The prevalence of elections – city elections fall every four years, the next one being in 2003 – keeps interest high. These are bruising and colorful affairs, with no restraint shown by the candidates when it comes to accusing opponents of every possible misdeed.

State elections are held every four years, two years off the federal cycle; the next Illinois elections are in 2002. These affairs often feature 'downstate-friendly' candidates, who represent the legions of Illinois farmers resentful of Chicago for gobbling up their taxes.

State Politics

For most of the history of Illinois, Chicago dominated state politics. Even when a Republican slipped in as governor on the strength of votes from the state's farmers – which has happened frequently – the city held sway in the Senate and House. But the shrinkage of Chicago's population in the 1970s, coupled with the resulting growth of the suburbs, has altered the balance. The suburbs are heavily Republican, and when they vote in combination with the farmers, Chicago's hegemony is no longer assured.

The Senate is controlled by Republicans and their leader, Pate Philip, who is known for his racist and sexist outbursts. The House lies in the control of Democrats with ties to the city. The governor is George Ryan, a genial Republican elected in 1998.

Sadly for Ryan, he looks to be a one-termer. In the best Illinois tradition, many misdeeds by his past subordinates have come to light. His popularity has suffered, and the prosecutors are circling ever closer.

County Politics

It's easy to forget that Chicago is part of Cook County, which is why the 'County' half of the County-City Building is frequently forgotten. Cook County is a diverse place, consisting of the city and the affluent and impoverished suburbs surrounding it. County government does little that affects the city – and usually falls into line with the mayor when it does. The present county president is John Stroger, a longtime politician who is the first African American to hold the job.

City Politics

Here's where the action is. Chicago's city government includes a mayor, elected every four years, who runs the executive branch and appoints managers in the various city departments, such as Planning, Aviation, Streets and Sanitation, etc. The city council consists of 50 aldermen who are elected every four years and represent small geographic districts.

Maintaining so many politicians and their related offices and staffs is expensive, but proposals to shrink the city council always run aground for the simple reason that the voters like things as they are. Certainly, this amount of bureaucracy is ripe for abuse and corruption (more on that later), but for the average Chicagoan it works well: You got a pothole in front of your house? Somebody stole your trash can? The neighbor's leaving banana peels all over your stoop? Mundane as they are, those are the kinds of matters that directly affect people's lives, and they can be taken care of with a call to the alderman.

With the districts so small in size, the politicians and their staffs can't afford to anger any voters, because angry voters start voting for somebody else. At the heart of this system is a phrase the late *Chicago Tribune* columnist Mike Royko used to say should be the motto for the city: 'Where's mine?' The entire system of city politics is based on a simple structure: the voter wants her alley cleaned, and the alderman wants her vote. If the alderman wants a lot of votes, he or she gets a bunch of plums for the district in the form of city jobs or big spending projects from the mayor. If the mayor wants votes for his or her programs from the city council, he or she doles out money in programs to the aldermen.

The Machine Chicago's vaunted machine is not even a shell of its former self. There was a time when politicians approved the hiring decisions in all departments of city government, which ensured armies of loyal workers at election time, but that era came to a crashing end in 1979, when political hiring was prohibited for all but top-echelon jobs.

Without all those jobs to give out, the power of the politicians – especially the aldermen – was sharply reduced. That helped Harold Washington win the mayoral election in 1983 and guarantees that the current Mayor Daley must appeal to a broad range of voters if he hopes to get reelected.

Ethics For a good laugh, stop by the information desk in front of the elevators at City Hall (121 N LaSalle St) and pick up the brochure from the Chicago Board of Ethics. It's a high-minded bunch of pap expressing the commitment of the city government to thwart such evils as theft from the city, the acceptance of bribes and the operation of a private businesses on city time, as well as a bunch of other malarkey about the need for honest government.

What makes this little brochure no better than twaddle are the antics of city officials and employees, most entertainingly covered in the local press. Examples follow.

In a sting dubbed 'Operation Greylord,' the federal government sent scores of county judges to the pokey in the 1980s after catching them literally stuffing cash in their pockets to fix cases. One memorable quote at the time came from one of the judges convicted of bribery and other crimes: 'I love people that take dough, because you know exactly where you stand.'

White Blight

Any Chicago politician can tell you that snow is a substance sent by God to ruin political careers, and because of that, the powers that be view each and every delicate little flake as an invader to be eradicated, whatever the cost.

At the first sign of flurries, official Chicago mounts a counterattack that rivals the Normandy invasion in its fury and single-minded sense of purpose. After all, everybody in city government remembers what happened to Mayor Michael Bilandic, who was sunning himself in Florida in January 1979, when the city was smothered by one of the worst blizzards of the century. Never mind that experts say the volume of snow precluded any response that would have saved the city from being buried for weeks. Images of the tanned Bilandic tut-tutting about the white stuff while people suffered heart attacks digging out their cars stuck with voters when they went to the polls two months later and sent a message that rocked Chicago's political machine.

Since then every mayor has gone to battle at the fall of the first flake. If you're in Chicago for a snowfall, you'll be treated to quite a show. First, more than 400 salt trucks with plows hit the streets with flashing yellow lights. Next come hundreds of garbage trucks hurriedly fitted with plows, followed by bulldozers, graders, dump trucks and other heavy equipment. Snow-parking rules go into effect, and any mope who leaves his or her car parked on an arterial street will find it towed.

At 10pm, watch the local newscasts. Each will have breathless reporters live at the command center of the Department of Streets and Sanitation, a milieu much like NASA's mission control, with reports of snow incursions immediately dispatched.

Tiny snowdrift forming at Clark and Diversey? Send in a platoon of plows! Patches of ice on the Randolph Bridge? Get a battalion of salt trucks over there! Homeless man refusing to leave box on Lower Wacker Dr? Send in a squad of cops to arrest him and toss him into a toasty cell. (Less stubborn sorts can avail themselves of the scores of 'warming centers' the city opens around the city.)

Outsiders might consider this response overkill, but Chicagoans take pride in this display of can-do attitude. No matter that the thousands of tons of salt dumped every year dissolve concrete, bridges, cars, trees, boots and everything else; nobody complains. In 1992 a deep cold snap hit the Midwest and several cities ran out of salt. 'What's the situation locally?' reporters asked. While cars skated on other cities' streets, everyone was delighted to learn that Chicago still had enough salt for several years, because each year the city buys at least three times what it needs. You can see some of these huge bluish-white mountains on vacant land around town.

Of course, anybody who has been to places such as Washington, DC, Atlanta or Dallas, where just a few flakes can cause pandemonium, might appreciate Chicago's war on the stuff. And they might enjoy the show as well.

US Representative Dan Rostenkowski, the third most powerful man in the United States Congress and a Bucktown resident, was caught masterminding scams for rewards worth little more than peanuts and was sent to jail in 1994.

In 1995 Representative Mel Reynolds was sent to prison for having sex with a minor. Among the evidence against him were tapes of a phone chat he had with a young girl concerning the color of her panties.

In a late 1990s scandal referred to as 'Operation Silver Shovel,' seven alderman were indicted for refusing no bribe, no matter how small. This is an ongoing operation mounted by the US Attorney's Office in Chicago, which stays busy prosecuting local politicians.

In 2000 former city treasurer Miriam Santos pleaded guilty to campaign extortion while she still had her job. She served time in the federal slammer.

During your visit to Chicago, you are bound to enjoy press coverage of the latest scandals. Odds are good that you may even enjoy an alderman's indictment or two.

ECONOMY

The value of Chicago's annual goods and services tops $150 billion. The service industries employ close to three-quarters of Chicago workers, in such areas as insurance, banking, accounting, commodities and options trading, retail sales, health care, advertising, entertainment, communications, hospitality, law and education.

Visitors, whether in Chicago for business, fun or both, were responsible for an estimated $15 billion in expenditures in 1999 and represent a vital part of the city's economy. The city averages about 30 million visitors a year, and numbers have been increasing by about 5% a year.

Fifteen *Fortune* 500 firms are based in Chicago, with another 20 in the surrounding suburbs. Among them are the following major players.

Bcom3 is the oddball name for one of the largest media firms in the world, with 1999 revenues of $2 billion. Its principal unit – also based in Chicago – is the huge Leo Burnett Advertising agency. Although Burnett's output is often banal, there's no doubt that Tony the Tiger, Mr Whipple, the Pillsbury Doughboy and a menagerie of other ad campaigns have found a place in the American psyche. On a darker note, the Burnett-hatched Marlboro Man has popularized and glamorized cigarette smoking worldwide.

Chicagoan Ray Kroc bought a successful hamburger stand from two brothers in California in 1955. He studied the concept and reduced it to its simple core of cheap assembly-line burgers of dependable, if not spectacular, quality served in squeaky clean surroundings. Since he opened up his first

The fast-paced scene on the trading floors of the Chicago Mercantile Exchange

RICHARD I'ANSON

McDonald's outlet, just beyond the city limits in Des Plaines, the world has not been able to get enough Bic Macs and fries.

The Sears merchandise group decamped for the suburbs in 1992, leaving their landmark building one-third empty. But the executive offices stayed on the high floors downtown, and the booming 1990s economy saw the Sears Tower fill right back up with new tenants.

United Airlines, the world's largest airline, has always been based at the world's busiest airport: first Midway and then O'Hare. Although O'Hare recently slipped to number two, United is in the process of moving its headquarters back into the city from the suburbs.

POPULATION & PEOPLE

Some 2.8 million people live in the city, a figure that has started to rise again after falling from the high of 3.6 million in 1950. Throughout the second half of the 20th century, the city's population fell due to two opposite factors: the economic and social devastation of some neighborhoods and, conversely, the economic success of others, where yuppies now live singly or in pairs in apartments that once housed whole families. The 2000 Census figures surprised many

with the news that Chicago had boosted a net population gain of more than 100,000 for the first time in 50 years.

Almost 40% of Chicagoans are African Americans, but the percentage is slowly diminishing as the Hispanic community expands and blacks move to surrounding suburbs.

Immigrants continue to arrive in droves. Many have long-established support groups that quickly find work for the new arrivals, which is why many newsstands are run by Pakistanis, many dry cleaners are run by Koreans and many of the office buildings are cleaned by Polish women.

The Hispanic community is the fastest growing in Chicago, constituting more than 20% of the total population. Its expansion has chiefly fueled the city's recent population gain. Chicago's diverse Hispanic population embraces sizable communities of Mexicans, Central Americans, Puerto Ricans and Cubans. Major Hispanic neighborhoods lie in northwest Chicago, in Pilsen and farther south through Canaryville.

Chinese American residents don't just live in Chinatown – they've also made their homes on Argyle St on the North Side, where they're part of a large Asian community alongside Vietnamese and Cambodians.

Chicagoans know how to have fun.

Koreans have made Lawrence Ave the center of their community, and many Indians and Pakistanis live near Devon Ave and throughout the far north neighborhoods. Asian Americas make up 4% of the city's population – a number that's growing fast.

Sometimes it seems there are more Irish in Chicago than Dublin. And that refers to those who were born in Ireland, not the millions of descendants of the first major group of Irish to inhabit the city. Many of the Irish-born people in Chicago work as nurses and construction workers for a few years and then return home.

Chicago has long welcomed Poles with open arms, and the city was an early supporter of the famous Solidarity movement in Poland. Along stretches of Milwaukee Ave you'll hear only Polish spoken.

ARTS

The arts community in Chicago is diverse thanks to its population, its long tradition of monetary support for the arts and its regional pull on young artists raised in the middle of the country, from the Rockies to Appalachia.

Businesses have come to recognize the economic potential of the arts that draw people to the city as tourists and as prospective employees. In the early 1990s the Chicago Symphony and the Lyric Opera challenged the corporate community to raise new money to renovate their homes and collected $100 million in short order. Leisure travelers who come to Chicago spend about 40% of their time visiting cultural attractions.

Of course, the big money doesn't always make it to the pockets of the artists themselves. Chicago actors who belong to Actors' Equity – the rough equivalent of a union – average only $5000 a year in pay. Non-Equity members often work free. The difficult existence of many artists bouncing from show to show, commission to commission or sale to sale has a hidden benefit for the city at large: to make ends meet, these smart and creative people often work in restaurants and bars, which often makes for a lively evening out in almost any place you choose.

Whether it is music, fine art, literature or drama, Chicago's creativity tends to reflect the city's personality: straightforward and unpretentious. Look for an honesty that goes right to the soul.

Music

Though most kinds of music are performed in the city, Chicago has exercised a special influence on a few genres. Jazz, blues and gospel – and by extension, rock – have enjoyed remarkable innovations thanks in some part to Chicago.

Blues The same Illinois Central trains that brought a generation of blacks to Chicago in the Great Migration brought the blues as well.

Early on, blues in the city closely resembled the variety played in the bayous of Mississippi and Louisiana. But the demands of noisy clubs and the pressures of urban life soon resulted in a more aggressive, amplified sound that is the basis of Chicago blues.

Muddy Waters arrived on the scene in 1943 and is widely regarded as the most important blues musician to work in Chicago. His influence runs deep, extending to early rock groups such as the Rolling Stones and the Paul Butterfield Band. His sideman in later years was Buddy Guy, whose electric-guitar work influenced musicians such as Eric Clapton, Stevie Ray Vaughan and Jimi Hendrix. Guy continues to operate the club bearing his name in the South Loop (see the Jazz & Blues section in the Entertainment chapter). Other important blues greats have included Willie Dixon, Sunnyland Slim and Koko Taylor, who also owns a club bearing her name.

Jazz In 1922 Louis Armstrong came to Chicago from New Orleans to join King Oliver's Creole Jazz Band, which cut some of the most influential recordings in jazz history the next year. His solo style soon flourished in the city, as he wowed crowds of fans in Bronzeville and elsewhere, giving his trumpet a workout only the toughest brass could withstand.

Like Armstrong, Jelly Roll Morton immigrated from New Orleans and gave Chicago jazz a freewheeling, powerful expression that defied the efforts of snobs to reduce jazz to static parlor listening.

Others who defined Chicago jazz included Benny Goodman, Bix Beiderbecke, Eddie Condon and Bud Freeman. In the 1960s a group of musicians formed the Association for the Advancement of Creative Musicians (more commonly known by its acronym, AACM), which continues to push the envelope of jazz, repeatedly redefining the genre.

The nonprofit Jazz Institute of Chicago (☎ 312-427-1676, 410 S Michigan Ave) labors ceaselessly to promote Chicago jazz. It's the creative force behind each year's jazz festival in Grant Park in June (see the Special Events section of the Facts for the Visitor chapter).

Many jazz greats of today live in Chicago, among them Von Freeman and Fred Anderson. The former plays regularly at the New Apartment Lounge while the latter hits the stage at his own Velvet Lounge. See the Entertainment chapter for details.

Gospel Blues and jazz planted the seeds of this soulful singing, which emanates from churches all over the South Side every Sunday. Huge choruses clap their hands, chant, shout, wail and create music that both inspires and speaks for the huge congregations of the primarily Baptist churches. Much of the credit for creating the gospel sound, at once mournful and joyous, goes to

Thomas A Dorsey, music director at the Pilgrim Baptist Church in Bronzeville, who died in 1993 at age 93. Mahalia Jackson is just one of the great Chicago gospel singers who have launched careers in South Side churches. Popular singers Ruth Brown and Faye Adams did as well, and so did Little Richard and Chuck Berry.

The Thompson Community Singers, a 50-year-old Chicago gospel choir, has attracted a huge following. Led by current musical director Percy Bady, the singers have headlined the Chicago Gospel Festival and produced some hot-selling CDs.

Closely related to gospel is soul, a genre that primarily emerged from Detroit's Motown sound, though Chicago also made contributions. Chicagoan Curtis Mayfield wrote, produced and performed through the 1960s and '70s. His musical additions to a series of the so-called blaxploitation films of the early 1970s are largely credited with the low-budget films' success. Check out his pulsing beat in the 1972 hit *Superfly*.

Rock Given rock's roots in the blues, you'd expect Chicago to have a strong rock music tradition. However, it wasn't until the 1980s that the city really made a name for itself in the rock world.

Steve Albini and Santiago Durango's guitar band Big Black exploded on Chicago stages in the mid-'80s. Their hard-driving punkish songs screeched at audiences and almost defied even fans' efforts to listen, but the band set the tone for what became a remarkable decade of alternative rock in the city.

In quick succession, Screeching Weasel, Urge Overkill and countless others defined a genre of music that featured lyrics probing the performer's psyches, souls and sex lives. Liz Phair, a suburban waif, became a sensation based on her brutally honest confessions in the album *Exile in Guyville*. But the biggest stars to come out of Chicago were the Smashing Pumpkins. Worldwide superstars, the Pumpkins sold millions of albums right through *Machina/The Machines of God*, their last release before their final concert at the Metro (see the Entertainment chapter) in 2000.

Although Bucktown – the center of Chicago's alternative rock world – no longer draws the same throngs of band wannabes on weekends, the local scene continues to produce new talent. Watch for eclectic efforts by the Blue Meanies, Frisbie, the Handsome Family, Everlast and Louise Post.

Fine Arts

Chicago art of 100 years ago was largely designed to show the world that Chicago was a city 'that got taste.' The industrialists funded works that evoked imperial Europe in their grand scale. Meanwhile, the same industrialists bought up the latest art Europe had to offer. During this period society matron Bertha Palmer and others gathered much of the Art Institute's wondrous collection of impressionist paintings.

During the 1920s Chicago art veered towards modernism and realism, led by the likes of Rudolph Weisenborn and Wassily Kandinsky. The gritty realm of the city proved a perfect inspiration for these new forms of art, with their hard-edged portrayals of urban life. Archiblad Motley Jr captured the essence of life on the South Side.

Styles fragmented with the emergence of the surrealism and abstract expressionism in the mid-20th century. Some Chicago artists who experimented with the new, unconventional techniques included Karl Wirsum, James Falconer and a group that came to be known as the Hairy Who.

Today, neighborhoods like Ukrainian Village and Wicker Park have drawn scores of young artists who enjoy the cheap rents and realism of city life while they try to express themselves as successfully as Ed Paschke, who found fame in the 1970s with his unusually conceived portraits, many of which can be seen at the Museum of Contemporary Art.

Chicago's resident artists, combined with the city's great museums and myriad galleries, make it a great place for art lovers. See the Things to See & Do chapter for more

RICHARD I'ANSON

A Chicago artist at work

information on Chicago's art museums. See the Shopping chapter for listings of galleries and neighborhoods where you can view and buy art.

Public Art In 1978 Chicago began to require that developers include financial provisions for public art in their projects, specifically 1% of the total cost. The decidedly mixed results can be seen throughout downtown. See the Things to See & Do chapter for a guide to the varied sculptures in the Loop, along with other notable examples of public art.

Architecture

See the special Architecture section for a full discussion of Chicago's place on the world stage of architecture and for a suggested walking tour of its rich architectural milieu.

Film

Few know that Chicago was a center of the American film industry until 1920. Charlie

Chaplin reigned as the star of Essanay Film Studios on Argyle St from 1907 to 1917, when the film industry heard that land could be bought for cheap out west in some new place called Hollywood.

Following that, filmmakers had trouble showing their faces back in Chicago. Mayor Richard J Daley did his best to bar them from the city, his hatred of the industry being one of his many quirks. His death in 1976 coincided with Hollywood's desire to find fresh locations. Chicago fit the bill perfectly, and for the past 20 years the city has starred in hundreds of films and TV shows. Sappy comedy director and producer John Hughes can't stay away.

The industry Daley shunned now pumps millions a year into the city economy and employs hundreds. Chicagoans acted like a bunch of star-struck rubes when the first wave of productions hit town, but they now hardly break their fast strides to give a location set a second glance.

Although Chicago has become a favored location for filmmakers, much of the city's homegrown talent still has to work out of Hollywood. The Cusacks, John and Joan, are but a tiny example.

Literature

In 1900 Theodore Dreiser wrote *Sister Carrie*. In a lot of ways, it is the perfect Chicago book: the mean streets of the city rob our heroine of her virtue, but in the best 'Where's mine?' tradition, she turns this seeming setback into profitable gain. This same gritty reality pervades much of Chicago's best literature.

Carl Sandburg's 1916 poem 'Chicago,' merely one in his exceptional collection titled simply *Chicago Poems*, captures a spirit of the city that endures even as the details have changed: 'Hog Butcher for the World, / Tool Maker, Stacker of Wheat, / Player with Railroads and the Nation's Freight Handler;/ …City of the Big Shoulders.'

The elusive Saul Bellow turns out high-profile works, which garnered him the Nobel Prize for Literature in 1976. His novels focus on the strengths and weaknesses of humanity through studies of flawed figures. These works include *Herzog*, *Humbolt's Gift*, *The Adventures of Augie March* and *The Dean's December*.

Gwendolyn Brooks became the first African American to win the Pulitzer Prize for her 1949 book of poetry *Annie Allen*. Some of her best-known works, which focus on African Americans in Chicago, use plain-spoken language to memorable effect. Brooks died in 2000 at age 83.

The classic Studs Lonigan trilogy, by James T Farrell, conveys the aspirations of Irish American immigrants and the nightmarish realities of their lives.

Leaving his CTA bus far behind, former driver Larry Heinemann based his first works on his experiences as a grunt in Vietnam. *Paco's Story* won the National Book Award for Fiction in 1987. His more recent novels have focused on the oddities of contemporary life in the city.

Before he was found hanging outside his Loop office window in 1996, Eugene Izzi made a name for himself by writing hard-edged mysteries set in the city. His last book was *A Matter of Honor*.

Cris Mazza, a University of Chicago creative writing professor, turns out books with such unusual plots that one right-wing Republican called her writing 'an offense to the senses.' Her recent novel *Dog People* features razor-sharp writing and a cast of colorful characters, among them a fascist dog trainer, a lesbian dancer and a loveless caterer.

Sara Paretsky's VI Warshawski detective novels at first seem like nothing more than escapist genre fiction, but within the gritty narratives about a woman private investigator, Paretsky weaves her own deep commitment to social justice.

Commonly known as 'an old man with a tape recorder,' the ageless Studs Terkel is much more; he's a compassionate chronicler of the lives of everyday people, making the seemingly mundane deeply moving. Among his works are *Division Street: America*, *The Good War: An Oral History of World War II* and *Working*.

A seemingly unstoppable producer of screenplays disguised as books, Scott Turow is actually more interesting than his plots, which

Nelson Algren

A product of the mean streets of the city, Nelson Algren (1909–81) was the quintessential Chicago fiction writer, crafting realist writing as no-nonsense as the city itself. He lived for many years at 1958 W Evergreen Ave in the then-sordid Wicker Park neighborhood, and he found his characters and places on the surrounding streets.

In 1950 Algren won the first National Book Award, bestowed by American publishers, for *The Man with the Golden Arm*, a novel set on Division St near Milwaukee Ave. Chronicling the lives of people struggling to survive within the confines of their neighborhood, this tale is shaped by varying degrees of desire, hope and loyalty, themes that have defined the lives of generations of Chicagoans. In the following excerpt, Algren explores the relationship between the deeply troubled central character, Frankie, and his sometime friend Sparrow:

> Sparrow himself had only the faintest sort of inkling that Frankie had brought home a duffel bag of trouble. The little petit-larceny punk from Damen and Division and the dealer still got along like a couple of playful pups. 'He's like me,' Frankie explained, 'never drinks. Unless he's alone or with somebody.'

Algren's other works include *The Neon Wilderness* (1947), *A Walk on the Wild Side* (1956) and *The Last Carousel* (1973).

always seem to feature a heroine destined to be played by Julia Roberts being pursued by Gene Hackman-like bad guys; Turow still works as a Loop lawyer and writes his books during his commute on the Metra train.

Theater

Moviegoers familiar with the carpet-chewing performances of John Malkovich and Gary Sinise already know the tenets of the Chicago style of acting, for which the two Steppenwolf Theater principals receive much credit: a fiery intensity marked by loud, physical acting.

In many ways the pair built on a tradition that had begun in the 1960s, when modern improvisational comedy, a Chicago invention, began leaving its mark on the actors who graced the stages. Improv called for deep commitment from the ensemble casts, in which everyone depended on everyone else for a performance to succeed.

Beginning in the 1970s, the tough, machine-gun-fire bursts of dialogue in David Mamet's taut dramas only added to Chicago theater's reputation for hard-edged, raw emotion. And legions of young actors and directors continue to fuel the theatrical fire with their burning desires to make their marks.

RELIGION

Chicago has the largest Catholic archdiocese in the country. Ongoing immigration from Catholic countries such as Mexico and Poland ensures that the city's large Catholic population will stay that way. Baptist churches are prevalent throughout the South Side. A large Jewish community established itself long ago.

The Yellow Pages lists thousands of churches, representing any of 119 denominations. The number and variety reflect the large and varied population. The choices include Russian Orthodox, Mennonite, Christian Chinese, Islamic and Armenian Apostolic.

LANGUAGE

As elsewhere in the US, English is the major spoken language here. In the heart of some ethnic enclaves you'll hear Spanish, Polish, Korean or Russian, but almost all business is conducted in English. Midwestern accents tend to be a bit flat with just a touch of nasal twang, but compared to other parts of the US, most of the English you'll hear is pretty standard – the middle of the country has always produced a large share of plain-spoken TV announcers.

You may also encounter 'Black English,' a variation of English that's spoken by many African Americans. Generally reserved for casual encounters with friends, its lexicon and cadences can be rather cryptic to nonnative English speakers.

CHICAGO ARCHITECTURE: A STUDY IN INNOVATION

Two great explosions of creative energy and innovation mark Chicago architecture. The first came after the 1871 fire (see the History section of the Facts about Chicago chapter), when architects from around the world flocked to the city for commissions. Most were young – the average age was under 30 – and had something to prove. They found a city happy to give them the scorched Loop as a stage, and within three decades they invented the modern skyscraper, with its steel frame, high-speed elevators and curtain walls of glass. These young architects also defined a new form of architecture that came to be called the 'Chicago School.' Tossed aside were the classical forms of Greece and Rome that architects the world over continued to apply to major works. The Chicago School stressed economy, simplicity and function.

These architects closely adhered to Chicago School architect Louis Sullivan's mandate that 'form follows function.' Though the basic tenet held true – the buildings did draw their facades from the underlying logic of the regular steel bracing beneath – that didn't result in a lack of adornment. The architects used a powerful language of simple geometric shapes, primarily strong vertical lines crossed by horizontal bands. Relief from the sharp lines came in the form of bay windows, curved corners, sweeping entrances and other details, which gave the buildings a pragmatic glory that reflected the city around them.

Chicago contributed again to world architecture after WWII. Led by Ludwig Mies van der Rohe, the new 'International Style' swept architecture. This style truly was the pared-down embodiment of Sullivan's mandate: the very structure of buildings – the steel frame – was no longer the inspiration for a building's look, it was the look. The oft-copied steel-and-glass towers, similar to the Federal Center (Dearborn and Adams

Above: Tiffany stained glass dome, Cultural Center
(RICHARD CUMMINS)

Right: Chicago's soaring skyline

DON EASTMAN

Sts), were built in every country around the world but often without Mies' careful eye for details.

From 1950 through 1980, the Chicago architectural firm of Skidmore, Owings & Merrill became the IBM of their day. No corporate manager was ever fired for hiring SOM and their bands of Mies disciples to design a building.

During the go-go era of the 1980s commercial space in the Loop almost doubled, and high-rise offices spread to the Near North. Many of these buildings were influenced by postmodernism, the movement that emphasized eclectic designs drawn from older styles and other art forms. The real estate crash at the end of the decade stalled new construction, but today occupancy in the Loop and surroundings is healthy, and another wave of construction has begun. It remains to be seen what architectural movement Chicago will next produce or embrace.

Architects

The following are some of the most important people associated with Chicago's architecture; their work can be found throughout the city.

Daniel Burnham He played a principal role in the development of the Chicago School of architecture (see the boxed text 'Make No Little Plans...').

Bertrand Goldberg He used concrete to create fluid structures such as Marina City (1959–67) and River City (1986).

Bruce Graham A leading partner at Skidmore, Owings & Merrill, Graham designed massive structures such as the John Hancock Center (1969) and the Sears Tower (1974), which continued Chicago's burly and aggressive style of architecture.

'Make No Little Plans...'

The lead planner of the 1893 World's Columbian Exposition, Daniel Burnham developed a concept known as 'City Beautiful,' which called for cities to be designed along a grand scheme that extended beyond buildings to streets, parks and the entire urban landscape. His 1909 plan for Chicago guided development for the next 30 years. Burnham's ideas influenced city design around the world.

Proving to be as good at quotes as he was at design, Burnham made the following exhortation to his colleagues:

Make no little plans; they have no magic to stir men's blood and probably themselves will not be realized. Make big plans; aim high in hope and work, remembering that a noble and logical diagram once recorded will never die, but long after we are gone will be a living thing, asserting itself with growing intensity. Remember that our sons and grandsons are going to do things that would stagger us. Let your watchword be 'order' and your beacon 'beauty.'

William Holabird & Martin Roche These partners took the Chicago School to commercial success, applying its tenets to more than 80 buildings in the Loop. Notable survivors include the Pontiac Building (1891) and the Marquette Building (1894).

Helmut Jahn This controversial architect reversed the Sullivan tenet and designed buildings in which function follows form. His early work, such as the modernist Xerox Centre, is overshadowed by his later showy works, such as the notorious James R Thompson Center (1985; see Part Four of the Loop Architecture Walking Tour) and the masterful United Airlines Terminal One at O'Hare (1988).

Fazlur Khan This structural engineer made the Hancock Center and Sears Tower not only possible but economically feasible. His prominent exterior cross-bracing on the Hancock Center was so efficient that material costs for the 100-story building were no more than those for a conventional 45-story affair.

Ludwig Mies van der Rohe The legendary architect brought his Bauhaus School ideas to Chicago when he fled the Nazis and Germany in the 1930s. His 860 and 880 N Lake Shore Dr apartments (1951) set the style for three decades of international architecture (see the Gold Coast section of the Things to See & Do chapter).

John Wellborn Root Burnham's partner, Root designed the Monadnock Building (1891) and the Rookery (1888), among many other Chicago School classics, before his untimely death at age 41.

Louis Sullivan A master of ornamentation, Sullivan brought his skills to bear on the entrance to Carson Pirie Scott & Co (1903) and on the now-destroyed Chicago Stock Exchange; you can see preserved bits of the latter at the Art Institute. Sullivan usually created his work in partnership with engineer Dankmar Adler.

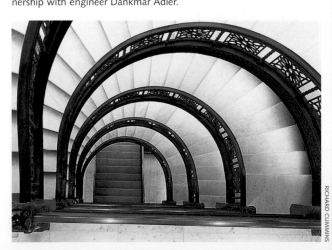

Right: Staircase in The Rookery, designed by Frank Lloyd Wright

RICHARD CUMMINS

Frank Lloyd Wright A visionary, Wright pioneered the revolutionary Prairie School style of architecture, which derived its form from its surroundings: buildings were low, heavily emphasizing the horizontal lines of the Midwestern landscape. In contrast to the simple lines of the architecture, Wright added myriad precise details, which you'll notice on closer inspection of his buildings. For more about Wright, see the Oak Park section of the Excursions chapter and the Robie House listing in the Hyde Park section of the Things to See & Do chapter.

Residential Styles

As you explore Chicago's neighborhoods, you will see several types of housing repeated over and over. The following styles are listed roughly in their order of appearance in Chicago.

Cottages & Frame Houses Chicago's great contribution to residential construction was the two-by-four. Until the system of knocking houses together from precut boards and mass-produced nails was developed in the city in 1833, building a house was a long and costly process of sawing timber and stacking rocks. Thousands of cottages and frame houses burned like matchsticks in the 1871 fire, but many more were built later in areas of the city where they weren't outlawed by the city's fire code. Look for them in Wicker Park, Old Town and Pilsen (see the Wicker Park walking tour in the Things to See & Do chapter).

Queen Anne Houses Commonly called Victorian houses, these residences proliferated in the late 19th century and featured a wealth of detail and ornaments, which the masses could afford thanks to assembly-line production techniques developed in lumber factories southwest of the Loop. The houses can be found throughout the north and northwest sides of the city.

RICK GERHARTER

Left: Victorian style in Old Town

Graystones Two and three stories tall, these dignified residences met the city's tough fire code and became popular refuges from 1890 to 1920. The expensive limestone was used only in front; the rest of the structures were made out of ordinary brick. Some were built as single-family homes, others as apartments. Graystones dot the city; the Wrigleyville neighborhood contains a huge concentration of them.

Apartment Buildings These come in all shapes and sizes, from three-story multi-unit affairs built in the late 1800s to the airy courtyard buildings of the 1920s to some really awful concrete high-rises that appeared after WWII. In the early 20th century Chicago's population density rose so much that by 1920 two-thirds of the city's residents lived in apartments.

Three-Flats Joined by their less ambitious cousins, the two-flats, these buildings filled many of the city's neighborhoods from the 1910s through today. Set on the usual narrow Chicago lot, the buildings feature apartments with light front rooms and airy back kitchens with wooden porches (many of which are now enclosed to increase living space). Dark bedrooms open off a long hall that runs the length of the apartment. Since the 1970s thousands of these buildings have been renovated throughout the North Side for a new generation of apartment dwellers and condo buyers.

Storefronts with Apartments Throughout the 20th century storeowners and developers have placed living spaces above small retail shops. Examples of this practice can be found along any of Chicago's retail streets, especially in the neighborhoods. To see a contemporary equivalent of this practice, look up at the condos high above the Michigan Ave vertical malls, such as Water Tower Place and 900 N Michigan.

Bungalows Built by the tens of thousands along Chicago's outlying streets from the 1920s through the 1950s, bungalows filled the subdivisions of their day. Aimed squarely at factory workers, these homes commonly cost only $1000 down, plus easy payments on builder-financed $5000 mortgages; the affordable prices brought single-family homeownership to a generation. Stolid and compact on lots 25 feet wide, the homes introduced the booming middle class to features their parents had considered luxuries: central halls, which gave privacy to bedrooms; ceramic-tiled bathrooms, which had hot and cold water; and kitchens with built-in cabinets and counters. Provisions were made for gas ranges, refrigerators and ever-growing collections of electrical appliances. Architectural details inspired by Frank Lloyd Wright's Prairie School brought character to the 'bungalow belts' that soon circled the city. These sturdy homes – most are still standing – have proven endlessly adaptable through the years. Roofs have been popped up to create full second floors; basements have been finished for rumpus rooms; kitchens and bathrooms have been remodeled to reflect the latest whims of design and convenience. Today a bungalow in good shape easily costs $180,000 or much more.

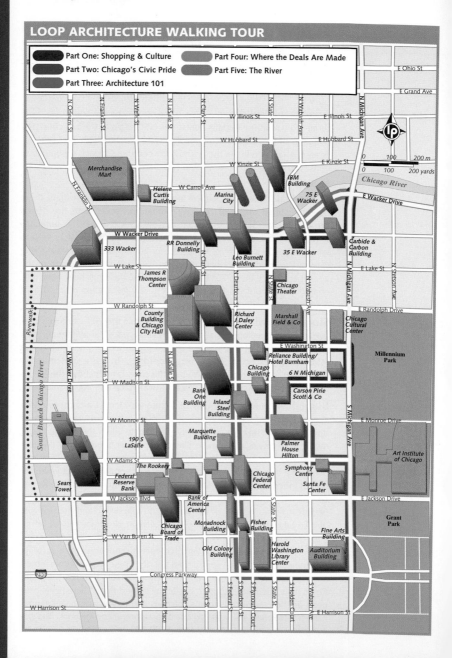

LOOP ARCHITECTURE WALKING TOUR

Part One: Shopping & Culture
Part Two: Chicago's Civic Pride
Part Three: Architecture 101
Part Four: Where the Deals Are Made
Part Five: The River

E Ohio St
E Grand Ave
N Orleans St
N Franklin St
N Wells St
N LaSalle St
N Clark St
N State St
N Wabash Ave
N Michigan Ave
W Illinois St
E Illinois St
W Hubbard St
E Hubbard St
W Kinzie St
E Kinzie St
0   100   200 m
0   100   200 yards
Merchandise Mart
W Carroll Ave
Helene Curtis Building
Marina City
IBM Building
75 E Wacker
Chicago River
E Wacker Drive
W Wacker Drive
333 Wacker
RR Donnelly Building
Leo Burnett Building
35 E Wacker
Carbide & Carbon Building
N Franklin St
W Lake St
E Lake St
N Stetson Ave
James R Thompson Center
N Dearborn St
N State St
N Wabash Ave
N Michigan Ave
W Randolph St
E Randolph Drive
County Building & Chicago City Hall
Richard J Daley Center
Chicago Theater
Marshall Field & Co
Chicago Cultural Center
Millennium Park
Riverwalk
E Washington St
Reliance Building/Hotel Burnham
Chicago Building
6 N Michigan
Carson Pirie Scott & Co
N Wacker Drive
N Franklin St
N Wells St
N LaSalle St
W Madison St
Bank One Building
Inland Steel Building
S Michigan Ave
Millennium Park
South Branch Chicago River
W Monroe St
E Monroe Drive
Marquette Building
Palmer House Hilton
Art Institute of Chicago
190 S LaSalle
W Adams St
The Rookery
Federal Reserve Bank
Chicago Federal Center
Symphony Center
Santa Fe Center
Sears Tower
W Jackson Blvd
Bank of America Center
E Jackson Drive
S Franklin St
S Wells St
S LaSalle St
Chicago Board of Trade
Monadnock Building
Fisher Building
Fine Arts Building
Grant Park
W Van Buren St
Old Colony Building
Harold Washington Library Center
Auditorium Building
290
Congress Parkway
S Financial Place
S Wells St
S LaSalle St
S Clark St
S Federal St
S Dearborn St
S Plymouth Court
S State St
S Holden Court
S Wabash Ave
W Harrison St
E Harrison St

Loop Architecture Walking Tour

The Loop abounds with important, beautiful and interesting architecture. Just by walking its streets for about half a day, you can trace the development of modern architecture in Chicago, the US and worldwide. This walking tour is arranged in five parts, which you can explore all at once or in stages – simply follow the map for each. You can explore the public spaces of most buildings during office hours on weekdays. Entering these buildings on the weekends is much more problematic. Note that the proper names for some buildings are actually their addresses.

Part One: Shopping & Culture

This walk passes structures that date from early in the 20th century, when the North Loop was the entertainment center of Chicago. Begin at the south end of the Michigan Ave Bridge and walk south.

❶ **Carbide & Carbon Building, 230 N Michigan Ave** Though it looks black, the exterior of this 1929 Burnham Brothers building is actually made of very dark green terracotta; it just could use a good cleaning. The tower, with its setback, is detailed in gold leaf.

❷ **35 E Wacker** Built as the 'Jeweler's Building' by Thielbar & Fugard in 1926, this spot once had an interior elevator that allowed tenants to park their cars securely near their offices. The four corner towers at the setback above the 24th floor hide water tanks. The domed pinnacle houses the offices of architect Helmut Jahn.

❸ **Chicago Theater, 175 N State St** Restored by the city in 1986, this 3800-seat theater is a grand example of the movie palaces of the 1920s. Its architects, Rapp & Rapp, cut their teeth on the 1921 commission and went on to design scores of theaters that increasingly came to resemble fantastic wedding cakes. The theater surrounds two sides of the Page Brothers Building, which was built in 1872 right after the fire. The building's Lake St facade is formed of cast iron, which makes it one of two such structures left in the city.

❹ **Marshall Field & Co, 111 N State St** Covering an entire block, Marshall Field's was built in five stages by Daniel Burnham and others between

RICHARD CUMMINS

1892 and 1914. The south-eastern corner (at Washington St and Wabash Ave) went up during the earliest stage and features massive load-bearing walls. On the State St side, the soaring ground-floor retail spaces are topped by Tiffany skylights. The whole store underwent a costly reconstruction in 1992, when a central escalator atrium was added.

❺ Reliance Building, 32 N State St Built in the early 1890s by Burnham & Root, the Reliance Building, with its 16 stories of shimmering glass framed by brilliant white terra-cotta details, is like a breath of fresh air. Its lightweight internal metal frame – much of which was erected in only 15 days – supports a glass facade that gives the building a feeling of lightness, a style that didn't become universal until after WWII. Narrowly avoiding demolition – a common fate for Chicago's architectural gems in a town where preservation often takes a back seat to commercial interests – the Reliance underwent an exterior restoration in 1995 and reopened as the chic Hotel Burnham in 1999 (see the Places to Stay chapter).

❻ Chicago Cultural Center, 78 E Washington St Thank the British for this beautiful 1897 public building. After the 1871 fire the Brits sent more than 8000 books to establish a free library for the people of Chicago. Many were autographed by the donors, such as Thomas Carlyle, Lord Tennyson and Benjamin Disraeli. The Chicago Public Library was established on the basis of that donation, and this building was created by Shepley, Rutan & Coolidge to house the collection. In 1977 the building was renovated for use as a cultural center. Today the books have found a home in the Harold Washington Library Center (see Part Two of this tour), but the magnificent public spaces remain. See the Loop section of the Things to See & Do chapter for details on the cultural center.

❼ 6 N Michigan From his corner office in this building, Montgomery Ward fumed as he saw developers encroaching on Grant Park (see the boxed text 'The Man Who Saved the Lakefront' in the Things to See & Do chapter). The 1899 structure, designed by Hugh MG Garden and Richard E Schmidt, has changed a lot from the way it looked when it

Left: Carbide & Carbon Building (foreground)

was the center of Ward's operations, but many charming terra-cotta details, such as reliefs of plants and animals, still exist – albeit under layers of grime.

❽ Carson Pirie Scott & Co, 1 S State St When the major part of this building was completed in 1906, critics said it was too ornamental to serve as a retail building. You be the judge, as you admire Louis Sullivan's superb metalwork around the main entrance, at State and Madison Sts. Though Sullivan insisted that 'form follows function,' it's hard to see his theory at work in this lavishly flowing cast iron. Amid the flowing botanical and geometric forms, look for Sullivan's initials, LHS. The rest of the building is clad simply in white terra-cotta. This was the first department store to have an all-steel frame.

Part Two: Chicago's Civic Pride

This segment of the tour passes by Chicago's cultural ground zero, along Michigan Ave. The sweep of buildings fronting Grant Park has received landmark status. The facades seen from Grant Park are a study in skyscraper development up to WWII. Only the Borg-Warner Building, just across from the Art Institute on the southwest corner of Adams St and Michigan Ave, rings a sour note, as welcome here as the Borg are on *Star Trek*.

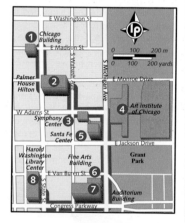

Begin at the southwest corner of State and Madison Sts, across from Carson Pirie Scott & Co.

❶ Chicago Building, 7 W Madison St This 15-story 1904 building is typical of many designed by the firm Holabird & Roche during the late 19th and early 20th centuries. The windows fronting State St show classic Chicago style: two narrow sash windows on either side of a larger fixed pane. After a modest career as home to miscellaneous small businesses, the building reopened in 1997 as a dorm for the School of the Art Institute – another innovative use of older Loop office buildings. The preserved cornice is unusual, since most older buildings have had theirs removed for maintenance reasons.

❷ Palmer House Hilton, 17 E Monroe St Completed in 1927, this luxury hotel, designed by Holabird & Roche, bears the name of former owner Potter Palmer. His Francophile wife Bertha's tastes were responsible for the ornate French lobby, with its ceiling of delicate mosaics. Enter on State St, pass through the shopping arcade and take the escalators up to the lobby before exiting onto Wabash Ave.

❸ **Symphony Center, 63 E Adams St and 220 S Michigan Ave** This complex consists of the original Orchestra Hall on Michigan Ave and a remodeled former liquor warehouse on Adams St. DH Burnham & Co designed the former in 1905, and Richard Schmidt and Hugh MG Garden engineered the transformation of the latter in 1904. The two buildings were joined by a soaring glass atrium in 1997, when the Chicago Symphony Orchestra completed the $110 million reconstruction of its headquarters and performance hall.

❹ **Art Institute of Chicago, S Michigan Ave at E Adams St** The classic approach to Chicago's premier cultural institution is to walk eastward on Adams in the afternoon and watch the sunlit facade slowly reveal itself. The original building, designed by Shepley, Rutan & Coolidge, dates from 1893 and has been expanded several times. Across the train tracks is the large Columbus Dr wing, designed by Skidmore, Owings & Merrill and added in 1977; the large Rice Building, designed by Hammond, Beeby & Babka, came along in 1988. The bronze lions fronting the main entrance have been beloved mascots since 1894.

❺ **Santa Fe Center, 224 S Michigan Ave** Architect Daniel Burnham kept his offices in this sparkling white terra-cotta building, which he designed in 1904. The unusual top-floor porthole windows make the structure stand out even more from its neighbors. Enter the lobby and look upward at the vast light well Burnham placed in the center. He gave this same feature to the Rookery (see Part Four of this tour). A 1985 renovation raised the glass canopy from the second floor to the building's top.

RICK GERHARTER

Left: Art Institute of Chicago

6 Fine Arts Building, 410 S Michigan Ave Built by Solon Beman in 1885, this building once housed the Studebaker carriage and automobile showrooms. In 1917 architect Andrew Rebori turned it into a home for the arts. Small music and literary companies still dominate its floors. Check out the murals on the 10th floor and the inner light well, overlooked by interior balconies. The rough stone exterior base was widely copied by the designers of neighboring buildings.

7 Auditorium Building, 430 S Michigan Ave This 1889 building, designed by Louis Sullivan with Dankmar Adler, is one of the city's greatest. Behind its granite and limestone facade hides a magnificent 4300-seat theater with some of the best acoustics and sight lines in the city. Inquire about viewing the theater, which still hosts performances. Originally a hotel and office space, the building is now largely occupied by Roosevelt University. The 10th-floor library used to be an ornate restaurant. The arcade on Congress Parkway was created when the sidewalk was sacrificed for the widening of the road in the 1950s.

8 Harold Washington Library Center, 400 S State St Named after the man dubbed 'the people's mayor' (see History in the Facts about Chicago chapter, earlier), this building serves as 'the people's library'; appropriately enough, the democratic process played a big role in its design. The city invited several architectural firms to submit designs, which were displayed in the Chicago Cultural Center (see Part One of this tour) for several months in 1989. Thousands of citizens inspected the competing proposals and voted for their choice. Robustly traditional, with details derived from many classic Chicago designs, this 1991 Hammond, Beeby & Babka building was the winner. Note the whimsical copper details on the roof, including studious-looking owls.

Right: Detail on the Harold Washington Library Center

RICK GERHARTER

Part Three: Architecture 101

Think of this march north on Dearborn St as an introductory course in architecture: in six blocks you'll find major works representing more than 100 years of architecture. The route passes several public sculptures (see the boxed text 'Loop Sculpture: From Historic to Incomprehensible' in the Things to See & Do chapter).

From the library, walk one block west on Congress Parkway.

① **Old Colony Building, 407 S Dearborn St** The rounded corner bays on this 1894 tower, designed by Holabird & Roche, were once a very common architectural feature. This building is the sole survivor of that era.

② **Fisher Building, 343 S Dearborn St** The main structure of this yellowish terra-cotta-clad building was completed in 1896; the simpler northern addition was added in 1907. Inspired by the name of the developer, Lucius G Fisher, architect Daniel Burnham gave the exterior a playful menagerie of fish, crabs, shells and other sea creatures.

③ **Monadnock Building, 53 W Jackson Blvd** Really two structures, an 1891 northern portion and an 1893 southern addition, this building can be considered the Loop Lourdes for architecture buffs on a pilgrimage: together the two parts represent a crucial juncture in American skyscraper development. The original portion of the building consists of traditional, load-bearing walls that are 6 feet wide at the base. Working with brick, architects Burnham & Root fashioned a free-flowing facade that becomes almost sensuous around the bottoms of the window bays. Constructed only two years later, the addition lacks the heavy walls and benefits from the latest advance in construction at the time: a then-revolutionary metal frame.

④ **Chicago Federal Center, Dearborn St between Jackson Blvd and Adams St** Ludwig Mies van der Rohe gave this complex his signature austere look in his original 1959 design. In 1964 the 30-story Dirksen Building became the first structure to be completed; it holds the federal courts. The 42-story Kluczynski Building came along in 1974; it's home to various federal agencies. The post office, finished the same year, completes the troika; Mies designed it to be as tall as the lobbies in its two

neighbors. *Flamingo*, a bright red sculpture by Alexander Calder, provides a counterpoint to Mies' ebony palette.

5 **Marquette Building, 140 S Dearborn St** Above its massive base, the Marquette is really an E-shaped building facing north. When Holabird & Roche designed it in 1893, the architects made natural light and ventilation vital considerations, because of the skimpy light bulbs and nonexistent mechanical ventilation of the time. The same firm took on the building's 1980 renovation. Tiffany and others created the sculptured panels above the entrance and in the lobby; these recall the exploits of French explorer and missionary Jacques Marquette.

6 **Inland Steel Building, 30 W Monroe St** Completed in 1958, this Skidmore, Owings & Merrill building was the first Loop high-rise with full central air-conditioning. Its innovations don't end there; the tower visible on Monroe St houses the elevators and mechanical services that allow the floors in the main portion of the stainless-steel-clad structure to remain unbroken by columns.

7 **Bank One Building, Dearborn St between Monroe and Madison Sts** The gracefully curving shape of this 60-story tower, designed by Perkins & Will and finished in 1969, gives this large bank (the longtime home of the First National Bank of Chicago, now absorbed into Bank One) a distinctive profile on the skyline. The multilevel plaza on Monroe St is popular at lunch. Marc Chagall's mosaic *The Four Seasons* recently gained an architecturally sensitive weather cover.

8 **Richard J Daley Center, Dearborn St between Washington and Randolph Sts** Another classic Chicago Miesian building, the 31-story Daley Center was called the Chicago Civic Center when it was completed by CF Murphy Associates in 1965. The building is clad in Cor-Ten steel, a

Right: Daley Center Plaza

type developed to avoid the need for paint: a layer of oxidation forms on the steel's surface, which protects it and gives the metal its distinctive bronze color. Inside, the scores of county courtrooms have ceilings two floors high. Outside, the plaza hosts regular performances and protests; it also holds what Chicagoans refer to simply as 'the Picasso,' an untitled sculpture by the great 20th-century artist.

Part Four: Where the Deals Are Made

Government and high finance coexist on LaSalle St. Chicago's corporate heart extends west past Wacker Dr to the canyon of high-rises surrounding the south branch of the Chicago River.

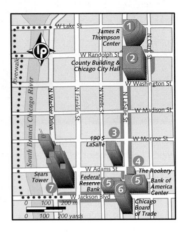

At the northwest corner of the Daley Center, cross Clark and Randolph Sts.

1 James R Thompson Center, 100 W Randolph St This bulbous building – completed as the State of Illinois Center in 1986 – features a shape reminiscent of its namesake governor, who commissioned it. Controversial from the start, the oddly shaped structure aroused ire with its all-glass design that extended deep inside. Architect Helmut Jahn thought the structure should be a metaphor for open government and left off doors, ceilings and walls from interior offices. As a result he produced a vast greenhouse filled with overheated bureaucrats, who held up thermometers showing temperatures of 110°F and higher for a gleeful media. When the imperious Jahn took a tour of what he had wrought, he was confronted by a secretary who complained about her heat stroke. Jahn suggested she get a new job. Vastly improved air-conditioning has lowered temperatures, and everybody loves the soaring atrium lobby.

2 County Building & Chicago City Hall, 121 N LaSalle St Designed by Holabird & Roche in 1911, this building that serves two government bodies is adorned with 75-foot columns that were a challenge to construct and support. Chicago proclaims its political dominance over Cook County by giving its half of the building (the west) much richer fixtures. Enter through Randolph St and exit at LaSalle St.

3 190 S LaSalle New York architect Philip Johnson's sole contribution to Chicago (1987) bows heavily to long-gone Chicago architectural gems. The gabled roof is inspired by surrounding buildings and is best viewed from the Sears Tower Skydeck. The lobby, with its vaulted ceiling covered in gold leaf and artwork, is designed to impress the building's lawyer tenants and to overwhelm their clients.

❹ The Rookery, 209 S LaSalle St Named after the pigeons that used to nest here, the Rookery (built from 1885–88) remains one of Chicago's most beloved buildings. The original design by Burnham & Root, with its load-bearing walls of granite and brick, surrounds a spectacular atrium space that was remodeled in 1907 by Frank Lloyd Wright. A lavish restoration in 1992 has returned the building to its peak grandeur.

❺ Bank of America Center, 231 S LaSalle St; Federal Reserve Bank, 230 S LaSalle St These buildings were constructed in 1922 and 1924, respectively, by Graham, Anderson, Probst & White. Their major exterior difference is that the federal building in-

RICHARD CUMMINS

corporates Corinthian columns, while its sibling's are Ionic. Formerly the Illinois Merchants Bank and later Continental Illinois Bank, the Bank of America Center contains a 2nd-floor public banking area that would do any Roman god proud. In fact, when he saw the finished work, Louis Sullivan suggested that the bankers wear togas.

❻ Chicago Board of Trade, 141 W Jackson Blvd The original 1930 Holabird & Root tower, fronting LaSalle St, is a classic 45-story art deco skyscraper topped with a statue of Ceres, the Roman goddess of agriculture. To the rear, a 1980 addition by Helmut Jahn nicely complements the original. Inside, the earlier building features a sumptuous lobby; the addition contains a 12th-floor atrium with a classic mural of Ceres that once adorned the original's main trading floor.

❼ Sears Tower, 233 S Wacker Dr The best view you'll have of this giant is from some other part of town. Up close all you can do is crane your neck and stare up at the dizzying height. By some factors still the world's tallest building (see the boxed text 'Tower Envy' in the Things to See & Do chapter), this 110-story tower, completed in 1974, owes its existence to the talents of Skidmore, Owings & Merrill architect Bruce Graham and structural engineer Fazlur Khan. It consists of nine structural square 'tubes' that rise from the building's base, two stopping at the 50th floor,

Right: Lobby of 190 S LaSalle

two more ending at the 66th floor, three more calling it quits at 90 stories and two stretching to the full height. Nobody ever liked the arrangement of the base, which mixed tourists with frazzled office workers. A 1985 remodeling helped, adding the odd Wacker Dr entrance, but it took a major 1992 reworking sparked by Sears' move to the suburbs to fix things for real. The building is now owned by an investment trust.

Part Five: The River

Walking toward Lake Michigan along the Chicago River is a quintessential Chicago experience. The rumble of the El trains crossing the river, the utilitarian charm of the drawbridges and the proliferation of proud buildings on both banks make the scene at once gritty and refined.

From the Sears Tower, cross the south branch of the Chicago River and walk north on the Riverwalk along the west bank. At Randolph St, jog slightly west and continue one block to Lake St. Walk back across the river on the north side of the bridge and continue walking east along the south bank of the river.

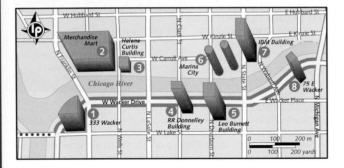

● **333 W Wacker** Completed in 1983, this curving green structure is the most popular Loop tower to emerge from the 1980s building boom. Architect William E Pedersen did a masterful job of utilizing the odd triangular site on the curve in the river. Water and sky play across the mirrored glass in an ever-changing kaleidoscope of shapes and colors. Pedersen's neighboring 1989 encore, at 225 W Wacker Dr, is much more conventional.

● **Merchandise Mart, north bank of the river between Franklin and Wells Sts** Graham, Anderson, Probst & White originally designed this building (1930) as a wholesale store for Marshall Field & Co, but the Kennedy family purchased it in 1945 and converted it into commercial space. The Merchandise Mart's 4.1 million sq feet are encased in a massive limestone exterior, which received a much-needed cleaning in 1992. The less said about the 1977 Apparel Mart immediately to the west, the better.

● **Helene Curtis Building, 325 N Wells St** Hired by the cosmetic giant Helene Curtis, Booth/Hansen & Associates gave this 1914 warehouse a

RAY HILLSTROM JR

gaudy makeover in 1984. The green glass seems as out-of-place today as green eye shadow.

4 **RR Donnelley Building, 77 W Wacker Dr** Spanish architect Ricardo Bofill drew inspiration from Greek and Roman temples for this 50-story tower. Completed in 1992 as a last gasp of the '80s building boom, it features a lobby made out of white marble quarried in Greece, with works by artists from Bofill's native Catalonia, Spain.

5 **Leo Burnett Building, 35 W Wacker Dr** Chicago's largest ad agency commissioned Kevin Roche–John Dinkeloo & Associates for this 1989 building. The incongruous metal pillars don't really mesh with the building's other details, which suggest a squarish Prairie School column. As is increasingly common, the structure goes beyond the standard, four-corner-offices-per-floor design and includes many of the prime office spots, to accommodate the demands of legions of corporate vice presidents.

6 **Marina City, north bank of the river between Dearborn and State Sts** Dominated by its twin 'corncob' towers, this mixed-use complex designed by Bertrand Goldberg has had a mixed history since its completion in 1967. The condos that top the spiraling parking garages are quite popular and especially picturesque at Christmastime, when the owners decorate the scalloped balconies with a profusion of lights. The marina at the foot of the complex does all right in the summer, but much of the rest of the space – intended for stores, restaurants, a bowling alley and other recreational services – was mired in bankruptcy court until the House of Blues opened in the long-dead theater (see the Entertainment chapter). The moribund office building reopened later as the House of Blues Hotel. Whoever allowed the incongruous Smith & Wollensky restaurant to be added in 1998 is a bonehead.

Right:
333 W Wacker

⑦ IBM Building, 330 N Wabash Ave Many consider this 1971 tower to be the signature office building by Mies van der Rohe; it was his last American commission. Here Mies' basic black palette gives way to an almost radical combination of rich browns. The building and its breezy plaza are fastidiously maintained by its persnickety owner.

⑧ 75 E Wacker Neighborless when completed by Herbert Hugh Riddle in 1928, this pencil of a building looked even more dramatic when it stood alone. The 42 terra-cotta-clad floors form the shape of a telescope, right up to the pointy top (which is being structurally repaired).

Other Notable Buildings

Not everything grand about Chicago architecture lies in the Loop or Near North. You can also find buildings of architectural significance in Wrigleyville, Wicker Park, the Prairie Avenue District, the University of Chicago and Oak Park. See those sections, and the Near North section, in the Things to See & Do chapter; for Oak Park, see the Excursions chapter.

BP-Amoco Building, 200 E Randolph St If it weren't in the aesthetic desert of Illinois Center (see the Five Ugly Buildings section, later), the 80-story BP-Amoco Building – Chicago's second tallest in overall height – might get some respect. Then again, it might not, owing to the comedy of errors that

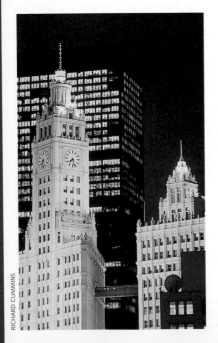

produced it. It is one of architecture's significant technical miscues. Constructed as the Standard Oil Building in 1973 by Perkins & Will, the building was clad in marble from the same quarry Michelangelo used, at the firm insistence of Standard Oil's then-chairman, John Swearingen, and his wife, Bonnie. To save money, the marble was cut more thinly than ever before, despite warnings from experts that, structurally, the marble would be too weak to withstand the very harsh Chicago climate. Within 15 years the owners knew they had a problem when the precious marble began falling off the building's 1136-foot facade. The

Left: The Wrigley Building (left)

RICHARD CUMMINS

43,000 panels covering the entire exterior had to be replaced with light-colored granite at a cost equal to the original construction.

Wrigley Building, 400 N Michigan Ave at the river The most photographed building in town was designed with a Hollywood flair: architects Graham, Anderson, Probst & White cast the white terra-cotta in six shades, which get increasingly brighter toward the top, ensuring that the building pops out of the sky whether it's high noon or midnight. Lights from neighboring buildings and across the river provide the nocturnal glow. The 'main building' actually occupies almost half the space of the much-larger northern addition. Both were designed and built between 1919 and 1924. The design combines European classicism with straightforward Chicago roots and makes for a grand entrance to the Magnificent Mile.

Tribune Tower, 435 N Michigan Ave, across from the Wrigley Building The self-proclaimed 'World's Greatest Newspaper' was never one to let modesty get in the way of bombast. When it announced an architectural competition in 1922 for a new headquarters, it asked for nothing less than 'the most beautiful office building in the world.' The chosen entry, by Howells & Hood, won out over 264 submissions; it borrowed elements of Gothic cathedrals such as flying buttresses and applied them to a skyscraper. Look up at the top of the building, where the purely decorative buttresses surround a small tower. As on cathedrals, carved figures frame the building's three-story entrance, although here they come from Aesop's fables rather than from the Scriptures. Completed in 1925, the tower gained its less-interesting addition to the north in 1934. Look for historic rocks embedded in the walls at its base.

John Hancock Center, 875 N Michigan Ave at Chestnut St Perhaps the most recognizable Chicago high-rise, the 100-story, 1127-foot John Hancock Center combines, from bottom to top, shopping, parking, offices, condos, tourist attractions and broadcast transmitters. The first major collaboration of the Skidmore, Owings & Merrill architect Bruce Graham and engineer Fazlur Khan, this 1969 building muscles its way into the sky atop a series of

Right: John Hancock Center (center)

RICHARD I'ANSON

cross-braces. If you look at the exterior, you can see where the shorter residential floors begin at the 44th floor. Some apartments even have balconies recessed behind screens.

Five Ugly Buildings

Along with world-class architectural triumphs, Chicago has some world-class duds. The following buildings may mess up the landscape, but at least they make their neighbors look good.

Illinois Center, south of the Chicago River, west of N Michigan Ave Not just one ugly building but a vast collection of them, this mixed-use development of offices, stores, apartments and hotels includes triple-decker roads and other atrocities that spoil the view from the river.

Shops at North Bridge This vast development anchored by the Nordstrom department store covers more than six blocks just west of N Michigan Ave along E Grand Ave and E Ohio St. Completed in 2001 after six years of construction, it shows what can result when a whole committee of architects designs the buildings: crap.

RICK GERHARTER

Apparel Mart, 350 N Orleans St, just west of the Merchandise Mart Check out the grime-streaked, windowless south side. This was commissioned by the same folks (the Kennedy clan of political fame) who own the regal Merchandise Mart next door.

1550 N Lake Shore Dr Who thought it would be smart to make the top of this high-priced condo look like a wicker basket?

Asbury Plaza, 750 N Dearborn St This structure breaks with high-rise apartment tradition by providing more walls than windows – the high-rise for people afraid of heights. It's a putrid green color, too.

Architectural Tours

If the walking tours here have whetted your appetite for more in-depth explorations of Chicago architecture, you might want to look into taking a guided tour.

The Chicago Architecture Foundation (CAF; ☎ 312-922-3432, www .architecture.org) provides a veritable supermarket of Chicago architecture tours. It's worth checking with CAF to see what tours have been added to the ever-growing roster, which includes Bridgeport,

Left: Apparel Mart

Jackson Park and LaSalle St in the Loop. The foundation operates two offices where the staff are ready to answer questions and sell you something neat: one is on the lower level of the John Hancock Center, 875 N Michigan Ave; the other is on the ground floor of the Santa Fe Center, 224 S Michigan Ave.

CAF leads more than 50 **walking tours** of the city and suburbs. Two start at the Santa Fe Center daily and cost $10 each ($15 for both): Early Loop Skyscrapers departs at 10 am, and Modern Buildings and Beyond begins at 1:30 pm. The Hancock Center office dispatches a tour of N Michigan Ave at 11:30 am daily; it costs $8. The tours last about two hours.

Ninety-minute **boat tours** led by CAF volunteers depart daily from early May through October; these leave from the southwest corner of the Michigan Ave Bridge and the Chicago River and cost $21 (for reservations, call ☎ 312-902-1500). On a tour boat with a wide, open upper deck, you'll explore both branches of the Chicago River. Besides the informed commentary, the best feature of the tour is the unusual view of the skyline you get from the south branch of the river near River City.

CAF also operates **bus tours** of Chicago, Prairie Ave, Hyde Park, Oak Park and other areas. During the summer it offers architectural **bike tours**. Call for schedules. One of the best deals is CAF's **El tours** of the Loop on summer Saturdays. These are free (!); call for details.

Right: Chicago's dizzying heights

RICK GERHARTER

Facts for the Visitor

WHEN TO GO

Depending on what you want to do, it may be wise to plan your visit to Chicago around the seasons. The summer is often hot and humid, and winter is usually shockingly cold, especially when you factor in the wind chill (the 'wind-chill factor' is an estimation of the temperature your skin feels when the effects of the cold are multiplied by the wind). Visitors should note two phrases endlessly repeated by local meteorologists: in summer, 'cooler near the lake'; in winter, 'warmer near the lake.'

January through March is the least busy time, when hotels and airfares are usually at their cheapest. Weatherwise it can be damp and cold or snowy for days on end. Temperatures in the teens are not uncommon, and combined with brisk winds they will guarantee that you spend a lot of time indoors.

Spring can be mild and sunny or it can be an extension of winter. Chances are, the capricious weather gods will bring a stretch of beautiful days in April and, conversely, some ugly gray days in June.

July is usually quite warm, but the sidewalks don't really start baking until August. Late summer is the peak of the festival season, with major events taking place in the parks and neighborhoods every weekend. See the Special Events section, later in this chapter, for a list of the major festivals.

September can be the nicest month of the year, with reliably warm days and fewer crowds once the American school year begins.

Trees in the parks change color about the second week of October. Expect mild days, with increasingly frosty nights. In the month from Thanksgiving until Christmas, the city bustles with shoppers. The weather tends to be gray, and the temperature hovers around freezing.

Besides the weather, another major consideration in your plans should be whether or not a big convention or trade show is coming to town during your visit. Pay close

RICK GERHARTER

The warmer months make prime times to visit.

attention to this detail if you plan to stay at a hotel, because there will simply be no room at the inn, anywhere, during major events. Even at dumpy places. However, if you don't need a hotel, don't worry. The city is so big, it easily accommodates even the largest influx of visitors.

WHAT TO BRING

Pack light, pack light, pack light. After doing that, take out half the stuff, shove it under the bed and depart for your trip. The first time you have to carry your stuff more than 20 feet, you'll thank me.

Chicago is a casual place. All but the most expensive restaurants will welcome you in anything better than rotten jeans and mangy shoes. Some sort of comfortable, non-sneaker walking shoes, dark pants or skirt and a casual shirt and sweater will cover you for 98% of what you might want to do. But because of the swings in temperature, plan for a few extremes; a pair of shorts and sandals could come in handy from May through September. Winter wear should include warm and water-resistant shoes, a warm jacket, gloves, a scarf and – as your mother may have nagged endlessly – something for your head.

Obviously, if hitting Charlie Trotter's, meeting clients, trying to impress skeptical in-laws or some other sartorially sensitive event is on your agenda, you'll want to bring something that involves a tie or black dress. And of course, there's casual and then there's casual. Wandering around in nylon sweats that look like they were salvaged from a crashed helium balloon will convince everyone that you really are a rube.

Sunglasses are good to carry throughout the year, especially in winter: when it gets sunny after a snowstorm, you'll want to avoid going blind. In the toiletry and personal-items department, be most concerned about hard-to-replace articles, such as prescriptions that might be difficult to fill away from home. One bit of advice I've been giving people for years is to carry the prescription for their eyeglasses or contact lenses with them. If, in a jet-lagged stupor, you step on your glasses or send your con-

Bad Dates

The following trade shows and expositions at McCormick Place are so huge that they might just gobble up every available room and restaurant table in town. Consider avoiding Chicago during these dates.

2001
- American Hardware Manufacturers Association: August 12 to 15
- Radiological Society: November 25 to 30

2002
- National Housewares Show: January 10 to 14
- National Manufacturing Week: March 18 to 21
- Comdex: April 22 to 25
- National Restaurant Association (over 100,000 people!): May 18 to 21
- NeoCon: June 10 to 12
- American Hardware Manufacturers Association: August 11 to 14

To find out if your intended visit coincides with a major show, you can try calling the Chicago Convention and Tourism Bureau (☎ 312-567-8500, www.chicago.il.org), but these folks – the ones who market McCormick Place – may not give you complete information on upcoming shows because of contractual agreements. The best sources are probably the major convention hotels, such as the Hyatt, Sheraton and the Hiltons. If they have rooms for the dates of your visit, then most other places will as well.

tacts swirling down the drain, you can get them replaced in an hour at LensCrafters (☎ 312-819-0205, 205 N Michigan Ave; Map 3), a somewhat pricey but very quick store with its own lab.

One consolation should you forget something or find yourself unprepared for a climatic swing is that you can buy almost anything you want easily, and visitors from abroad will likely pay less than at home. See the Shopping chapter for plenty of details.

Finally, if your hotel has a pool or Jacuzzi, bring a bathing suit. The lake is always open for swimmers, although those who aren't members of the Polar Bear Club (and don't want to hack a hole in the ice in January) will find it most accommodating from late June through mid-September. See the boxed text 'Lakefront Parks & Beaches' in the Things to See & Do chapter for details on beaches.

ORIENTATION

Chicago will be the easiest city you've ever navigated outside of your hometown. Thanks to Edward P Brennan (see the boxed text 'Why You Can't Get Lost'), the streets follow a logic you wouldn't expect in a town with such a turbulent past.

The intersection of Madison and State Sts is ground zero in a numbering system that lets you navigate without knowing any street names. From that point, all street numbers are predicated on north, south, east or west, depending on which way they radiate; street signs note the direction you're heading. If you tell me to meet you at 800 West and 3200 North, I will show up at Halsted St and Belmont Ave.

The numbers follow a system that remains constant through the city. 1600 W Madison St is the same distance west as 1600 W Chicago Ave. Each increase of 800 in numbers corresponds to a mile. For every increase of 400, there is a major arterial street. For instance, Division St (1200 N) is followed by North Ave (1600 N) and Armitage Ave (2000 N) and so on. Most arterial streets have their own CTA bus line.

RICK GERHARTER

Ground zero

Most of the streets are arranged true to the compass: north-south streets run due north and due south. A few major streets, such as Clark St, Lincoln Ave and Milwaukee Ave, are arranged on diagonals.

Chicago is known as a 'city of neighborhoods.' You will soon discover there is not a square meter of the city that doesn't have some moniker, such as the Gold Coast, Lake View, Wrigleyville and many, many others. Neighborhood boundaries are sometimes defined by residents down to the inch, while others, such as that between Wicker Park and Bucktown, are open for broad interpretation. Neighborhood names are shown on the maps, and I have used them where appropriate to organize chapters.

MAPS

Maps are widely sold at hotels, drug stores and newsstands. Try Lonely Planet's *Chicago* city map, a laminated map that folds into a compact size. Rand McNally's Chicago map is also popular, but it doesn't show El lines or stations and is better for driving than walking or touring. It also hasn't kept up to date with roadway developments in the River North and lakefront areas. And it calls Walton St 'Walnut.'

Some other tourist maps cover only the Loop and Near North, but there's no reason you should restrict yourself to those neighborhoods. Many of the free maps found at the tourist information office, on brochure racks, in visitor magazines and such suffer the same short-sighted restrictions on territory.

The maps in this book are quite comprehensive. You'll really need to supplant them only if you have serious exploration in mind; if that's the case, look for a map that includes the whole city and also shows the El.

TOURIST OFFICES

The main Visitor Information Center is in the Chicago Cultural Center (☎ 312-744-2400, TTY 312-744-2947, 800-226-6632 outside the Chicago area, 77 E Randolph St at Michigan Ave; Map 3), just to the left as you enter the building. The center offers hundreds of brochures and booklets and maps of varying quality. The staff will endeavor to answer your questions as well. You can sit down with your piles of information and figure things out at the tables and chairs here. The center is open 10am to 6pm weekdays, 10am to 5pm weekends.

A second location, the Chicago Visitor Center in the Water Tower Pumping Station (same telephone numbers as above, 163 E Pearson St at Michigan Ave; Map 5) is quite impressive. Besides the usual plethora of brochures, you'll find helpful employees, a good café, a sitting area with a fireplace, free chilled water, free treats for dogs (!) and a small art gallery. You can also tour the historic old pumps in the basement. The center is open 8am to 7pm daily.

The center with the longest hours is at the Illinois Marketplace Visitor Information Center in Navy Pier (700 E Grand Ave; Map 3). It's open 10am to 9pm Sunday to Thursday and 10am to midnight Friday and Saturday.

For information about events such as festivals and exhibitions, contact the Chicago Office of Tourism at the Chicago Cultural Center (☎ 312-744-2400, 78 E Washington, Chicago, IL 60602 USA). You can also visit the Web site www.ci.chi.il.us.

Hotel rooms usually come with free visitor magazines such as *Where*, but these contain so many ads that it's hard to tell the difference between promotional material and editorial content.

TRAVEL AGENCIES

Council Travel (☎ 312-951-0585, 1160 N State St; Map 5) is good at arranging budget as well as student travel. American Express (☎ 312-435-2595, 122 S Michigan Ave; Map 3) operates a full service travel agency in the Loop.

DOCUMENTS
Passports

With the exception of Canadians, who need only proof of Canadian citizenship with photo ID, all visitors to the US must have a valid passport and may also require a US visa (see the next section). Check these regulations carefully with the US embassy in

Why You Can't Get Lost

As you make your way through Chicago's orderly system of streets and numbers, radiating from ground zero at State and Madison Sts, you can thank the persistence and zeal of a frustrated bill collector for your ease of navigation. Scouring the city in search of deadbeats, Edward P Brennan got fed up trying to decide which of the city's 10 Oak Sts or 13 Washington Sts or eight 42nds might contain the address he was looking for. And those were just a few of his problems. Some streets changed their names every few blocks, and house numbers followed no set pattern.

In 1901 Brennan proposed a new system based on a regular grid and numbering system. Exhibiting a timeless skepticism of the Chicago City Council's ability to discern the wisdom of the plan, Brennan said of his proposal, '[It] may be another job for the undertaker, as its fate is likely to be early death and burial.'

To his surprise, however, the plan was adopted and implemented beginning in 1909. During the next 30 years, Brennan attended more than 600 council meetings to see his plan to maturity, and after researching historical figures in the city's short history he renamed 300 duplicate street names. The only memorial to this toil – for which he refused payment – is a short street named Brennan Ave in Beverly at 2300 East, from 9600 South to 9772 South.

your country before you depart. Conservative legislators in the US government have enacted laws that allow Immigration and Naturalization Service (INS) officials at airports to toss you in jail overnight and then ship you home on the first flight out without a chance for appeal.

Your passport should be valid for at least six months longer than your intended stay in the US, and you'll need to submit a recent photo with your visa application. Documents of financial stability or guarantees from a US resident are sometimes required, particularly for people from Third World nations. In special cases, the INS can demand that someone entering the country be 'sponsored' by a citizen who promises to provide them with financial support.

Although most visitors to the US have no problem entering the country, you should

HIV & Entering the US

Anyone entering the US who is not a US citizen is subject to the authority of the Immigration and Naturalization Service (INS; www.ins.usdoj.gov), which has the final say about whether you can enter or not and has full power to send you back to wherever you came from. Being HIV-positive is not grounds for deportation, but it is grounds for exclusion. What this means is that once in the US, you cannot be deported for being HIV-positive, but you can be prevented from *entering* the US.

The INS does not test people for HIV when they try to enter the US, but the form for nonimmigrant visas asks, 'Have you ever been afflicted with a communicable disease of public health significance?' If you answer yes to this question, the INS may try to exclude you when you reach the US.

If you are HIV-positive but can prove to the consular officials to whom you have applied for a visa that you are the spouse, parent or child of a US citizen or legal resident (green-card holder), you may be exempt from the exclusionary rule; decisions on this waiver are made on a case-by-case basis. A manual on immigration and HIV is available free of charge from the San Francisco AIDS Foundation (☎ 415-487-3080, PO Box 426182, San Francisco, CA 94142).

For legal information and referrals to immigrant advocates, potential visitors should contact the National Immigration Project of the National Lawyers Guild (☎ 617-227-9727, 14 Beacon St, Suite 602, Boston, MA 02108) and the Immigrant HIV Assistance Project, Bar Association of San Francisco (☎ 415-782-8995, 465 California St, Suite 1100, San Francisco, CA 94104).

tread carefully from the time you exit your international flight until you have passed through all the formalities and are in the actual arrivals area of the terminal. In addition to the INS people, who will inspect your passport and 'papers,' you will encounter customs officials, who might search your bags, and a Drug Enforcement Agency dog that might sniff your leg and luggage.

The vast majority of these personnel are polite and, in the case of the animals, well behaved. However, if you have problems with any of them, the last thing you should do is argue or otherwise cause them further irritation. The simple truth is that until you have passed through the last formality, you have few if any rights. If various government officers so desire, they can find an excuse to detain you and make your life miserable. It is not uncommon for foreign nationals to be detained for hours over minor procedural questions. If that happens, try to get word to an airline official or even another traveler, who can then notify the people waiting for you outside.

If you are a person of color, the ugly truth is that the odds of your being questioned or searched or of having your luggage inspected are greater. All the agencies involved will vigorously deny that, but I spent a lot of time with these inspectors and agents for a news story once, and they all confirmed, far off the record, that this is exactly what happens. If it does, endure the procedure without complaint. If you feel especially aggrieved, contact one of the news agencies listed in the Newspapers & Magazines section (you'll find their phone numbers and addresses in the Chicago phone book) and tell them your story. They're always looking for juicy examples of government malfeasance.

Visas

A reciprocal visa-waiver program applies to citizens of certain countries, who may enter the US for stays of 90 days or fewer without having to obtain a visa. Currently these 29 countries are Andorra, Argentina, Australia, Austria, Belgium, Brunei, Denmark, Finland, France, Germany, Iceland, Ireland, Italy, Japan, Liechtenstein, Luxembourg, Monaco, the Netherlands, New Zealand, Norway, Portugal, San Marino, Singapore, Slovenia, Spain, Sweden, Switzerland, Uruguay and the UK. Under the visa-waiver program, you must possess a roundtrip ticket on an airline that participates in the program; you need proof of financial solvency, such as credit cards, a bank account with evidence of a balance beyond two figures or employment in your home country; you must sign a form waiving the right to a hearing over deportation (!); and you will not be allowed to extend your stay beyond 90 days. Consult with your airline or the closest US consulate or embassy for more information.

Other travelers (except visitors from Canada) will need to obtain a visa from a US consulate or embassy. In most countries the process can be done by mail, but in some – notably Turkey, Poland and Russia – you'll need to go to a US consulate or embassy in person. Visa applicants may be required to 'demonstrate binding obligations' that will ensure their return back home. Because of this requirement, those planning to travel through other countries before arriving in the US are generally better off applying for their US visa while still in their home country, rather than while on the road.

The validity period for US visitor visas depends on what country you're from. The length of time you'll be allowed to stay in the US is ultimately determined by the INS officers at the port of entry, such as an airport.

Visa Extensions Tourists using visas are usually granted a six-month stay on first arrival. If you try to extend that time, the first assumption will be that you are working illegally (an assumption often right on the mark), so come prepared with concrete evidence that you've been behaving like a model tourist: receipts to demonstrate you've been spending lots of your money from home in the US or ticket stubs that show you've been traveling extensively. Requests for visa extensions in Chicago are entertained at the INS office (☎ 800-375-5283, www.ins.usdoj.gov, in the Kluczynski Building of the Federal Center, 10 W Jackson Blvd, Suite 600; Map 3).

Travel Insurance

A travel insurance policy to cover theft, loss and medical problems is a good idea. Some policies offer lower and higher medical-expense options; the higher ones are chiefly for countries such as the USA, which have extremely high medical costs. You'll find a wide variety of policies available, so check the small print. Some policies specifically exclude 'dangerous activities', which can include scuba diving, motorcycling, even hiking.

You may prefer to get a policy that pays doctors or hospitals directly rather than your having to pay on the spot and submit a claim later. If you have to claim later, make sure you keep all documentation. Some policies ask you to call (collect) a center in your home country where the staff can make an immediate assessment of your problem.

Check that the policy covers ambulance services or an emergency flight home.

Driver's License & Permits

You'll need a driver's license to rent a car. You may want to obtain an International Driving Permit, usually valid for one year, from your national automobile association before leaving for the USA. Local traffic police are more likely to accept the IDP as valid identification than an unfamiliar document from another country. Of course, in Chicago, you'll be smart not to drive at all.

If you're a young person from the US or Canada (and, thus, traveling without a passport), you should always have your driver's license on hand if you plan on going to the bars. Bouncers will check the birth date on your license and refuse to let you past if you're not 21 years old.

Student & Youth Cards

In Chicago your student ID card can sometimes get you discounted rates at museums and other attractions.

Copies

All important documents (passport data page and visa page, credit cards, travel insurance policy, air/bus/train tickets, driver's license, etc) should be photocopied before you leave home. Leave one copy with someone at home and keep another with you, separate from the originals.

EMBASSIES & CONSULATES

It's important to realize what your own embassy or consulate can and can't do to help you if you get into trouble. Generally speaking, your embassy or consulate won't be much help in emergencies if the trouble you're in is remotely your own fault. Remember that you are bound by the laws of the country you are in. Your embassy or consulate will not be sympathetic if you end up in jail after committing a crime locally, even if such actions are legal in your own country.

In genuine emergencies you might get some assistance, but only if other channels have been exhausted. For example, if you need to get home urgently, a free ticket home is exceedingly unlikely – the embassy or consulate would expect you to have insurance. If you have all your money and documents stolen, your embassy might assist with getting a new passport, but a loan for onward travel is out of the question.

US Embassies Abroad

A full list of US missions abroad can be found at the Web site www.usembassy.state.gov. US diplomatic offices abroad include the following:

Australia (☎ 02-6214-5600), 21 Moonah Place, Yarralumla, ACT 2600

Canada (☎ 613-238-5335), 490 Sussex Dr, Ottawa, K1N 1G8

France (☎ 01 43 12 22 22), 2 rue Saint Florentin, 75382 Paris

Germany (☎ 030 8305 0), Neustädtische Kirchstr. 4-5, 10117 Berlin

Ireland (☎ 1 668 8777), 42 Elgin Rd, Ballsbridge, Dublin 4

Japan (☎ 3-3224-5000), 10-5 Akasaka, 1 Chome, Minato-Ku, Tokyo 107-8420

Mexico (☎ 5209-9100), Paseo de la Reforma 305, Col. Cuauhtémoc, 06500 Mexico City

New Zealand (☎ 644-472-2068), 29 Fitzherbert Terrace, Thorndon, Wellington

UK (☎ 020 7499 9000), 5 Upper Grosvenor St, London W1

Consulates in Chicago

A number of nations maintain consular offices in Chicago – check the Yellow Pages under Consulates. Australia closed its Chicago consulate in a budgetary cutback in the early 1990s. The closest representation is the embassy in Washington, DC: (☎ 202 797-3000), 1601 Massachusetts Ave NW, Washington, DC 20036-2273.

Canada (☎ 312-616-1860), 180 N Stetson Ave, Suite 2400

France (☎ 312-787-5359), 737 N Michigan Ave, Suite 2020

Germany (☎ 312-580-1199), 676 N Michigan Ave, Suite 3200

Ireland (☎ 312-337-1868), 400 N Michigan Ave, Suite 911

Japan (☎ 312-280-0400), 737 N Michigan Ave, Suite 1100

Mexico (☎ 312-855-1380), 300 N Michigan Ave, Suite 200

Poland (☎ 312-337-8166), 1530 N Lake Shore Dr

South Africa (☎ 312-939-7929), 200 S Michigan Ave, Suite 600

Sweden (☎ 312-781-6262), 150 N Michigan Ave, Suite 1250

UK (☎ 312-346-1810), 33 N Dearborn St, Suite 900

CUSTOMS

International travelers will be familiar with the red-and-green line system at O'Hare. Those with nothing to declare can opt for the green line and hope they are not singled out for a spot check.

Those with something to declare should definitely do so, because if you try to smuggle something in – especially drugs – and are caught, your day will immediately go downhill. Remember, until you clear all the formalities, you have no rights.

Non-United States citizens over the age of 21 are allowed to import 1 liter of liquor and 200 cigarettes (or 100 non-Cuban cigars) duty free. Gifts may amount to no more than $100 in value.

You may bring any amount of money less than $10,000 into or out of the US without declaration. Amounts greater than $10,000 must be declared. There is no legal limit to the amount of US and foreign cash and traveler's checks you can bring in, but undeclared amounts of more than $10,000 can be confiscated. For more information, visit the Web site www.customs.gov/travel/travel.htm.

MONEY

Nothing works like cash, but in the US most merchants accept most forms of payment. How to get cash is another matter. Read the Exchanging Money section, below, to consider your options.

Currency

Most of the world knows that the US currency is the dollar ($), divided into 100 cents (¢). Coins come in denominations of 1¢ (penny), 5¢ (nickel), 10¢ (dime), 25¢ (quarter), 50¢ (half dollar – rare) and $1 (silver dollar – rare). A new, gold-colored coin, introduced in 2000, has been snapped up by American collectors (or Americans aspiring to be collectors), so you're not likely to see many of these coins in circulation yet, but keep your eye out for the face of Sacagawea, a Native American commemorated on the new coin. Notes ('bills') come in denominations of $1, $2 (rare), $5, $10, $20, $50 and $100.

Exchange Rates

At press time, exchange rates were as follows:

country	unit		dollar
Australia	A$1	=	US$0.55
Canada	C$1	=	US$0.67
Euro	€1	=	US$0.14
France	FF10	=	US$1.40
Germany	DM1	=	US$0.48
Hong Kong	HK$10	=	US$0.13
Japan	¥100	=	US$0.87
New Zealand	NZ$1	=	US$0.45
UK	UK£1	=	US$1.48

Exchanging Money

Wherever possible, use credit cards and withdraw money from your home account using ATMs; this will get you the best exchange rates. You'll find that exchanging foreign cash and non-US dollar traveler's checks in Chicago is a hassle, although it can be done.

Cash & Traveler's Checks Traveler's checks are usually just as good as cash in the US, provided they are in US dollars. Most places will accept them as long as you sign them in front of the cashier, waiter, etc.

Even if you plan to get cash using your ATM card or to charge everything on your credit card, it is a good idea to have some backup funds in the form of traveler's checks, in case your card stops working, is eaten by an ATM or falls victim to some other calamity.

The arrivals area of Terminal 5, the international terminal at O'Hare, has a foreign exchange service that is generally open for incoming flights. Otherwise, to exchange cash and traveler's checks in foreign currencies, try Thomas Cook Currency Services (☎ 312-807-4941, 800-287-7362, 9 S LaSalle St; Map 3) or American Express, with a Loop location (☎ 312-435-2595, 122 S Michigan Ave; Map 3) and a Lincoln Park location (☎ 773-477-4000, 2338 N Clark St; Map 6). World's Money Exchange (☎ 312-641-2151, Suite M-11, 203 N LaSalle St; Map 3) offers the largest selection of foreign currency, accepting bills from 120 countries.

Chicago's largest bank, Bank One, will chase you off if you proffer them foreign currency. Try bringing it to American National Bank & Trust (☎ 312-661-5000, 1 N LaSalle St; Map 3) or Northern Trust Bank (☎ 312-630-6000, 50 S LaSalle St; Map 3)

One cautionary note: shortly after arriving in Chicago, you will begin noticing garishly lit 'currency exchanges' on many street corners. They are not what you might think. These primarily serve people without bank accounts who want to 'exchange' their 'currency' in return for services such as money orders or check-cashing. If you slip your German marks, French francs or other currency under the bulletproof divider at a currency exchange, they will come sliding right back, possibly with an ill-tempered tirade from the clerk.

If your traveler's checks are lost or stolen, call the check issuer:

American Express	☎ 800-221-7282
MasterCard	☎ 800-223-9920
Thomas Cook	☎ 800-223-7373
Visa	☎ 800-227-6811

ATMs The vast majority of ATMs in Chicago operate under the 'Cash Station' moniker. You will find them almost everywhere – in convenience stores, gas stations, shopping malls, bars and even banks. In the central part of the city, there's always one within a block or two. If in doubt about where to look, remember that the ubiquitous Jewel grocery stores, White Hen Pantry convenience stores and all bank branches contain Cash Stations.

The Cash Station network is linked up with Cirrus and Plus, the two largest ATM networks worldwide. In addition, the machines will cheerfully accept your Master-Card or Visa for cash advances. Some will also take your American Express card, and still others will take Discover as well. Because banks can now dock your account up to $3 for using a nonlocal card, they are all too happy to make sure that these little devices accept any card you might offer; ATMs have become profit centers. Foreign visitors should note that the exchange rate in an ATM transaction is usually the very best available, much better than what you'll get with traveler's checks. However, fees for using your card may nullify that advantage.

Wherever you're from, be sure to check with your card issuer to confirm that your card will work. At the very least you need to have a four-digit password. Finally, there have been some well-publicized robberies of people using ATMs, so exercise your usual amount of caution when withdrawing money.

Credit Cards

Major credit cards are widely accepted by car rental firms, hotels, restaurants, gas stations, shops, large grocery stores, movie theaters, ticket vendors and other places. In fact, you'll find certain transactions impossi-

ble to perform without a credit card: you can't reserve theater or other event tickets by phone without one, nor can you guarantee room reservations by phone or rent a car. Even if you want to avoid running up a huge balance that takes the balance of your life to pay off, it is good to have a major credit card in case of an emergency. In bars and nightclubs, cash is still the best bet.

The most commonly accepted cards are Visa and MasterCard. American Express is widely accepted but not as universally as the first two. Discover and Diners Club cards are usually good for travel tickets, hotels and rental cars, but they're less commonly accepted in other situations.

If your credit card is lost or stolen, call the card issuer:

American Express	☎ 800-992-3404
Diners Club	☎ 800-234-6377
Discover	☎ 800-347-2683
MasterCard	☎ 800-307-7309
Visa	☎ 800-336-8472

Security

Be cautious – but not paranoid – about carrying money. If your hotel or hostel has a safe, keep your valuables and excess cash in it. Don't display large amounts of cash in public. A money belt worn under your clothes is a good place to carry excess currency when you're on the move or otherwise unable to stash it in a safe. Avoid carrying your wallet in a back pocket of your pants – this is a prime target for pickpockets, as are handbags and the outside pockets of day packs and fanny packs (bum bags). See Dangers & Annoyances, later in this chapter, for other cautions to heed.

Costs

People moving to Chicago from New York get down on their knees and kiss the ground the first time they find out how little the apartments cost. Such budgetary enthusiasm extends to other expenses as well, for Chicago is moderate in cost compared to other US urban areas. You can eat very well for $25 a day. Pints of beer average $3.50, and since you can walk most places, transportation costs are low. Figure on about $50 a day for costs not associated with accommodations and you won't have to skimp.

You should be able to find decent hotel accommodations for $80 a day for one or two people, or much more depending on your tastes. If money is no object, you'll find no shortage of world-class hotels, restaurants, shops and more. Enjoy!

Tipping

Tipping is a US institution that can be confusing to foreign visitors (just as the tipping habits in their countries tend to confound American visitors). Restaurant wait staff, hotel maids, valet car parkers, bartenders, bellhops and others are paid a mere pittance in wages and expect to make up the shortfall through tips. There's no reason to feel sorry for people working for tips; I know many waiters who make a small fortune because they are good at what they do. And of course, working for tips does contribute to a service worker's desire to deliver good service.

So you have to tip, unless the service is really *appalling*. I have been tempted not to leave a tip just a couple of times. But whom to tip? And how much?

Bartenders – 50¢ to $1 per drink

Bellhops – from $2 total to $1 per bag or more, depending on the distance covered

Cocktail servers – at least 10% to 15%, when you pay for the drinks

Concierges – nothing for answering a simple question, $5 or more for securing tickets to a sold-out show

Doormen – $1 to $2 for summoning you a cab, depending on the weather

Hotel cleaning staff – $1 to $2 per day, left on the pillow each morning

Restaurant wait staff – 15% is standard, but leave 20% if you're really pleased with the service; an easy rule is to pay the same amount as the tax (which is 18.5% in Chicago restaurants)

Skycaps – at least $1 per bag

Taxi drivers – 10% to 15%, even if the individual needs immediate psychiatric attention

Valet car parkers – $2, when the keys to the car are handed to you

Whom not to tip: cashiers, ticket vendors working in booths, the employees who staff hotel front desks.

Taxes

You will encounter a thicket of taxes as you spend money in Chicago. Sadly for the visitor, many of the taxes are aimed right at you, since you can't vote for (or against) the local politicians who impose them. Calculate the taxes into your budget estimates, because along with tips, they can greatly increase your costs.

The basic sales tax is 8.75%. Some grocery items are taxed at only 2%. Newspapers and magazines, but not books, are tax free. The hotel tax is 14.9%; the car rental tax is 18%. And for meals in most parts of town you are likely to visit, there's an extra 9.75% that goes right into funding things like all those pretty flowers in planters.

POST & COMMUNICATIONS
Post

The good news is that compared to other countries, sending mail in the US is cheap. The bad news is that Chicago regularly finishes dead last in the US Postal Service's own rankings of service quality. If you're lucky, you won't have to wait for any mail to be delivered to you while you're in Chicago; otherwise, you might never leave. Mail carriers are regularly arrested for throwing away mail they didn't feel like delivering.

Letters mailed to other parts of the city are often delivered the next day; to other places in the Midwest, in two to three days; to the coasts, in four to five days; and to overseas destinations, in seven days or more.

Postal Rates Rates rise frequently. At press time, it costs 34¢ to mail a 1oz 1st-class letter within the US. Each additional ounce costs 21¢. Postcards cost 20¢.

It costs 60¢ to mail a 1oz letter to Canada or Mexico, 80¢ for other international destinations. Attach 50¢ of postage for postcards to Canada and Mexico, 70¢ for those going overseas. All aerogrammes cost 70¢.

Parcels mailed to foreign destinations from the US are subject to a variety of rates. First class can be very expensive. If you're not in a hurry, consider mailing your items fourth class, which goes by boat. Those rates can be very low, but delivery to Europe, for instance, takes six to eight weeks. If all you are sending is printed matter such as books, you qualify for an extra-cheap rate.

Sending Mail The following three post offices offer a full range of services and accept general delivery mail. Try to avoid them at lunchtime on weekdays, when they are swamped.

Main Post Office (☎ 312-654-3895, 433 W Harrison St, Chicago, IL 60607; Map 10), open 24 hours

Loop Station (☎ 312-427-4225, 211 S Clark St, Chicago, IL 60604; Map 3)

Fort Dearborn (☎ 312-644-7528, 540 N Dearborn St, Chicago, IL 60610; Map 3)

Receiving Mail Poste restante is called 'general delivery' in the US. If you're sending (or expecting) mail to be held at the post office in Chicago, it should be addressed to one of the post offices above as follows:

```
Your Name
  c/o General Delivery (Station Name)
  Chicago, IL, Zip Code
  USA
```

Mail is usually held for 10 days before it's returned to the sender; you might ask your correspondents to write 'hold for arrival' on their envelopes. When you pick up your mail, bring some photo identification. Your passport is best.

Alternatively, have mail sent to the local office of American Express or Thomas Cook, which provide mail service for their clients.

Telephone

Area Codes The city has two area codes, with more soon to come as the proliferation of pagers, faxes and Internet connections sops up the available supply of numbers. The area code 312 serves the Loop and an area bounded roughly by 1600 North, 1600 West and 1600 South. The rest of the city falls in area code 773. The northern suburbs use area code 847, those close to the west and the south 708, and the far west suburbs 630.

Dialing All phone numbers within the US and Canada consist of the three-digit area code followed by a seven-digit local number. If you are calling locally, just dial the seven-digit number. If you are calling to another area code, dial 1 + the three-digit area code + the seven-digit local number. In the city, if you don't use the area code when you should or you do use it when you shouldn't – both of which are common mistakes – you'll get an ear-shattering screech, followed by advice on what to dial.

The country code for the US is 1. The international access code is 011 for calls you dial directly, 01 for calls made collect or on a calling card; dial it first, before you dial the country code. To find out the country code of the place you're trying to call, look in the front of the local phone directory.

Toll-free phone numbers start with the area codes 800, 877 or 888. Numbers that begin with 900 could cost you a small fortune (up to several dollars per minute). You'll most often see such numbers advertised late at night on TV in ads asking, 'Lonely? Want to have some hot talk?'

Local directory assistance can be reached by calling ☎ 411 or ☎ 555-1212. If you are looking for a number outside of your local area code but know what area code it falls under, dial ☎ 1 + the area code + 555-1212. These calls are no longer free, even from pay phones, which no longer have phone books.

To obtain a toll-free phone number, dial ☎ 800-555-1212.

Pay Phones Coin phones have been deregulated and now charge whatever the market will bear. A variety of companies operate them. Ameritech phones, by far the most reliable, cost 35¢. Some pay phones are operated by companies just this side of crooks. If you try to make a long-distance call using their phones and punch in your credit card or calling card number, you will later be horrified that the operator charged you $5 per minute, or some other extortionist rate.

American pay phones have not yet adopted the convenient card technology found elsewhere. Have plenty of quarters, dimes and nickels ready (but see the Prepaid Calling Cards section, below).

Hotel Phones Here's a paradox for you: the cheaper the hotel, the more likely you'll pay nothing to make phone calls from your room. On the dubious theory that if you're paying $300 a night for your room then you won't mind being gouged for a call, some of the very best hotels nick you for $1.50 every time you pick up the receiver, even for local or toll-free calls.

Long Distance Hundreds of companies compete for your long-distance business. If you are using a pay phone, check to see which carrier is the default long-distance

provider (the company's name is listed in very small type on the rate card, displayed on every phone). Sprint, MCI and AT&T are not the very cheapest, but they refrain from scams. You should also check who the default long-distance carrier is for your hotel-room phone, so you won't end up paying a price equivalent to the one you paid for the room.

Collect Calls You can call collect (reverse the charges) from any phone. The main service providers are AT&T (☎ 800-225-5288) and MCI (☎ 800-365-5328). These generally charge rates that will be less stressful to the lucky recipient of your call than the fees levied by local phone companies or the dreaded third-party firms.

Prepaid Calling Cards Convenience stores and other places sell phone cards good for a prepaid amount of long-distance phone time; these are typically available in amounts of $5, $10, $20 and $50. To use one, you dial an 800 number and then enter the code number on your card. The company's computer keeps track of how much value you have left. At a prompt, you enter the number you are calling. These cards are often a good deal and a good way to circumnavigate the swamp of phone-call-making minutiae.

Lonely Planet's eKno global communication service provides low-cost international calls. It also offers free messaging services, email, travel information and an online travel vault, where you can securely store all your important documents. You can join on the Web at www.ekno.lonelyplanet.com, where you'll find the local-access numbers for the 24-hour customer-service center. Once you've joined, always check the eKno Web site for the latest access numbers for each country and updates on new features. The eKno access number in the US is ☎ 800-706-1333.

Mobile Phones The US uses a mess of incompatible formats for mobile (or 'cell') phones. Many still use an old analog format, while the newer digital models primarily use the competing TDMA or CDMA formats. Few use the GSM format that is popular in the rest of the world. If you want to bring your mobile phone, check with your service provider to see if there's any hope it will work in the US.

Fax

Pay fax machines are located at shipping outlets such as Mail Boxes Etc, copy places such as Kinko's and hotel business centers. Prices can be high, as much as $1 per outgoing page to a US number or $4 a page to Europe. Receiving faxes costs about half as much.

Email & Internet Access

If you set up an email account with a free Internet access service such as Hotmail (www.hotmail.com) or Yahoo (www.yahoo.com), you can access your email from any computer with a Web connection. Otherwise, check with the provider of your account to see how (or if) you can access it from Chicago.

The US uses the standard RJ-11 telephone plug, and most computer equipment now comes equipped with these plugs.

If you're traveling with a computer and modem, you will likely be able to connect to the Internet from your hotel room. Many hotel phones now have standard RJ-11 jacks labeled 'Data,' into which you can safely plug your modem cord. Before you plug into a regular wall-mounted phone jack, ask if it's connected to a PBX (ie, a private branch exchange, found mainly in big hotels and office buildings). If it is, it may fry your modem. What you want is a normal 'analog' phone jack.

If you just want to get on the Web, try the Internet café Screenz (☎ 773-388-8300, 2717 N Clark St; Map 6) or the Harold Washington Library Center (☎ 312-747-4300, 400 S State St; Map 3). Internet access is free at the library; see the Libraries section, later in this chapter, for information about hours.

DIGITAL RESOURCES

The World Wide Web is a rich resource for travelers. You can research your trip, hunt down bargain air fares, book hotels, check on weather conditions or chat with locals and other travelers about the best places to visit (or avoid!).

There's no better place to start your Web explorations than the Lonely Planet Web site (www.lonelyplanet.com). Here you'll find succinct summaries on traveling to most places on earth, postcards from other travelers and the Thorn Tree bulletin board, where you can ask questions before you go or dispense advice when you get back. You can also find travel news and updates to many of our most popular guidebooks, and the subWWWay section links you to the most useful travel resources elsewhere on the Web.

CitySync Chicago is Lonely Planet's digital city guide for handheld computers (currently available for Palm Computing, Handspring and other Palm OS organizers). With CitySync you can search, sort and bookmark hundreds of Chicago's restaurants, hotels, attractions, clubs and more – all pinpointed on scrollable street maps. Sections on activities, transportation and local events give you the big picture plus all the little details. Purchase or demo CitySync Chicago at www.citysync.com.

BOOKS

For information on literary books about Chicago, see the Literature section in the Facts about Chicago chapter.

Most books are published in different editions by different publishers in different countries. As a result, a book might be a hardcover rarity in one country while it's readily available in paperback in another. Fortunately, bookshops and libraries search by title or author, so your local bookshop or library is best placed to advise you on the availability of the following recommendations.

Most of the books listed here are available in the US, although some may need to be specially ordered.

Lonely Planet

Lonely Planet's *Great Lakes* and *USA* are good companions to this book if your travels will take you farther. *Great Lakes* covers the Midwestern states of Illinois,

Indiana, Wisconsin, Minnesota, Michigan and Ohio. If, like, you don't, like, speak, like, American, you might like to, like, consider the *USA Phrasebook*.

History

Real estate mogul Dempsey J Travis has developed a productive sideline gig writing well-regarded books about African Americans in Chicago. His book *Harold: The People's Mayor* is the authorized biography of Chicago's first black mayor, Harold Washington. Travis has also known and heard every jazz great for more than half a century. His 1983 bestseller *An Autobiography of Black Jazz* is a rich chronicle of Chicago jazz and the society that spawned it.

David D Perata's book *Those Pullman Blues: An Oral History of the African American Railroad Attendant* traces the life of a Pullman employee during the time when these employees played a vital role in the civil rights movement. *Chicago's South Side, 1946–1948* is a stunning book of photos taken during this turbulent period in Chicago's black neighborhoods. The photos by Wayne F Miller are intimate portraits of everyday life.

David Farber's *Chicago '68* tells the story from all sides of the disastrous Democratic convention that ended in a police riot. James R Grossman's *Land of Hope* documents the huge migration of blacks from the South to Chicago. The late, legendary Chicago journalist Mike Royko wrote *Boss*, one of the best political books ever penned; it tells the story of Richard J Daley, the mayor who ruled Chicago from 1955 to 1976.

For a completely different history of Chicago, check out William Cronon's *Nature's Metropolis*, which discusses the city's development from an environmental perspective. Cronon shows how exploiting the land drove the development of the city and the region.

Another good, general-purpose book on Chicago's history is Donald L Miller's highly readable *City of the Century*.

Robert J Schoenberg's definitive work on the famous gangster, *Mr Capone*, shows that when the romanticizing is over, Capone was an amoral violent thug. Bad morals of a different sort are documented in the best-selling *Eight Men Out: The Black Sox and the 1919 World Series*. Written by Eliot Asinof and Stephen J Gould, it shows what happened when the White Sox took money to throw the World Series.

Lois Wille's *Forever Open, Clear, and Free* is a textbook study of how the dedicated efforts of a few can thwart the corrupt ambitions of many. The heroes of this book have spent a century preventing developers and crooked politicians from turning the lakefront into a high-rise hell.

General

AIA Guide to Chicago, by the American Institute of Architects Chicago and other groups, is an excellent one-volume source of informed commentary about architecture in the Windy City.

Lois Wille's *At Home in the Loop: How Clout and Community Built Chicago's Dearborn Park* shows the forces behind the conversion of the blighted rail yards south of the Loop into a booming community.

The fans' profitable fascination with the losing Cubs is at the center of Peter Golenbock's *Wrigleyville*. The chapters on the era of owner Philip K Wrigley are a fascinating read about the oddest man to ever own a baseball team.

Local author Richard C Lindberg has filled *Quotable Chicago* with little choice nuggets, like this one from the first Mayor Daley: 'They have vilified me. They have crucified me. Yes, they have even criticized me.'

Not just for architecture buffs, *Building Images: 70 Years of Photography at Hedrich Blessing* is a gorgeous album filled with images of local buildings shot by the noted Chicago firm of Hedrich Blessing.

FILMS

Some notable films have been shot in Chicago, including the following. *Call Northside 777* (1948), an often ignored Jimmy Stewart vehicle about a cynical reporter, was filmed on location throughout the West Side. It features excellent shots of gritty city blocks later demolished for expressways.

The middle part of the Hitchcock classic *North by Northwest* (1959), starring Cary Grant, contains scenes filmed on location at the Omni Ambassador East, on N Michigan Ave, at the now demolished Dearborn Station train shed and at Midway Airport.

Nightmare in Chicago (1964), a forgotten early thriller by director Robert Altman, was shot entirely in the city. The gripping story follows a psychopath who terrorizes the town.

In *The Blues Brothers* (1980), possibly the best-known Chicago movie, Second City alums John Belushi and Dan Aykroyd tear up the city, including City Hall. But the scenes with the hapless Nazis in the Pinto were filmed in Milwaukee.

Ordinary People (1980), Robert Redford's Oscar-winning directorial debut, is an intelligent and engrossing drama about a really screwed-up rich family. In Steve McQueen's final film, *The Hunter* (1980), a car takes a sublime swan dive into the river from Marina City; otherwise this one is a dud.

The Blues Brothers

In *Risky Business* (1983), a darkly satiric parable about all the things not to do when the folks leave home, Tom Cruise and Rebecca De Mornay enjoy the most pleasurable El ride of all time. Chuck Norris single-handedly cleans up Chicago in *Code of Silence* (1985), featuring an excellent chase on top of the El.

David Mamet's play *Sexual Perversity in Chicago* inspired *About Last Night* (1986), a watered-down snoozer made by Hollywood execs terrified by the original name. It shows off some of the worst bars in town.

The Color of Money (1986), Martin Scorsese's sequel to *The Hustler*, portrays Paul Newman and Tom Cruise cruising the West Side. *Ferris Bueller's Day Off* (1986), director John Hughes' cinematic postcard

for the city, revolves around a rich North Shore teen discovering the joys of the city.

Based on the 1940 novel of the same name by Richard Wright, *Native Son* (1986) plays out the disturbing repercussions of a young white woman's accidental murder by Bigger Thomas, a poor young black man. Much of this tense drama, directed by Jerrold Freedman, was shot in Hyde Park and the South Side.

Gregory Hines and Billy Crystal team up in *Running Scared* (1986), a buddy movie about wisecracking Chicago cops. There's a splendid car chase *on* the El and a great shoot-out in the State of Illinois Building.

Kevin Costner saves Chicago from Al Capone in *The Untouchables* (1987). The infamous baby-carriage scene was filmed in Union Station, the exploding grocery store stood at Clark and Roscoe, the ball-bat banquet happened in the Blackstone Hotel and the trial took place in the Cultural Center.

John Candy and John Hughes just couldn't get enough of this city. They filmed portions of *Planes, Trains and Automobiles* (1987) and *Uncle Buck* (1990) in Chicago. Gene Hackman stars in *The Package* (1989), a political thriller that uses Chicago's dismal gray winters to dramatic advantage.

Lots of abandoned buildings went up in flames in *Backdraft* (1991), director Ron Howard's ode to those regular-guy Chicago firefighters. *Only the Lonely* (1991) features John Candy in his least-stupid role as a cop who has to choose between mom and girlfriend. The Music Box Theater stars.

Harrison Ford stars as the falsely accused main character in the action film *The Fugitive* (1993), with great scenes in City Hall and the Chicago Hilton & Towers and on the El. The author of this guide found himself standing next to Ford during the filming of the chase through the actual St Patrick's Day Parade.

Go Fish (1994), director Rose Troche's somewhat experimental film, shows what it takes for one Chicago lesbian to get a date.

The stirring documentary *Hoop Dreams* (1994) follows the high school basketball careers of two African American teenagers from the South Side. Filmmakers Frederick Marx, Peter Gilbert and Steve James interview the young men and their families, coaches, teachers and friends over several years, showing how the dream of playing college and pro ball – and escaping the ghetto – influences their life choices.

In *While You Were Sleeping* (1995), Sandra Bullock portrays the kind of CTA ticket vendor who could only exist in the movies. Cameron Diaz co-stars as the daughter of the White Sox owner in *My Best Friend's Wedding* (1997) – fortunately dad isn't the real-life owner, Jerry Reinsdorf, a man Sox fans love to hate. Julia Roberts is typically goofy as a woman who falls in love with her best friend on the day of his wedding.

High Fidelity (2000) stars native son John Cusack. Although the city looks great here, you can't get away from the fact that this movie is based on Nick Hornby's book, which is set in London. And it's a great London book.

In addition, although it was filmed entirely in Hollywood, *His Girl Friday* (1940) is a marvelous remake of Ben Hecht's *The Front Page* (1931). Hecht, who scripted both, worked as a Chicago reporter during the peak of the newspaper circulation wars in the 1920s. He based these movies on his experiences covering trials at the old Criminal Courts Building, which still stands at Kinzie and Dearborn Sts, although it's now used as an office building.

The TV series *ER* features exterior scenes filmed in Chicago in every episode. These tend to be postcard stuff and Chicagoans love to laugh at their ludicrous lack of continuity: characters manage to jump miles around town during one short stroll.

NEWSPAPERS & MAGAZINES

Chicago boasts a diverse range of publications serving every segment of the population. The city has a long tradition of newspapers and is one of the few remaining American cities to support separately owned and competing major dailies. Reading one, if not both, of the two major dailies is a great way to start the day. On Friday, both papers publish good guides to current entertainment and events.

Author and playwright Ben Hecht worked in Chicago for many years early in the century, immortalizing the rough-and-tumble world of newspapering in his play *The Front Page*, which later became the movie *His Girl Friday* (1940).

Chicago Tribune

The largest newspaper in the Midwest, the *Chicago Tribune* has come far from its quirky days under publisher Robert R McCormick. The *Tribune* is known for employing good writers who are experts in their areas of coverage, and it publishes a fair amount of foreign and national news from its bureaus worldwide. Its coverage of the city is often overshadowed by its aggressive coverage of the surrounding suburbs and their affluent readers, whom the paper covets.

The *Tribune* excels at highbrow arts and culture coverage. At the other end of the extreme, it also features the best comics section in town. The Sunday *Trib* weighs in at several pounds and boasts more than 1,000,000 readers. However, in recent years there's been a growing feeling that the paper has become complacent. David Halberstam summed it up this way in the magazine *Brill's Content:* '[The *Tribune*] seems to be going through the motions with its flagship paper…operating without genuine passion or purpose.' The paper has suffered from the fact that some of its best talents have either died or quit in recent years.

You can read the newspaper online at www.chicagotribune.com. For entertainment and dining information, check out the Web site www.metromix.com, also operated by the *Tribune*.

Chicago Sun-Times

The tabloid competitor to the *Tribune*, the *Chicago Sun-Times* concentrates most of its much smaller resources on comprehensive coverage of the city. The paper has spent years recovering from a disastrous period in the mid-1980s, when it was owned by Rupert Murdoch, whose efforts to turn it into a trashy tabloid drove away hundreds of thousands of readers. Recently it has drawn criticism for its palpable lean to the far right under the ownership of conservative Conrad Black. Its endorsement of George W Bush for president in 2000 sparked a boycott by its many black readers.

The *Sun-Times* is known for its columnists. Robert Feder is the premier media columnist in the country. Gossip columnist Bill Zwecker comes up with scores of salacious scoops on notable folks, and the legendary veteran Irv Kupcinet has been churning out prose for more than 50 years. Famous movie critic Roger Ebert is a workhorse, reviewing up to six movies a week. On the editorial pages, Pulitzer Prize–winning cartoonist Jack Higgins skewers the high and mighty with a daily bit of hilarity. *Next*, a new essay section in its lagging Sunday paper, holds great promise; it's quite readable.

Many Chicagoans read the *Sun-Times* for local news and the Midwest edition of the *New York Times* for news from farther afield. Visit www.suntimes.com for the online version.

Other Newspapers

Readily available national newspapers include the *New York Times*, *USA Today* and the *Wall Street Journal*.

With its daily circulation down to 20,000, the *Chicago Defender* shows few signs of the pivotal role it once played in the black community, not just in Chicago but across the nation (see the boxed text 'The Great Defender').

Many of Chicago's ethnic communities support newspapers such as the Spanish-language *El Heraldo*, the *Polish Daily News* and the *Korean News*. These are available on newsstands or in stores serving those communities.

The Great Defender

After World War I the *Chicago Defender*, founded in 1905 by Robert S Abbott, was the most important black newspaper in the country and the most popular newspaper among Southern blacks.

A complex distribution system, which included Pullman sleeping-car porters throwing bundles off at every stop, meant each week's edition was read by hundreds of thousands of African Americans. So effective was the *Defender* that racist whites, fearing the paper's influence, murdered its readers and tortured its distributors.

The paper played a pivotal role in the Great Migration, the movement of millions of southern blacks to Chicago and other northern cities in the early years of the 20th century (see the History section in the Facts about Chicago chapter). Abbott knew that the influx of thousands of blacks into the city would increase the community's clout – and by sheer numbers alone, it did. Abbott, the city's first black millionaire, reveled in the Great Migration. By 1929 the *Defender*'s circulation was 230,000. After Abbott's death in 1940, however, the paper's influence steadily declined. Today it is but a shadow of its former self.

Each Thursday two free weeklies hit the streets. Be careful that you don't get hit by the *Chicago Reader*. This mammoth four-section tabloid lists virtually everything going on in town, from theater to live music to offbeat films to performance art. Navigating your way through this behemoth, which brims with ads for futon stores and coffeehouses, can take hours. Reading the personal ads is a great way to pass time in a bar while waiting to meet someone. You can also find the Reader on the Internet at www.chicagoreader.com.

The other weekly, *New City*, is a nimbler and hipper publication. By no means complete, it lists major goings-on of interest to younger, more 'alternative' readers.

Unfortunately, the accuracy of its information can sometimes be as haphazard as its design.

The *Chicago Free Press* is the city's main gay and lesbian weekly, with local, national and entertainment news. *Streetwise* is a bi-monthly sold by the homeless and others down on their luck. It's a worthy enterprise aimed at getting people back on their feet through work.

Magazines

The monthly magazine *Chicago* features excellent articles and culture coverage. But for visitors, the magazine's greatest value lies in its massive restaurant listings. The hundreds of expert reviews are up to date and indexed by food type, location, cost and more. It's worth picking up to find the latest and greatest places in Chicago's vibrant dining scene.

Moguls and would-be moguls consult *Crain's Chicago Business*, a business tabloid that regularly scoops the dailies despite being a weekly.

You'll find scores of free publications piled on the floors of bookstores, bars and restaurants throughout the city. Pick up a few and see if you find one you like.

RADIO

The radio spectrum screeches with a cacophony of local stations. National radio personalities who work in Chicago include Paul Harvey, the amazingly stalwart conservative fossil on WGN, and Jim Nayder, host of WBEZ's *The Annoying Music Show*, which plays such duds as Leonard Nimoy crooning 'Proud Mary' and the Brady Bunch demolishing 'American Pie.'

During some parts of the day, WGN (720 AM) broadcasts from its street-level studio in the Tribune Tower overlooking N Michigan Ave. You can press your nose up against the glass and make stupid faces at hosts such as the duo of Kathy O'Malley and Judy Markey, two irreverent delights.

WBEZ (91.5 FM), the National Public Radio affiliate, is well funded and popular. It's the home station for the hit NPR show *This American Life*. Located on Navy Pier, WBEZ (☎ 312-832-9150) produces radio dramas and dramatic readings. Some of these recordings are taped before a live audience; call for details.

WBBM (780 AM) blares news headlines all day long, with traffic reports every 10 minutes. Newcomers to the US will want to listen to talk radio on WLS (890 AM) for a few minutes to hear a succession of the kind of paranoid blabbermouths who give the nation a bad rep.

You'll find the most interesting music on WXRT (93.1 FM), a rock station that aggressively avoids falling into any canned format trap. Other notables in Chicago are:

WSCR	670 AM, sports talk
WLIT	93.9 FM, 'lite' rock
WBBM	96.3 FM, top 40
WFMT	98.7 FM, classical
WOJO	105.1 FM, Spanish
WGCI	107.5 FM, urban contemporary

TV

Chicago's local network affiliates are little different from their counterparts in other large cities. WLS (channel 7, the ABC affiliate) is generally the ratings leader for newscasts, covering the latest murders and mayhem from the streets. WMAQ (channel 5, the NBC affiliate) is a ratings loser after years of being adrift. WFLD (channel 32, the Fox affiliate) features the usual Fox neon effects. In 2000 WBBM (channel 2, the CBS affiliate) tried an innovative hard news format that lacked sensationalism. Led by the estimable Carol Marin, it was loved by the critics and shunned by the viewers (who evidently do like their blood glowing).

Other stations in town each have their own niches. WGN (channel 9) is owned by the Tribune Company. Its meteorologist, Tom Skilling, will tell you more than you could ever want to know about the weather, but that's good if you're traveling. The station also shows all the games played by fellow Tribune-empire denizens, the Cubs.

WTTW (channel 11) is a good public broadcasting station. *Chicago Tonight*, at 7pm weekdays, takes an in-depth look at one of the day's news stories.

WSNS (channel 44) is a Spanish-language station.

VIDEO SYSTEMS

Overseas visitors should remember that the USA and Canada use the National Television System Committee (NTSC) color TV and video standard, which is not compatible with the PAL and SECAM standards used in Africa, Europe, Asia and Australia unless converted. If you buy an NTSC video movie and put it in your PAL or SECAM video-cassette player, you'll get only garbled images and sound.

PHOTOGRAPHY & VIDEO

All major brands of film and US-format video cassettes are available at reasonable prices in many stores, including any Walgreens or Osco pharmacies. These outlets stock a wide range of popular films at competitive prices and offer a range of developing services. Processing a roll of 100 ASA 35mm color print film with 24 exposures costs about $7 for regular service. Look for special offers.

Wolf Camera and Ritz Camera also have dozens of locations. Neither one offers particularly good prices on film, although they both keep more esoteric types of slide film in stock.

Central Camera (☎ 312-427-5580, 232 S Wabash Ave; Map 3) sells every kind of camera and related equipment imaginable for low prices that belie its Old World appearance. The folks behind the counter know what they're talking about, and if you are looking for a new lens for some ancient Nikon willed to you, you'll find it here.

Best Buy (☎ 312-988-4067, 1000 W North Ave; Map 6) is a huge electronics store at the back of a large strip mall that's about a 10-minute walk from the North/Clybourn El stop. This outlet of the electronics chain consistently sells film for $1 to $2 less per roll than the competition. While you're there, check out the CD prices – they're usually the lowest around.

TIME

There's never enough, right? Chicago falls in the US Central Standard Time (CST) zone. 'Standard time' runs from the last Sunday in October to the first Sunday in April. 'Day-

RICHARD CUMMINS

light saving time,' when clocks move ahead one hour, runs from the first Sunday in April to the last Sunday in October, when clocks go back to standard time.

Chicago is one hour behind Eastern Standard Time, which encompasses nearby Michigan and Indiana, apart from the northwestern corner of Indiana, which follows Chicago time. The border between the two zones is just east of the city. Note that Indiana doesn't take a cotton to notions like daylight saving time. In the summer Indiana keeps the same time as Chicago; in winter, with the exception of its northwestern corner, it is one hour ahead.

The city is one hour ahead of Mountain Standard Time, which includes much of the Rocky Mountains, and two hours ahead of Pacific Standard Time, which includes California.

Chicago is six hours behind Greenwich Mean Time (but remember daylight saving time).

ELECTRICITY

Electric current in the US is 110-120 volts, 60 Hz AC. Outlets accept North American standard plugs, which have two flat prongs and an occasional third round one. If your appliance is made for another system, you will need a converter or adapter. These are best bought in your home country. Otherwise, try a travel bookstore (see Books in the Shopping chapter).

WEIGHTS & MEASURES

The US continues to resist the imposition of the metric system. Distances are measured in inches, feet, yards and miles; weights are measured in ounces, pounds and tons.

Gasoline is sold in US gallons, which are 20% smaller than the Imperial version and the equivalent of 3.79 liters. Once you have that down, it will become apparent what a bargain gas is in the US. Beer on tap in bars is often sold in US pints, which are three sips short of international ones. Sandwiches often come with a quarter-pound of meats or cheese. Temperatures are given in degrees Fahrenheit. When it is 65° to 85° outside, it's nice. Water freezes at 32°. Your body is normally 98.6°.

LAUNDRY

Swank hotels will do your laundry for you, but it won't be cheap. Expect to pay $2 to $5 or more per item. You'll have to decide if the convenience of having someone haul your dirty duds away and bring them back sparkling clean is worth it. Dry cleaners abound, with one on almost every block. Coin-operated laundries are cheap and plentiful. A wash in a large machine costs about $1.50, with large dryers costing 25¢ for 10 minutes. Laundromats usually contain machines dispensing little boxes of detergent and the like.

Riverpoint Coin Laundry (☎ 773-549-5080, 1730 W Fullerton Ave), in the Riverpoint Plaza, features a 125-gallon fish tank complete with an exhaustive sign detailing the inhabitants. This upscale suds house is open 24 hours and offers free coffee from midnight to 9am. You can stock up on supplies at the huge Omni supermarket, in the same complex and also open 24 hours, while your clothes spin.

Laundryland (☎ 773-528-0350, 2206 N Halsted St; Map 6) is a large laundry in a posh neighborhood.

Wrigleyville's Saga Laundry Bar (☎ 773-929-9274, 3435 N Southport Ave; Map 7)

has an attached sports bar and café for your entertainment; it's open 7am to 11pm (last wash) weekdays and Sunday, 7am to 5pm Saturday. Other good bars and cafés lie just across the street.

You'll find laundries in the Spincycle chain all over town. These clean, air-conditioned facilities have TVs. To find the nearest location, call ☎ 800-973-7746.

TOILETS

When it's time to see a man about a horse, to drop the kids off at the pool or whatever euphemism you prefer for bladder or bowel evacuation, you'll face several challenges. In fact, perhaps you need to be your own nagging mom and repeatedly ask yourself before you set out each day, 'Are you sure you went?'

The main challenge faced by all is finding a place to go. Try shopping malls, department stores, large bookstores (the Borders at N Michigan Ave and Pearson St contains basement restrooms) train stations and other large public places. Hotels often have downright swank facilities somewhere past the front desk, often by the telephones. Museums usually place the toilets past where you pay admission. The Chicago Park District has begun a push to clean and sanitize the toilets in its parks and beaches. Many are now much improved and optimistically called 'comfort stations' on park district maps. In a dire emergency, no restaurant or bar should refuse you. Those ubiquitous McDonald's are good for one thing: generally clean and open toilets.

Foreign visitors face the additional problem of figuring out what goofy terminology your chosen establishment uses to indicate where the toilets are. Here are synonyms in a rough descending order of frequency: bathroom, restroom, facilities, men's/ladies'/women's room, little boy's/little girl's room, powder room, latrine, john, lavatory, way station, potty. Worse yet, once you get to the restroom doors, this nonsense is often replaced by cryptic signs that bear little relationship to your immediate needs. Confronted by two doors, each with a non-gender-specific animal head on it, what do

FACTS FOR THE VISITOR

you do? Try the one on the left. If screams from the opposite sex result, try the one on the right.

HEALTH

Chicago is a typical first-world destination when it comes to health. The only foreign visitors who may be required to get immunizations are those coming from areas with a history of cholera and yellow fever.

Excellent medical care is readily available, but if you are not properly insured, a collision with the US health care system could prove fatal to your budget.

If you require a certain medication, take an adequate supply with you and bring the prescription as well, in case you lose your supply. You won't have trouble buying most nonprescription medications.

Precautions

The water is fit to drink, and restaurant sanitation is good. The only health risks you face in Chicago are related to accidents, violence or the weather. The first is somewhat preventable, the second easy to minimize by reading the Dangers & Annoyances section, later. Weather can be almost entirely eliminated as a health risk by following certain rules. In the winter, when it's cold, bundle up. That sounds absurdly simple, and it is, but many people coming from perennially warm regions don't understand it. When the weather forecasters say there is a 'wind-chill factor' of 15 degrees or colder, then you should not expose any parts of your body to the air. (The 'wind-chill factor' is an estimation of the temperature your skin feels when the effects of the cold are multiplied by the wind.) Wear warm and solid footwear with wool socks to avoid frostbite. The key to preventing frostbite is to listen to your body. If your toes, ears or other easily chilled parts of you feel cold, numb or worst of all, painful, then you need to take action to warm them.

People from mild climates can have problems during the warm summer months also. Chicago is not in the tropics, but on a hot, sunny day fair-skinned people can burn quickly. Use sunscreen with an SPF of 30 or more. Dehydration is also a problem; drink plenty of fluids. If the temperature climbs well into the 90s, those not acclimated to that kind of heat shouldn't spend all day in it. Spend time in air-conditioned places and don't overexert yourself.

Health Insurance

Be sure that you have some form of health insurance that will pay your US medical bills in full should you need medical care while in the USA. Bills for an illness that requires hospitalization can easily exceed $1000 or even $2000 per day, and you will be expected to pay even at publicly supported government hospitals unless you can show that you are destitute. For information on insurance, see Travel Insurance, earlier in this chapter.

Medical Services

If you are ill or injured and suspect that the situation is in any way life-threatening, call ☎ 911 immediately. This is a free call from any phone, and you don't have to make a deposit in a pay phone first. This number will connect you to a Chicago emergency services operator, who will dispatch the appropriate people to assist you.

If you have a less serious malady, such as the flu or a sprained ankle, and want to see a doctor, ask your hotel for a recommendation. Though Chicago is filled with clinics and doctors, none of their services come cheap, so make sure you have insurance. To get prescriptions filled, call Walgreens' 24-hour pharmacy (☎ 312-664-8686).

The following hospitals offer medical services through their emergency rooms. If your condition is not acute, call first, because many also operate clinics that can see you in a more timely and convenient manner.

Northwestern Memorial Hospital (☎ 312-926-2000, 2251 E Huron St; Map 3) is the most convenient hospital to the Near North and Gold Coast.

Illinois Masonic Hospital (☎ 773-975-1600, 836 W Wellington Ave; Map 7) is in Lincoln Park, just west of Halsted St.

University of Chicago Hospital (☎ 773-702-1000, 5841 S Maryland Ave; Map 12) is in Hyde Park, just north of 59th St at the west end of campus.

Children's Memorial Hospital (☎ 773-880-4000, 2300 N Lincoln Ave; Map 6), in Lincoln Park, is one of the nation's leading medical centers for children.

Howard Brown Health Center (☎ 773-388-1600, 4025 N Sheridan Rd; Map 7) is the Midwest's largest lesbian, gay and bisexual health organization, although it has no ER as such.

If you are broke and have no insurance, head to Cook County Hospital (☎ 312-633-6000, 1835 W Harrison St; Map 10), one block south of the Medical Center El stop on the Blue Line. If your problem is not life-threatening, you will be seated in a waiting room where you will do just that for perhaps 12 hours while you're surrounded by people sicker than yourself. However, if you have been shot, stabbed or injured in a horrific accident, you will come here by ambulance and will receive the best trauma care in the world. This is where the concept was invented, in 1966. The TV show *ER* was inspired by this place. Sometime in 2001 or 2002 the hospital will move to a new location immediately west.

WOMEN TRAVELERS

Women will be safe alone in most parts of Chicago, though they should exercise a degree of caution and awareness of their surroundings. The El is safe, even at night, though you might want to seek out more-populated cars or the first car, to be closest to the driver. Or you can take one of the buses that parallel many train lines.

In the commonly visited areas of Chicago, you should not encounter troubling attitudes from men. In bars some men will see a woman alone as a bid for companionship. A polite 'no thank you' should suffice to send them away. Chicagoans are very friendly, so don't be afraid to protest loudly if someone is hassling you. It will probably send the offending party away and bring helpful Samaritans to your side.

Women travelers face the extra threat of rape. The best way to deal with this threat is to avoid the same kind of risky situations that might leave you open to other types of violent crime. Be alert if somebody seems to be following you to your hotel room or if someone is trailing you down a street. Conducting yourself in a commonsense manner will help you avoid most problems. Self-defense experts advise that if you're attacked in any way, immediately start screaming as loudly as possible.

If you are attacked, call ☎ 911 from any phone. You will be connected with an operator who can dispatch the appropriate assistance. The Chicago Rape Victim Emergency Assistance 24-hour hotline number is ☎ 312-744-8418.

GAY & LESBIAN TRAVELERS

The heart of Chicago's large and vibrant gay and lesbian community lies on N Halsted St between Belmont Ave and Addison St, but Andersonville, Lincoln Park, Bucktown and other neighborhoods are also gay- and lesbian-friendly. Outside of the Halsted neighborhood, however, open affection between same-sex partners often draws confused or disapproving stares.

Horizons (☎ 773-472-6469, 961 W Montana St) serves the gay community with referrals to social services. Horizons' 24-hour LGBT Help Line (☎ 773-871-2273), staffed by volunteers, offers advice for lesbians, gays, bisexuals and transgendered people who've been the victims of violence.

For AIDS- and HIV-related questions, try the AIDS Foundation of Chicago (☎ 312-922-2322, 411 S Wells St, Suite 300); it's open 9am to 5pm weekdays. You can also call the Illinois AIDS Hotline (☎ 800-243-2437 in Illinois).

Other information services include Chicago Black Lesbians & Gays (☎ 312-409-4917, PO Box 14811, Chicago, IL 60614 USA), the Chicago Area Gay & Lesbian Chamber of Commerce (☎ 773-871-4190, 3713 N Halsted St, Chicago, IL 60613 USA, www.glchamber.org) and the Chicago Women's Health Center (☎ 773-935-6126, 3435 N Sheffield Ave), which is open noon to 4pm weekdays.

DISABLED TRAVELERS

Chicago is not an accommodating place for people with reduced mobility. The preponderance of older buildings means that doorways are narrow and stairs prevalent. Most of the El is inaccessible. If you do find a station with an elevator, make sure that there's also one at your destination. You can get from O'Hare to the Clark and Jackson Stations on the Blue Line in the Loop. From Midway, you can ride the Orange Line to the Library, Washington and Clark Stations in the Loop.

Half the CTA buses are not equipped with wheelchair lifts. Even those that are equipped sometimes speed past people in wheelchairs because the driver doesn't want to stop and work the lift. Metra and Amtrak trains are supposedly accessible, but boarding them is usually a major undertaking, so you're best off getting to the station early. Call ☎ 836-7000, preceded by the area code for whatever area of Chicago you are in – 312, 708, 847, 630 or 773 – for details on the CTA and Metra services; for Amtrak, call ☎ 800-872-7245.

For hotels, you are best off with the newest properties. But call the hotel itself – not the 800 number – and confirm that the room you want to reserve has the features you need.

The Mayor's Office for People with Disabilities (☎ 312-744-6673, TTY 312-744-7833, 121 N LaSalle St, Room 1104, Chicago, IL 60602) is a good spot to start asking questions about the availability of services.

Organizations

A number of organizations and tour providers around the world specialize in the needs of disabled travelers.

In Australia, try Independent Travelers (☎ 08-232-2555, 167 Gilles St, Adelaide, SA 5000).

In the UK, try RADAR (☎ 020 7250 3222, radar@radar.org.uk, 250 City Rd, London, EC1V 8AF).

In the US, try Mobility International USA (☎/TTY 541-343-1284, fax 541-343-6812, info@miusa.org, PO Box 10767, Eugene, OR 97440), a program that advises disabled travelers on mobility issues and runs an educational exchange program. You also can try the Society for the Advance-

ment of Travel for the Handicapped (SATH; ☎ 212-447-7284, sathtravel@aol.com, 347 5th Ave, Suite 610, New York, NY 10016 USA).

Twin Peaks Press (☎ 360-694-2462, 800-637-2256, twinpeak@pacifier.com) publishes several useful handbooks for disabled travelers, including *Travel for the Disabled* and *Directory of Travel Agencies for the Disabled*. Address requests for these guides to PO Box 129, Vancouver, WA 98666 USA.

Based in Belgium, Mobility International (☎ 2 201 56 08, fax 2 201 57 63, secretariat@mobility-international.org, 18, Bd Baudouin, B-1000 Brussels) is an organization for disabled travelers.

SENIOR TRAVELERS

Though the age at which senior benefits begin varies, travelers 62 and older (though sometimes 50 and older) can expect to receive discounts from hotels, museums, tours, restaurants, and other places. Some US advocacy groups that help seniors in planning their travels are:

American Association of Retired Persons (AARP; ☎ 312-458-3600, TTY 312-458-3613, 800-424-3410, member@aarp.org, 601 E St NW, Washington DC 20049)

Elderhostel (☎ 877-426-8056, 978-323-4141, TTY 877-426-2167, 75 Federal St, Boston, MA 02110)

National Council of Senior Citizens (☎ 301-578-8800, 888-373-6467, membership@ncscinc.org, 8403 Colesville Rd, Suite 1200, Silver Spring, MD 20910)

CHICAGO FOR CHILDREN

Chicago can seem like a big mean city to kids, but it doesn't have to be. Almost all the museums have installed special areas aimed at entertaining, amusing and even (don't let this one slip) educating them. Here are some of the major sites that work at being kid-friendly (see the Things to See & Do chapter for addresses and more information):

Chicago Children's Museum – on Navy Pier, an obvious place to start, followed by the rest of the pier itself

Art Institute of Chicago – features an excellent hands-on art area

Field Museum of Natural History – dinosaurs everywhere!

Lincoln Park Zoo – contains a special children's area where kids can commune with rodents

Museum of Science & Industry – a perennial favorite of kids

Shedd Aquarium – with lots of neat fish

Child Care

Check with your hotel for baby-sitting recommendations. Also try the state-licensed American Registry for Nurses & Sitters (☎ 773-248-8100, 800 240 1820, 3921 N Lincoln Ave). Sitters are subject to reference checks and are proficient in child and infant CPR. They have been minding the little dears since 1950.

LIBRARIES
Harold Washington
Library Center

The Harold Washington Library Center (☎ 312-747-4300, TTY 312-747-4314, 400 S State St at Van Buren St; Map 3) opened in 1991 after an architectural competition in which the citizens of Chicago were allowed to vote on their choice of several designs. You can while away hours wandering the

nine floors of this great free library. The basement features rotating historical and art expositions. The 2nd floor contains the children's library. The main collections begin on the 3rd floor. Here's a guide to some of what might interest you:

3rd floor – newspapers from all over Illinois and the US; English-language papers from around the world; microfilm of old newspapers going back to the founding of the city

4th floor – foreign-language newspapers from around the world

6th floor – travel books and guides for the entire world, as well as atlases, maps, and comprehensive worldwide airline and train schedules

7th floor – special section devoted to Chicago authors

8th floor – section on Chicago architecture

9th floor – winter garden atrium, a cheery place to read a book

Copy machines are located throughout the building. Copies cost 15¢ each, but if you buy a special card on the 3rd floor, the price drops to 13¢ each. The collection catalog is in a database that you can search from computer terminals scattered all over the library. You can also access major information

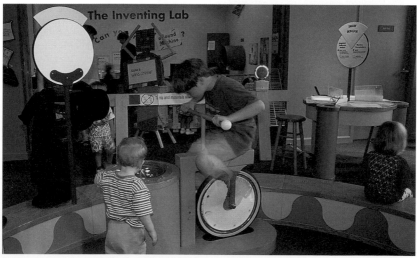

Hands-on fun at the Chicago Children's Museum

databases, as well as the Internet, on other terminals.

The library is open 9am to 7pm Monday to Thursday, 9am to 5pm Friday and Saturday, 1pm to 5pm Sunday.

Other Libraries

The Newberry Library (☎ 312-943-9090, 60 W Walton St; Map 5) is a huge research facility geared toward scholars. Its 1.5 million volumes cover specialties such as the Italian Renaissance, cartography and genealogy. The vast and diverse collection contains such inestimable gems as the papers of Ben Hecht, a former Chicago newspaperman turned Hollywood screenwriter whose play *The Front Page* became the basis of the film *His Girl Friday*. Visitors are welcome, but remember that nothing circulates, so you can't take that first edition of the King James Bible home with you. The Newberry also often features interesting special exhibits.

The Gerber-Hart Library (☎ 773-381-8030, info@gerberhart.org, 1127 W Granville Ave), in the far northern reaches of the city, is one of the nation's oldest and largest gay and lesbian libraries. Its more than 50,000 books are augmented by magazines and archives.

UNIVERSITIES

Chicago has four major universities. The farthest north, Northwestern University lies in somewhat sleepy Evanston, with its law and medical schools in Streeterville. This private school, one of the best institutions in the US, excels in the liberal arts. See also the Evanston section of the Excursions chapter for more information.

DePaul University, a Catholic school located in gentrified Lincoln Park, is primarily an undergraduate institution, although it operates a law school in the Loop. See the Lincoln Park section of the Things to See & Do chapter for more details.

The University of Illinois at Chicago is the fast-growing local campus of the state's main university, which is in Champaign-Urbana. Once a commuter school, the Chicago branch is building dorms to make the campus more residential. See the West Side section of the Things to See & Do chapter for more details.

The University of Chicago is another top university with a long history and numerous Nobel prizes to the credit of its faculty. The campus makes an excellent location for strolling. See the Hyde Park section of the Things to See & Do chapter for more details.

CULTURAL CENTERS

The Chicago Cultural Center is a fascinating and useful place for the visitor, with a tourist information center, a large sitting area where you can chill out for as long as you want and a decent café. Local music groups representing many different cultures give live performances most days at lunchtime. See the full details in the Loop section of the Things to See & Do chapter.

Chicago's other cultural centers include the French Alliance Française (☎ 312-337-1070, www.afchicago.com, 810 N Dearborn St) and the German Goethe Institut (☎ 312-263-0472, www.goethe.de/uk/chi, 150 N Michigan Ave).

Newberry Library

DANGERS & ANNOYANCES

Parts of Chicago are as safe as you'll find in any American city; other parts are virtual killing fields, with several murders a day. Fortunately, there is little reason for you to go to the unsafe parts of the city, although you should be aware of their existence – not just for your own safety, but so that you have a balanced image of Chicago.

Unsafe Areas

Unless noted otherwise, the areas written about in this book are reasonably safe during the day. At night the lakefront, major parks (with the exception of Grant Park during any kind of festival or concert) and certain neighborhoods (especially south and west of the Loop) can become bleak and forbidding places. The Loop, Near North, Gold Coast, Old Town, Lincoln Park, Lake View and Wrigleyville neighborhoods are safe at night, especially on the busy commercial streets.

Be aware that neighborhoods can change in just a few blocks. Four blocks west of the Gold Coast and south of Old Town lie the Cabrini-Green housing projects, where schoolchildren are ordered to lie down under their desks when gunfire breaks out.

Scams

Destroy your credit-card carbons when you make purchases and don't give your card number out to anybody unless it is a business you have called.

If anybody offers you anything on the street (gold jewelry, sports tickets and the like) for absurdly low prices, you can assume that the goods are stolen.

You may be propositioned by urchins claiming that the money from the candy bars they're selling supports their sports team. The goods have usually come from a vandalized container in the vast rail yards, and the sports team or club often doesn't exist.

Chicago's winters make it an inhospitable place for the homeless. However, you will encounter people selling the newspaper *Streetwise* year-round. This worthy enterprise provides health, housing and job-training services to its homeless vendors and requires them to follow a code of conduct.

Crime

Most of Chicago's violent crime is perpetrated by street gangs battling over drug turf. The gangs are often centered around public-housing projects, where 95% of the residents are honest people held hostage by the mayhem.

The kind of crime you should be most aware of in Chicago is the same type that exists throughout the world: pickpocketing, purse- or jewelry-snatching, auto break-ins and bike stealing. Basically, if you leave something accessible to crooks, they will try to steal it.

Finally, use your common sense. If a neighborhood, street, El station or any other situation doesn't seem right or something about it worries you, don't stick around.

EMERGENCIES

Dial ☎ 911 for police, fire or ambulance services. Chicago emergency services have a good record of arriving within three minutes for life-threatening situations.

For any disaster in the lake, call the Coast Guard at ☎ 773-768-4093.

To report a picked pocket or other minor crime for which speedy police response is useless, dial ☎ 312-746-6000. You will need a police report to file for an insurance claim in most cases.

If you need to visit a police station, try the East Chicago district station (☎ 312-744-8230, 113 W Chicago Ave in River North; Map 3), where the cops have seen it all.

LEGAL MATTERS

In a big city like Chicago, the cops usually have better things to do than hassle tourists. Usually. If at any time a police officer gives you an order of any kind (such as 'Get outta the road!' or 'Move on!'), do not, I repeat do not seize upon that moment for a debate. I have had good experiences with Chicago cops through the years; they've pulled me out of a few jams and averted their eyes when I messed up but seemed genuinely contrite.

But I also have witnessed scores of cops showing zero tolerance for back talk. They'll happily throw you in a lockup for a few hours while you reconsider your argument.

Then again, if you have a problem or question, feel free to take it to the nearest cop. Often the response will be an entertaining spiel delivered in pure 'Chicagoese.'

If you are arrested, you have the right to remain silent. There is no legal requirement to speak to a police officer if you don't want to, but never walk away from one until given permission. Anyone who is arrested is legally allowed (and given) the right to make one phone call. If you don't have a lawyer or friend or family member to help you, call your consulate. The police will give you the number upon request.

It's generally against the law to have an open container of an alcoholic beverage in public, whether in a car, on the street, in a park or at the beach. But during festivals and other mass events, this rule is waived. If the people around you are enjoying a beer and they don't look like candidates for a 12-step program, then join in.

The drinking age of 21 is pretty strictly enforced. If you're younger than 35 (or just look like it), carry an ID to fend off overzealous barkeeps and the like.

There is zero tolerance at all times for any kind of drug use.

See the Car & Motorcycle section in the Getting Around chapter for the scores of ways a car can get you in trouble.

BUSINESS HOURS

Office hours in Chicago are typically 8am to 5pm, although masters of the universe and their overworked minions often work many more hours than that.

Shops are usually open at least until 7pm, and most keep Sunday hours. The Loop tends to close earlier than the Near North. During the Christmas season, stores will often stay open until 9pm every night. You'll find plenty of convenience stores and supermarkets open 24 hours a day. Banks increasingly keep longer hours like stores, including Bank One (☎ 888-963-4000);

several of its branches are now open on Sunday.

Movie theaters and many bars and restaurants are open every day of the year. Smaller restaurants are often closed one or two days a week, frequently early in the week. Most theaters that stage live productions are 'dark' (closed) on Monday.

PUBLIC HOLIDAYS & SPECIAL EVENTS

On national public holidays, banks and many businesses close, and public transportation, museums and other services operate on a Sunday schedule. The number of national holidays that shuts down retail stores keeps dwindling (as more and more store owners discover that workers with the day off might want to go shopping), but commerce does generally come to a halt on Thanksgiving and Christmas. Most public holidays always fall on Monday. If a holiday falls on a Saturday, it's generally observed on the preceding Friday; if it falls on Sunday, it's celebrated on the following Monday.

Dates of special events can shift from year to year, so if any these events are essential to you, confirm the dates with the Chicago Office of Tourism (☎ 312-744-2400, www.cityofchicago.org/tourism) before you make your travel plans.

Music festivals in Grant Park are held at the Petrillo Music Shell. For information about any events below with no phone number listed, contact the Chicago Office of Tourism for information. Also note that some events float within a range of weeks from year to year.

January

New Year's Day January 1 is a widely observed public holiday.

Martin Luther King Jr Day The birthday of the civil rights leader is celebrated with a public holiday on the third Monday of the month.

Navy Pier Art Fair Displays by local artists take place all month; call ☎ 312-595-7437.

Chinese New Year A massive celebration with millions of little firecrackers, a parade and more takes place in Chinatown. Exact date varies according to the ancient Chinese calendar; call ☎ 312-225-6198.

February

African American History Month Displays and live events take place all month at Navy Pier; call ☎ 312-225-6198.

Winterbreak This celebration of winter was designed to fill a desolate period in the city's events calendar. The hodgepodge of events, which take place the first two weeks of the month, include ice sculpture contests on the Mag Mile; call ☎ 312-744-3315.

President's Day This public holiday pays tribute to George Washington and Abraham Lincoln on the third Monday in February.

Chicago Auto Show Detroit, Tokyo and Bavaria all introduce their latest to the excited gearheads in a huge show mid-month at McCormick Place; call ☎ 630-495-2282.

March

Pulaski Day On the first Monday of the month, Chicagoans honor a Polish icon who fought the Russians and then helped Americans fight the British during the American Revolution.

St Patrick's Day Parade Every year on March 17, this Chicago institution starts at the river, dyed green for the occasion, and snakes south on Dearborn St. Look to see which politicians are jostling to be at the very front – the best part; call ☎ 312-744-3370.

April

Spring and Easter Flower Show Zillions of blooms are at their best at the Lincoln Park Conservatory (☎ 312-742-7736), just north of the zoo, and at the Garfield Park Conservatory.

Smelt Season Tiny bony fish swarm near the lakeshore, to be snared by nighttime anglers, who then deep-fry 'em.

Earth Day Tree huggers and other good people gather on the fourth Saturday of the month at the south end of Lincoln Park for music, poetry, and liberal talk; call ☎ 312-629-1770.

Cinco de Mayo Festival On the last weekend of the month, a large celebration at McCormick Place honors the Mexican holiday.

May

Art Chicago This massive mid-month festival at Navy Pier attracts international artists; call ☎ 312-587-3300.

Printer's Row Book Fair This event features thousands of rare and not-so-rare books on sale, plus author readings, on the last weekend of the month; call ☎ 312-987-9896.

Memorial Day The last Monday in May is a public holiday.

June

Chicago Blues Festival This highly regarded three-day festival happens in Grant Park on the first weekend of the month; call ☎ 312-744-3315.

57th St Art Fair Roving artists hawk their wares in Hyde Park on the first weekend of the month; call ☎ 312-684-8383.

Chicago Gospel Festival Hear soulful gospel music on the second weekend of the month in Grant Park; call ☎ 312-744-3315.

Old Town Art Fair Held on the second weekend of the month, this fair offers a wonderful excuse for strolling around and partying. The art is not always the best, but the mood is; call ☎ 312-337-1938.

Andersonville Midsommerfest This traditional Swedish festival has become a rollicking street fest north of Foster Ave on Clark St. It takes place on the weekend closest to June 21.

Country Music Festival A hoedown takes over Grant Park on the last weekend of the month; call ☎ 312-744-3315.

Gay & Lesbian Pride Parade A most flamboyant spectacle parades through Lake View, usually on Belmont Ave and Broadway, to Lincoln Park. The Dykes on Bikes are a perennial favorite, as are the Proud Parents, who cause more than a few eyes to go misty. Look for the parade on the last Sunday of the month; call ☎ 773-348-8243.

Taste of Chicago This enormous festival closes Grant Park for the 10 days leading up to Independence Day on July 4. More than 100 local eateries serve some of the greasiest food you've ever tried to rub off your fingers. Live music on several stages drowns out the rumble of the belches from the 3.5 million people who attend each year; call ☎ 312-744-3315.

July

Independence Day Concert and Fireworks Though it really happens the day before Independence Day, on July 3, the city pulls out all the stops for this concert, which features a really long fireworks show and Tchaikovsky's '1812' Overture, played with gusto by the Grant Park Symphony Orchestra. For the best view, try the embankment east of Randolph St and Lake Shore Dr; call ☎ 312-294-2420.

RAY HILLSTROM JR

Taste of Chicago takes over Grant Park.

Independence Day July 4 is a public holiday. The Chicago Historical Society marks the occasion with events that focus on the roots of the day. These take place around the Lincoln statue in Lincoln Park behind the museum; call ☎ 312-642-4600.

Chicago to Mackinac Island Yacht Race Usually held on the third weekend of the month, this race holds near-mystic significance to its participants. The town is witness to the amusing antics of drunken sailors in bars the nights before the kickoff. Monroe Harbor is a good place to watch the boats depart; call ☎ 312-861-7777.

World's Largest Block Party The savvy pastor of Old St Patrick's Church, in the West Loop, sponsor this huge singles' bash. Tens of thousands of single, primarily Catholic Chicagoans drink beer and exchange Catholic grade-school horror stories on the third weekend of the month. The church is fully booked for weddings for months afterward; call ☎ 312-648-1021.

Black Expo Chicago Businesses, volunteer groups and anybody else trying to reach African Americans take part in a McCormick Place exhibition on the third weekend of the month; call ☎ 312-791-7000.

Sheffield Garden Walk Ostensibly a chance to tour the lovely gardens of some of Lincoln Park's gentrified homes, this is really an excuse for a huge street party with music, food and beer; call ☎ 773-929-9255.

Venetian Night Late in the month, yacht owners decorate their boats with lights and parade them at night in Monroe Harbor to the adulation of the rabble. A fireworks display follows; call ☎ 312-744-3315.

August

Gold Coast Art Fair On the second weekend of the month, traveling artists staff loads of booths centered on the blocks near State and Division Sts; call ☎ 312-744-2400.

Bud Billiken Parade & Picnic Named after a merry and mythical figure in the black community, this huge parade is a local institution founded by the late John H Sengstacke; it runs south on Martin Luther King Jr Dr from 39th to 55th Sts, with a huge Washington Park picnic afterward. The festivities usually take place on the second Saturday of the month; call ☎ 312-225-2400 for details.

North Halsted Market Days The gay neighborhood's street festival features lots of people wearing costumes usually seen in S&M nightmares. Open to all, it's really quite an enjoyable event. The only 'market' the name refers to is a meat market; call ☎ 773-883-0500.

Chicago Air and Water Show Your tax dollars at work: the latest military hardware flies past the lakefront from Diversey Parkway south to Oak St Beach. Acrobatic planes and teams perform both afternoons on the third weekend in August. The water part of the show is always a dud, featuring a couple of speedboats most people can't see. The best views are those from high-rises overlooking the lake; call ☎ 312-744-7431.

Viva! Chicago This Latin music festival takes place in Grant Park, usually on the last weekend of the month; call ☎ 312-744-3315.

September

Labor Day The first Monday of the month is a public holiday.

Chicago Jazz Festival Loads of national and local groups play on Labor Day weekend in Grant Park; call ☎ 312-744-3315.

Around the Coyote A once cutting-edge festival now gone mainstream, this event features all forms of art by local artists in their Wicker Park and Bucktown studios. There's something for everyone; try to find the worst and best of the performance art. The quarrelsome artists are always feuding on exact plans, but usually they agree to hold the festival on the second weekend of the month; call ☎ 773-342-6777.

Mexican Independence Day Parade You'll see lots of cute kids dressed to the nines at this colorful and loud event, held on the second Saturday of the month.

Berghoff Oktoberfest The Berghoff restaurant's Oktoberfest holds true to the traditional German dates in mid-September. Huge crowds cram Adams St in front of the Berghoff during the week; call ☎ 312-427-3170.

German-American Festival This much more enjoyable Oktoberfest happens on the third weekend of the month in the heart of the old German neighborhood at Lincoln Square, 4700 N Lincoln Ave.

World Music Festival Musicians and bands from around the world perform around Chicago late in the month; call ☎ 312-742-1938.

October

Chicago International Film Festival Early in the month, scores of films compete during this weeklong event, which always produces some sleepers and some stinkers; call ☎ 312-644-3400.

Columbus Day The second Monday in October is a public holiday.

Windy City Marathon Runners from all over the world compete on the usual 26-mile course. If there is such a thing as slacker runners, this is the marathon for them, because the city is dead flat; for dates, call ☎ 312-904-6174.

November

Day of the Dead The traditional November 1 Mexican celebration of spooks and souls includes displays at the Mexican Fine Arts Center Museum; call ☎ 312-738-1503.

Magnificent Mile Lights Festival The increasingly commercialized lighting of all 600,000 lights on the trees lining the streets takes place mid-month, after which the little fellas twinkle sweetly on Michigan Ave north of the river through January. Ask for the program at a hotel or store – it lists all sorts of free events and giveaways; call ☎ 312-642-3570.

Veterans Day This public holiday happens on November 11, but some celebrate it on the nearest Monday.

Thanksgiving Day The fourth Thursday of the month is a major public holiday, kicking off the Christmas holiday season.

Official Tree Lighting Ceremony The city's Christmas tree lights up on Daley Plaza on Thanksgiving Day; call ☎ 312-744-3315.

December

Carol to the Animals Hordes of people sing Christmas tunes to perplexed zoo critters at the Lincoln Park Zoo in this goofy event on the second Sunday of the month. The question on all the inmates' minds: 'When's feeding time?' Call ☎ 312-742-2283.

Kwanzaa The increasingly popular African American holiday celebration adds new events and locations each year; call ☎ 312-744-2400.

Christmas Day December 25 is a major public holiday.

Long-Term Events

Under the Picasso Local and visiting bands, dancers and other entertainers give performances almost every weekday, roughly between noon and 1pm, either inside or outside the Daley Center; call ☎ 312-744-3315.

Downtown Thursday Night Special events at businesses, bars, restaurants and museums throughout the Loop happen every Thursday night; call ☎ 312-742-1171.

Grant Park Music Festival Performances take place June though August; see the Classical Music section in the Entertainment chapter for details.

Neighborhood Festivals

From May through September, just about every neighborhood throws a street party one weekend. These usually feature live music, lots of beer and gourmet treats like corn dogs. They vary greatly in size and make excellent events for people-watching. Many festivals take on the ethnic character of their neighborhoods. In Lincoln Park that means everybody sports new polo shirts; in Pilsen it means that the tacos are excellent and cost less than $1. Check with the Mayor's Office of Special Events to see what's on where; call ☎ 312-744-3315.

WORK

It is very difficult for foreigners to get legal work in the US. Securing your own work visa without a sponsor – meaning an employer – is nearly impossible. If you do have a sponsor, the sponsor should normally assist or do all the work to secure your visa.

Foreign visitors can always find work in the US if they are willing to work in low-paid menial jobs, such as cleaning hotel rooms or working at McDonald's or at even more frightful third-rate fast-food places with names like Peanut World II. However, you should know that from the first minute you accept a job in the US without a hard-to-get work visa, you become an illegal alien. If you are caught, the full weight of the anti-immigration sentiment in the US government will crash down on you. Expect to be immediately deported and barred from the US for at least five years. This is not be taken lightly, because the deportation can now occur the same day the INS finds you. There will be no time to gather belongings or notify friends or loved ones.

Getting There & Away

AIR

Chicago is served by two main airports. O'Hare International (ORD) is the world's busiest hub. Midway (MID) is much smaller and is primarily served by discount carriers. The Getting Around chapter offers full details on the myriad options for getting from the airports to central Chicago.

The US and Chicago both levy airport taxes on travelers; however, these are included in the price of the ticket, so you won't have to pay a departure tax at the airport.

O'Hare International Airport

Sixty-five million passengers – one-quarter of the population of the US – pass through O'Hare (ORD; ☎ 800-832-6352) each year, continuing Chicago's historic role as a US transportation hub. Each day flights depart to over 300 cities around the world, a figure unmatched by any other airport anywhere. The airport's Web site (www.ohare.com) offers details on weather conditions and flight

arrival and departure information. Get all your bad news on the many flight delays here.

The place is huge. The best advice for navigating O'Hare is to tread slowly because, while the signs and maps aren't bad, the sheer scope of the place can intimidate even grizzled travelers. Domestic flights and international departures for domestic airlines depart from Terminals 1, 2 and 3. All international arrivals, as well as departures for non-US airlines, are in Terminal 5. There are some exceptions to this rule: Lufthansa, for instance, departs out of United's Terminal 1. The listing of airlines below gives terminal information.

United's **Terminal 1**, designed by Helmut Jahn, is the largest hub of the world's largest airline, hosting over 800 flights a day. The soaring concourses, underground New Age light show and tunnel between Concourses B and C are attractions in themselves. There are moving sidewalks and escalators galore, and for such a huge place it is really quite

---

What's an ORD? Who's O'Hare?

In 1942 fighter pilot Edward 'Butch' O'Hare shot down five Japanese planes that were attacking his ship, the USS *Lexington*, during the Battle of the Coral Sea. He became America's first fighter ace of World War II and was an immediate national hero at a time when the nation had few.

One year later, O'Hare himself was shot down and killed. The Chicago City Council moved to rename a small airport then called Orchard Field, on the city's northwest side, in honor of the pilot, and O'Hare Airport was born.

At the time it had already acquired the three-letter code ORD, for Orchard. This technical designation has remained on international rosters and continues to adorn millions of bags every year.

During the 1950s the world's busiest airport was Midway, on Chicago's southwest side. But hemmed in by houses on all sides, it couldn't be expanded for the new jets and huge growth in air travel that followed. Looking about for an alternative, Chicago settled on the still-sleepy O'Hare. Runways and terminals were built within just a few years, and O'Hare began its unbroken tenure as the busiest airport in the world, with 67 million people passing through in 1997.

For years, there was little information at the airport about why it's named O'Hare or who O'Hare might have been. That has changed dramatically. A restored version of an F4F Wildcat fighter, the kind flown by O'Hare, is on display in Terminal 2 and features the complete story about O'Hare and the vast airport that came to bear his name.

Air Travel Glossary

Bucket Shops These are unbonded travel agencies specializing in discount airline tickets.

Cancellation Penalties If you have to cancel or change a discounted ticket, heavy penalties are often involved; insurance can sometimes be taken out against these penalties. Some airlines impose penalties on regular tickets as well, particularly against 'no-show' passengers.

Courier Fares Businesses often need to send urgent documents or freight securely and quickly. Courier companies hire people to accompany the package through customs and, in return, offer a discount ticket that's sometimes a phenomenal bargain. However, you may have to surrender all your baggage allowance and take only carry-on luggage.

Lost Tickets If you lose your airline ticket, an airline will usually treat it like a traveler's check and, after inquiries, issue you another one. Legally, however, an airline is entitled to treat it like cash: if you lose it, it's gone forever. Take good care of your tickets.

Onward Tickets An entry requirement for many countries is a ticket out of the country. If you're unsure of your next move, the easiest solution is to buy the cheapest onward ticket to a neighboring country or a ticket whose price can later be refunded if you do not use it.

Open-Jaw Tickets These roundtrip tickets permit you to fly out to one place but return from another. If available, this can save you backtracking to your arrival point.

Overbooking Since every flight has some passengers who fail to show up, airlines often book more passengers than they have seats. Usually excess passengers make up for the no shows, but occasionally somebody gets 'bumped' onto the next available flight. Guess who it is most likely to be? The passengers who check in late.

Promotional Fares These are officially discounted fares, available from travel agencies or directly from the airline.

Reconfirmation If you don't reconfirm your flight at least 72 hours prior to departure, the airline may delete your name from the passenger list. Call to find out if your airline requires reconfirmation.

Restrictions Discounted tickets often come with various restrictions – for example, they may need to be paid for in advance, or altering them may incur a penalty. Other restrictions include minimum and maximum periods you must be away.

Round-the-World Tickets RTW tickets give you a limited period (usually a year) in which to circumnavigate the globe. You can go anywhere the carrying airlines go as long as you don't backtrack. The number of stopovers or total number of separate flights is decided before you set off, and these tickets usually cost a bit more than a basic roundtrip flight.

Transferred Tickets Airline tickets cannot be transferred from one person to another. Travelers sometimes try to sell the return half of their ticket, but officials can ask you to prove that you are the person named on the ticket. On an international flight, tickets are compared with passports.

Travel Periods Ticket prices vary with the time of year. There is a low (off-peak) season and a high (peak) season and often a low-shoulder season and a high-shoulder season as well. Usually the fare depends on your outward flight – if you depart in the high season and return in the low season, you pay the high-season fare.

user-friendly. United's partner Lufthansa also departs from here.

Continental, Northwest, US Airways, TWA and Air Canada are located in **Terminal 2**, the building right across from the Hilton Hotel. After United, the other major carrier at O'Hare is American Airlines, which operates a hub out of **Terminal 3**, a facility whose cut-rate renovation a few years ago (the concourses have long walks unbroken by moving sidewalks) befits American's number-two status. Delta is here as well.

Terminal 5 is the international terminal; all foreign airline departures (except Lufthansa's) and flights to Canada take off from here. Built in the early 1990s, the terminal is designed to minimize walks to and from the planes. Arriving passengers are treated to a large immigration and customs facility. They are also treated to a great collection of local art, but it's doubtful that the bleary-eyed arrivals notice the works.

Careful counters will note the lack of a Terminal 4; it was a temporary facility used while Terminal 5 was being built.

The terminals and the main long-term parking lot are linked by a 'people mover' tram system. The service is frequent, quick and runs 24 hours a day. Be certain to get on the train going in the direction you want. Short-term parkers can use the main parking garage, a vast facility where the fee starts at $3 and increases by $2 an hour thereafter. Fees at the long-term parking lots are about $12 a day. On nice days, the top level of the main parking garage offers good views of the runways and makes a good place for some 'fresh' air if you're stuck between flights.

Information City-run information booths are located in the baggage claim areas of Terminals 1, 2 and 3. In Terminal 5 the desk lies between the two customs exits. The employees have undergone training in courtesy from the Disney organization. The results have paid off: the red-jacketed people working these booths are not only polite but often enthusiastic. Many of them speak a range of languages. Unless you are familiar with Chicago, it's worth visiting these booths for advice and armloads of maps and brochures. You may have to look carefully for the booths, since the directional signs are inconsistent.

Large boards between the exit doors provide hotel and motel information for hundreds of places that are all in the suburbs. Pass these right by.

Amenities & Services You'll find scores of ATMs accepting every card known to humankind throughout the airport. Full-time currency exchanges operate in the arrivals area of Terminal 5 and Concourse K of Terminal 3, where the American Airlines flights to Europe depart. Some low-tech currency exchange carts try to snag customers near the departure gates for international flights elsewhere.

You'll find food courts with wide selections of chow on Concourse C and on the departure level of Terminal 5. Goose Island, a good local microbrewery, has opened bars in Concourses H and K in Terminal 3. The Berghoff, a legendary Loop restaurant, operates an outpost in Terminal 1. If you have a long time to kill between flights, the Hilton Hotel in the middle of the terminals contains a good sports bar and a fine Italian café. Take the pedestrian tunnels down from the baggage claim areas to get there.

The airport limits its retail stores mostly to small shops selling travel goods, newspapers and magazines, souvenirs and the like. The British bookstore chain Waterstones operates decent outlets in the concourses of Terminals 1, 2 and 3; buy your Lonely Planet guide to your next destination there.

Unlike other major airports, O'Hare still boasts large seating areas with large windows, so you can get plenty comfortable while you wait out the frequent delays. But you can also bide your time amid the amusements of Terminal 2, which features a large children's recreation area sponsored by the Chicago Children's Museum, as well as a branch of the Museum of Broadcast Communications showing classic TV shows and a huge exhibit dedicated to the airport's namesake (see the boxed text 'What's an ORD? Who's O'Hare?').

If you require any medical services, the University of Illinois at Chicago operates a clinic (☎ 773-894-5100) in Terminal 2. The general-service facility can help with minor problems, such as the after effects of that bad airplane food.

Midway Airport

Home to cut-rate carriers such as Southwest, Midway (MDW; ☎ 773-838-0600) long had a reputation for its suitably low-rent ambience. But that's about to change, once the city finishes building a grand new terminal, due to be completed in 2004. In 2001, meanwhile, a vast and light new main terminal building opened on the east side of S Cicero Ave to rave reviews. Later in 2001, a vastly improved selection of restaurants and shops will debut in a new concessions area. During the following years new concourse and gate areas will replace decrepit facilities that date back to the 1950s, when Midway was the busiest airport in the world.

A city information center, in the baggage claim area of the new terminal building, offers transportation and accommodations information.

Airlines

Airlines serving Chicago include those on the following list. Note that, especially at Midway, scheduled service by low-fare airlines changes frequently. Also, most of the following airlines have at least one city ticket office, while United and American have scores. Check with the airline for the location nearest you and its hours.

The letter M following the airline name indicates an airline serving Midway. The letter O indicates an airline serving O'Hare. The letters M, O indicate an airline serving both airports.

Aer Lingus (O)
  ☎ 800-223-6537, www.aerlingus.ie

Aeroflot (O)
  ☎ 312-819-2350, www.aeroflot.com

Air Canada/Canadian Airlines (O)
  ☎ 888-247-2262, www.aircanada.ca

Air France (O)
  ☎ 800-321-4538, www.airfrance.com

AirTran (M)
  ☎ 800-247-8726, www.airtran.com

Alitalia (O)
  ☎ 800-223-5730, www.alitaliausa.com

America West Airlines (M, O)
  ☎ 800-235-9292, www.americawest.com

American Airlines (O)
  ☎ 800-433-7300, www.aa.com

American Trans Air (M)
  ☎ 800-435-9282, www.ata.com

ANA (O)
  ☎ 773-380-6080, www.ana.co.jp

Austrian Airlines (O)
  ☎ 800-843-0002, www.austrianair.com

British Airways (O)
  ☎ 800-247-9297, www.british-airways.com

Continental Airlines (M, O)
  ☎ 800-523-3273, www.continental.com

Delta Air Lines (O)
  ☎ 800-221-1212, www.delta-air.com

El Al Israel Airlines (O)
  ☎ 800-223-6700, www.elal.co.il

Iberia (O)
  ☎ 800-772-4642, www.iberia.com

Japan Airlines (O)
  ☎ 800-525-3663, www.jal.co.jp

KLM (O)
  ☎ 800-374-7747, www.klm.nl

Korean Air (O)
  ☎ 800-438-5000, www.koreanair.com

LOT Polish Airlines (O)
  ☎ 312-236-3388, www.lot.com

Lufthansa (O)
  ☎ 800-645-3880, www.lufthansa.com

Mexicana Airlines (O)
  ☎ 800-531-7921, www.mexicana.com.mx

National Airlines (M)
  ☎ 800-757-5387

Northwest Airlines (M, O)
  ☎ 800-225-2525, www.nwa.com

Sabena (O)
  ☎ 800-955-2000, www.sabena.com

SAS (O)
  ☎ 800-221-2350, www.scandinavian.net

Southwest Airlines (M)
  ☎ 800-435-9792, www.southwest.com

Swissair (O)
  ☎ 800-221-4750, ww.swissair.com

TWA (O)
☎ 800-221-2000, www.twa.com

United (O)
☎ 800-241-6522, www.ual.com

US Airways (O)
☎ 800-428-4322, www.usairways.com

Virgin Atlantic (O)
☎ 800-826-4827, www.virgin-atlantic.com

Buying Tickets

An air ticket alone can gouge a great slice out of anyone's budget, but you can reduce the cost by finding discount fares. Stiff competition has resulted in widespread discounting – good news for travelers! The only people likely to be paying full fare these days are travelers flying in 1st or business class. Passengers flying in economy class can usually manage some sort of discount. But unless you buy carefully and flexibly, it is still possible to end up paying exorbitant amounts for a journey.

When you're looking for bargain airfares, look in the newspapers for ads about discount fares before you try calling the airlines directly. From time to time, airlines do offer promotional fares and special offers, but generally they only sell fares at the official listed price. Many airlines, though, will sell cheaper tickets through their Web sites. And plenty of ticket consolidators also offer discount fares on the Web. These include www.cheaptickets.com, www.priceline.com and www.travelocity.com.

If you go to a travel agent, note that commissions for discount tickets have been cut to the bone, and it doesn't really pay for them to spend much time looking for a cheap fare. But travel agents can be a necessity if you're trying to build a complicated itinerary with a lot of stopovers and if you don't have much flexibility in your travel schedule.

So-called 'bucket shops' advertise last-minute fares in the travel sections of major newspapers; they can offer good prices because they unload all the seats that the airlines couldn't sell. Be aware that these tickets are highly restricted and may not leave you with many rights if your flight is canceled. After you've made a reservation or paid your deposit to a bucket shop, call the airline and confirm that the reservation was made. Paying by credit card generally offers protection in case you fall prey to a scam.

You may decide to pay more than the rock-bottom fare by opting for the safety of a better-known travel agent. Firms such as STA Travel, which has offices worldwide, Council Travel in the USA and Usit Campus (formerly Campus Travel) in the UK are not going to disappear overnight, and they do offer good prices to most destinations. See Europe, below, for information about contacting these agencies.

It's important to keep in mind that the tickets with the greatest discounts are heavily restricted, which means that you will have to buy your ticket at least 14 days in advance and stay over a Saturday night. If you just want to fly one way, it's often cheaper to buy a heavily discounted roundtrip ticket. Fly on the one half and toss the return ticket (you can't really give it away or sell it, because the airlines now

Warning

The information in this chapter is particularly vulnerable to change. Prices for international travel are volatile, routes are introduced and canceled, schedules change, special deals come and go, and rules and visa requirements are amended. Airlines and governments seem to take a perverse pleasure in making price structures and regulations as complicated as possible. You should check directly with the airline or a travel agent to make sure you understand how a fare (and any ticket you may buy) works. In addition, the travel industry is highly competitive, and there are many lurks and perks.

The upshot of this is that you should get opinions, quotes and advice from as many airlines and travel agents as possible before you part with your hard-earned cash. The details given in this chapter should be regarded as pointers and are not a substitute for your own careful, up-to-date research.

check the identification of passengers for security reasons).

Visit USA Passes Before coming to the US, many non-US citizens can buy coupons good for flights within the States (although US carriers generally exclude citizens of North and South America from these coupon deals). United offers the most flights to the most places from Chicago, so here's its program: three coupons cost about $379. That's a fantastic deal, because you can fly from Chicago to, say, Seattle, then to Los Angeles and then back to Chicago. You could never do that for so little money with regular tickets (even discounted regular tickets). The coupons can be purchased in whatever amount you wish and get progressively cheaper the more you buy. Six cost about $600, which is a mere $100 a flight.

Round-the-World Tickets If you are coming from overseas, you should include the joys of Chicago on a round-the-world itinerary. These kinds of tickets typically cover East or West Coast cities in the US, but you can usually get them to include Chicago as well. They offer substantial savings over individual tickets in all three classes of service.

The USA

United may not always offer the lowest fares, although its fares usually are competitive. This giant airline is likely to be your carrier to Chicago simply because of the sheer volume of nonstop flights it offers. However, its image was tarnished in 2000, when labor problems forced it to cancel thousands of flights, stranding tens of thousands at O'Hare.

American is the other major carrier at O'Hare, though unlike United, its primary hub is not in Chicago. It doesn't offer quite as many flights to as many places as United.

Unless you happen to be going to one of their hubs, keep in mind that all the other major domestic carriers at O'Hare will likely route you through one of their hubs, which means changing planes someplace else.

At Midway, Southwest is the major carrier. It offers frequent flights to many Midwestern cities at cheap fares (although if you can plan in advance, the major carriers usually match them). The airline has a flawless safety record, but I personally find certain aspects of its service a bit annoying: there's no advance seat selection, nothing beyond a beverage in flight and not much room between the seats. Southwest flies to all points of the compass from Midway, but none of these flights is very long. A $199 fare to California sounds good until you find out it's via St. Louis and Phoenix, for an all-day aviation adventure.

Midway also hosts numerous other discount airlines. Be careful which cheap airline you pick, because many offer only one flight a day, and if for some reason it's canceled, you might be stuck, since the bargain carriers don't sell tickets that other airlines will honor. Another consideration is that if your cheap airline goes out of business – which they do with alarming regularity – you can end up with no ticket and no money.

Here's a very rough idea of what you can expect to pay for flights using the most heavily restricted (and therefore cheapest) roundtrip tickets to and from Chicago:

Major cities within 500 miles	$150 to $300
The South and the East Coast	$250 to $400
The West and the West Coast	$350 to $550

As you try to make sense of all of the flight options, you can take heart that unlike many frequent fliers, you won't have to change planes at O'Hare.

Canada
American, United and Air Canada offer regular service to locations throughout Canada, including Montreal, Toronto and Vancouver. Look for fares in the $300 to $500 range.

Central & South America
American and United operate flights to Mexico and points south. Mexicana serves Mexico and Varig serves Brazil. Fares from

Mexico City range from $400 to $500; from Brazil, they average $800 to $1000.

Europe

American, British Airways, United and Virgin Atlantic each offer multiple flights a day to and from London's Heathrow Airport; the flight takes about eight hours. Other major European carriers have nonstop flights serving their capitals, such as Swissair to/from Zurich, KLM to/from Amsterdam and Sabena to/from Brussels. O'Hare serves as American Airlines' base for European flights; flights go directly to Paris, Frankfurt, Milan and other cities. United offers flights to Frankfurt, Düsseldorf, Paris and Amsterdam. In the summer, European service increases dramatically.

European fares follow a fairly predictable pattern. Except for the Christmas season, flights from November through March cost $400 to $600 roundtrip. During the 'shoulder' months of April, May, September and October, fares average $500 to $700. In summer and at Christmastime, expect to pay $700 to $1000 – if you can find a seat on the always jammed flights. Tickets bought in Europe are roughly equivalent to these prices, depending on the vagaries of exchange rates.

In London, *Time Out* runs several pages of ads for discount tickets. Also try calling any of the following travel agencies:

Usit Campus Travel
☎ 020-7938-2188, 174 Kensington High St, London W8 7RG, www.usitcampus.co.uk

STA Travel
☎ 020-7465-0484, 117 Euston Rd, London NW1 2SX, www.statravel.co.uk

Trailfinders
☎ 020-7937-5400, 215 Kensington High St, London W8 6BD, www.trailfinders.co.uk

Travel Cuts
☎ 020-7255-2082, 295A Regent St, London W1R 7YA, www.travelcuts.co.uk

Australia & New Zealand

Service to and from down under requires a change of planes in either Los Angeles or San Francisco. Both cities make attractive stopover points. Qantas and Air New Zealand offer flights to Los Angeles. United serves Auckland, Melbourne and Sydney nonstop from LA and Sydney nonstop from San Francisco. With flights between the US and the South Pacific averaging 14 hours, the idea of a stopover becomes much more appealing. Fares from Melbourne and Sydney can vary widely with the seasons – by as much as $1200 to $1800.

The usual advice for finding cheap tickets applies to travel from these two nations: look in the newspapers. In Australia, the Flight Centre and STA travel agencies in Melbourne and Sydney sell competitively priced tickets. STA also has offices in Auckland, New Zealand.

Asia

American, ANA, JAL and United offer daily flights to Tokyo. United also serves Hong Kong and Shanghai and offers many connections through its Asian hub in San Francisco. Korean Air flies to Seoul. The wealth of service to Tokyo keeps fares around $900. Hong Kong requires more shopping, with huge variations on fares through the year – anywhere from $1200 to $2000.

BUS

The striking, modern main bus station (☎ 312-408-5980, 630 W Harrison St between Desplaines and Jefferson Sts; Map 10) is often referred to as 'the Greyhound station.' The Clinton El stop on the Blue Line is two blocks away.

Greyhound

Greyhound (☎ 312-408-5980, 800-231-2222, www.greyhound.com), the sole national bus line – called 'The Dog' by veteran riders – sends dozens of buses in every direction every day. The seats are narrow but otherwise comfortable, the windows are big and the passengers are a polyglot lot. The buses also stop frequently – not because of the most important reason (since they all have toilets) but because they must pick up passengers from countless small towns that otherwise have no connection with the outside world except by car. That slows progress considerably, and the bus always takes longer than even a car obeying the speed limit would.

While conditions are not posh, neither are the prices. The eight buses a day to Memphis and the nine buses a day to Minneapolis, for example, charge a full fare of only $61. The bone- and butt-numbing journey to San Francisco, 48 hours straight, costs a mere $105. These fares include the option of bringing a companion along free and also tend to get cheaper when Greyhound is offering one of its many bargains. If you buy your ticket more than 21 days in advance, you pay $49 to $109 for any destination in the US.

Visitors to the US may become Doglovers when they see the prices for the Ameripass. If you have a non-US passport, seven days of unlimited travel everywhere Greyhound runs cost $155. Prices climb to $449 for 60 days of riding. If anyone takes advantage of this deal, please let me know

the gory details. If you are from the US, the same deal costs $185 and $509, respectively.

Indian Trails

This is a regional line (☎ 800-231-2222) operating buses similar to Greyhound's. It serves Michigan from the main Chicago bus station and offers similar bargain-basement fares.

TRAIN

Visitors from Europe will be appalled at the state of train travel in the US. The quasi-government agency Amtrak is the sole provider of interstate service, and it provides very little.

Thanks to penurious government funders, trains in the US are slow and infrequent (Chicago's superb Metra commuter rail system is an exception). But if that keeps most Americans from using trains to get anywhere, it shouldn't stop you. The slow pace of the trains is perfect for sightseeing, and many of the routes run past magnificent scenery. In urban areas, the trains provide a view into residents' back-

yards, giving you an unvarnished look at how people really live. One thing that's immediately apparent is that Americans keep a lot of crap.

Amtrak

Chicago is the hub for Amtrak's national and regional service, so it has more service than any other city. During much of the year it's crucial to reserve your Amtrak tickets well in advance. In the summertime, sleeper space and even simple seats are gone weeks ahead. The same situation exists at holidays. If you call the reservation phone system (☎ 800-872-7245), you'll often get a busy signal or wind up on hold for a mind-numbing period. Try going in person to Union Station (210 S Canal St between Adams St and Jackson Blvd; Map 3), where all the Chicago trains depart. Amtrak's Web site (www.amtrak.com) works well.

Fares Amtrak travel can be cheap. The three daily trains to Detroit have discount seats available right until departure for $20 to $29. That is about the same price as the bus, but the train is more comfortable and faster.

Expect to pay $20 to Milwaukee, $27 to St. Louis, $90 to New York, $160 to San Francisco for regular seats. Prices for sleeper cars depend on their level of luxury; a basic room for two can cost $150 to $300. These accommodations can be a pretty good deal because they include all meals, some drinks and other treats, including coffee in bed.

Except during the summer and Christmas, Amtrak sells Explore America tickets, which can be an excellent bargain. The US is divided into four regions – the West, Central (including Chicago), the East and Florida. The tickets allow you to make up to three stopovers on a roundtrip. Travel in one region costs $179; in two adjacent regions, $239; and the whole country, $299. Some itineraries from Chicago include these: New Orleans–San Antonio–Kansas City for $179; Boston–New York–Washington DC for $239; or a 4,000-mile trip through some of the best western scenery on the Seattle–San Francisco–Los Angeles

route for a ridiculously cheap $239. You have to make your plans in advance, and sleeping cars cost extra.

If you take advantage of a special deal between Amtrak and United Airlines, you can ride the train one way and fly back. This way, you can enjoy the scenery on your way to someplace like Portland, but then avoid chugging back through the same sites on your return to Chicago. This deal, imaginatively called 'Air-Rail,' has a special reservations number (☎ 800-437-3441).

Trains & Routes The trains themselves are very comfortable. Lacking speed and frequency, they boast plenty of amenities to lure people aboard. Dining cars and lounge cars dispense food and drink, and on long-distance trips special sightseeing cars have extra-large windows that encompass part of the roof, making the good views even better. Sleeping cars come in a variety of sizes and budget levels, and even lowly coach class on long-distance trains contains seats roughly equivalent to those in business class on long-distance flights. The lounge cars are a unique American institution. Selling cheap drinks well into the night, they soon fill up with former strangers cheerfully chatting away.

Amtrak's three trains from Chicago to the West Coast can be vacation experiences in themselves. They utilize the line's cushy 'Superliner' equipment and come with a full range of amenities. Each takes upward of three days and two nights to reach its destination. And don't plan any split-second connections: Amtrak is notoriously late, sometimes by several hours.

The *Empire Builder* goes to Seattle and Portland, passing through the beautiful northern Rockies and the 'big sky' country of Montana. The *California Zephyr* passes through dramatic canyons in the Rockies in Colorado and the Sierra Nevada in California. The *Southwest Chief* traces the route of the legendary *Super Chief*, once run by the Santa Fe Railroad. It speeds through the striking painted deserts of New Mexico and Arizona and usually carries Native American guides to point out and describe the sights.

Other long-distance trains entail an overnight journey and serve Texas, Washington, DC, and Boston. The *Lake Shore Limited* to New York City makes a dramatic run at dawn along the old Erie Canal and Hudson River (unless it's late; then it's a dramatic mid-morning run). And the *City of New Orleans* covers the same route immortalized in the Arlo Guthrie song.

Short-distance trains run more than once a day and go to Detroit, St. Louis and Grand Rapids, Michigan. Five trains a day go to downtown Milwaukee in slightly more than 90 minutes, better than you can do by car.

CAR & MOTORCYCLE

Interstate highways converge on Chicago from all points of the compass. None is especially scenic or otherwise recommended, although if you are coming from the east, follow the Indiana Toll Road all the way to the border and then spring for the $2 skyway. You'll save a good 30 minutes or more, compared to curving around on I-94.

Try to time your arrival so as not to arrive during the worst weekday rush hours, from 6am to 9am and 4pm to 7pm. Your nerves and passengers will thank you. See the Radio section in the Facts for the Visitor chapter for a list of radio stations that offer frequent traffic updates.

HITCHHIKING

Hitchhiking is never entirely safe in any country in the world, and we don't recommend it. Travelers who decide to hitchhike should understand that they are taking a potentially serious risk. If you do choose to hitchhike, you'll be safer if you travel in pairs and let someone know where you're planning to go.

Americans in particular frown on hitchhiking, and it may be downright illegal on major highways. If you do try to hitchhike in the US, you might wait quite a while for a ride. Many drivers will refuse to pick you up, out of fear for their own safety. Don't count on getting anywhere fast by hitchhiking.

Getting Around

Often you will find that the best way to get around Chicago is by foot. It's flat and easy to navigate, and walking is the best way to get the flavor of the city. But when your feet need a break, public transit here is not bad by American standards. This is one of the few American cities you can fully enjoy without a car. In fact, having a car in Chicago would seriously *detract* from your enjoyment.

TO/FROM THE AIRPORTS

There is no best way to and from O'Hare and Midway. Each option discussed here requires a tradeoff between cost and convenience. Details specific to each airport are listed separately.

Cabs are plentiful around the clock at the airports and will always very happily take you anywhere in town. Their large trunks will swallow up all your luggage. But taxis are stuck with the same traffic jams as everybody else, despite your cabbie's best efforts to drive on the shoulder, maniacally switch lanes, etc. Cabs are the most expensive option, but they are the only option with direct door-to-door service.

During rush hours, which seem to occur on Chicago expressways for the majority of each day, the CTA's El is the quickest way to and from the airports. At $1.50, it is also by far the cheapest. But the trains are not designed for people with luggage, and at the airport the stations are a long and sometimes confusing walk from the gates. The stations downtown have few escalators and fewer elevators, so be prepared to schlep your bags.

Shuttles leave at regular intervals from the airports to the major downtown hotels and vice versa. But they, too, are vulnerable to traffic woes, and unless you are the last

ANN CECIL

aboard, you may have to spend a frustrating half-hour or more waiting as the shuttle collects or drops off passengers at various terminals or hotels. Shuttle fares fall midway between those for the CTA and taxis.

See the Driving section for details on reaching the city by car.

O'Hare International Airport

You'll want to leave O'Hare as quickly as possible. Fortunately, your choices are many. The Loop is 17 miles southeast.

Taxi Each terminal has one taxi stand outside the baggage claim area; you may have to line up. The fare to the Near North and Loop runs $28 to $35, depending on tip (usually about 10% to 15%) and traffic (taxi meters keep running even when the car is stuck in a standstill). Extra passengers cost 50¢ each. If there are other travelers heading downtown, it may make sense to use the Share-a-Ride program (some signs may read 'Share-a-Cab' or 'Ride Sharing'), by which a cab takes you to the city for a flat $19 per passenger. However, make certain you inform the driver you want to do that before you start off.

The El The CTA offers frequent train service on the Blue Line to and from the Loop. Unfortunately, the O'Hare station is buried under the world's largest parking garage. Finding it can be akin to navigating a maze like a rat – and there's no cheese waiting at the end to guide you. Directional signs are variously marked as 'CTA,' 'Rapid Transit' and 'Trains to City.'

From Terminals 1 and 3, look for the escalators down from the baggage claim areas. There you will encounter a vast curving corridor that will lead you via a series of moving sidewalks to the CTA station. From Terminal 2, take the escalator down from baggage claim to a corridor that runs under the Hilton Hotel. This leads to the station.

If you're coming from Terminal 5, prepare for an adventure. The journey takes 15 minutes and is a fair hike, involving several modes of transport. When you exit customs, proceed up two levels to the tram station. Take a tram going to the main terminals, and be careful which one you board: it's easy to go the wrong way and end up in a remote parking area. Get off at the first station, which is Terminal 3. Go up the escalator and turn left into the parking garage, not right to the terminal. In the parking garage, head to the elevator bank on the right. Ignore all the buttons bearing the logos of Chicago sports teams (a clever device to help drivers remember where they parked their cars) and take the elevator down to the level marked 'Hilton CTA.' Follow a narrow corridor to a much larger one, and you are on your way to the station.

At the station you might want to buy a fare card right from the start. (Full details on fare cards can be found in the CTA section.) Unless you are staying right in the Loop, you will have to transfer to another El or bus to complete your journey. For recommendations on which one to take, ask your hotel when you reserve your room. A good alternative is to ride the El as close as you can get to your hotel and then take a taxi for the final few blocks. Again, ask your hotel or consult the neighborhood map in this book to see which El stop is closest to your hotel.

Shuttle Airport Express (☎ 312-454-7800, 800-654-7871, www.airportexpress.com) has a monopoly on services between the airport and hotels in the Loop and Near North. The fare is $17.50 per person, plus the usual 10% to 15% tip. Once downtown, you may ride around while others are dropped off before you. You also may have to wait until the van is full before you leave the airport. If there are two or more of you, take a cab – it's immediate, direct and cheaper per person.

Limo Limos may sound expensive, but they often are not. They easily hold four people and accommodate piles of luggage. They charge a flat $40 an hour no matter how many people ride, and the fee is prorated. So if your trip lasts 45 minutes, you pay $30. To arrange for a limo, look for the 'Pre-Arranged Ride Directory' in the baggage area of each terminal. Use the phone to find a company that can take you immediately. If you want to plan ahead, here are the numbers for four large companies:

American Limousine	☎ 630-920-8888
My Chauffeur Limousine	☎ 847-671-3600
One Magnificent Limousine	☎ 312-944-1317
Safe Limousine Co	☎ 773-275-7796

Regional Buses For trips farther afield, regional bus companies serve southern Wisconsin, suburban Illinois and northwest Indiana from the Bus/Shuttle Center, installed in the ground level of the central parking garage. Use the tunnels under the Hilton Hotel to get there from Terminals 1, 2 and 3. Terminal 5, the international terminal, has its own pickup area.

Midway Airport
Many of the transportation details for Midway are the same as for O'Hare. The differences follow. Midway is 12 miles southwest of the Loop.

Taxi The fare to the Loop is $18 to $25 plus tip. The Share-a-Ride fare is $14 plus tip.

The El The CTA Orange Line goes to Midway from the Loop elevated tracks. The trains go around clockwise on the inner set of tracks. The new Midway terminal building has a good connection to the El.

Because the Orange Line goes around the Loop elevated tracks, it is especially cumbersome to transfer from it to the Red Line, which in the Loop is in a subway. Follow the directions carefully at the State St Station, where you obtain a free transfer to the subway.

Shuttle The Airport Express monopoly (☎ 312-454-7800, 800-654-7871, www.airportexpress.com) charges $12.50 per person plus tip to get you downtown.

Car To reach the city from Midway, drive north on Cicero Blvd, the major road in front of the airport exit, for 2 miles, until you reach the Stevenson Expressway (I-55). Veer right and head northeast into the city.

PUBLIC TRANSPORTATION
Chicago Transit Authority
The Chicago Transit Authority (CTA), the underfunded public transportation system serving the city, consists of the El and buses. You will soon find that there are a dearth of helpful signs or maps for the El at its stops, so use the one in the back of this book (Map 2) or ask for a free map at the information booths in El stations. The system has its roots in a slew of private and competing companies that provided transit in the city before World War II. Almost 60 years later, the myriad routes are still not well integrated.

Bring something to read – even though the CTA has posted schedules for the El in the stations, they are really best-case scenarios and have little bearing on how long you will actually wait. You won't find any published schedules for buses.

The system is fairly safe. Statistics show that crime is less prevalent on the CTA than on the streets as a whole. Avoid deserted El stations late at night, although stations between the Loop and Addison, with the exception of North/Clybourn, are populated around the clock. Whether on the El or buses, watch out for pickpockets.

Information Bus drivers, El conductors and station attendants may give you detailed and friendly transit advice or they may tell you to get lost. You can also contact the CTA (☎ 888-968-7282, www.transitchicago.com). Definitely ask an El attendant or bus driver for the excellent free CTA map.

Fares The fare on a bus or the El is $1.50. Within the El system, you can transfer between as many lines as you like without paying extra. But to transfer between the El and buses or vice versa, or just between buses, you must pay 30¢ for a transfer, which is good for two hours after you buy it. Note: You have to buy your transfer when you pay your first fare.

The CTA uses fare cards called Transit Cards, which have replaced cashiers and ticket booths at El stations. Some turnstiles accept $1.50 in change, but the vast majority take only a transit card. Purchase these at the vending machines located in every El station for any value you wish between $3 and $100. Note that for every $13.50 in value you put on the card, you actually get credit for $15. A minor bargain! The El turnstiles automatically deduct the cost of your ride from the card.

On the buses you can pay your fare in exact change and cash (buses accept dollar bills) and buy a transfer good for another ride on the bus or the El, or if you have a transit card, you can use that by swiping it through a machine. (You cannot buy a transit card on the buses, however.) It knows if you are transferring and will deduct 30¢ from the card instead of the full $1.50.

So what happens when your card has some useless amount like 60¢ left on it? You add value to the card using one of the vending machines. Also, more than one person can use one card by having each rider insert it separately. Children younger than seven ride free. Those seven to 11 ride at half price, but you have to go through the hassle of proving their age to the bus driver or station attendant.

Tourist Pass The CTA sells visitor passes good for unlimited riding for a specific number of days. The cost for 1/2/3/5 days is $5/9/12/18, which can be a good deal. The only problem is that the passes are hard to buy. You can purchase them from vending machines at the O'Hare and Midway Stations and you can buy them at the Chicago Visitor Information Centers (see the Tourist Offices section of the Facts for the Visitor chapter for locations), as well as at a few other scattered outlets. Contact the CTA (see Information, above) to purchase the passes in advance or to find out where to buy them.

The El The CTA likes to call its train service 'Rapid Transit.' I've never heard anyone refer to it that way – everybody just calls it the El, whether the specific service they are referring to runs above ground, below ground or somewhere in between. For simplicity, this book does the same thing.

There are seven color-coded lines on the El: Red, Blue, Purple, Orange, Brown, Green and Yellow. Most visitors should be

able to use the system for almost all their transit needs, the exception being those going to Hyde Park, certain areas of Lincoln Park near the Lake and the area east of N Michigan Ave that includes Navy Pier.

Cars are air-conditioned as well as heated and have large windows for good viewing when above ground. (See the boxed text 'An El of a Tour' for an excellent tour of the city courtesy of the CTA.) During the day you shouldn't have to wait more than 15 minutes for a train. Late-night service varies. The Red Line and the Blue Line between Forest Park, the Loop and O'Hare operate 24 hours a day, but other lines and many stations may not run or may be closed.

The Orange Line to and from Midway Airport is closed from 11:20pm to 5am, as is the airport itself.

Bus CTA buses go almost everywhere, but they do so on erratic schedules. The bus stops are clearly marked, with signs showing which buses stop there but little else. Buses make frequent stops and don't go very fast. At rush hour you'll have to stand, and during the summer many buses lack air-conditioning (to tell whether or not a bus is air-conditioned, look to see whether the windows are open or closed).

The following routes come in handy for visitors and run from early in the morning until late in the evening.

No 22 Clark – runs north on Dearborn St until Oak St and then on Clark St all the way to the north end of the city. This is a good bus for getting to the parts of Lincoln Park that are a hike from the Fullerton El stop, such as the zoo. It's also a good way to shuttle up and down the North Side.

No 29 State – runs on State St through the Loop and River North, then east on Illinois St to Navy Pier. These buses have large 'Navy Pier' signs on their fronts.

No 36 Broadway – mostly mirrors the No 22 Clark route going north, until it reaches Diversey Parkway, where it veers off on Broadway. It's a good way to reach east Lake View.

No 72 North – runs on North Ave and makes a good route between Bucktown/Wicker Park and Lincoln Park.

No 73 Armitage – runs parallel to the 72 but four blocks north.

No 146 Marine-Michigan – runs from the Berwyn El stop in Andersonville south along the lakefront all the way to N Michigan Ave. This tourist-friendly route travels through the Loop via State St, then cuts through Grant Park on Balbo Dr and Columbus Dr en route to the Museum Campus. Note that on weekdays it runs express between Belmont Ave and N Michigan Ave.

No 151 Sheridan – runs from Union Station through the Loop and then up N Michigan Ave until Lake Shore Dr, where it takes local streets through the heart of Lincoln Park; it stops right in front of the zoo.

Metra

A web of commuter trains running under the Metra banner serves the 245 stations in the suburbs surrounding Chicago. The primary riders are people who work in the city and live elsewhere. These customers don't tolerate delays, and the trains almost always run on time. The clean Metra trains have two levels, with the second offering tight seating but better views.

Some of the Metra lines run frequent schedules seven days a week; others operate only during weekday rush hours. The four main Metra stations in Chicago have schedules for all the lines and other information. The Metra information line is an excellent service that can tell you what combination of CTA, Metra and Pace (a very limited suburban bus service) can get you from where you are to where you want to go. The information number is ☎ 836-7000 and requires no area code if dialed from one of these area codes: 312, 708, 847, 630, or 773. From elsewhere, dial ☎ 312-836-7000. The Web site (www.rtachicago.com) is also useful.

Short trips start at $1.75; long journeys cost up to $6.60. Buy tickets from agents and machines at major stations. At small stations where nobody is on duty, you can buy the ticket without penalty from the conductor on the train; normally there is a $1 surcharge for doing this.

On weekends adults can buy a ticket good everywhere Metra goes for $5. You can use these tickets on both Saturday and Sunday, and each holder can bring along up to three children younger than 12. This is an excellent deal – just make certain that the lines you want to take operate on those days.

Stations Derived from the services once run by the many competing railroads in the region, the Metra's 12 lines depart from four stations ringing the Loop :

Union Station (210 S Canal St between W Adams St and W Jackson Blvd; Map 3) – This grand station will make you wish that the trains lived up to the grandeur of the main waiting area. Scores of restaurants and shops serve commuters. All Amtrak trains also depart from here.

Richard B Ogilvie Transportation Center (500 W Madison St at Canal St; Map 3) – Formerly called Northwestern Station, a moniker it's bound to keep for most people, this airy station is built into the base of Helmut Jahn's 1986 re-creation of a 1930s radio. It contains many food stalls and shops.

Randolph St Station (below street level at E Randolph St and N Michigan Ave; Map 3) – This station is linked to the underground Pedway system that lets you walk past Marshall Field's to destinations in the central Loop without sampling Chicago's sometimes horrid weather. Besides being a starting point for the Metra electric service to Hyde Park and beyond, the station is the terminus for the South Shore trains to the Indiana Dunes and South Bend. The facilities are in the midst of a multiyear rehab tied to the construction of Millennium Park, above the station; amenities are sparse.

LaSalle St Station (414 S LaSalle St between W Congress Parkway and W Van Buren St; Map 3) – As businesslike as the Chicago Stock Exchange above it, this station has a tiny waiting room and next to no shops. Trains depart for Joliet on the Metra/Rock Island District line.

RICK GERHARTER

An El of a Tour

For $1.50 you can see Chicago in its glory and despair and get an up-close tour of many of the city's most interesting neighborhoods. From your (usually) climate-controlled car on the El, you'll enjoy a vantage point that's impossible from the street. You can see how neighborhoods have grown and declined while tracing the city's history.

Any of the lines pass interesting sights, but the following tour on the Orange and Brown Lines will give you the most varied experience. Station names are shown in boldface.

Start by boarding an Orange Line train at **Clark**, which is part of the bulbous glass monster known as the James R Thompson State of Illinois Center. At **State**, the next stop, look right. Next to the Chicago Theater is the Page Brothers Building, with a cast-iron facade. Before the great fire in 1871, most of the Loop's buildings resembled this one.

The train turns south and runs above Wabash Ave. Through the upper-floor windows of buildings on both sides, you can catch myriad glimpses of urban life that are denied pedestrians. This is one of the busiest stretches of the Loop tracks, which opened in 1897 to unite the various elevated lines built by several different companies. The tracks have survived several proposals through the years to replace them, their longevity mostly thanks to a lack of public funding for the construction of anything better.

As you leave the Loop, you penetrate what was once known as 'the Levee District,' a notorious area populated from about 1890 to 1910 by prostitutes, gamblers and other vice-seekers. Around **Roosevelt** you'll see a residential development called Central Station, a vast project that will be under construction for years to come. This is where Mayor Daley lives. The old warehouses in the surrounding blocks are undergoing renovation, and the area is quickly gaining popularity with artists and professionals.

After the tracks split, the Orange Line heads southwest and traverses acres of vacant land once used for railroad yards servicing the hundreds of daily passenger trains that made Chicago the rail transit hub of the country.

Continuing southwest, the line is hemmed in by the Stevenson Expressway and the Chicago River. Past **35th St/Archer** the tracks climb to their highest point for the best view of the skyline from anywhere on the El system.

Just before **Western**, look left to see a relic from the city's days as a major meat processor. The cattle ramps and holding pens look out of place today.

After **Kedzie** the line overlooks block after block of tidy bungalows before it reaches Midway Airport, where the planes take off above the trains. At **Midway**, which is the end of the line, cross the tracks and return downtown.

When you reach the Loop, the train will turn left, heading west, and stop at the **Library** station. Two pioneer office towers flank Dearborn St, to the right of your train. On the east side of the street, the Fisher Building dates from 1896. Look for the terra-cotta fish and other seashore critters decorating the exterior. On the west side is the world-famous Monadnock Building, built from 1889 to 1893.

One block west of the Fisher and Monadnock Buildings on Clark St, the Chicago Metropolitan Correctional Center, built in 1975, cuts its unique angle to the left of the tracks. The building houses people awaiting trial for federal crimes; believe it or not, its 5-inch-wide plastic windows allowed a few inmates to escape before bars were added on the inside.

The most delightful station out of a mostly dreary lot in the Loop is **Quincy**. Originally built in 1897 and restored by the city in 1988, it shows what all the stations once looked like.

An El of a Tour

Get off when you reach **Clark** and cross over the tracks to board a Brown Line train. One of Chicago's most famous views occurs right as the trains leave the Loop and cross the Chicago River.

Between **Chicago** and **Armitage** there used to be seven stations; now there is only one. This run gives a stark illustration of the disparities in wealth in the city. To the east is the Gold Coast, one of the nation's wealthiest neighborhoods; to the west, Cabrini-Green, one of the poorest. Notice how upscale developments are hemming the low-income housing projects in on all sides.

The sharp turns at Halsted St, a daily annoyance to thousands of standing commuters, are a legacy of the free-enterprise roots of the El system. During the line's construction in the 1890s, the German farmers in the area held out for higher prices for their land. Instead of negotiating, the then-private El company simply went around them.

Beginning at **Armitage**, the tracks run north through gentrified Lincoln Park. After **Belmont** the line heads west and offers some of the most varied views in the city. The distant lakefront, numerous vintage buildings and industrial water towers all combine for constantly changing urban panoramas.

West of the **Western** stop, which serves the old Lincoln Square German neighborhood, the line descends to ground level. There's a nice crossing of the Chicago River before the tracks terminate at **Kimball**, in Albany Park. From here you can explore the neighborhood, which has many Middle Eastern and Asian shops, or you can return to the Loop. Alternatively, take a No 81 Lawrence Ave CTA bus east to the **Lawrence** El stop on the Red Line. From here you can ride south past Wrigley Field back to the Loop.

RICK GERHARTER

GETTING AROUND

Important Lines The following Metra lines can help tourists get around the city and beyond. The stations where the trains originate are listed in parentheses and are indicated on the Loop map (Map 3).

Metra Electric (Randolph St, Van Buren St) – This is the best way to get to Hyde Park and the Museum of Science & Industry (15 minutes, $1.95). Trains run at least hourly every day. It's also an excellent means of transportation to McCormick Place (10 minutes, $1.75).

South Shore Line (Randolph St, Van Buren St) – This historic line with modern electric trains serves northwest Indiana. It's the best way to visit the Indiana Dunes (75 minutes, $5.75) and South Bend (2½ hours, $9.40). Trains run daily, but not all of them travel the entire route, so definitely check schedules first. The ride through the Gary steel mills is a lesson in the brutal grandeur of 20th-century industry.

Metra/BNSF (Union Station) – This line goes to the western suburbs, with at least hourly service daily. The Hollywood stop serves the Brookfield Zoo (23 minutes, $2.75).

Metra/Union Pacific North Line (Ogilvie Transportation Center) – The line provides frequent service all the way to the Wisconsin border, with stops at affluent North Shore suburbs, including Wilmette and Winnetka, on the way.

CAR & MOTORCYCLE

In most cases, once you are in the city, you can forget about your car. Whether it's for the day or for a week, park it and forget it. Better yet, don't bring it. Parking expenses will rapidly eat through your wallet. Riding a motorcycle is a good idea only during the temperate months, and finding secure parking for it is even more of a concern than for cars.

Chicago's streets, with their logical layout and numbering system, are easy to navigate, but drivers do not take dawdlers lightly, and horns are sounded with little provocation. If you can possibly avoid it, don't drive during rush hours (6am to 9am and 4pm to 7pm), when circulation becomes an artery-clogged nightmare – conditions that mimic the heart attack you may suffer while jammed in frustrating traffic. Weekends, when residents are out trying to run errands, can be even worse.

Driving outside of the city brings its own set of challenges. People accustomed to numerical designations for US highways (such as I-80) will be in for confusion in northern Illinois, where the roads are more commonly identified by honorary names rather than numbers. Many people you ask for directions will know the highways only by their names, not their numbers (see the boxed text 'Major Freeways').

Even the variations on the word 'highway' can be confusing. Roads without tolls are called expressways, not freeways. Those that charge money are called tollways or toll roads. If this doesn't cause you enough stress,

Major Freeways

Edens Expressway (I-94)
From Kennedy Expressway north to North Shore suburbs and Milwaukee

Tri-State Tollway (I-94/I-294)
From southern suburbs east to Indiana

Northwest Tollway (I-90)
From O'Hare International Airport west to Schaumburg

John F Kennedy Expressway (I-90/I-94)
From downtown west to O'Hare International Airport

Dwight D Eisenhower Expressway (I-290)
From West Side west to Oak Park and Schaumburg

East-West Tollway (I-88)
From Eisenhower Expressway west to Oak Brook and Aurora

Adlai Stevenson Expressway (I-55)
From Dan Ryan Expressway southwest to Midway Airport and Joliet

Dan Ryan Expressway (I-90/I-94)
From downtown south to I-57 and I-94

Chicago Skyway (I-90)
From Dan Ryan Expressway east to Indiana Toll Road

the Illinois Department of Transportation promises to raise your blood pressure with its notoriously bad signage. Also, sometimes you'll find that roads are designated 'east' when they're going due south. So don't use your compass. But bring a good map, a hopefully good navigator and plenty of patience.

Note that gasoline bought in the city is subject to lots of taxes. If you're embarking on a big journey out of town, wait until you're well clear of the city before filling up. You'll easily save 30¢ or more per gallon.

Road Rules

Chicago's abundant nightlife is a good excuse not to drive for two reasons. First, the blood-alcohol level considered legally drunk is now only .08, the equivalent of about four beers. Cops love to toss drunk drivers in jail overnight. Second, there still are plenty of drunk drivers out there, and you're far better off not tangling with them.

Anyone driving or riding in the front seat of a car must wear a seatbelt. Motorcyclists are not required to wear helmets, leaving them free to suffer the kinds of head trauma that keep ERs busy.

Parking

Trying to park your car will soon make you wish it would be stolen. In the Loop and Near North there are plenty of parking garages, but they charge $18 a day or more. The lots are usually secure, even the ones where the attendant asks you for the keys so he or she can move your car around through the day. If you're staying in a hotel, find out what the parking charges are before you commit; otherwise, that bargain room may cost $20 a day or more extra. Conversely, during slack times hotels may offer free parking to entice you.

Some parking garages and hotels and many restaurants offer valet parking. You pull up and a person in a red cap takes your key and drives away. The fees vary widely, but remember to tip the person who retrieves your car at least $1.

Parking meters line most streets in the Near North area. Competition for these spaces, which average 25¢ for 15 minutes, is heated. Parking enforcers patrol constantly and will cheerfully slap a ticket on your windshield within seconds of the meter expiring. You can toss the ticket away, but the city is adept at tracking down in-state and

Lincoln Bandits

You need to run into a store for some simple item. You can't find a place to park, but then you spy an empty space in an alley. You leave your car for a moment, complete your business, come back and find your car gone. Was it thieves? Possibly, but more likely it was the zealous trolls working for Lincoln Towing (☎ 773-561-4433), a private firm with contracts to police most of the private parking lots, alleys and other places that might tempt you to leave your car.

Employing dozens of spotters and commission-based drivers, Lincoln Towing snatches scores of cars every day, towing them – often with car alarms shrieking like an animal caught in the jaws of a predator to its lot at 4882 N Clark St. The frustration of the hapless car owners is evident in the office area: the entrance bears traces of fires, graffiti and possible assault with a vehicle; the employees work behind heavily scarred bulletproof glass. The anger on the part of car owners stems partly from the inconvenience and expense ($105) of retrieving one's car, but it is greatly compounded by the Lincoln Towing personnel, who revel in abusing their 'clients' with a stream of invective. When I called to ask about the pricing structure, this was the response I got from the representative on the phone: 'When your car gets towed, get your ass up here and I'll let you know what it will run you.'

Oh, and if you think your car was towed by mistake, tough luck. Short of evidence you can use in court – numerous witnesses, photos, etc – you can forget getting the fee waived. Pay your money (cash only!), check carefully for damage and avoid these vultures like off-color meat.

out-of-state offenders. Don't think a rental car will shield you, either. The rental company will simply put the charge on your credit card a few months later.

The situation is no better in the neighborhoods, many of which have adopted some sort of permit scheme that prevents nonresidents from parking for any length of time.

Finally, if you do find a place to park, make certain that it is not a tow-away zone. Both the city and private companies make big profits from snatching illegally parked cars. The city charges a cool $110 plus the cost of the parking fine to retrieve your car. In fact, most people who report cars stolen later find them in city or private auto impound lots. (See the boxed text 'Lincoln Bandits.') If you suspect your car has been towed, check the place where you parked to see who has jurisdiction over towing there; if it was a public street, call the Chicago Police Department at ☎ 312-746-6000 to find out which lot to contact (there are several).

Rentals

If Chicago is your first stop on a tour of the Midwest, then wait to pick up a rental car until you're ready to leave the city. If you're staying in Chicago and just need a car for a couple of days, try to time your rental for the weekend, when the rental lots are full of cars unwanted by business travelers. Like hotels, car rental agencies offer a variety of deals. Most are in force from about noon on Thursday until Monday morning.

Make reservations in advance to ensure the best deal, and shop around carefully to get a good rate. Look out for any deals offered by your credit card, frequent flier program or even your employer.

To rent a car, you usually have to be at least 25 years of age with one good credit card. Beware of firms that put a huge hold on your card, leaving you with no credit line and in deep doo-doo when you try to check out of a hotel. Renting a car without a credit card is conceivable but requires advance planning with the company. Renting a car when you are younger than 25 is also possible with some companies, but sometimes they charge you an extra fee.

Midweek rates for a compact car are $45 to $60 a day. Weekly rates can be much cheaper, at $135 and up. You can also find weekend deals for $29 a day. As you ponder these figures, add in the special city and state car rental tax of 18%.

Your credit card or personal auto insurance may give you some coverage that will help you avoid the insurance costs, which can add $15 or more a day to your bill. But check very carefully, as you don't want to be stuck owing Mr Hertz $19,000 for that wrecked rental. Rentals almost always include unlimited mileage, but again, it's well worth double-checking.

Try to buy gas outside of town to avoid noxious city taxes. But also remember to return your car with a full tank to avoid even more noxious refueling surcharges, which the rental companies just love to add.

You will probably be offered the latest car rental scam by the brightly smiling counter clerk when you pick up the car; a chance to 'buy' your full tank of gas at a going rate. A good deal? Unless you're prepared to calculate your fuel usage so that you return the car with just fumes in the tank, you will be giving Ms Avis free gas. And it's unlikely she'll say 'thanks.'

All the major car rental companies have outposts at the airport and in the city. For the best deals, you may have to go to the airport to pick up your car from one of the vast lots out there. The best way to get there is to take the El to the airport and then transfer to one of the free car rental shuttle buses.

The following agencies rent cars at O'Hare; most also maintain offices downtown and at Midway.

Alamo	☎ 800-327-9633, www.alamo.com
Avis	☎ 800-831-2847, www.avis.com
Budget	☎ 800-527-0700, www.budget.com
Dollar	☎ 800-800-4000, www.dollar.com
Hertz	☎ 800-654-3131, www.hertz.com
National	☎ 800-227-7368, www.nationalcar.com
Thrifty	☎ 800-367-2277, www.thrifty.com

The following firms have Loop or River North locations (call the numbers listed above for general information, hours and reservations):

Avis	214 N Clark St
Budget	65 E Lake St
Hertz	401 N State St
National	203 N LaSalle St
Thrifty	180 N Franklin St

TAXI

Taxis are easy to find in many of the northern parts of the city, from the Loop through Wrigleyville. Raise your arm and one will promptly cut a few cars off and zip over to the curb to pick you up. In other parts of the city, you can either call a cab or face what may be a long wait for one to happen along. When the cab's top light is on, it means it is ready for a fare (although many of the lights are broken and remain on even when the back seat is full).

The major cab companies are Yellow Cab (☎ 312-829-4222), Checker Taxi (☎ 312-243-2537) and Flash Cab (☎ 773-561-1444). The first two companies have the same owners and supply the majority of cabs on the streets. Flash is very popular with locals because it has a reputation for hiring older, more experienced drivers; it's worth calling first. When hailing a cab, there's no reason to get picky.

Driving a cab is hard work, with very long days and some risk of robbery. Lots of recent immigrants work as cab drivers, and they may have only limited English skills and patchy knowledge of the city. However, most are fairly polite and will do what you ask, such as turning on the air-conditioning on a hot day or turning down the talk radio. Cases of meter-fraud are not common.

Fares are $1.90 when you enter the cab and $1.60 for each additional mile; extra passengers cost 50¢ apiece. Drivers expect a 10% to 15% tip. A ride from the Loop into Lincoln Park will cost about $10, including tip. The same under-publicized Share-a-Ride program that can save airport passengers a bit of money also applies at McCormick Place: a ride to or from the vast convention center from downtown or Near North costs $5 per person. Make certain you explain to the driver that you want to ride-share before you set off in a cab.

To report a taxi problem (the number one reason why people complain to the city), call the taxi complaint hotline (☎ 312-744-9400). Mayor Daley will personally come and refund your fare. Well, not exactly…

BICYCLE

Curbs are the highest mountains you'll find in Chicago, making the town ideal for biking. The popular, 18½-mile lakefront path, from Hollywood Ave in the north to 71st St in the south, suffers from its own traffic jams on warm weekends. The path is an excellent way to see the city from top to bottom, and in the hot weather the lake offers cooling breezes.

Lincoln Park is another good spot for biking, with paths snaking around the small lakes and the zoo. Chicago streets themselves, while flat, are not terribly accommodating: bike lanes don't exist, except in a couple of places, where they have become de facto double-parking zones, and many streets are just wide enough for speeding traffic and parked cars. And it's both illegal and bad form to ride on the narrow sidewalks. One way to beat cars is to ride down small side streets in the neighborhoods; these are less hectic and more pleasant.

Finally, lock your bike, lock your bike, lock your bike. Oh, and did I mention to lock your bike? And choose a busy location. The number of broken, supposedly thief-proof U-locks you see in the gutters should tell you about the kind of opposition you're up against.

Rentals

The cool company Bike Chicago (☎ 312-944-2337, 800-915-2453), open 9am to 7pm daily, deserves praise and business. From April 15 to October 15, it rents Trek mountain bikes, big cruisers with fat tires, bicycles built for two and kids' bikes. The company runs a main office at Navy Pier (600 E Grand Ave; Map 3); when the weather's nice, it also operates out of trailers at Oak St Beach, Lincoln Park Zoo and Buckingham

Fountain (call first to confirm). As part of the deal, you can pick your bike up at one location and return it to another for no extra charge.

If you rent for an entire day, Bike Chicago will bring the bike to your hotel in the morning. Rates start at $8.75 per hour and $34 per day, with significant reductions for additional days. The cost of the rental includes locks, helmets and maps that show the 18½-mile lakefront path in detail.

Here's one of the coolest offers: each day a Bike Chicago guide leads 15 riders on a two-hour tour. It's free and open to people who didn't even rent from Bike Chicago. To join a tour, all you have to do is call and secure your place in advance. You can also rent in-line skates at lower rates than those for bikes.

In Lake View, the Bike Stop (☎ 773-868-6800, 1034 W Belmont Ave; Map 7), two blocks west of the El stop, rents mountain bikes and in-line skates.

WALKING

Except when huge chunks of windblown sleet are smacking you in the face, the best way to see the city is on foot. (When the aforementioned weather conditions are in force, I recommend fantasizing about the city while sitting next to the fireplace in a cozy bar.)

The city is flat and very simply laid out – you know that by now, right? Walking the sidewalks, you can discover for yourself the myriad little shops, cafés, corner pubs, architectural gems and scores of other treats that make Chicago such an interesting place for residents and visitors.

Don't let winter put you off, either. After a fresh snow, the sounds of traffic are muffled and the fresh flakes make a seductive crunch-crunch under your feet. Of course, once the snow gets old, dirty, and slushy, then you're better off back by the fireplace.

See the boxed text 'Streetwalking' for a few routes to get you started.

ORGANIZED TOURS

Guided tours abound here. Especially in the warmer months, you can go by land or lake.

The choice of bus versus boat depends on the experience you want. You cover more territory on a bus, but you can't duplicate the views from the water. If nothing else, boats let you see how badly the undersides of the city's bridges need paint, and they show you the lock into Lake Michigan, plus the canyon effect of the buildings along Wacker Dr and the occasional dead fish. Also, for whatever reason, the friendly citizens of Chicago wave constantly at people on boats. When you're on the bus, nobody waves at all.

Buses excel at covering a lot of territory, especially the longer tours. Heading north and south, you get away from Michigan Ave and the Loop and can glimpse more of Chicago's diversity. Buses also have the advantage of year-round service.

For in-depth tours, try one of the several walking tours, which offer detailed information on selected areas.

Bus Tours

American Sightseeing (☎ 312-251-3100) departs from the Palmer House Hilton and other downtown hotels. The buses are of the big air-conditioned and tinted-glass variety, which means that you're definitely insulated from the sights you see. The 14 tours include the North tour, which covers the Loop, the many commercial pleasures of River North, Lincoln Park and Wrigley Field; and the South tour, which visits Grant Park, Hyde Park and historical areas of the city that few people take the time to see, such as Prairie and Woodlawn Aves. Two-hour tours cost $16/8 for adults/children. Specialized tours on black Chicago and other topics are sometimes available. American Sightseeing operates similar tours under the Gray Line brand name (☎ 312-251-3107).

Okay, it's a personal opinion, but I always think that the people bouncing around the city's streets on the fake trolleys run by the Chicago Trolley Co (☎ 773-648-5000) look like nitwits. These gas-powered vehicles, which have both open and air-conditioned areas, might remind you of a kid's ride. The service itself is not a bad idea, though: you pay one price and ride the trolleys all day, hopping on and off at all the major tourist

GETTING AROUND

attractions over a good portion of the city. If you opt for this ride, on-and-off tickets cost $18/8 for adults/children. Call to find out the stop closest to you.

Boat Tours

Chicago has two main boat-tour companies offering similar 90-minute tours of the river and lake for similar prices. The guides are often perfunctory, offering bad jokes and limited information. Be aware that passing through the locks to and from the lake can take up a fair part of the tour.

Mercury Chicago Skyline Cruises (☎ 312-332-1353) depart from the southwest corner of the Michigan Ave Bridge and the river (Map 3) and cost $15/7.50 for adults/children. Wendella Sightseeing Boats (☎ 312-337-1446) depart from the northwest corner of the Michigan Ave Bridge and the river (Map 3) and charge $12 to $16. Both also offer other tours and night cruises.

About the only factor that you should consider when deciding between Wendella and Mercury is which side of the river you're on. They're that similar. The Wendella boats don't place you under as much

blue plastic as Mercury's, but that can be a bad thing on a breezy ride. One thing you'll notice about the locks while waiting: seemingly every seagull in the Midwest lives on the breakwater there, and seagulls foul their nests. It stinks.

For a much more learned approach to water touring, take the Chicago Architecture Foundation River Cruise. See the Architectural Tours portion of the special Architecture section for details on these highly recommended tours.

Navy Pier The south side of the pier features a row of tour and dinner-cruise boats that avoid the time-consuming locks into the Chicago River but also miss the close-up views of a river tour. Schedules change with the seasons, so confirm them in advance. Also, the air over Lake Michigan can be pretty cold even when the city is warm, so bring a sweatshirt or jacket.

Shoreline Sightseeing (☎ 312-222-9328) offers 30-minute lake-only tours. You'll see lots of postcard views on these tours, which leave from Navy Pier, the lake in front of Buckingham Fountain and the Shedd

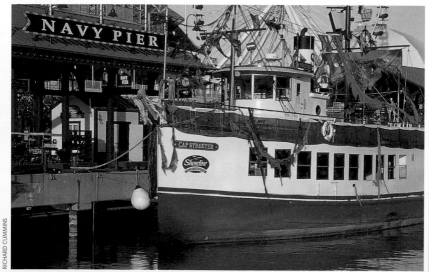

Hop on a boat at Navy Pier.

RICHARD CUMMINS

Aquarium. Tours cost $9/4 for adults/children, but you can get a ticket good just for cruising from one site to the next. Printed translations of the narration are available in 12 languages, including French, Spanish, German, Polish, Arabic, Japanese and Hindi.

Odyssey Cruises (☎ 888-741-0282) operates a sleek cruise boat that looks like a huge yacht. Two-hour cruises, which sail throughout the year, include a meal and music. Glamour doesn't come cheap, and the company suggests that you should dress up for the experience. Brunches and lunches cost $36 to $44. Dinners are a pricey $77 to $90. A moonlight cruise during the summer costs $30 and leaves at midnight.

The *Spirit of Chicago* (☎ 312-836-7899) offers slightly downscale lunch and dinner cruises (wear what you want), departing year-round except when the lake is frozen. Lunch cruises cost about $38, dinner about $75 and various party cruises (no chow) about $27 to $35. The boat has lots of open space on deck for enjoying the view.

When the wind blows, which is most of the time, the *Windy* (☎ 312-595-5555), a 148-foot, four-masted gaff topsail schooner, plies the lake from May to September. A class B tall ship, she is the only certified four-masted traditional sailing vessel in the US. Passengers can play sailor by helping to raise and lower the sails. A better deal is to play skipper by trying your hand at the wheel. With only the sound of the wind in your ears, the *Windy* is the most relaxing way to see the skyline from offshore. Ninety-minute tours cost $25/15 for adults/children.

Walking Tours

The Chicago Architecture Foundation offers a long list of walking tours. See Architectural Tours in the Architecture section

---

Streetwalking

Wandering the streets of Chicago is one of the city's greatest pleasures. There are no points awarded for doing so in the Near North – it's fun and fascinating, but you won't need any guidance there; just start walking.

This book offers self-guided architecture walks of the Loop and the University of Chicago; it also offers a sculpture tour of the Loop. (See the Architecture special section for the Loop tour, the Things to See & Do chapter for the rest.) But I can't stress enough that you should find some area or site you like the sound of and then just start walking. The maps in this book will guide you, and the number of routes is infinite.

Following are four ideas to help send you on your way. See the appropriate sections in the Things to See & Do and Shopping chapters for guidance to sights. The Places to Eat and Entertainment chapters will offer suggestions for refreshment and frolic. Use these streets and landmarks as starting points. Wander off them in any direction and see what you find.

Wells St and Lincoln Ave The walk north from Division St to Diversey Parkway covers the heart of Old Town and Lincoln Park in 2.3 miles.

Clark St The 3.4-mile trek north from North Ave to Irving Park Rd goes from gentrified Lincoln Park through lively Lake View and Wrigleyville.

Lincoln Park Start where Dearborn St ends at North Ave and head north; when you reach Diversey Parkway, head east to the lake and you can keep going all the way to Hollywood Ave, 1.7 to 5.4 miles. This is the most bucolic long walk in the city.

Loop to the Museum Campus Take S Michigan Ave south from Madison St to Roosevelt Rd and east to the Museum Campus, 1.8 miles. This walk encompasses the grandeur of Michigan Ave, Grant Park and the museums.

for details. See the Things to See & Do chapter for some self-guided walking tours of Wicker Park and Hyde Park.

Special Interest

You can find a tour for every taste, ranging from cultural to offbeat to downright weird. Chicago Neighborhood Tours (☎ 312-742-1190), run by the city's Department of Cultural Affairs, offers nine tours throughout the year, with one every Saturday on a rotating basis. Local experts lead each tour, which lasts four hours and gives a detailed look at one or two neighborhoods. Among the neighborhoods explored are Bronzeville, Humboldt Park, Uptown, Devon Ave and Pilsen. Local businesses contribute free food and gifts. I highly, highly recommend these tours. Call to confirm the details, but in 2000 you had to be at the Chicago Cultural Center (77 E Randolph St at Michigan Ave; Map 3) at 9:30am for the 10am bus departure, and the tours cost, on average, $30.

Black CouTours (☎ 312-233-8907) offers 2½-hour bus tours that focus on African American history in Chicago with a generous dash of soul. This is an excellent way to see parts of the South Side ignored by major tours. Tickets cost $25/20/15 for adults/seniors/children. Daily departures happen at 9am, noon and 3pm.

Chicago Supernatural Tours (☎ 708-499-0300) offers five-hour tours every day in the summer and on weekends the rest of the year. The ghoulish itinerary takes in murder sites, cemeteries, supposedly haunted houses and all sorts of other places with some kind of spiritual connection (at least in the minds of the tour leaders). Tours cost $30.

Horse-drawn carriages depart from the Water Tower throughout the year, day and night. These attract lots of suburban teens who are in town for a prom and want to smooch. Rates start at $35 for a minimum of 30 minutes; each half hour thereafter costs another $35. Drivers will hope for a tip, whether they give witty commentary or leave you to your romance. You can choose a route or let the driver pick one for you. Call ☎ 312-664-6014 for advance reservations.

Untouchable Gangster Tours (☎ 773-881-1195) leads comic tours through gangland Chicago in an old bus. See the boxed text 'Capone's Chicago' in Facts about Chicago for more information.

If you want to see the real, and I mean *real,* Chicago, Dennis McKenna (☎ 312-315-6374), a retired Chicago cop, will take you on a tour of the city and show you what's really going down. He's seen it all and will love to show you. Call for information.

Things to See & Do

Chicago is a vast place with enough to keep you busy for a few years. Places of interest, museums, sights and other diversions are listed by neighborhood. For information on recreational activities throughout the city, see the end of the chapter.

THE LOOP (Map 3)

The Loop is the historic center of the city, drawing its name from the elevated tracks that circle it. It's a fascinating place to walk around, and its buildings constitute a virtual textbook of American architecture. During the daytime it hums with shoppers, office workers and tourists. Once quiet at night, it now boasts a burgeoning nightlife thanks to the addition of new residents and the development of the Loop Theater District (see the Entertainment chapter).

Through the 1960s the Loop served as both the commercial hub and the entertainment center of Chicago. Grand movie palaces, chic restaurants and nightclubs drew the masses. The 1970s and 1980s saw much of the focus shift to the Near North, Gold Coast and other neighborhoods. A disastrous effort that turned State St into a

pedestrian mall in 1979 proved a 15-year failure that primarily benefited exhaust-belching buses. Most of the remaining theaters and entertainment venues closed or moved. At night the streets needed only a few urban tumbleweeds to complete the bleak tableau.

But during this same period the city doggedly kept trying to resuscitate the area. Tax breaks were offered to developers, and State St eventually was attractively remodeled – with new street lamps, El entrances and other classical details – and reopened to traffic.

Now that the new Loop Theater District has further helped to revive the neighborhood, developers have hit upon innovative schemes for some of the older office buildings. Previously these architecturally significant buildings would have been torn down because their small floors, low ceilings and other details make them unsuitable for modern offices. Now, however, developers have realized that those small floors are perfect for residences and hotels. As part of this trend, the number of people living in the Loop and its environs has grown by 45% in 10 years.

The landmark Reliance Building (32 N State St) has become the Hotel Burnham; the Chicago Building (7 W Madison St) has been converted to artists' lofts; condos are on sale at the McCormick Building (330 S Michigan Ave); and many more projects are in the works.

See the Architecture section, earlier in the book, for a Loop architecture walking tour.

Sears Tower

It may be the world's tallest building, or it may not be (see the 'Tower Envy' boxed text), but there's no doubt that the Sears Tower (☎ 312-875-9696, 233 S Wacker Dr) has become a symbol of Chicago. It boasts the kind of stats that make good grade-

Top 10 Destinations

Here are Chicago's favorite sites and their number of visitors in 1999:

Navy Pier	7.5 million
Lincoln Park Zoo	3.5 million
Shedd Aquarium	1.85 million
Museum of Science & Industry	1.65 million
Field Museum	1.5 million
Sears Tower Skydeck	1.4 million
Art Institute of Chicago	1.35 million
Chicago Cultural Center	675,000
Adler Planetarium	460,000
Chicago Children's Museum	459,000

Tower Envy

The Sears Tower was the undisputed size champ in the tallest-building category until the 1996 opening of the Petronas Towers in Malaysia. But the matter wasn't that simple. The 88-story Petronas Towers were shorter than the Sears Tower until two 111-foot decorative towers were added, topping the 110-story Sears Tower by 20 feet.

Chicago's civic boosters licked their erectile wounds until the Council on Tall Buildings and Urban Habitat, the international group that certifies tall buildings, came to the Sears Tower's rescue. In 1997 the council expanded the categories of tallest buildings from one to four:

- height to structural or architectural top
- height to the highest occupied floor
- height to the top of the roof
- height to the top of antenna

Under this scheme, Petronas wins the first category, Sears takes the second and third and the taller of New York's World Trade Center towers garners the fourth. So, thanks to the Council on Tall Buildings and Urban Habitat, Chicago and the Sears Tower still win two out of four.

RICK GERHARTER

school presentations: 43,000 miles of phone cable, 2232 steps to the roof, enough concrete to build an eight-lane highway 5 miles long.

Much of what's inside the 110-story, 1454-foot building is mundane office space. But the lure of the world's highest observation deck draws more than 1.5 million people a year. You can join the mobs on the **Skydeck** (☎ 312-875-9696; admission $9.50/6.75 for adults/children; open 9am-10pm daily, until 11pm Mar-Sept) or visit my preferred choice, the John Hancock Center Observatory (see the Gold Coast section, later).

The Skydeck entrance is on the Jackson Blvd side of the block-size building, which is also bounded by Wacker Dr, Adams and Franklin Sts. Your journey to the top starts with a slow elevator ride down to the charmless waiting area, where visitors queue for tickets. A sign will tell you how long you'll have to wait to get to the top. On busy days it can be an hour or longer, so this is a good

time to confirm the visibility – before you invest your time and money. Even days that seem sunny can have upper-level haze that limits the view. On good days, however, you can see for 40 to 50 miles, as far as Indiana, Michigan and Wisconsin.

A dark series of rooms follow the ticketing area and cleverly disguise the full scope of the waiting line. Eventually, you reach a theater (on my most recent visit, a saddened child whined: 'Do we have to go in there? Can't we just go to the top?'), where you have to watch a film titled *Over Chicago*. Political junkies will be reminded of *Morning in America*, the short film about a mystical America that Ronald Reagan used for his election campaign in 1984. The syrupy narration of the aerial footage of Chicago seems endless, but the film lasts only 15 minutes.

More lines after the film mean that any lingering nausea will subside before the 70-second elevator ride to the top in the world's fastest elevators. Your ears will definitely pop on the way up. Once there, you're bound to think the view was worth the price paid in money and patience: the entire city stretches below, and you can take the time to see exactly how Chicago is laid out. You should be able to pick out most of the major features on the maps in this book.

You'll probably find more lines of visitors waiting to descend in one of the two elevators, but you can linger as long as you like at the windows. Sunsets can be quite stunning, and the emergence of lights at twilight is charming.

Trading Floors

The profit motive leads to all-out anarchy on Chicago's crazy trading floors. Hands fly, shouts ring through the air and a few shoving matches break out in these chaotic scenes, as traders compete to buy or sell commodities and options for the best price.

Trading Nothing

Hand signals flash, papers fly and voices frantically call out. What explains the din and confusion? Money in sums that defy comprehension. It's the hottest futures market in a town that has become the world center for futures trading. At the Eurodollar trading pit in the Chicago Mercantile Exchange, contracts worth more than $470 billion are traded each day. Annual volume of the pit: $1.21 followed by 14 zeros. Try writing that. Brash, rough-edged, never refined, the Chicago markets have elbowed their way to a dominant position in global finance.

In the trading pits, contracts can be purchased for almost anything with a fluctuating value, such as metals, foreign currency, grains, bonds and much more. But whereas futures contracts on grain or even bonds represent something that you could conceivably hold in your hand, Eurodollars represent the ultimate embodiment of the legalized gambling that is futures trading: nothing. They don't exist; you can't hold one in your hand. They are based on the euro-denominated interest rates on US money held in foreign banks. The futures traders are betting on what that value will be at some distant date. If they're right, they make money, maybe a fortune. If they're wrong, they can lose their shirts.

It's a high-stakes business that favors the young and manic. When trading gets heated, brawls and mayhem can erupt. A badge of honor among the mostly male traders is a scar on the cheek caused by accidental pencil jabs from others frantically signaling in the pits.

The whole wild business began after the Civil War, when the Chicago Board of Trade revolutionized the way grain prices were set by instituting a uniform and dependable system. It soon became common to trade 'futures,' in essence, speculative bets based on the future price of commodities such as wheat. Farmers were guaranteed set prices, which reduced their risk. However, the suspicion has always lingered throughout the Midwest that the traders in Chicago somehow manipulate prices at the expense of the farmer.

When a split-second's miscalculation can cost $10,000 or more, the stakes are as high as the energy levels. These people take caffeine to relax.

The two main futures trading organizations have free viewing areas overlooking their trading floors. Both take commendable steps to explain the impenetrable world of futures trading, where people make money by spending money they don't have on goods they can't buy and which really don't exist. It's a fascinating show.

Inside the main building of the **Chicago Board of Trade** – a beautiful 1930 structure with a four-story lobby decorated in marble, brass and platinum – the trading floor (☎ *312-435-3500, 141 W Jackson Blvd at LaSalle St; admission free; open 8am-2pm weekdays*) is a riot of color.

You'll find the **Chicago Mercantile Exchange** in a modern building with a good view of the river. The trading floor (☎ *312-930-8249, 10-30 S Wacker Dr; admission free; open 7:30am-3:15pm weekdays*) matches the Board of Trade's for mania.

You can meet the traders after work (usually starting about 3pm), when they begin their energetic decompression from their incredibly high-pressure jobs at the legendary **Alcock's Inn** (☎ *312-922-1778, 411 S Wells St*). Some of the patrons are newly rich and others newly broke, but most of them are drunk.

For more information about futures trading and watching the action, see the boxed text 'Trading Nothing.'

Art Institute of Chicago

One of the world's premier museums, the Art Institute of Chicago (☎ *312-443-3600, www.artic.edu, Adams St at S Michigan Ave; admission $10/7 for adults/children, free Tues; open 10:30am-4:40pm Mon, Wed, Thur, Fri, until 8pm Tues, 10am-5pm weekends*) has found generous patronage among Chicago's wealthy. Their money has funded a collection that spans 5000 years of art from around the globe. The museum's collection of impressionist and postimpressionist paintings is second only to collections in France; it represents the purchased booty of generations of touring patrons, led by the indomitable society matron Bertha Palmer.

Here's a brief rundown of the types of art you'll find: African and ancient American art; American art from the 17th century through 1955; ancient Egyptian, Greek and Roman art; architecture; Chinese, Japanese and Korean art, beginning 5000 years ago; European decorative arts since the 12th century; European painting and sculpture from 1400 to 1800; 19th-century European painting; photography; prints and drawings; textiles; furniture; and 20th-century painting and sculpture.

The main entrance is the original 1893 Allerton Building, where Adams St meets Michigan Ave. The bronze lions flanking the steps are Chicago icons. The Art Institute decorated them with giant Bears football helmets in 1985, during that team's championship season. Purists cried foul, but everyone else enjoyed the gesture. The steps themselves become one of the city's prime rendezvous points on fair days.

Chicago Board of Trade

[continued on page 124]

Loop Sculpture: From Historic to Incomprehensible

In 1967 the arrival of the Picasso sculpture at what's now the Richard J Daley Civic Center began a veritable sculpture frenzy that culminated in a city council decree in 1978, when the powers that be decided that new or renovated public buildings had to include public sculptures.

Here are a few of the notable works in the Loop, from north to south.

Michigan Ave Bridge Since 1928 the four bridge towers have featured sculptured relief panels celebrating Chicago's early history. On the northeast, James Earl Fraser's *The Discoverers* shows explorers Louis Jolliet and Jacques Marquette and others. On the northwest, Fraser's *The Pioneers*

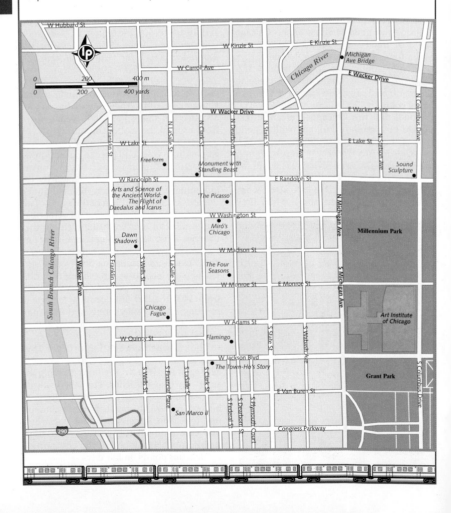

Loop Sculpture: From Historic to Incomprehensible

depicts John Kinzie, a fur trader. On the southwest, Henry Hering's *Defense* portrays the 1812 Fort Dearborn massacre; note the odd looks on the faces of the Potawatomi Indians as they prepare to wield their hatchets. On the southeast, Hering's *Regeneration* shows the rebuilding of the city after the 1871 fire.

Freeform Two-and-a-half stories tall, Richard Hunt's 1993 free-form aluminum sculpture decorates the facade of the Illinois State Office Building (160 N LaSalle St).

Monument with Standing Beast In 1984 French sculptor Jean Dubuffet created this characteristic collection of blobs for the state's James R Thompson Center (100 W Randolph St).

Sound Sculpture Henry Bertoia's 1975 metal sculpture recalls fields of wheat and makes various noises in the wind. It's on the east side of the BP-Amoco Building (200 E Randolph St).

Arts and Science of the Ancient World: The Flight of Daedalus and Icarus This large 1991 mosaic by Roger Brown, over the entrance to 120 N LaSalle St, shows dad and son escaping the labyrinth of the Minotaur.

'The Picasso' Officially it's untitled, but Chicagoans soon adopted their own no-nonsense name for the huge work made out of Cor-Ten steel (the same material that clads the Daley Center, behind it). Bird, dog, woman – you decide. The base makes a great slide for kids. You can easily view it from both Washington and Dearborn Sts.

Dawn Shadows Louise Nevelson's 1983 steel sculpture, painted black, takes its inspiration from the configuration of the El (maybe after a wreck). It dominates the entrance to Madison Plaza (200 W Madison St).

Miró's Chicago Joan Miró hoped to evoke the 'mystical force of a great earth mother' with this 39-foot sculpture, made with various metals, cement and tile in 1981. You'll find it in a dark plaza across Washington St from Daley Plaza.

The Four Seasons Russian-born artist Marc Chagall loved Chicago and donated this grand 1974 mosaic on the Dearborn St side of Bank One Plaza (formerly First Chicago Plaza) in 1974. Using thousands of bits of glass and stone, the artist portrayed six scenes of the city in hues reminiscent of the Mediterranean coast of France, where he kept his studio. Chagall continued to make adjustments, such as updating the skyline, after the work arrived in Chicago. Recently, the bank built a roof over it to protect it from the elements.

Chicago Fugue The soaring lobby of the 190 S LaSalle St building makes a suitable home for this 28-foot tall bronze by Anthony Caro.

Flamingo Alexander Calder's soaring 1974 free-standing steel sculpture, on N Dearborn St between Adams St and Jackson Blvd, provides some much-needed relief to the stark facades of the federal buildings around it. Actually, a flock of flamingoes wouldn't be a bad idea.

The Town-Ho's Story This 6½-ton work, made of industrial junk, occupies the lobby of the Ralph H Metcalfe Federal Building (77 W Jackson Blvd). Part of artist Frank Stella's 'Moby Dick' series, the sculpture seems to depict what would have happened if Moby had swallowed a garbage scow and later fell ill.

San Marco II Inspired by the four horses that grace the facade of St Mark's Basilica in Venice, artist Ludovico de Luigi created this stone sculpture on the plaza outside one of the main entrances to the 440 S LaSalle St building (access the sculpture from Financial Place).

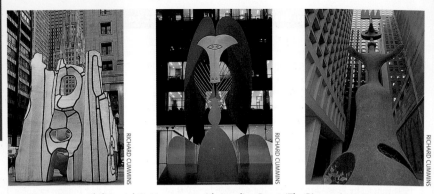

Loop sculptures (left to right): *Monument with Standing Beast*, 'The Picasso,' Miró's *Chicago*

[continued from page 121]

The modern 1977 Rubloff Building, accessed via the Columbus Dr entrance, houses the School of the Art Institute, where the number of pierced body parts far exceeds the student body. The Rice Building was added in 1988.

The Art Institute is huge but not unmanageable, given the scope of its works. See the accompanying special section, 'The Art Institute in 90 Minutes,' for a 90- to 120-minute tour that covers both major and interesting minor works. Excellent color maps of the institute are available free at the many information booths in the museum. You can use them to plot a visit that concentrates on specific aspects of the collection or leads to a grand tour. The quality of the documentation with the works gets better each year, as the curators share more of their wisdom about the displayed pieces.

Many – but not all – of the impressionist paintings are displayed in luminous skylit rooms. If your visit will coincide with dusk, head to these rooms before dark. The museum's good café and restaurant are open for lunch daily and stay open until 7pm Tuesday.

Millennium Park

A new 16-acre extravaganza, Millennium Park is rising above the grim Metra Randolph St Station tracks and the desolate parking field in the shadow of Illinois Center. The park occupies a prime location between Randolph and Monroe Sts that's desperately needed work for decades.

The portion of the park closest to Michigan Ave will feature a formal design incorporating ponds that will harmonize with Grant Park to the south. But the major portion of Millennium Park will feature a huge outdoor music pavilion that can accommodate 30,000 people. This will replace the unacceptable Petrillo Band Shell in Grant Park, where only the 5% of people closest to the stage can actually see the performers. The new design is by Frank Gehry, the trendsetting architect whose Guggenheim Museum in Bilbao, Spain became one of the most significant structures built in the 1990s. Like the Guggenheim, Gehry's pavilion will make bold use of curving stainless steel.

It all sounds good and it likely will be, but this being Chicago, there have been a few problems. The original contractor – a chum of Mayor Daley's – had to be fired after the park went $100 million over budget and missed various deadlines. The new contractors, brought in at the last moment and at huge expense (not unlike the opening credits of *Monty Python and the Holy Grail*) now hope to have large areas complete later in 2001 or 2002. Complicating the process is the fact that the park is being built atop new underground parking garages, which in turn have to span the Metra tracks below.

THE ART INSTITUTE IN 90 MINUTES

This eclectic and highly personal tour takes in the greatest works of the Art Institute while giving an idea of the breadth of the collections. Give yourself 90 minutes if you follow this closely, more if you use it merely as a starting point to begin your own explorations. It starts with sculpture, pottery and other three-dimensional works from all ages worldwide before beginning a backward march through the history of painting.

Pick up one of the color floor plans from an information desk and note that some pieces listed here may move from time to time, as curators try new groupings. If you can't find something, ask the omnipresent guards – they are usually quite knowledgeable.

After clearing the entrance gates on the Michigan Ave side, take the stairs down to the lower level.

Room 11 contains the Thorne Miniature Rooms, a fascinating series of 68 small rooms showing the progression of interior design from the 13th century to 1940. These are intricately detailed works of art in their own right. Kids love 'em too. Look for A30, a Georgia double parlor that needs only a dotty aunt to be complete, and A37, a California hallway right out of a Raymond Chandler novel.

Room 1 holds temporary photo exhibits that are always worth a look.

Return to the 1st floor and head up the first set of eight steps to the Asian collections on the right. Pass through Rooms 131A and 131B to **Room 132**, where bronze works date from 2000 BC and feature some artful and witty details; look for the water vessel with the arched cat used as the handle.

Right: Outside the Art Institute

RICHARD CUMMINS

Cut through Room 133 and take a right into **Room 105**. The stunning statues all around you are funeral earthenware from the Tang Dynasty (AD 618–907). Prior to archaeologists' efforts to unearth them, these vibrant and animated figures might have made only one public appearance – during the funeral procession – before being placed in a tomb. Horses were highly prized. Note the quiet dignity the artists gave both human and beast.

Exit back the way you came and turn right outside Room 131A into Gunsaulus Hall, the link over the train tracks. Suits of armor dominate the room and get the most attention here; these have the same metallic charm as the scores of other, similar suits in museums worldwide. Along the right wall you'll find much-overlooked examples of European decorative arts. The Italian wine cistern dating from 1553 leads the brilliant collection of majolica, a tin-glazed earthenware with bright colors and animated decoration.

Once through Gunsaulus Hall, you descend into a hall called Room 150; turn right into the Rice Building and descend to the 1st level. Pass forward through the sculpture court and into **Room 167**. Here you'll see

Left: Grant Wood's *American Gothic*, 1930 (Room 244)

©THE ART INSTITUTE OF CHICAGO

companion portraits of Daniel Hubbard and his wife, painted in 1764 by John Singleton Copley, a self-taught portrait painter from Boston who was known for his careful detail. Quiet, intelligent Mrs Hubbard contrasts with her smirking husband, who looks like he swallowed a canary. Imagine this pair bad-mouthing the British amid the early American furnishings in the next few rooms.

Room 177 will move you closer to the modern age. The highlights include a 1906 Vienna Secessionist coffee set in gold, blue, red and black. Exit the 1st level and go to the lower level of the Rice Building.

The star of this area, which is devoted to European decorative arts from 1600 to 1900, is the 1640 Augsburg Cabinet in **Room 71**. There's more to this ebony-and-ivory masterpiece than meets the eye. You'd never know it (which is the idea), but the cabinet contains a bevy of hidden drawers and cubbyholes. Five medicine canisters and 22 drug-related utensils were once secreted away in the compartments. Move through Rooms 66 and 65 to **Room 64** for a hidden gem that is a favorite of the curator. Unlike many of its contemporaries, the French chest of drawers from 1770 features large drawers that would actually hold things, as well as delicate floral inlays. Imagine keeping your yearly change of underwear in that (that's right – way back in the olden days people only changed underwear once a year).

Exit the Rice Building and take a well-deserved rest on the benches in **Room 150**, facing the azure windows donated to Chicago in 1977 by artist Marc Chagall to honor both America's bicentennial and Mayor Richard J Daley, who had only recently died.

Right: Edward Hopper's *Nighthawks*, 1942 (Room 244)

Walk to the right of the stained glass and enter **Room 159**, which highlights American art completed after 1901. Gifford Beal's *Puff of Smoke* (1912) captures the raw power and destruction that industry rapidly

brought to the US. Continue to **Room 157**. One of the best-preserved works of its kind, the Ayala altarpiece dates from 1396 and shows the kind of vanity art popular in the 14th century, with members of the commissioning Spanish family from Castille making guest appearances in scenes from the life of Jesus.

Through the windows you can see the shady McKinlock Court Garden, with fountains and a café serving above-average food. A jazz band performs on Tuesday evening, which makes this one of the classiest places in town for a casual date.

Continue around the courtyard in Rooms 156 through 153, which house various ancient arts from Egypt, Greece, and Southeast Asia. Many guidebooks urge you to make a detour at **Room 153** to see the Chicago Stock Exchange Trading Room, which dates from 1893–94. This admittedly spectacular space is almost all that survives of its namesake building, demolished in 1972 despite its status as one of the most significant buildings in the city. Displaying this fragment of a willfully destroyed masterpiece is, to me, akin to putting the heart of a dead person in a jar and displaying it because the person 'had a good heart.' There's something ghoulish about the whole thing.

An exquisite collection of Indian and Asian art starts in **Room 152**. The 12th-century granite Buddha looks like it's about to come to life, thanks to the skill of the Tamil carvers.

Proceed back around to Room 150 and the stairs leading up to the 2nd level, where a procession of masterworks begins. **Room 246** holds a changing display of Picassos from the Art Institute's huge Picasso collection.

Next door, **Room 244** packs a lot of work into a small space. Here you'll see a painting that rivals the Mona Lisa for the number of times it has been bastardized by marketers: *American Gothic* (see page 126). Grant Wood's

Left: Georges Seurat's *A Sunday on La Grande Jatte – 1884*, 1884-1886 (Room 205)

1930 study of a fictional Iowa farm couple looks to Flemish Renaissance art for its formal composition. The image has been altered so many times that now even the real thing borders on self-parody, so take time to study the long faces Wood gave to the models: his sister and dentist.

Nearby, the exuberant nightclub studies by Archibald J Motley Jr provide a lively contrast to Wood's work. His *Nightlife* (1943) explodes in neon colors. And another icon hangs here as well: *Nighthawks* (see page 127), Edward Hopper's 1942 study of four isolated people in an anonymous diner, which has become one of the best-known images of 20th-century painting. Hopper said he wasn't trying to convey bleakness, but that 'unconsciously, probably, I was painting the loneliness of a large city.'

In **Room 243** take time to notice an interesting early Picasso work: the 1921 *Mother and Child*. In a fascinating twist Picasso altered the image to give the originally pictured father the boot. The kid isn't reaching for mom, but rather a fish that the father had been holding before he was eradicated from the picture.

Exit ahead, out Room 240, and cut to the left through Rooms 230 to 236. In **Room 237A**, you'll find a painting with all the subtlety of bathroom graffiti. All but the dimmest bulbs will get the symbolism of Salvador Dalí's 1930 *Anthropomorphic Tower*. The challenge: count the penises.

Work your way back to **Room 206**. The 'money room' for many visitors, this prime spot features a passel of Monets, including *Parliament* (1889), *Water Lilies* (1906) and six examples of his original 15 *Grainstacks*

Right: Gustave Caillebotte's *Paris Street: Rainy Day*, 1877 (Room 201)

©THE ART INSTITUTE OF CHICAGO

(1890–91). Often called *Haystacks* or *Wheatstacks*, these works depict symbols of sustenance and survival caught in nature's temporal cycle.

In **Room 205**, Georges Seurat practically anticipated the invention of process color printing with *A Sunday on La Grande Jatte – 1884* (see page 128), his painting of Parisians enjoying a day in the park. Consider the number of dots Seurat painted and you'll see why it took him awhile (from 1884 to 1886) to complete the sofa-size work in pointillist style. He spent six months in the park just sketching possible subjects.

At the center of this part of the museum (the Allerton Building), **Room 201** houses brooding paintings of Paris that convey more feeling than any photograph. Gustave Caillebotte's 1876–77 *Paris Street: Rainy Day* (see page 129) shows the artist's view of then-modern and bleak Paris. It moodily prefigures Seurat's work. Monet's 1877 *Arrival of the Normandy Train* is but one of 12 studies he did of this scene. In contrast to the bleak Paris streetscape, the luminous scene in Pierre Auguste Renoir's *Two Sisters (On the Terrace)* (1881) makes this work one of the all-time favorites of Art Institute patrons. But Mrs Potter Palmer, whose impressionist collection formed the basis of the museum's holdings, must have liked Renoir's *Jugglers at the Circus Fernando* (1878–79) even better: after she purchased it, she kept it with her at all times, even on trips, before it found a permanent home here.

Head down the hall past Rooms 226 through 223 to **Room 222**. This gallery shows the diversity of European painting in the 1800s before impressionism. Joseph Mallord William Turner conveys the insignificance of humans in the face of nature in *Fishing Boats with Hucksters Bargaining for Fish* (1837–38). Look at how he captured the roiling waves. Across the room, Alberto Pasini's 1880 *Cicassion Calvary* evokes strong emotion, and Constant Troyon shows his mastery with cattle in *The Road to Market* (1858).

Walk back through European art until you reach the 16th century in **Room 215**. Spanish master El Greco, who earned the named because of his Grecian birth, painted *Assumption of the Virgin* (1577) as his first major commission after arriving in Spain. The Virgin rises from her tomb and seems almost ready to burst from the canvas in an explosion of color. Match the holy men below her with the following emotions: awe, excitement, disbelief and confusion. The mounting was added by the Art Institute in 1987 to re-create the feel of the painting's original setting and possibly to keep Mary from heading right on up through the roof.

Return to the central stairs and descend to the point where your tour began, safe in the knowledge that with just several more hours you could see everything.

Chicago Cultural Center

Galleries, exhibitions, beautiful interior design and a permanent museum all make the block-long Chicago Cultural Center (☎ 312-346-3278, 78 E Washington St at N Michigan Ave; admission free; open 10am-7pm Mon-Wed, to 9pm Thur, to 6pm Fri, to 5pm Sat and 11am-5pm Sun), in the city's former main library, an interesting place to wander around. The exhibitions on three floors change frequently, so take a moment as you enter on either Randolph or Washington Sts to find out the schedule of events. The grand staircases at both of these entrances are works of art: the one on the Randolph side is decked out in pink marble and complex mosaics; the one on the Washington side is clad in white marble, and its classical lines appear to hang in space.

Excellent guided tours (☎ 312-742-1190; admission free; 1:15pm Tue-Sat) leave from the Randolph St lobby. Free lunchtime concerts take place on weekdays.

Inside the Chicago Cultural Center

RICHARD CUMMINS

Museum of Broadcast Communications

In the early days of television most shows were produced live at the individual stations rather than picked up from networks. Chicago enjoyed a long tradition of live programming that extended back through the radio era.

Filled with memories for many Chicagoans, this fascinating museum (☎ 312-629-6000, 1st floor, Chicago Cultural Center; admission free; open 10am-4:30pm Mon-Sat, noon-5pm Sun) takes a trip back to simpler days, before digital broadcasting and the proliferation of hundreds of channels.

The TV area displays clips of shows that bring wistful smiles to adults who grew up with Garfield Goose and Kukla, Fran and Ollie. Famous local moments are also replayed, including the Kennedy-Nixon debate of 1960, which many argue Nixon lost because on television his shifty eyes and heavy beard made him look like a crook. (Who says TV lies?)

Visitors can view tapes from a large library of shows. They can also pose as a newscaster on an old WGN set and buy a videotape of their sensational performance for $19.95.

For radio buffs, local stars Fibber McGee and Mollie, Edgar Bergen and Charlie McCarthy evoke that memorable era.

Gallery 37

A pet project of mayoral wife Maggie Daley, Gallery 37 (☎ 312-744-8925, www.gallery37.org, 66 E Randolph St; admission free; open varying hours) combines art galleries and performance spaces. You can

Bad-Weather Refuges

Some aspect of Chicago's weather that never turns up in tourist brochures rears its head – what do you do? Eventually, shopping, museums, eating, drinking and other indoor pursuits lose their charm. And you don't want to go back to the hotel room. If it was nice, you'd sit in the park, but the present storm makes that an untenable option. Here are two places where you can just hang out, catch your bearings and plan for your next adventure:

Chicago Cultural Center You can buy stamps at the main tourist office or explore a few galleries and museums at the Cultural Center (☎ 312-346-3278, 78 E Washington St at N Michigan Ave; admission free; open 10am-7pm Mon-Wed, to 9pm Thur, to 6pm Fri, to 5pm Sat and 11am-5pm Sun; Map 3). But best of all is the large area inside the Randolph St entrance, where you can relax on comfortable chairs, write post cards at tables or stare at the wall. An outlet of the Corner Bakery provides battery-recharging refreshments.

Harold Washington Library Center Within this vast building (☎ 312-542-7279, 400 S State St; open 9am-7pm Mon-Thur, 9am-5pm Fri & Sat, 1pm-5pm Sun; Map 3) you'll find a good ground-floor coffee bar, scores of nooks and crannies where you can kick back and more books than you can count. Floors 3 through 8 feature quiet sitting areas along the exterior walls. Some of the alcoves contain windows and tables. The 9th-floor winter garden boasts even comfier chairs, but you can't take any library books there – which may be the point.

browse works by local artists or attend plays, poetry readings, music performances and even cooking demonstrations.

Ellen Lanyon Murals

Sixteen murals have been placed along the walkway on the south bank of the Chicago River where it crosses under the west side of Lake Shore Dr. Produced by artist Ellen Lanyon, the large panels depict the history of the river.

GRANT PARK (Maps 3 & 4)

After Montgomery Ward saved the marsh that was to become Grant Park from developers (see the boxed text 'The Man Who Saved the Lakefront'), the Olmsted Brothers architecture firm published plans for the park, which they hoped to model on the formal lines of Versailles. Executing the plan would take more than 20 years. It was completed just in time for the 1933-34 Century of Progress exposition, on the lakefront near where Soldier Field and McCormick Place are today.

Over the years the park, often called 'Chicago's front yard,' has suffered depriva-

tions more befitting a back yard. Through much of the 20th century, commissioners bowing to the tyranny of the auto allowed Lake Shore Dr, Columbus Dr and Congress Parkway to be developed into major thoroughfares, robbing the park of many of its best open areas. (Every year the huge Taste of Chicago festival closes Columbus Dr and Congress for two weeks, and the world doesn't come to an end.)

Somnolent care from the Chicago Park District saw the entire place give way to weeds, dead trees and other neglect. The sad situation changed dramatically in the early 1990s, when Soldier Field won its bid to host the opening ceremonies for the 1994 World Cup. Realizing that thousands of impressionable visitors would stroll through Grant Park on their way to the stadium, the city began an ambitious program to spruce up the place.

Hundreds of new trees have since been planted, sidewalks have been replaced and Buckingham Fountain has been repaired. Now looking much better, Grant Park makes an excellent place both to visit and to travel through on your way to and from the Museum Campus.

Buckingham Fountain

Kate Sturges Buckingham, a very wealthy widow, gave this magnificent fountain *(10am-11pm daily May 1-Oct 1)* to the city in 1927 in memory of her brother, Clarence. She also wisely left an endowment to maintain and operate the fountain.

It's twice the size of its model, the Bassin de Latone at Versailles. The central fountain is meant to symbolize Lake Michigan, with the four water-spouting sea creatures representing the surrounding states. The fountain presents a subtle show rather than randomly spraying its 1.5 million gallons. Like so much in life, the spray begins small. Each successive basin fills, stimulating more jets. At the climax the central fountain spurts up to its full 150 feet. The crowd sighs in awe and is thankful that smoking is allowed. The fountain climaxes once an hour, and mood lighting (colored lights timed to match the fountain's 'moods') comes on at 8pm; the best time to experience the full melodic effect is 9pm.

At the four corners of the gravel expanse that surrounds the fountain, pavilions have toilets and sell refreshments.

Wildflower Works

Up until 200 years ago, much of the land in northern Illinois was prairie, a vast undulating expanse that bloomed with a rainbow of wildflowers through the growing season. Early settlers who crossed it said it was like sailing in an ocean of color.

With farming and development, this delicate ecosystem died out, as nonnative plants muscled their way into the region. In 1985 artist Chapman Kelly received permission to plant 1.5 acres near the Daley Bicentennial Plaza with native wildflowers. With a team of dedicated volunteers, Kelly found seeds for the long-forgotten plants. Often the volunteers had to go to rural rail lines, where land between the tracks had been left alone, to harvest seeds.

The first few years were difficult for the group – the wildflowers were laggards when it came to germination and would have perished had invading wind-borne seedlings not been uprooted by hand. It was very hard work. I was a volunteer then and crawled around picking out weed seedlings about the size of a bean sprout. The toughest part was differentiating between the good and

The nightly light show at Buckingham Fountain

bad plants. I'm afraid that in my zones the slaughter might have been indiscriminate.

More than 15 years later, the Illinois wildflowers are much better established. Their scores of seeds and root systems make outside invasion much more difficult. From April through October a constantly changing panoply of flowers in all shapes and sizes takes its turn on Kelly's stage. Take some time here to wander around, listen to the bumblebees and imagine the flowers in front of you stretching as far as the eye can see.

Statues

Edward Kemeys' bronze **lions** have become Chicago icons since they began flanking the entrance to the Art Institute in 1894.

Augustus Saint-Gaudens' **'Sitting Lincoln,'** Chicago's second sculpture of Abraham Lincoln, the 16th US president, contrasts with the artist's more animated study in Lincoln Park. In this 1908 statue President Lincoln shows the isolation of his office as he sits alone in a chair.

Architect Daniel Burnham's observation that no one had ever personified the Great Lakes inspired Lorado Taft to create *Fountain of the Great Lakes*, a large bronze work, in 1913. Partially hidden by surrounding shrubs, it's worth seeking out. Here's the artist's description of what the five conchshell-holding women are up to: 'Superior on high and Michigan on the side both empty into the basin of Huron, who sends the stream to Erie, whence Ontario receives it and looks wistfully after.' This progression duplicates that of the Great Lakes.

The Bowman and the Spearman by Ivan Mestrovic consists of two 17-foot-high bronze figures of Native Americans. Both created in 1923, they symbolize the struggle between Indians and whites as the latter moved west and settled there. Mestrovic depicted the figures in the act of using their weapons, which are left to the imagination of the viewer. Originally much closer together, they were separated by the 1956 intrusion of Congress Parkway, which destroyed the grand steps that once led to a plaza beyond.

The *Theodore Thomas Memorial* shows a 15-foot bronze woman straddling a globe and listening to a chord on her lyre. This 1923 work by Albin Polasek honors the founder of the Chicago Symphony Orchestra.

The famous British sculptor Henry Moore created *Large Interior Form*, a bronze form suggesting the human figure, in 1983.

Trees

Replanting is restoring the diversity of native and imported trees that once grew in the park. The following species are listed in ascending order of size; the original designers of the park intended for the trees to become gradually larger as the rows progressed away from open spaces.

The small flowering crab apples blossom throughout May and are later covered with fruit.

One of Chicago's best-known residents guards the Art Institute.

The Man Who Saved the Lakefront

When Chicagoans frolic at the lakefront's vast expanse of beaches and parks, they should thank Montgomery Ward, founder of the department stores bearing his name, who led an impassioned crusade to save the shore from development.

For two decades beginning in 1890, Ward invested a good chunk of his fortune in legal battles to block various projects that would have used a little bit of the shoreline here and a little bit there until all that would have separated the city from the lake was a wall of buildings. Although he was up against the three forces that have shaped the city – greed, power and corruption – Ward steadfastly defended Chicago's original charter, which stipulated that the lakefront should remain 'forever open, clear and free.' Although his many critics thought of him as a populist dilettante, Ward saw the parks as a 'breathing spot' for the city's teeming masses.

After Ward's death in 1913, many others continued fighting for his cause. They had their work cut out for them, as a steady stream of politicians viewed developing the empty real estate of the lakefront and beaches as 'progress.' For example, during the 1960s Mayor Richard J Daley and his cronies hatched schemes that would have put huge overpasses and cloverleaves at both Oak St Beach and 57th St Beach. Fortunately, both schemes died after massive protest.

The one major loss of lakefront occurred in the 1950s, when the *Chicago Tribune* decided it wanted a mammoth convention center on the lake. McCormick Place is named after its sponsor, Colonel Robert R McCormick, editor of the *Tribune*, who used his newspaper to get the complex built on 34 acres of lakefront property, far from hotels and transportation.

As for Ward's own business, his legacy was less lasting. In 2000, after decades of mismanagement, Montgomery Ward ceased operations and closed all of its stores.

The small, thorny hawthorns that flower in May are native to the area. Honey locusts, another native species, are used to line streets because they seem impervious to salt, dogs, barbecue embers and other urban hazards.

When the park was built, its designers planted elms, long considered the most graceful of shade trees. More than 75% of the original 3000 elms have died from Dutch elm disease. Their replacements are hybrid American elms – less graceful but much more resilient.

Other Sights

The **Stock Exchange Arch** is a relic amputated from the great building when it was demolished in 1972. The *AIA Guide to Chicago* calls it the 'Wailing Wall of Chicago's preservation movement.'

The park's **Rose Gardens** contain 150 varieties best viewed from mid-June to September.

To watch Chicagoans at a favorite pastime, stop by **Hutchinson Field**, where

scores of amateur league softball games are played each summer.

In warm-weather months, visitors can play a set at Grant Park's tennis courts. In winter they can skate at **Daley Bicentennial Plaza** (see the Activities section at the end of the chapter for more information).

NEAR NORTH (Map 3)

An assortment of warehouses, factories and association headquarters once filled the area west of N Michigan Ave between the river and Chicago Ave – until the 1970s. After that the neighborhood rapidly changed. The grimy old users were sent packing and were replaced by galleries, trendy shops, hotels and the highest concentration of restaurants in the city.

Near North, a generic term for the area north of the river, includes several distinct neighborhoods. River North, west of State St, stretches north of the river to Chicago Ave and contains the River North Gallery District, where art galleries have taken

Holy Cow!

In June 1999 a herd of 300-plus life-size fiberglass cows hit the streets of Chicago. The bovines were bolted into sidewalks through the Loop and Near North area and soon struck some chord in a city where millions of cows once met their deaths in the old stockyards. Each of the plastic-horned critters sported a unique look courtesy of a local artist or designer. Chicagoans embraced the cows, and by the end of the summer the livestock impersonators had become a major tourist attraction.

The success of this stunt presented city officials with a new problem: how to top it. In 2000 the city's Office of Special Events placed Ping-Pong tables all over the city – a marginally successful effort at best. In 2001 the office came up with Suite Home Chicago, a scheme to place plastic versions of living room furniture, such as sofas, all over the Loop and Near North. Like the cows, the pieces would be decorated by various artists. However, compared to a cow, a plastic ottoman lacks that *je ne sais quoi*. What will the city try in 2002 and beyond? Stay tuned. Some wags have suggested that ubiquitous city critter, the rat.

RICHARD CUMMINS

over renovated warehouses in the area around Superior and Huron Sts and near the El tracks (see the Shopping chapter for details).

East of State St you'll find the upscale shopping heaven of N Michigan Ave, known as the Magnificent Mile (see the Shopping chapter for details). The area east of Michigan Ave is called Streeterville in honor of one of the city's great characters, George Wellington Streeter. A skipper who would have been at home on *Gilligan's Island*, Streeter and his wife were sailing past Chicago in the 1880s, purportedly on their way from Milwaukee to the Caribbean (!) when they ran aground on a sandbar near what is today Chicago Ave and Lake Shore Dr. Streeter built a little causeway to the mainland and convinced developers to dump excavated dirt on the site. Soon the area had grown to several acres, and Streeter seceded from the city and Illinois.

Not surprisingly, the city was not impressed. Various efforts to evict Streeter and a band of loyal squatters who had joined him ended in fiasco. The entire matter was finally laid to rest in the courts in 1918. Streeter lost. Today Streeterville contains some of Chicago's most valuable property, much of it home to hotels, expensive high-rise condos and offices. The River East Center is being built on several blocks east of Columbus Dr along Grand Ave. The huge project will include hotels, movie theaters and the requisite shops.

The blocks surrounding Ohio and Ontario Sts west of Michigan Ave have become an increasingly notorious zone filled with theme restaurants and nightclubs. During the weekends and all summer long the sidewalks crawl with Chicagoans and out-of-towners visiting the place of the moment and usually leaving with a bulging stomach and an even more bulging bag from a gift store. A city spokesperson has compared the area to Las Vegas and Disney World.

The Hard Rock Cafe and the Rock & Roll McDonald's opened their doors in the mid-1980s – now the area is exploding with development, as entertainment conglomerates race to establish themselves. Disney built a high-tech theme park called DisneyQuest across Rush St from the block-square Marriott and installed an ESPN sports bar nearby, all part of the infamous North Bridge project, an overdeveloped and poorly designed complex.

As the economy has boomed and living in the city has become widely fashionable, concrete high-rise apartments and condos have shot up throughout the Near North like bamboo in the spring. Few have any architectural merit at all.

River Esplanade

Beginning with the oddly proportioned curving staircase at the northeast tower of the Michigan Ave Bridge, this carefully detailed walkway extends east along the river past the Sheraton Hotel. The views of the river are great, the only sour note being the multilevel roadways at Illinois Center.

Where the sidewalk meets McClurg Court, **Centennial Fountain** burbles away peacefully for most of the hour. But on the hour, from 10am to 2pm and again from 5pm to midnight, it shoots a massive arc of water across the river for 10 minutes. The entire exercise commemorates the reversal of the Chicago River in 1900, which prevented sewage from flowing into the lake, where it was sucked into the intake pipes that supplied the city with water.

As the neighborhood east of here rapidly develops, plans call for the esplanade to be extended past Lake Shore Dr to Navy Pier.

Navy Pier

From 1918 to 1930, Navy Pier (☎ *312-595-7437, www.navypier.com, 600 E Grand Ave; admission free; see the later paragraphs of this section for the complex hours)*, more

Sunrise over the Chicago River

ANDRE JENNY

than half a mile long, served as the city's municipal wharf. Later it was the first home of the University of Illinois at Chicago. During the 1970s and '80s it languished like a dead 800lb gorilla: huge, difficult to dispose of and with no obvious use.

After Mayor Daley was elected in 1989, plans that had been drawn up by his rich political ally John Schmidt were quickly enacted. Some $200 million in public funds later, the entire length of the pier had been massively rebuilt into a combination amusement park, meeting center and food court. The result has proven to be a hit, with more than 7 million people trekking out to the pier each year. Many of them come to the exposition space that covers half the pier; it's managed in conjunction with McCormick Place (see the Near South Side section, later).

A visit here can easily consume half a day, much of it spent wandering the great length of the pier. Grab a free map at the entrance to navigate. The views from the very end are excellent, and there's no charge just to wander around or get wet in the fountains. However, costs can mount perilously if you start taking advantage of the amusements, boat tours, souvenir stands and restaurants.

From May through September, the pier is open 10am to 10pm Monday to Thursday, 10am to midnight Friday and Saturday, 10am to 9pm Sunday; from October through April it's open 10am to 9pm Monday to Thursday, 10am to 10pm Friday and Saturday, 10am to 7pm Sunday. Note that individual restaurants and attractions may have different hours.

The pier is about a 15-minute walk from Michigan Ave. To get to Navy Pier by car, take the Grand Ave exit from Lake Shore Dr. There's parking on the pier itself and in lots to the west. A free shuttle trolley runs daily between the pier and the Grand Ave El stop on the CTA Red Line. It departs about every 20 minutes from 10am to 11pm.

Among CTA buses, the No 29 State provides the most frequent service. It runs on State St through the Loop until it takes a right on Illinois in River North. The No 56 Milwaukee runs from Milwaukee Ave, past the Richard B Ogilvie Transportation Center (formerly called Northwestern Station) and on through the Loop to Navy Pier.

The lakefront bike path goes right past the entrance. In the summer Shoreline Sightseeing (☎ 312-222-9328) runs a water taxi between Navy Pier, the river near the Sears Tower and the Shedd Aquarium.

Chicago Children's Museum The target audience of this attraction (☎ 312-527-1000, www.chichildrensmuseum.org; admission $6.50, free Thur after 5pm; open 10am-5pm Tues, Wed & Fri-Sun, until 8pm Thur) will love the place. Designed to challenge the imaginations of kids ages one through 12, the colorful and lively museum near the main entrance to Navy Pier includes numerous politically correct exhibits.

The Stinking Truth about Garbage takes kids on a trip to an imaginary landfill and impresses on them the virtues of recycling. The Grandparents exhibit teaches kids to love guess who (it's evidently assumed that the immediate older generation is beyond redemption) in a family-tree-building game. Dinosaur Expedition explores the world of paleontology.

An exhibit with a game-show motif, Face to Face teaches the young ones how not to grow up to be jerks by cautioning against prejudice and discrimination. Designing your own flight of fancy is the goal at the build-your-own-airplane Inventing Lab. Other exhibits let kids get wet just when they've finally dried out from the Navy Pier fountains.

Other Sights The 150-foot **Ferris wheel** ($3 per ride) moves at a snail's pace, but that's good for enjoying the views. Not so good is the insipid piped-in narration that reminds you that McDonald's sponsors the ride. The **merry-go-round** ($2) is a classic, with bobbing carved horses and organ music.

A variety of acts appears through the summer at the **Skyline Stage** (☎ 312-595-7437), a 1500-seat rooftop venue with a glistening white canopy. See the Entertainment chapter for details on the IMAX Theater and the Chicago Shakespeare Theater.

Some of Navy Pier's free amusements include the **fountains** at the entrance to the

MARK E GIBSON

Survey Chicago from the top of the Ferris wheel at Navy Pier.

pier. It's as much fun to watch the cavorting kids as the fountain itself; scores of water jets squirt at unpredictable intervals, and everyone's encouraged to get wet. The upper-level Crystal Gardens fountains feature delightful water jets that appear out of nowhere and lazily arc over the heads of the unsuspecting.

If you're looking for further diversions, a flotilla of competing **tour boats** lines the dock. For the skinny on what's available, see the Organized Tours section of the Getting Around chapter for details.

The front of the main building contains numerous **shops**, most of which sell the kind of nonsensical knickknacks that fill closets for decades.

Shops at North Bridge

This vast new retail complex that stretches west of N Michigan Ave along Grand Ave and Illinois St is the work of developer John Buck. Home to shops, hotels, a Nordstrom department store and various restaurants, it has had a huge impact on the area – and not all for the good. In fact, *Sun-Times* architecture critic Lee Bey likened the complex to a

bomb, calling the Shops at North Bridge mall and the Nordstorm building 'Fat Man and Little Boy.'

DisneyQuest (*☎ 312-222-1300, 55 E Ohio St; admission $26 for unlimited play, $10 for limited play; open 11am-10pm daily)* is like a video arcade that's gone, well, Disney. Five floors of virtual reality games simulate everything from fantasy settings to roller coasters. Open since 1998, this portion of the North Bridge complex is showing signs of waning popularity; admission prices have been falling.

Terra Museum of American Art

Amid the commercial confines of the Mag Mile, this modest little museum (*☎ 312-664-3939, 666 N Michigan Ave; admission $7/3.50 for adults/children, free Tue & 1st Sun of month; open 10am-8pm Tue, 10am-6pm Wed-Sat, noon-5pm Sun)* displays an overview of American art since 1800. Founded by Daniel J Terra, a self-made millionaire, the museum has its own custom-built stairway and entrance building, though the galleries occupy a renovated space next door.

The collection includes lesser works by Winslow Homer, James Whistler, John Singer Sargent, Mary Cassatt and others, including a passel of works by Andrew Wyeth. Special exhibitions focus on American artists at work abroad and at home.

In 2000 the museum became embroiled in controversy after Terra's widow Judith announced she wished to move it to Washington, DC.

Holy Name Cathedral

It's ironic that in a town with so many grandiose churches, the Chicago Archdiocese would call this modest Gothic church home (☎ 312-787-8040, 735 N State St; admission free; open 7am-7pm daily). It's even more ironic when you consider that the archdiocese has had to close some of its most beautiful churches because of declining membership in some parishes.

Built in 1875 to a design by the unheralded Patrick Keeley, the cathedral has twice been remodeled in attempts to spruce it up. The latter effort in fact covered up bullet holes left over from a Capone-era hit across the street (see the boxed text 'Capone's Chicago' in the Facts about Chicago chapter).

The cathedral does provide a quiet place for contemplation, unless the excellent choirs are practicing, in which case it's an entertaining respite. Open most of the day, it holds frequent services.

Other Sights

Not the living kind but life-size nonetheless, **whales** cavort on the east wall of the Hotel Inter-Continental Chicago (505 N Michigan Ave), part of a mural unveiled in 1997. The 25-story painting was done by Wyland, a one-named artist whose paintings of marine life have made him a millionaire many

Gaze at the Loop...

times over. The Chicago mural is his 73rd in a series of 100 he is donating worldwide.

The **Floor Clock** takes up part of a city block. Its hands – the minute hand is 20 feet long – run on tires as they make timely cruises past gigantic numbers. The best way to appreciate this work by Vito Acconci is from a room at the Sheraton, where you can look down on the spectacle. The clock is on the block bounded by Columbus Dr and E Illinois, E North Water and N New Sts; it's east of the NBC Tower and north of the Sheraton Hotel.

Colonel Robert McCormick, eccentric owner of the *Chicago Tribune*, collected – and asked his overworked reporters to send – rocks from famous buildings and monuments around the world. These are now implanted all around the base of the **Tribune Tower** *(435 N Michigan Ave)*. See how many of the 138 you recognize. In 1999

the Tribune added a moon rock brought back by the Apollo 15 mission. It's on display in the lobby 24 hours a day. In the lobby you'll also find a rack of good brochures describing the rocks outside.

With all the appeal of an aluminum can, the headquarters of the ***Chicago Sun-Times*** *(401 N Wabash Ave)*, the most-read paper in the city, does not lure admirers, but it does boast a nice outdoor plaza, which overlooks the river and the Loop skyline from the east side of the building. Trees, lawns you can sit on and many, many benches make this a wonderful spot to rest your weary dogs on a decent day. A branch of the ubiquitous McDonald's and a small grocery store provide sustenance.

Designed by Japanese architect Kenzo Tange and opened in 1990, the headquarters of the **American Medical Association** *(515 N State St)* is proof that all that glitters is not gold. Managerial miscues and blunders have

RICK GERHARTER

...from Grant Park.

RICK GERHARTER

Tribune Tower (foreground)

Tigerman's parking garage at 60 E Lake St in the Loop looks like an old Bentley.

Built during the World's Columbian Exposition in 1893, the fascinating **Tree Studios** were designed to encourage artists to remain in Chicago (but a condo conversion today is driving them away). Check out the very well-preserved facade, on the east side of State St between Ontario and Ohio Sts. The most interesting details are hidden from the street: huge greenhouse windows on the back of the building, overlooking a lovely enclosed courtyard.

Behind the Tree Studios and facing Wabash Ave, the **Medinah Temple** was built in 1913 by the Shriners, who chose a flamboyant Moorish design for their festival hall. However, both the temple and the Tree Studios were threatened in the late 1990s by rapacious developers coveting their locations. After an outcry from preservationists in 2000, a typically Chicago deal was cut: the facades and courtyard were preserved but developers were allowed to transform the loft-

helped drive membership in the association to record lows. Now fewer than 40% of American doctors belong.

Note the distinctive four-story cutout at the top of the building's profile and then consider that upon the building's opening, employees were told that the hole would help them find the building. This conjured visions of AMA staffers dopily wandering the city, asking: 'Have you seen the building with the hole?'

Stanley Tigerman, the architect of the **Anti-Cruelty Society building** *(159 W Grand Ave)*, is known for his witty creations. He meant for the facade facing LaSalle St to resemble a basset hound.

like art studios into expensive condos (bye-bye, artists). Meanwhile, the Medinah Temple's exterior survived, but developers converted the interior to – of all things – a Bloomingdale's furniture store.

Like the Loop, the Near North area contains a number of public sculptures. Commissioned by the tool and die industry, *Being Born* is a 1983 stainless steel sculpture by Virginio Ferrari. It symbolizes both precision, with its two fitted rings, and economic growth, with its open outer ring. Lots of Chicagoans have had the opportunity to contemplate this piece, for it sits at the confluence of Ohio and Ontario Sts where they meet the entrance to the Kennedy Expressway.

Artist Ginny Sykes' *Rora* symbolizes the Chicago River. The huge mosaic of glass tile has been installed where W Erie St meets the north branch of the Chicago River.

SOUTH LOOP (Map 4)
The South Loop resurged in the 1980s with the renovation of the Chicago Hilton & Towers, the success of the Dearborn Park and Central Station developments and the emergence of Printer's Row as a gentrified district of converted lofts. It continues to prosper as its vibrancy spreads south and the Museum Campus, to the east, draws more and more visitors.

Printer's Row
Chicago was a center for printing at the turn of the century, and the rows of buildings on Dearborn St from Congress Parkway south to Polk St housed the heart of the city's publishing industry. By the 1970s the printers had left for more economical quarters elsewhere, and the buildings largely emptied out, some of them barely making it on the feeble rents of obscure nonprofit groups.

In the late 1970s savvy developers saw the potential in these derelicts, and one of the most successful gentrification projects in Chicago began. Virtually every building turned into mid-price and luxury rentals and condos. The following describes some of the notable buildings if you're traveling from north to south.

A snazzy renovation of the **Mergenthaler Lofts** *(531 S Plymouth Court)*, the 1886 headquarters for the legendary linotype company, included the artful preservation of a diner storefront.

The **Pontiac Building** *(542 S Dearborn St)*, a classic 1891 design by Holabird & Roche, features the same flowing masonry surfaces as the firm's Monadnock Building, to the north.

A massive and once-windowless wreck, the 1911 **Transportation Building** *(600 S Dearborn St)* enjoyed a 1980 restoration that assured that the neighborhood had arrived.

The **Second Franklin Building** *(720 S Dearborn St)*, a 1912 factory, shows the history of printing in its tiled facade. The roof slopes to allow for a huge skylight over the top floor, where books were hand-bound, for this building existed long before fluorescent or high-intensity lamps did. The large windows on many of the other buildings in the area serve the same purpose.

Once the Chicago terminal of the Santa Fe Railroad, the 1885 **Dearborn St Station** *(47 W Polk St)* used to be the premier station for trains to and from California. Today it merely sees the trains of parent-propelled strollers from the Dearborn Park neighborhood, built on the site of the tracks to the south.

Museum of Contemporary Photography
Located in one of the many buildings of Columbia College, this museum *(☎ 312-663-5554, 600 S Michigan Ave; admission free; open 10am-5pm weekdays, until 8pm Thur, noon-5pm Sat)* focuses on American photography since 1959. Once primarily a venue for student work, it has won widespread support as the only institution of its kind between the coasts. The permanent collection includes the works of Debbie Fleming Caffery, Mark Klett, Catherine Wagner, Patrick Nagatoni and 500 more of the best photographers working today. Special exhibitions augment the rotating permanent collection.

Spertus Museum
An excellent small museum devoted to 5000 years of Jewish faith and culture, the Spertus *(☎ 312-922-9012, 618 S Michigan Ave; admission $5/3 for adults/children, free Fri; open 10am-5pm Sun-Wed, 10am-8pm Thur, 10am-3pm Fri)* boasts an equally excellent corps of volunteers. The museum's exhibits juxtapose aspects of Jewish life and religion to convey the diversity of both. The Zell Holocaust Memorial features oral histories from survivors who immigrated to Chicago, as well as the names of Chicagoans' relatives who died.

The museum mounts well-curated special exhibitions that cover topics as diverse as Biblical images in classic art and Jewish humor in the US. The basement is devoted to a children's area called the 'ArtiFact

Center,' where kids can conduct their own archeological dig for artifacts of Jewish life.

River City

Architect Bertrand Goldberg followed up his famous Marina City project 20 years later with the much less famous River City *(800 S Wells St)*. The undulating 1985 buildings reflect the course of the river and have their own marina. Plans to expand the development by a factor of 10 have yet to materialize – which is what you'd expect Captain Kirk to do in these futuristic confines.

MUSEUM CAMPUS (Map 4)

A recent Chicago creation, the Museum Campus brings together three museums devoted to land, sea and sky. The institutions have been around a long time, but until 1996, when the northbound lanes of Lake Shore Dr were moved west of Soldier Field, they've been separated from each other by a constant roar of traffic. People familiar with the old setup can only smile now, as they stroll from the Field Museum to the Shedd Aquarium and the Adler Plan-

etarium without fear of becoming a hood ornament on a speeding sedan.

A pedestrian underpass makes the campus either a 15-minute walk east from the Roosevelt El stops or a longer but very enjoyable sojourn through Grant Park and along the lakefront from the Loop. Alternatively, the CTA No 146 bus makes the run from N Michigan Ave and State St in the Loop. Parking is easy for a change, as the commodious lots around Soldier Field have plenty of room (except during Bears games and huge conventions).

Field Museum of Natural History

This old and storied research institution *(☎ 312-922-9410, www.fieldmuseum.org, 1400 S Lake Shore Dr; admission $8/4 for adults/children, some exhibits extra, free Wed; open 9am-5pm daily)* contains 20 million artifacts, including mummies, stuffed animals, Native American artifacts, and dinosaurs and more dinosaurs (especially one named Sue; see below). Only a small fraction of these (about 4%) is on display; the rest fills countless storage areas.

Free Days at Chicago Attractions

Here's an easy reference for saving on admission fees at Chicago attractions:

Adler Planetarium	Tuesday
Art Institute of Chicago	Tuesday
Chicago Academy of Sciences	Tuesday
Chicago Children's Museum	Thursday after 5pm
Chicago Historical Society	Monday
DuSable Museum of African American History	Sunday
Field Museum	Wednesday
Museum of Contemporary Art	Tuesday
Museum of Science & Industry	Thursday
Spertus Museum	Friday
Terra Museum of American Art	Tuesday and first Sunday of month

The following attractions are always free:

Chicago Cultural Center	Mexican Fine Arts Center Museum
International Museum of Surgical Science	Museum of Broadcast Communications
Jane Addams Hull House	Museum of Contemporary Photography
Lincoln Park Zoo	

One of the Field Museum's many permanent and changing exhibits

The museum has been doing an excellent job of replacing its musty exhibits with fascinating interactive ones over the past 20 years. (For an example of how things used to be, take a gander at the orderly rows of display cases in the Indians section, then flee.)

The Building Money for the building was donated by Marshall Field, who decreed that he wanted 'a grand museum of natural history.' Constructed on marshland from 1915 to 1921, the building features a 706-foot-long colonnaded facade of Georgia marble.

Entrances on the north and south sides lead to the dramatic 300-foot-long, two-story-high Stanley Field Hall. The scope becomes apparent when you see how small the life-size skeleton of the Brachiosaurus looks. And the two huge stuffed elephants look almost pint-size in the space, which is often used for gala benefit dinners. (Being seated at a table under the elephants' rumps is a sign that you definitely have not arrived.)

Most of the museum's displays radiate off the main floor of the hall or are on the floor overlooking the hall or in the basement below it. A simple deli and a McDonald's are in the basement.

The Collections The big – and I mean big – news at the Field involves a dinosaur named **Sue**. Specifically it's the most complete Tyrannosaurus rex ever discovered, standing 13 feet tall and stretching 41 feet long. Sue takes its name from Sue Hendrickson, the fossil hunter who found the 90%-complete skeleton in South Dakota in 1990. The Field paid more than $8 million for Sue, which explains why you see those logos for McDonald's and Disney, who helped foot the bill. The display is drawing record crowds to the museum.

The head honchos at the Field read *Variety* and know the business *Jurassic Park* did. That's why Sue is just one of many dinosaur-related exhibits. The permanent **Dinosaur Hall** contains a range of real and replica skeletons of the beasts who measure their age in the tens of millions. A Dino-Store sells anything that can possibly be linked to dinosaurs.

The other big news at the Field is actually quite small: **Underground Adventure**, a vast permanent exhibit that opened in 1999, explores the habitats of animals and insects that live underground.

An ambitious walk-through exhibit on **Africa** attempts to capture the scope of the continent by taking visitors from the streets of Dakar to Saharan sand dunes. You'll explore aspects of life in the bush before the path leads through the hold of a slave ship, with its grim shackles and collars.

A clever blend of the fanciful with a large amount of Field artifacts, the **Inside Ancient Egypt** exhibit re-creates an Egyptian burial chamber on three levels. The mastaba (tomb) contains 23 actual mummies and is a reconstruction of the one built for Unis-ankh, the son of the last pharaoh of the Fifth Dynasty, who died at age 21 in 2407 BC. The bottom level, with its twisting caverns, is especially cool. The reeds growing in the stream are real.

One of the first exhibit areas to open after the Field adopted a more user-friendly approach – but before the museum got clever with its names – the well-thought-out **Maritime Peoples of the Arctic & Northwest Coast** combines life-size models and dioramas showing the precarious lives of the people native to the far north.

Other displays worth your time include Gems, Plants of the World, Traveling the Pacific and Messages from the Wilderness, an exhibit showing the perils of pollution and extinction.

Visiting the Field can cause extinction of even the most burning enthusiasm. The oversize rooms seem deceptively manageable. Just trying to navigate the Life Over Time exhibit will take the better part of a day if you try to absorb all the details, and it will certainly feel like a lifetime. At the west end of the 1st floor, the Rice Wildlife Research Station is a refuge where you can sit on comfortable chairs while you sort out your Albertosaurus from your Parasaurolophus.

Few feet, especially little ones, can hope to survive a visit dedicated to seeing every last Maori bead and stuffed marmot. Use the cheerfully distributed maps to find your favorite spots.

Shedd Aquarium

The world's largest assortment of finned, gilled, amphibious and other aquatic creatures swims within the marble-clad confines of the John G Shedd Aquarium (☎ 312-939-2438, www.shedd.org, 1200 Lake Shore Dr; admission $15/11 for adults/children, 30% discount for Chicago residents; open 9am-5pm weekdays, until 6pm weekends).

Most of the 8000 species represented live in fairly small tanks that pale in comparison to the flashy, shark-infested aquariums in other cities. However, the Shedd has created a spectacular draw, the controversial Oceanarium (see The Collections, below).

The Building The original 1929 building houses 200 tanks in a compact octagonal shape. Patterns of waves and shells repeat throughout the building's details, both large and small. Note Neptune's trident atop the dome. The 1991 Oceanarium is a spectacular space where the huge mammal pools seem to blend into the lake outside the floor-to-ceiling windows.

The Shedd is an easy place to navigate. The original building is compact, and displays radiate from the coral reef tank. In addition to the exhibits mentioned below, the premises also include a food court and sit-down restaurant, both of which often get mobbed at lunchtime.

The Collections The aquarium has made a commitment to change its tanks in the original building from those you might find in an upscale dentist's office to miniature ecosystems where fish swim amid the plants and bugs that they'd be hanging with in the wild.

The large new exhibit **Amazon Rising: Seasons of the River** opened in 2000. It traces the world's longest river through its many twists, turns, environments and seasons. Besides an array of authentic flora, the exhibit features such fauna as piranhas, stingrays, birds and sloths (my favorite – what a life!).

Long popular, the centrally located 90,000-gallon **coral reef** tank got an overhaul in 1998 and holds 500 tropical fish, from placid nurse sharks to less-neighborly moray eels. The water swirls create a current. Divers frequently pay visits with food to keep some of the more cannibalistic residents content.

Among the highlights in the darkened **galleries** of the original building, by gallery number, are (1) colorful Caribbean fish, (2) even more colorful warm-water Pacific fish, (3) a recently built northwest Pacific tidal-surge zone, (4) playful river otters, (5) a 50-year-old snapping turtle that comes up for air once an hour, and (6) well-fed piranhas and a river ecosystem from Thailand that no longer exists in the wild. In the same gallery, check out the employees' favorite fish, a wonderfully homely 60-year-old Australian lungfish.

With its huge windows and seemingly seamless transition to the lake beyond, the multilevel **Oceanarium** seeks to replicate the northwest coast of North America through real and fake foliage, geographic features and some native inhabitants. The most controversial residents are the five beluga whales. Two of the four 1200lb adults were plucked from their Arctic homes and brought to Chicago, while the other two adults are on loan from a museum in Washington; the fifth whale was born to great acclaim at the Shedd in 1999. All get to exhibit 'natural behavior' in return for fish. Ethics of their capture aside, they are remarkably cute creatures that come from the pint-size end of the whale scale. Their humped heads and natural 'smiles' make them look eerily human. You'll also see

Pacific white-sided dolphins, harbor seals, sea otters and penguins (which come from the Southern Hemisphere, but let's not quibble, okay?). Don't linger only on the main floor – you can go underneath the cement seats and watch the mammals from below through viewing windows. You need to buy a separate ticket for the Oceanarium; to reserve the best Oceanarium times, call ☎ 312-559-0200.

A large new exhibit devoted to the Indo-Pacific is slated to open in 2002. A long, long overdue exhibit devoted to Lake Michigan and Illinois rivers (some would have thought those would be priorities, given the Shedd's location) will open sometime thereafter.

Shedd Aquarium

Adler Planetarium

The Adler Planetarium & Astronomy Museum (☎ *312-922-7827, adlerplanetarium .org, at the end of Solidarity Dr; admission $5/4 for adults/children, free Tue; open 9am-5pm weekdays, 9am-5pm weekends*) has seen visitor numbers soar since a large new addition opened in 1998.

To see the sky, you head underground. From the entrance to the Adler, visitors descend below the 1930 building, which has 12 sides, one for each sign of the zodiac. The 60,000-sq-foot addition enjoys great views that take advantage of the museum's lakefront location and includes the requisite café and gift shops.

In the new wing a digital sky show re-creates such cataclysmic phenomena as supernovas. Interactive exhibits allow you to simulate cosmic events such as a meteor hitting the earth (this one is especially cool).

The original planetarium does a good job planning special events around celestial occurrences, be they eclipses or NASA missions. In the Sky Theater a mechanical Zeiss projector can create huge varieties of nighttime sky effects.

The Adler staff comes up with new shows every year. Some of the memorable efforts include 'African Skies,' which showed how various stellar observations influenced folktales on the continent. Each year at Christmas the Adler re-creates the heavens as they would have looked at the time of the birth of Jesus, which allows visitors to search for scientific answers to such legends as the Star of Bethlehem.

The Adler does a commendable job of involving visitors in astronomy, with live video links to various telescopes around the world and research facilities that are totally accessible to visitors. The sky-show programs last about 50 minutes. The whole place can be easily covered in less than two hours. A cafeteria serves all the usual stomach-filling burgers, sandwiches and such.

Other Sights

The stretch of grass on the lake between the Shedd and the Adler may be the setting for more amateur and postcard photos than any other place. One look toward the skyline will show you why: the view is good year-round; on clear days in winter, when the lake partially freezes and steam rises off

RICHARD CUMMINS

The Adler aglow

the buildings in the Loop, it verges on the sensational.

Near the entrance to the Adler, a 12-foot **sundial** by Henry Moore is dedicated to the golden years of astronomy, from 1930 to 1980, when so many fundamental discoveries were made using the first generation of huge telescopes. About 100 yards west in the median, the **bronze statue** of 16th-century Polish astronomer Nicolaus Copernicus shows him holding a compass and a model of the solar system. Near the western end of the median, the *Thaddeus Kosciusko Memorial* honors the Polish general who fought on the winning side of the American Revolution and then returned to help his nation's fight for freedom. The last two monuments inspired the city to rename the street Solidarity Dr in 1980 to honor the Lech Walesa–led movement in Poland.

Near the Field the city has installed **Olmec Head No 8**. Over 7 feet tall, it's a copy of one of the many amazing stone carvings done by the Olmec people more than 3500 years ago in what is now the Veracruz state of Mexico. No one has been able to figure out how the Olmec carved the hard volcanic rock.

The huge hulk to the south of the Field Museum is **Soldier Field**. Built from 1922 to 1926, the oft-renovated edifice is in line for a huge $600 million reconstruction.

The planes overhead come from nearby **Meigs Field**, used almost exclusively by corporate jets, commuter flights to and from Springfield for politicians and lobbyists and the occasional pilot-tourist. Mayor Richard M Daley has attempted to close the airfield to convert it into a park, but the state bureaucrats who like the airfield's proximity to the Loop have successfully kept it open.

The **Burnham Park yacht harbor** completes this increasingly bucolic picture. During the summer people work in the Loop by day and sleep on their moored sailboats by night.

NEAR SOUTH SIDE (Map 4)

One hundred years ago, the best and worst of Chicago lived side by side south of the Loop. Near the lake around Prairie Ave, the top millionaires of the day, such as Marshall Field and George Pullman, lived on 'Millionaire's Row,' between 16th St and 20th St (now called Cullerton).

In contrast, four blocks to the west was the Levee District, an infamous area known for its saloons, brothels, opium dens and virtually any other vice that money could buy. With four major train stations near the neighborhood, Chicago became the sin capital of the Midwest. Legend has it that the 'Mickey Finn' knockout cocktail was invented here when the first of generations of conventioneers came to Chicago itching for fun and left with merely an itch.

Corrupt politicians ran the ward. 'Bathhouse' John Coughlin and Michael 'Hinky Dink' Kenna staged annual Levee District orgies that attracted scores of politicians, business leaders and police. The bacchanalia lasted for days. Eventually this drunken spectacle became too much even for the city government, and the area became a warehouse district. Meanwhile, the crooked politicians took their vices to City Hall, where they began the long Chicago government tradition of shakedowns and kickbacks.

A taste of the district's past returned in the late 1920s, when Al Capone set up shop at the Lexington Hotel, at the corner of Michigan Ave and Cermak Rd. This location achieved fame again in 1986, when pompous talk-show host Geraldo Rivera opened a supposedly 'secret' vault on live TV and discovered nothing.

Today the entire area is undergoing a renaissance. The Dearborn Park neighborhood has become home to 15,000 people on the site of the old Santa Fe rail yards, running south from Polk St to 15th St. The Central Station neighborhood is being built on the old Illinois Central yards east of Michigan Ave and south of Roosevelt Rd. Mayor Daley caused a minor uproar when he moved here in 1994 from his traditional Bridgeport home. The once musty warehouses are fast becoming lofts, and trendy restaurants and businesses are beginning to move into the area.

The Roosevelt El stops on the CTA Red and Green Lines serve the north end of the neighborhood. Otherwise, the No 3 King Dr bus starts at the intersection of Chicago Ave and N Michigan Ave and stays on Michigan all the way south to Roosevelt, where it shifts one block east to Indiana Ave and covers the length of the neighborhood. The area is improving, but the streets can be quite bleak and empty at night.

Prairie Ave Historic District

By 1900 Chicago's crème de la crème had had enough of the scum de la scum over in the Levee. Potter Palmer led a procession of millionaires north to new mansions on the Gold Coast. The once-pristine neighborhood, which lined Prairie Ave for two blocks south of 18th St, fell into quick decline as one mansion after another gave way to warehouses and industry.

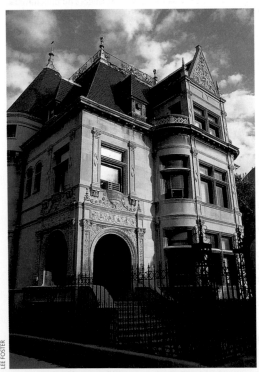

LEE FOSTER

One of the grand homes in the Prairie District

In 1966 the Chicago Architecture Foundation was formed to save the Glessner House and other survivors from demolition. The area's fortunes slowly improved thereafter, accelerating in recent years. Streets have been closed off, making the neighborhood a good place for a stroll. A footbridge over the train tracks links the area to Burnham Park and the Museum Campus.

John J Glessner House The Glessner House (☎ 312-326-1480, 1800 S Prairie Ave; tours $11/9 for adults/children, free Wed; open for tours at noon, 1pm & 2pm Wed-Sun) is the premier survivor of the neighborhood. Famed American architect Henry Hobson Richardson took full advantage of the corner site for this beautiful composition of rusticated granite. The classic, arched motif over the doorways invites a third and fourth look. A recent exterior cleaning has helped the overall effect.

Built from 1885 to 1887, the L-shaped house, which surrounds a sunny southern courtyard, got a hundred-year jump on the modern craze for interior courtyards. Much of the home's interior looks like an English manor house, with heavy wooden beams and details. More than 80% of the current furnishings are authentic, thanks to the Glessner family's penchant for family photos. The Glessners lived in the house for more than 50 years and by every indication loved every minute of it.

Tours of the Glessner House include the nearby Clarke House.

Henry B Clarke House When Caroline and Henry Clarke built this imposing Greek Revival home in 1836, log cabins were still the rage in Chicago residential architecture. Constructed on what were then sand dunes, the Clarke House (1855 S Indiana Ave; same hours, admission as Glessner

House) was considered a country home far from downtown. Now it's the oldest structure in the city. The sturdy frame paid off, because during the past 160 years the house has been moved twice to escape demolition. The present address is about as close as researchers can get to its somewhat undefined original location.

The interior has been restored to the period of the Clarkes' occupation until 1872. The tall, narrow windows make the simple rooms bright and airy. The children enjoyed a bed made to look like a sleigh. Other period toys dot the rooms. Given what the area looked like when the house was constructed, one expects to see a sand pail and shovel as well.

Other Historic Homes Generally, you can't visit the following houses, but you still can admire them from the outside. Modeled after 15th-century French chateaus, the **William K Kimball House** *(1801 S Prairie Ave)* dates from 1890 to 1892. Sadly, this former home of an organ maker can't help looking like a French postcard in comparison to the Glessner House, across the street.

The **Joseph G Coleman House** *(1811 S Prairie Ave)* exhibits a more restrained Romanesque style than the Kimball House. Limestone puts a glitzy facade on the brick **Elbridge G Keith House** *(1900 S Prairie Ave)*, an early 1870 home that is now home to a 1st-floor art gallery. A house restorer looking for a huge challenge can find a life's work at the remains of the **Marshall Field Jr House** *(1919 S Prairie Ave)*. The hulking structure used to be a 44-room mansion; it awaits a few million dollars and months of work.

Hillary Rodham Clinton Women's Park Fronting on Prairie Ave, with the Glessner House to the north and the Clarke House to the west, the 4-acre park is named for former first lady, now US Senator Hillary Rodham Clinton, who grew up in suburban Park Ridge and calls herself a lifelong Cubs fan (though that slipped her mind when she also pledged her loyalty to both the Mets and the Yankees in her successful bid to become a New York senator).

Although dedicated in 1997, now little more than some fer and uncleared rubble from demo sions. Plans to turn it into a public space honoring Chicago's women seem to have faded since Hillary decided to run for senator in New York, rather than her native Illinois.

Now subject to an inauspicious future, the park already has a notorious past. The Fort Dearborn massacre, in which some Native Americans rebelled against the incursion of white settlers, is thought to have occurred on this very spot in August 15, 1812.

Second Presbyterian Church Designed by James Renwick, the architect of St Patrick's Cathedral in New York and Washington, DC's, original Smithsonian Institution building, the 1874 church *(☎ 312-225-4951, 1936 S Michigan Ave; call for hours)* is a neo-Gothic limestone celebration accented by Tiffany stained glass.

Vietnam Veterans Art Museum Opened in 1996, the National Vietnam Veterans Art Museum *(☎ 312-326-0270, 1801 S Indiana Ave; admission $5/4 for adults/children; open 11am-6pm Tues-Fri, 10am-5pm Sat, noon-5pm Sun)* displays the art of Americans who served in the military during the Vietnam war. Spread over three floors in an old commercial building, it features a large and growing collection of haunting, angry, mournful and powerful works by veterans.

Cleveland Wright's *We Regret to Inform You* is a heartbreaking look at a mother in her kitchen at the moment she learns of her son's death. Ned Broderick's *VC Suspect* shows the bleak future of a prisoner. Joseph Fornelli's sculpture *Dressed to Kill* comments on the role of the average grunt in Vietnam. Some 58,000 dog tags hang from the ceiling, a haunting reminder of the Americans who died in the war. A small café here serves snacks.

Willie Dixon's Blues Heaven

From 1957 to 1967, this humble building *(☎ 312-808-1286, 2120 S Michigan Ave; admission varies; open noon-2pm Mon-Sat or call for an appointment)* was Chess Records, a temple of blues and a spawning ground of rock and roll. The Chess brothers, two Polish Jews, ran the recording studio that saw – and heard – the likes of Muddy Waters, Bo Diddley, Koko Taylor and others. Chuck Berry recorded four top 10 singles here, and the Rolling Stones named a song '2120 S Michigan Ave' after a recording session at this spot in 1964. (Rock trivia buffs know that the Stones named themselves after the Muddy Waters song 'Rolling Stone.')

Today the building belongs to Willie Dixon's Blues Heaven, a nonprofit group set up by the late musician to promote blues and preserve its legacy. A gift store is open in front, while the old studios are upstairs. There are many artifacts on hand as well. More often than not visitors will meet Shirli Dixon Nelson, the daughter of Willie Dixon, the blues great who recorded often at the studios. During the summer occasional concerts happen in the open space next door to the building.

McCORMICK PLACE (Map 4)

Called the 'mistake on the lake' for its prime location in Burnham Park, the McCormick Place convention center (☎ 312-791-7000) is an economic engine that drives up profits for the city's hotels, restaurants, shops and airlines. 'Vast' isn't big enough to describe it, nor 'huge,' and 'enormous' doesn't work, so settle for whatever word describes the biggest thing you've ever seen. The 2.2 million sq feet of meeting space spreads out over three halls.

The East Building (now called Lakeside Center) interrupts the sweep of the lakefront. The oldest part of today's complex, it was completed to replace the original fireproof McCormick Place, which burned down in 1967. The *Chicago Tribune* played a disgraceful role in the original building's construction, with its owner Col Robert R McCormick using all of his hefty political weight to get it built on the lake. (Politicians who opposed the project were threatened with investigative stories.)

RICK GERHARTER

McCormick Place

The North Building, a barn of a place, accrued huge cost overruns during its construction in 1986. The newest addition, the South Building, was finished in 1997. The best of the lot, it features the Grand Concourse, a bright and airy hall linking all the buildings.

In a place this big, any of the four million people who visit annually can get lost easily. The distances and the scale of the halls combine to make you feel as small as a bug. Escaping the place for a stroll along the lake or north to the Museum Campus is a challenge. When I tried that in both 1997 and 1998, several employees were stumped at how to get out of the complex. I finally found an escape but only after hours spent wandering endless and windowless carpeted halls.

Here's how to flee: Go to Level Two of the Lakeside Center (the East Building) and proceed north to the 'Burnham Park Parking' exit. You'll emerge in a small park overlooking the yacht harbor; the museums are a 15-minute walk north.

Conventioneers have whined about the quality and prices of food and drink at McCormick Place for decades. There's no reason to stop now. I ate a $3 cookie before setting off to find the lakeside exit. It stunk.

The Chicago Convention and Tourism Bureau handles all convention and show questions at ☎ 312-567-8500.

It's easy to get a cab to McCormick Place but much harder to get one leaving at, say, 5pm, when everyone is trying to catch a ride. The scene can get quite chaotic. Try arranging a Share-a-Ride for $5 a person. A great insider's tip is the 23rd St Metra train station, hidden in the lowest level of the North Building. You won't see many signs, so ask for directions at the information booths. Trains to and from the Randolph St and Van Buren St Stations, in the Loop, stop often during rush hour. Midday Monday through Saturday, they depart from Randolph St at 20 minutes past the hour and take 7 minutes to reach McCormick Place. On Sunday the trains run about every 90 minutes. The fare is $1.75.

Parking can be a hike from the buildings and is expensive. If you're hoofing it, the pleasant walk from Michigan Ave and the river through Grant Park and the Museum Campus is a little over 3 miles. The main entrance to McCormick Place now lies on Martin Luther King Jr Dr, just north of the Stevenson Expressway.

CHINATOWN (Map 4)

To experience the full charm of Chinatown, wander its streets and browse in its many varied small shops, especially in the retail heart of the neighborhood, on Wentworth Ave south of Cermak Rd. Other interesting parts include Cermak itself and Archer Ave just to the north. The neighborhood is one of the city's most vibrant, and its affluent residents are developing land in all directions even as more immigrants continue to arrive.

The Cermak-Chinatown El stop on the CTA Red Line is just to the east of the action. East of the stop itself is a dicey area dominated by a housing project. But the busy streets of Chinatown itself tend to be safe.

The **On Leong Building** (2216 S Wentworth Ave) once housed various neighborhood service organizations and some illegal gambling operations that have led to spectacular police raids. It now houses the Chinese Merchants Association. Built in 1928 and also known as the Pui Tak Center, the grand structure is a fantasy of Chinese architecture that makes good use of glazed terra-cotta details. Note how the lions guarding the door have twisted their heads so they don't have to risk bad luck by turning their backs to each other.

On much of the rest of Wentworth you'll find a blend of typical Chicago and Chinese architecture. The characteristic arch near Cermak was added in the 1970s. The continually growing **Chinatown Square** (Archer Ave at Cermak Rd) dates from 1992 and combines ground-floor shops with upper-level apartments for their owners.

GOLD COAST (Map 5)

In 1882 Potter and Bertha Palmer were the power couple of Chicago. His web of businesses included the city's best hotel and a huge general merchandise store later sold

Chinatown's On Leong Building

to a clerk named Marshall Field. When they relocated from Prairie Ave north to a crenelated castle of a mansion at what's now 1350 N Lake Shore Dr, the Palmers set off a lemminglike rush of Chicago's wealthy to the neighborhood around them. Showing the kind of shrewd judgment that had made him a millionaire, Palmer purchased much of what later became the Gold Coast *before* he moved there. He later subdivided his land and quadrupled his money.

Development centered on Astor St, and within 40 years most of the plots were covered with grand mansions. After WWII, surging demand for lake-view apartments led to the wholesale slaughter of mansions

on Lake Shore Dr; in their place some of the most hideous high-rises in Chicago went up and quickly filled. As the wave of construction threatened to move inland, preservationists managed to save most of the blocks from development, although the occasional 1960s high-rise draws attention to the bankrupt aesthetic values of that era. Today most of the district has been placed on the National Register of Historic Places.

While the area east of Clark St prospered, the area west became a notorious slum known as Little Hell. European immigrants who arrived in the 19th century were later joined in the tenements by blacks from the South. After WWII, two projects dramatically altered Little Hell's future: the city cleared the slums west of Orleans and built the Cabrini-Green housing project. The first units constructed were simple two-story townhouses, but in the late 1950s, because of budget woes, 15 high-rises from seven to 19 stories high were built. Meanwhile, just to the east, a huge middle-class development known as Sandburg Village mixed townhouses and high-rises on the blocks between LaSalle and Clark Sts north of Division St.

Little did anybody know, the latter would prove an effective lure for young college-educated professionals. Soon demand for space spread to Old Town and Lincoln Park, two neighborhoods that were in tatters. Some urbanologists have gone so far as to say that Sandburg Village saved the North Side of Chicago, because it proved there was demand for inner-city housing among the middle class at a time when developers were bulldozing cornfields and carving out suburbs as quickly as they could.

The lesson of the Cabrini-Green projects, however, has been unremittingly grim.

Rundown and crime-ridden, they are the legacy of a Chicago Housing Authority (CHA) that, until Harold Washington's election in 1983, was controlled by whites with little regard for black tenants. Instead of being affordable homes for the working poor, they became warehouses for the chronically underemployed and unemployed. Single mothers – the vast majority of CHA households are headed by single women – found it impossible to supervise their kids playing 15 stories away. Gangs soon took over many of the buildings.

By the early 1990s the CHA had given up on these projects; the agency is now slowly demolishing the high-rises. Many of them have been empty for years, illegally populated by drug dealers and gangs. With gentrification now encroaching on all sides, developers are visibly licking their chops at the prospect of covering the land with expensive townhouses. The city, desirous of the tax revenue, is sending the poor residents to live in other parts of town.

A visit to Cabrini-Green, which runs east of Orleans St and north of Chicago Ave, is a bad idea day or night. Sniper gunfire regularly rings out in a place that's as much a Little Hell now as it was 100 years ago.

Water Tower

It's hard to believe that the 154-foot Water Tower *(806 N Michigan Ave)*, a city icon and focal point of the Mag Mile, once dwarfed all the buildings around it. Built in the late 1860s, the Water Tower and its associated building, the Pumping Station across the street, were constructed with local yellow limestone in a Gothic style popular at the time. This stone construction and lack of flammable interiors saved them in 1871, when the great Chicago fire roared through town.

The complex was obsolete by 1906, and only concerted public outcry saved it from demolition three times. Whether Oscar Wilde would have joined the preservationists is open for debate: when he visited Chicago in 1881, he called the Water Tower 'a castellated monstrosity with salt and pepper boxes stuck all over it.' Yet by 1883 his attitude had somewhat softened: 'It was not until I had seen the water-works at

The prosperous Gold Coast

RICK GERHARTER

Chicago that I realized the wonders of machinery; the rise and fall of the steel rods, the symmetrical motion of the great wheels is the most beautiful rhythmic thing I have ever seen.'

A major restoration in 1962 ensured the tower's survival. It is surrounded by a pleasant park. The Pumping Station houses the tourist office.

Museum of Contemporary Art

The MCA (☎ *312-280-2660, www.mcachicago .org, 220 E Chicago Ave; admission $8/5 for adults/children, free Tues; open 10am-8pm Tues, 10am-5pm Wed-Sun)* has prospered since its new building opened in 1996. Visits have increased substantially, and the museum now has four times more space for exhibits than it did in its old location in a converted

bakery. Though it began as a second-rate facility with a limited catalog, the MCA is rapidly building its permanent collection with works by major artists and promising lesser names.

This museum generally believes that 'modern art' covers works since 1945. The permanent collection includes art by Franz Kline, René Magritte, Cindy Sherman and Andy Warhol, with displays arranged to show the gradual blurring of the boundaries between painting, photography, sculpture, video and other media. The MCA also mounts large special exhibitions, among them one devoted to the brilliant desert photos of Richard Misrach.

Anyone who has ever found themselves staring at some noted modern work and wondering what the hell it is will appreciate the copious curator's notes that accompany the exhibits. For instance, wall panels give maximum explanation of artistic movements such as minimalism.

Designed by Berlin architect Josef Paul Kleihues, the MCA's boxy building and its imposing entry stairs have been likened to the works of Albert Speer, Adolf Hitler's architect. You decide.

The metallic exterior panel is designed to age to a sort of dull gray. Inside, things get brighter. A curving staircase on the north side of the building presents an invitation few can refuse. On the top floor you'll find four galleries with soaring, barrel-vaulted, skylit roofs. Puck's at the MCA, a café overlooking Lake Michigan, attracts crowds with its fine views of the sculpture garden and lake beyond, as well as its creative food. See the Places to Eat chapter for details.

Tours, included with the cost of admission, take place

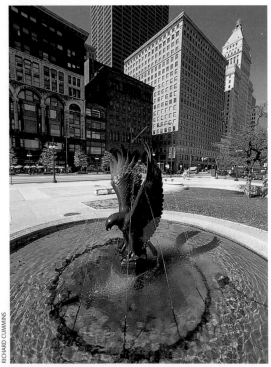

RICHARD CUMMINS

The eagle has landed on Michigan Ave.

at 1pm Tuesday to Sunday, with an additional tour at 6pm Tuesday.

860–880 N Lake Shore Dr

The International Style of high-rises got its start here. Built from 1949 to 1951, the twin towers were the manifestation of designs that architect Mies van der Rohe first put forward in 1921. The idea of high-rises draped only in a curtain of glass and steel was so radical at the time that psychologists speculated about the impact of living in a transparent home.

When the buildings opened, few guessed how easily Mies' precepts would be bastardized by legions of untalented architects. The aesthetic nightmares just up the road are immediate examples. How their bone-headed architects managed to screw up Mies' design tenets is remarkable.

John Hancock Center

The world's tallest 'mixed-use' building (meaning that it contains both residential and commercial space), the Hancock *(875 N Michigan Ave)* is the third-tallest building in Chicago, at 1127 feet. A remodeling of the plaza below street level has added a nifty fountain whose curtain of water muffles traffic noise above.

Much less popular than the Sears Tower's Skydeck, the **John Hancock Observatory** *(☎ 312-751-3681, admission $8.50/6 for adults/children; open 9am-midnight)* benefits from having shorter lines and no sappy film. The friendly employees guide you to the fast – 23 mph – elevators for the 40-second ride to the 94th floor. In many ways the view here surpasses the one at the Sears, because from the Hancock you can see the Sears and appreciate just how tall it is compared to the rest of the Loop skyline.

Another plus at the Hancock is the screened, outdoor area that lets you listen in on the sounds of the city. When you're that far above the street, there's something almost lyrical about the dull roar of traffic punctuated by jackhammers, sirens and the like.

Look for some of the clever details built into the waiting area, which evoke the original Hancock construction site. Hint: one of the workers didn't like pickles.

Fourth Presbyterian Church

This 1914 church *(☎ 312-787-4570, 126 E Chestnut St at Michigan Ave)* belongs to one of the city's wealthiest congregations. It brings to mind a bunch of dons in some old Gothic school guzzling port and eyeing the choirboys. Lurid fantasies aside, the church provides a welcome break from the commercial blocks and offers a reminder of the not-so-long-ago times when low-rise mansions dominated the neighborhood. Occasional organ recitals take place in the splendid sanctuary.

Washington Square

A center of 1855's beer riots (see the 'Beer Riots' boxed text in the Entertainment chapter), this rather plain park across from the Newberry Library has had a colorful and tragic history. In the 1920s it was known as 'Bughouse Square' because of the communists, socialists, anarchists and other -ists who gave soapbox orations here.

In the 1970s, when it was a gathering place for young male prostitutes, it gained tragic infamy as the preferred pickup spot of mass-murderer John Wayne Gacy. Gacy took his victims back to his suburban home, where he killed them and buried their bodies in the basement. Convicted on 33 counts of murder (although the actual tally may be higher), he was executed in 1994.

Delaware Place and Walton, Clark and Dearborn Sts border the park.

Astor St

This street of mansions has retained the grandeur lost to high-rises elsewhere. For a quick idea of what Lake Shore Dr once looked like, trot over to the lake and check out Nos 1250, 1254 and 1258. All three narrowly averted the fate of their brethren.

Astor St is lined with gems; take your time strolling and be sure to note the following standouts.

Originally four, now three, the 1887 homes at **Nos 1308-1312** feature a lovely sculptured quality that extends to the turrets, gables and dormers. The architect, John Wellborn Root, was so pleased with his efforts that he moved into **No 1310**.

Once one home, now several apartments, the 1887 mansion at **No 1355** represents the full flower of Georgian revival. Note the alternating skulls and animal heads above the windows.

While he was still working for Louis Sullivan, Frank Lloyd Wright designed the large but only 11-room **Charnley-Persky House** (☎ 312-573-1365, 1365 N Astor St) and he proclaimed with his soon-to-be-trademarked bombast that it was the 'first modern building.' Now home to the National Society of Architectural Historians, the house is sometimes open for tours. Call for times and prices.

A late arrival on the street, the 1929 **Russell House** (1444 N Astor St) is art deco French at its most refined.

The 1880 mansion that serves as the **Archbishop's Residence** (1555 N State St) spans the entire block to Astor. Built in the Queen Anne style that later became known generically as 'Victorian,' this comfortable place looks like it would provide solace to any archbishop pondering the sins of the flock.

Other Notable Buildings

Walking south from State St and North Ave, look for the following buildings.

French elegance came to Chicago in a manner as humble as Napolean's ego with the 1912 apartment house at **1550 N State St**, which once boasted a mere one unit per floor.

The sexual revolution perhaps started in the basement 'grotto' of the otherwise unremarkable 1899 mansion at **1340 N State**, which belonged to *Playboy* impresario Hugh Hefner in the 1960s and '70s. Later a dorm for the School of the Art Institute (imagine the pickup lines!), it was gutted in 1993 and turned into four very staid but very expensive condos.

Built in 1919 in a flamboyant Gothic style, the stunning **Archbishop Quigley Preparatory Seminary** (☎ 312-787-8625, 831 N Rush St; admission free; open 11am-3pm Mon-Sat May-Sept, noon-2pm other times) holds the magnificent Chapel of St James, which was ambitiously modeled after Sainte-Chapelle in Paris. With 45,000 panes of glass in its impressive windows, it comes close to the original. Local choral groups often perform in the chapel, a recommended and ennobling treat.

The **St Benedict Flats** (42-50 E Chicago Ave) offer an unusual glimpse of French Second Empire architecture. I once lived here briefly. I hope my millions of roach roommates were eradicated during a complete renovation that saw the place turned into condos.

International Museum of Surgical Science

Home to an eclectic collection of surgery-related items, the Museum of Surgical Science (☎ 312-642-6502, 1524 N Lake Shore Dr; admission free; open 10am-4pm Tue-Sat) features such a poorly marked assortment of medical items that at first the museum seems like nothing more than a place to escape a vicious lake squall. But start exploring and you'll soon be rewarded with fascinating thematic displays, such as the one on bloodletting, the act of bleeding patients to death to 'cure' them. The undeniable gems of the collection are the 'stones,' as in 'kidney stone,' 'gallstone,' etc. All of the spectacularly large specimens were passed by patients who may have wished instead for a good bloodletting.

OLD TOWN (Map 6)

This once-simple neighborhood of wood houses was one of the first in the city to gentrify in the 1960s. The original artist residents, with plenty of late 1960s inspiration, made the neighborhood Chicago's funky hippie hangout; the requisite string of head shops once lined Wells St.

Today the only haze over Wells St comes from cigar-puffing swells at the many swank restaurants of Old Town, now one of the city's most affluent neighborhoods. The old wood houses have been fixed up and modified in ways their builders never would have imagined. But those are the lucky ones; many other simple old homes have been demolished by greedy owners whose replacement houses fill the lots to bursting in all their extravagance.

Wells St north of Division St is safe, although the neighborhood to the west calls for caution. North of North Ave and west of Wells St, you'll find a jumble of narrow streets that are perfect for wandering. Also try the area bordered by North Ave, Wells St, Lincoln Ave, Armitage Ave and Larrabee St – a safe spot filled with surprises.

The facades of the 1890 vintage apartments of **Crilly Court**, a single block off Eugenie St, are charming stone variations of Queen Anne architecture, but the real surprise is the back of the units, which line a private alley between St Paul Ave and Eugenie St. These have wrought-iron porches right out of the French Quarter in New Orleans.

The **Henry Meyer House** (*1802 N Lincoln Park West*) offers a rare glimpse at how Chicago's houses looked before the 1871 fire. This one was built right afterward – the flames roared through here – but just before the arrival of laws that banned wood structures in the area devastated by the fire.

The **Frederick Wacker House** (*1838 N Lincoln Park West*) is another wooden example built during the same brief window of opportunity as the Meyer House. Imagine whole blocks of these homes and you'll start to get an idea of the horror of the fire.

LINCOLN PARK (Map 6)

Chicago's most popular neighborhood stays alive day and night, with people in-line skating, walking dogs, pushing strollers and driving in circles for hours looking for a place to park. The humble origins of most of the blocks away from the lake have been lost under the waves of renovation and gentrification that began in the mid-1970s. Notable highlights are few, but the entire neighborhood, which stretches roughly from North Ave north along the lake to Diversey Parkway and west to Clybourn and Ashland Aves, makes a pleasant place for a stroll. See the Places to Eat, Entertainment and Shopping chapters for more about the area's attractions.

Gentrified Old Town

RICK GERHARTER

Lincoln Park Proper

The neighborhood gets its name from this park, Chicago's largest. Its 1200 acres stretch for 6 miles, from North Ave north to Diversey Parkway, where it narrows along the lake and continues until the end of Lake Shore Dr. The park's many lakes, trails and paths make it an excellent place for recreation. Cross-country skiing in the winter and sunbathing in warmer months are just two of the activities Chicagoans enjoy in Lincoln Park. Many buy picnic vittles from the markets on Clark St and Diversey Parkway.

Most of Lincoln Park's pleasures are natural. Some of the highlights include the following. (For major sights, see separate headings, later.)

In contrast to his 'Sitting Lincoln' in Grant Park, sculptor Augustus Saint-Gaudens in his

John Dillinger

Unlike Al Capone, John Dillinger wasn't part of Chicago's criminal mobs. He was a bank robber whose daring exploits throughout the Midwest made him a celebrity. Many Midwestern towns contain a bank once robbed by Dillinger. Despite being on the FBI's 10 Most Wanted List, the wily criminal managed to evade police time and time again. The following example comes from William J Helmer, Chicago gangster expert and co-author of *Dillinger: The Untold Story*:

Dillinger didn't confine his thrill-seeking to robbing Midwestern banks. During his leisure time, the Chicago resident liked the thrills of the rides at the old River View Amusement Park at Belmont and Western Avenues. While partaking of these pleasures on a spring day in 1934, Dillinger was alarmed when suddenly all the power to the park was shut off and patrons told to leave through one exit. Fearing he'd been recognized by the police, the 31-year-old robber ran up to a woman who was loudly complaining about the shutdown and said, 'Hey, they've got Dillinger trapped by the roller coaster.' The woman began screaming this news about Chicago's most wanted criminal. In the ensuing hubbub, Dillinger slipped past the waiting police and into an unattended police car. Roaring out the gates of the park, he encountered more cops and yelled, 'Hey they got Dillinger, I'm going for reinforcements.' Making good his escape, he ditched the car and vanished.

It was later that year, on July 22, that Dillinger was betrayed by the infamous 'lady in red' and gunned down by the FBI outside the Biograph Theater (2433 N Lincoln Ave; Map 6) in Lincoln Park.

'Standing Lincoln' shows the 16th president deep in contemplation right before he delivers a great speech. Saint-Gaudens based the work on casts made of Lincoln's face and hands while Lincoln was alive. The statue stands in its own garden east of the Chicago Historical Society.

Near the southeast corner of LaSalle Dr and Clark St, the **Couch Mausoleum** is the sole reminder of the land's pre-1864 use: the entire area was a municipal cemetery. Many of the graves contained hundreds of dead prisoners from Camp Douglas, a horrific prisoner-of-war stockade on the city's South Side during the Civil War. Trying to move all the bodies proved a greater undertaking then the city could stomach, and today if you start digging at the south end of the park you're liable to make some ghoulish discoveries.

From a little dock in front of pretty **Cafe Brauer**, a 1908 Prairie School architectural creation, you can rent two-person **paddleboats** and cruise the South Pond, south of the zoo. A more bucolic cruise can be had

on the North Pond, which doesn't have the zoo crowds; rent boats from the little boathouse east of where Deming Place meets the park. The rental season at both ponds is roughly May through September.

Chicago Historical Society

The history of the Lincolns, Capones, Daleys and other notables gets some attention here, but this well-funded museum (☎ *312-642-4600, www.chicagohistory.org, 1601 N Clark St; admission $5/3, free Mon; open 9:30am-4:30pm Mon-Sat, noon-5pm Sun*) focuses on the average person. The role of the commoner in the American Revolution sets the tone for the humanistic exhibits. One, titled Fort Dearborn and Frontier Chicago, shows how settlers and Indians changed each other's lives. The Pioneer Court offers hands-on demonstrations in the intricacies of making candles, weaving blankets and knitting clothes. None of the work was easy.

Much of the 2nd floor is devoted to Chicago's development and history, with

RICHARD CUMMINS

Inside the Lincoln Park Conservatory

displays that explore the roles of immigration and industry, as well as the problems of slums and the lives of the rich. Special exhibitions – the museum's strong point – cover such diverse topics as how bungalows allowed almost every family to afford a home, and Chicago's role in the birth of gospel music.

The Big Shoulders Cafe serves soups and sandwiches. The bookstore is excellent.

Lincoln Park Zoo

The zoo (☎ 312-742-2000, www.lpzoo.com, 2200 N Cannon Dr; admission free; open 9am-5pm daily, until 7pm May-Sept) is one of Chicago's most popular attractions not just because of the free admission but also because of its wide range of exhibits, which feature 1600 animals on a compact 35-acre setting. Founded in 1868, the zoo enjoys considerable community support. Wealthy patrons, including Joan Kroc, wife of McDonald's founder Ray Kroc, have donated millions of dollars over the last three decades to renovate old facilities and build new ones.

CTA buses Nos 22, 36, 146 and 151 all pass close to the zoo. Parking is among the worst in the city. Crowds are a problem on sunny weekends, but during colder months a visit can be an almost intimate experience. Food options have improved greatly in recent years, with good cafés both inside and out.

You can easily reach the zoo from most parts of the park; there are entrances to it on all sides. The following tour starts at the main, west entrance on N Cannon Dr and proceeds around the zoo in a clockwise direction. Free maps of the zoo are readily available.

Once inside you encounter the crowd-pleasing antics of the sea lions, which frolic day and night. Especially at night: I once lived across the street and can attest to their boisterous antics in the wee hours.

Walking Tour Take a trip to Antarctica at the **Penguin/Seabird House**. Eighteen penguins from three species stoically stare out from their refrigerated quarters. The big ones are kings.

Turn left as you leave and follow your nose to the **Joseph Regenstein Large Mammal Area**. You'd normally find the elephants, giraffes and the like here, but because the building is undergoing a major reconstruction until 2003, all the animals have moved to other zoos for the duration. Just east of the construction, you'll find the **polar bear exhibit**. The two huge white beasts spend much of the summer in their pool. To see them at their best, drop by in January.

From here, head south past the exhibit of the other bears, which seem to be in year-round hibernation. The **McCormick Bird House**, the next stop on the tour, can be one of the most rewarding exhibits at the zoo, but you have to work at it. Visitors in a hurry won't see a majority of the species on display, because it takes time to locate the birds among the natural foliage in the 10 habitat areas.

Contrary to popular belief, not all birds sit in trees; many spend their lives wandering the ground. For example, the cape

RICK GERHARTER

You can lead a kid to water – and make him drink – at the Lincoln Park Zoo.

thick-knee, a relative of the roadrunner, stalks about in the savanna exhibit. In the tropical river area, look for the green imperial pigeon, whose gold neck feathers stand up during breeding.

Opened in 1997, the glass-domed **Regenstein Small Mammal–Reptile House** houses scores of beady-eyed rodents, amphibians and other critters. The curving walkway snakes through open and glassed-in areas designed to give the animals a natural habitat while offering visitors a close look. Among the highlights: huge monitor lizards, Galapagos turtles, naked mole rats, fruit bats and spiders. (Arachnophobes beware!) Everybody comes to see the koalas but nobody sees much: the Australian tree-huggers are about as active as your teddy bears at home.

As you continue on the tour, skirt the lion house for now and continue south. Renovated in the early 1990s, the **Helen V Branch Primate House** has come a long way from its earlier days, when the animals were kept in sterile cages. To get a feeling for what it might have been like for them, sit in the metal seat of Bushman the gorilla (dead since 1951 and stuffed at the Field Museum) and stare out through the bars. The crowd-pleasers here are the white-faced gibbons, which like to come right up to the glass to inspect visitors. Also look for two small holes in the big stump in the lemur area. They're part of a system that releases termites into the exhibit for the animals to track down and eat.

The zoo has been a world leader in gorilla breeding, with more than three dozen born here since 1970. Two distinct family groups of gorillas live in the **Lester E Fisher Great Ape House**. A smaller chimp population also calls this house home. All the primates enjoy private areas far from the prying eyes of Homo sapiens.

Rather than walking quickly through this circular building, derisively comparing the primates' behavior to those of relatives, stop and watch their complex interactions as family groups. The facial expressions and eyes of the animals show such a range of emotions that it's almost eerie. Look for 350lb Frank. In the past 18 years he has adopted almost a dozen baby gorillas into his family – behavior that's rare for his species. Although gorillas tend to be good parents, it's not uncommon for mothers to abandon a baby or, worse, for lead males to kill the infants of young females joining the group. Another stellar ape is Debbie, who has helped raise several infants.

If you're lucky, the chimpanzees will be drawing on poster board with crayons. Some of their works have been shown in galleries.

Walk past the hoofed-animals area toward the small pond. Continue around until you see the apocryphal vision of an Illinois farm, south past Cafe Brauer. **Farm in the Zoo**, the place where many urbanites first learn that milk comes from cows instead of cardboard containers, features a full range of barnyard animals in a faux farm setting just south of the zoo. Frequent demonstrations of cow milking, horse grooming, butter churning and other chores take place. The exhibits don't make any bones about the ultimate fate of most livestock. For instance, those cute piglets head to the slaughterhouse only four to six months after birth.

From the farm, head back north past the flamingo pond toward the roar of the big cats. Lions and tigers receive their grub at various intervals throughout the day at the **Kovler Lion House**, where you won't find any posted feeding times. Watching a 600lb Siberian tiger devour a hunk of horse meat is an eye-opening experience. Also note the white spots on the back of the tiger's ears; they're the signals baby tigers use to follow their mothers through grasslands.

Once you've had enough of these scary beasts, revisit the kinder, gentler sea lions and veer left to the low-slung brown building. At the **Pritzker Children's Zoo** kids can cuddle the usual lineup of furry creatures, such as guinea pigs, or catch a glimpse of their young animal counterparts in the zoo's nursery, behind a glass wall. Although visitors thrill at the sight of baby animals in cribs, zoo keepers don't. Animals end up in the nursery only if the natural parents haven't been able to care for them.

Other Sights Just north of the zoo are two other worthy sights that keep the same hours. Near the zoo's north entrance, off Stockton Dr, is the **Lincoln Park Conservatory** (☎ 312-742-7736), two gardens first planted in 1891; these bloom year-round under three acres of glass. The 1887 statue *Storks at Play*, outside the conservatory, has enchanted generations of Chicagoans.

The stone walls of the **Zoo Rookery**, created in 1937, resemble the stratified canyons of the Wisconsin Dells. When not overrun with people, the Rookery makes a magical setting, especially in winter. Planted with native Midwestern species, it's at the north end of the zoo near Fullerton Ave.

Chicago Academy of Sciences

Always a snoozer, this museum slumbered for more than 100 years in a building near the zoo. It never became the powerhouse research institution envisioned by its founders (the Field Museum assumed that role) but instead offered nature exhibits as dry as the dust on its taxidermy collection.

All that changed with the 1998 opening of the Academy's Peggy Notebaert Nature Museum (☎ 773-755-5100, 2430 N Cannon Dr just off Fullerton Ave; admission $6/4/3 for adults/seniors and students/children, free Tue; open 9am-4:30pm weekdays, 10am-5pm weekends), which transformed the entire institution. The many features of the new building include one of those trendy rooms where you can walk among butterflies. Other exhibits show how many different wild animals live in urban Chicago, both inside and outside. A computer lab allows visitors to solve environmental problems.

In perhaps the most interesting exhibit visitors can take water from the adjoining North Pond and examine it under a microscope. Considering that I once passed a floating French tickler in my rented paddleboat there, I'd say that the results could be interesting.

Other Sights

The Elks Club, once a hugely popular men's social club, has fallen on hard times all over the US, but during its heyday it built the impressive **Elks Veterans Memorial** (☎ 773-528-4500, 2750 N Lakeview Ave; admission *free; open 9am-4pm daily*) to honor members killed at war.

Istanbul's Hagia Sophia inspired the restored Byzantine mosaics that grace the dome of the 1918 **St Clement's Church** (☎ 773-281-0371, 646 W Deming Place), a Catholic church built in 1918. When the University of Notre Dame football team loses, Sunday masses are a sea of red eyes in this parish, which caters to young, single college grads. The church sits on a street lined with gracious mansions with extra-wide front lawns.

So taken by Chicago that you want to move here? You might consider hiring the **Reebie Storage & Moving Company** (☎ 773-549-0120, 2325 N Clark St) for its legacy of wit alone. The 1923 building carries its King Tut–inspired theme right down to the hieroglyphics below the statue of Ramses II on the right; these read, 'I give protection to your furniture.'

Bounded by Geneva Ave, Webster Ave and Halsted St, **Oz Park** is celebrating its name thanks to the generous donations of neighborhood's rich. The Tin Man stands at the northeast corner of the park, wondering which passersby might have a heart for him, while a yellow brick sidewalk stretches from that same corner into the park. Those neighborhood dollars also bought Oz the best playground in the city.

DePaul University (☎ 773-325-7000, 2320 N Kenmore Ave) is charming, efficient or ugly, depending where you are. The campus stretches east and west of the El south of Fullerton Ave. Chalmers Place is a scholarly square east of the El. The row houses were built for a seminary that has since been absorbed by DePaul.

West of the Fullerton El stop, the Academic Center and the University Center were built in 1968 and 1978, respectively, in an architectural style that's aptly named 'brutalism': both monstrosities look like they're meant to be last redoubts in case of urban assault. The 1992 library marks a new and vastly improved era of DePaul design. Notice how the architects have tried to camouflage some of the Academic Center.

THINGS TO SEE & DO

The Tin Man in Oz Park

LAKE VIEW & WRIGLEYVILLE (Map 7)

These neighborhoods have become just as popular as Lincoln Park, to the south, but their younger residents give them more of an edge. While you won't find many specific sights to see here, strolls along Halsted St, Clark St, Belmont Ave or Southport Ave, as well as the side streets, can yield delights. The stretch of Halsted St north of Belmont Ave is the vibrant heart of Chicago's gay community. Shops, bars and restaurants abound here.

Lake View begins at Diversey Parkway and stretches from the lake to Ashland Ave. Near Addison St, what was North Lake View has adopted the name of the Cubs stadium, thanks mostly to the efforts of real estate agents who determined that Wrigleyville adds cachet.

The Belmont and Addison El stops serve the area well, with able bullpen support from the Diversey, Wellington, Southport and Sheridan stops. Check the map in the back of the book for details.

Wrigley Field

This legendary baseball park *(1060 W Addison St)* draws plenty of tourists, who pose year-round under the classic neon sign over the main entrance. See the Entertainment chapter for details on the Chicago Cubs, who play here. If you don't have tickets or don't want to see the Cubbies lose, stroll over to Sheffield St and chat with the guys who hang around all day, waiting for a ball to be hit out of the park. Notice, too, how the surrounding three-flats have adapted their roofs for watching games.

Alta Vista Terrace

Chicago's first designated historic district is worthy of the honor. Developer Samuel Eberly Gross re-created a block of London row houses on Alta Vista Terrace in 1904. The 20 exquisitely detailed homes on either side of the street mirror each other diagonally, and the owners have worked hard at maintaining the spirit of the block. Individuality isn't dead, however: head to the back of the west row and you'll notice that every house has grown to the rear in dramatically different fashions.

Reaching the small, historic block can be a challenge; use Map 7 to trace your way one long block east of Clark St along Grace St or one long block north of Wrigley Field on Seminary Ave.

Graceland Cemetery

Why go to Memphis to see ostentatious memorials to the dead when you can go to Graceland right in Chicago? The local version *(☎ 773-525-1105, 4001 N Clark St; admission free; open 8am-4:30pm daily)* is in much better taste and is the final resting place for some of the biggest names in Chicago history. Most of the notable tombs lie around the lake, in the northern half of the 121 acres. Buy one of the 25¢ maps at the entrance to navigate the swirl of paths and streets.

Many of the memorials relate to lives of the dead in symbolic and touching ways:

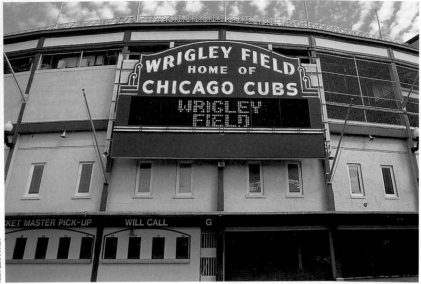

RICK GERHARTER

National League founder William Hulbert lies under a baseball; hotelier Dexter Graves lies under a work titled *Eternal Silence*; and George Pullman, the railroad car magnate who sparked so much labor unrest, lies under a hidden fortress designed to prevent angry union members from digging him up.

Daniel Burnham, who did so much to design Chicago, gets his own island. Photographer Richard Nickel, who helped form Chicago's nascent preservation movement and was killed during the demolition of his beloved Chicago Stock Exchange Building (the 1972 accident was unrelated to the demolition), has a stone designed by admiring architects. Other notables interred here include architects John Wellborn Root, Louis Sullivan and Ludwig Mies van der Rohe, plus retail magnate Marshall Field and power couple Potter and Bertha Palmer.

ANDERSONVILLE (Map 8)

Once little more than celery farms, Andersonville grew up around the turn of the 20th century. Lots of Swedes settled here, and their legacy continues today in the names of many of the stores, such as the Swedish Bakery (see the Places to Eat chapter). Andersonville kept its traditional residents long after other neighborhoods had undergone rapid ethnic turnover; as a result, it remained one of the city's most stable enclaves.

Now most of the residents are Swedish only by chance. The blocks surrounding Clark St from about Argyle St through Bryn Mawr Ave have become popular with young professionals. The once-low rents attracted graphic artists and other creative types in the 1980s and '90s. Many lesbians have found a home among the widely varied residents. Sadly, the neighborhood's popularity means that a Starbuck's coffee house has arrived; in Chicago this usually heralds the arrival of sharply escalating rents and condo conversion of apartments.

Even now, the shopkeepers and condo owners routinely sweep their sidewalks each day, as per Swedish tradition, although now these broom-wielding businesspeople are as likely to be Lebanese or gay as they are the stolid older Nordic residents.

The Berwyn El stop on the Red Line is a 10-minute walk east of Clark St. Simply walk up Berwyn Ave. The No 22 Clark bus also cuts through the heart of Andersonville.

Swedish-American Museum Center

The permanent collection at this small storefront museum *(☎ 773-728-8111, 5211 N Clark St; admission $4/2 for adults/children; open 10am-4pm Tues-Fri, 10am-3pm Sat & Sun)* focuses on the lives of the Swedes who originally settled Chicago. In that sense it reflects the dreams and aspirations of many of the groups who have poured into the city since it was founded. Look at some of the items people felt were important to bring with them both because they thought they would need the items and because they wanted to remember their homeland: butter churns, traditional bedroom furniture, religious relics and more.

Lakewood-Balmoral

These residential blocks draw their name from the two streets they are centered on: Lakewood and Balmoral Aves. You can explore this area when you're walking to and from the El. An integral part of Andersonville, it lies midway between Clark St and the El.

The houses here all date from the turn of the 20th century. Quite large, they were built as single-family homes for upper-middle-class families who often employed Swedish servants. Among the variety of designs: **5222 N Lakewood Ave,** which looks like something out of *Hansel and Gretel*; **5347 N Lakewood Ave**, an example of the Craftsman style that emphasized careful detailing; and **St Ita's Church** *(1220 W Catalpa Ave)*, which is in the 13th-century French Gothic style.

WICKER PARK & BUCKTOWN (Map 9)

For more than 100 years generations of Central European immigrants lived in simple wood-frame residences in these working-class neighborhoods (the 1871 fire didn't come through here, so wood houses were still legal).

In the 1980s yuppies and artists discovered Bucktown and quickly gentrified the area on either side of Damen Ave north of the railroad tracks that bisect the area at 1800 North. Wicker Park, south of the tracks and surrounding the namesake park, retains an edge, as yuppies, artists, musicians, Hispanic immigrants and others all mix in a mostly harmonious manner. Mellow cafés, exquisite restaurants and dives peddling brain tacos for a buck line Milwaukee Ave. In a disturbing trend, however, those shoddy, newly constructed two- and three-flats blighting the city are growing here like weeds (see the boxed text 'Here Today, Gone Tomorrow').

In both neighborhoods a stroll down the residential streets will reveal scores of

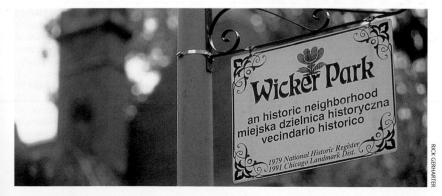

Here Today, Gone Tomorrow

Sturdy two- and three-flat buildings line many of Chicago's streets. Built over a 50-year period beginning in about 1890, these buildings are just what their names imply: multi-family dwellings with one flat – or apartment – per floor.

The ingredients of these structures are simple. The exteriors feature a solid facade of brick or stone, while the rest of the walls are solid brick. The back porches and exterior stairwells are made of wood. Inside, the flats have solid wood floors – usually oak – and plaster walls. Together, these materials make for a building that survives the wear and tear of human habitation for generations. Every so often the floors can be sanded and refinished, the walls replastered and the back stairs replaced – which extends the life of the house for another few decades. Update the kitchen and the bath every so often, and you've got a great home.

In the 1980s developers on the North Side seized upon this classic design to start filling in vacant lots. City living had become cool, and yuppies were demanding more housing. Unfortunately, the greedy developers and builders made a few modifications to the classic design; these included facades made from wafer-thin stone and brick veneers, walls fashioned from hollow cement block, fake floors consisting of artificial wood products and interior walls made from thin wallboard. As a result, these new buildings have no structural soul and often start falling apart within years of their construction.

A *Sun-Times* investigation found that many of these thousands of new two- and three-flats are fatally flawed and may have to be torn down, leaving their upscale owners holding the bag. Meanwhile neighborhoods like Wrigleyville and Bucktown are blighted by these things. How to spot them? Easy – in their greed the developers often built the buildings both taller and closer to the street than any other structure on the block. As many a neighbor has said, 'Oh well, the @£%$£ thing will soon fall down anyway.'

houses built before the Chicago street level was raised in the late 19th century to make way for sewers. The yards of these houses sit below the sidewalks, and stairs lead a half-flight up to what once was the second floor.

With a dome modeled on St Peter's in Rome, the huge **St Mary of the Angels Church** (☎ *773-278-2644, 1850 N Hermitage Ave at Cortland St*) dominates both Bucktown and the view from the Kennedy Expressway. Built with money from Polish parishioners prodded by a zealous pastor, the church features angels on the parapet, in the nave and possibly in the heavens above as well.

Certainly the church is blessed, as proven by its ability to cheat death. Only 60 years after its completion in 1920, its maintenance costs – which had gone through the holey roof – and its declining membership made it a prime candidate for an early demise. But a grassroots campaign arose to save the church, drawing support from the community and people across the city. In 1992 the repairs, which cost more than the original construction bill, were completed, and the invigorated parish has drawn many new members.

At **Wicker Park**, the neighborhood's triangular focal point just south of the Damen El stop, buffed bods walk pedigreed dogs past retirees playing chess. Note the fenced area where those dogs can give each other a sniff while their often-single owners can do the same – albeit mentally.

In the **Nelson Algren House** (*1958 W Evergreen Ave*), a three-flat one block south of the park, the writer created some of his greatest works about gritty life in the neighborhood (see the boxed text 'Nelson Algren' in the Facts about Chicago chapter). You can't go in, but you can admire it from the street.

Wicker Park Walking Tour

The streets northwest of Wicker Park have been called 'the ethnic Gold Coast.' German and Scandinavian immigrants who made it big in the late 19th century built their mansions here. Although they could have put their grand homes on Prairie Ave or the Gold Coast, they preferred to live where the people they ran into on the streets spoke the language of the old country.

From the Damen El stop on the CTA Blue Line, walk two blocks northwest on Milwaukee Ave to Caton St. Turn left and begin the tour. You'll notice that the neighborhood gets gentrified the moment you leave shabby Milwaukee Ave.

At **2138-2156 W Caton St** you'll see an 1891 minidevelopment of five large homes, each with a different exterior design and theme. Among the variations: No 2142, Queen Anne; No 2146, Swiss; No 2152, Renaissance. The stone-and-brick home at No 2156 used to belong to Norwegian Ole Thorp, who built the houses.

The large 1891 turreted house at **2159 W Caton St** is a good example of Queen Anne

style. At the intersection of Caton and Leavitt Sts, cross Leavitt.

To make the upscale apartment flats at **1644 & 1658 N Leavitt St** fit in with nearby mansions, builders used high-quality materials such as limestone and cut glass and included ornately carved wooden details.

Head south on Leavitt St for one block. The 1893 mansion at **2156 W Concord Place** features a proud conical tower and an interesting curved front.

Continue south on Leavitt St; cross North Ave and turn east (left) on Pierce Ave. The three similar houses at **2146, 2150** and **2156 W Pierce Ave** date from 1890. Note how the limestone at 2150 has held up better than the sandstone at 2156 and 2146.

An architectural relic survives in Wicker Park.

RICK GERHARTER

See all that woodwork on **2138 W Pierce Ave**? You'd never guess that the original owner, John D Runge, owned a wood-milling firm. Notice the Masonic insignia under the eaves of the dormer.

The 1899 house at **2135 W Pierce Ave** includes more detail (in pressed metal, wood and brick) than the eye can soak up. The side porch overlooking a garden was a popular detail in the neighborhood. Note the polychromatic paint job.

At the end of the block, turn south (right) onto Hoyne Ave. Germans liked sculpted figures of women, as seen on the 1886 house at **1520 N Hoyne Ave**, which was actually built for a Russian lumber baron.

The porch of the 1895 turreted Queen Anne house at **1521 N Hoyne Ave** features wood carved to resemble lace. The **Wicker Park Lutheran Church** (*N Hoyne Ave at LeMoyne St*) was built in 1906 with granite salvaged from an upscale Levee District brothel.

Ripe for restoration, the 1879 Italianate house at **1417 N Hoyne Ave** includes a typical side porch. The proud French Second Empire mansion at **1407 N Hoyne Ave**, dating from 1879, features a cast-iron porch.

Turn east (left) on Schiller St and proceed one block; cross Damen Ave. The 1891 house at **1941 W Schiller St** is a prime example of Queen Anne architecture in all of its styling. It's been beautifully restored.

After your tour, rest up across the street in Wicker Park.

UKRAINIAN VILLAGE (Map 10)

This ethnic enclave is still heavily populated with its original residents or their descendants. The No 66 Chicago Ave bus runs through the heart of the neighborhood, which radiates from the intersection of Chicago and Oakley Aves.

Inside a bright white storefront, the **Ukrainian Institute of Modern Art** (☎ 773-227-5522, 2320 W Chicago Ave; admission free; open noon-4pm Wed-Sun) displays works by artists of Ukrainian descent. The growing permanent collection rotates through one gallery, while special mixed-media exhibitions occupy the others. The museum also sponsors the work of native Ukrainians.

The **St Nicholas Ukrainian Catholic Cathedral** (☎ 773-276-4537, 2238 W Rice St at Oakley Ave) is the less-traditional of the neighborhood's main churches. Its 13 domes represent Christ and the Apostles. The intricate mosaics – added to the 1915 building in 1988 – owe their inspiration to the Cathedral of St Sophia in Kiev.

Liturgical differences led the traditionalists at St Nicholas to build the showy **Saints Volodymyr & Olha Church** (☎ 312-829-5209, 739 N Oakley Ave) in 1975. It makes up for its paucity of domes – only five – with a massive mosaic showing the conversion of Grand Duke Vladimir of Kiev to Christianity in AD 988.

WEST SIDE (Map 10)

The flat expanse west of the Loop and affluent lakefront is a patchwork of ethnic neighborhoods, urban renewal, blight, gentrification and a lot of sleepy areas that defy description. The area west of Milwaukee Ave, the Loop and S Halsted St has always been a working-class part of town. Neighborhood names such as Greek Town, Little Italy and others reveal the origins of their early residents.

The far West Side neighborhoods that radiate out from W Madison St, such as Lawndale, are some of the worst in the city. After Martin Luther King Jr was assassinated in 1968, this part of the city literally went up in flames during several nights of rioting that saw the destruction of the commercial districts, businesses and many factories. As is so often the case with urban riots, the rioters destroyed their own neighborhoods. After the fires were put out, the rioters were much worse off than before and any hope of new capital investment had literally gone up in smoke.

Safety is definitely a consideration when visiting many sites on the West Side. The areas discussed here are okay during the day, and some are okay at night as well. Individual cautions, as well as transportation options, are covered in each neighborhood section. If you have a car, you can cover the entire area in an afternoon.

Polish Museum of America

Rather than focusing on Poles in America, this large museum (☎ 773-384-3352, 984 N Milwaukee Ave at Augusta Blvd; admission $2/1 for adults/children; open 11am-4pm daily) focuses on Poles in Poland. In its heyday during the decades after WWII, the museum sought to portray Poland's long history of art, culture and science, a heritage largely ignored by the Communists.

The exhibits mix art, artifacts (such as ubiquitous suits of armor) and displays on the lives of such notable Poles as Chopin, Copernicus and Pulaski. The last, who has had a major Chicago street and a city holiday named in his honor, was a Polish general who fought with the Americans in the Revolutionary War. One of his greatest achievements was covering the retreat of George Washington from a battle gone bad. He died fighting the British in 1779.

The Division El stop on the CTA Blue Line is three blocks north of the museum on Milwaukee Ave.

Public Sculptures

Josh Garber's large *Episodic* is mounted at Grand and Western Aves. Assembled from chunks of light poles that have been welded together, it looks sort of like a demented blue screensaver for a computer.

Another piece of city-funded public sculpture sits at the intersection of Ashland and Ogden Aves and Madison St. Created by Herbert Ferber – who couldn't create a name for it beyond *Untitled* – the heavy piece is a huge cube of brown metal.

United Center

Built for $175 million and opened in 1992, the United Center arena (*1901 W Madison St*) is home to the Bulls and the Blackhawks

THINGS TO SEE & DO

RICK GERHARTER

Michael Jordan immortalized at the United Center

(see Spectator Sports in the Entertainment chapter for details) and is the venue for special events such as the circus. The most notable thing about the building is its huge size, with an interior similar to other big stadiums in the US.

The statue of an airborne Michael Jordan in front of the east entrance pays a lively tribute to the man whose talents made the financing for the edifice possible. The center, surrounded by parking lots, is okay by day but should be avoided at night – unless there's a game, in which case squads of cops are everywhere in order to ensure public safety.

For the 1996 Democratic Convention at the United Center, the city remodeled Madison St all the way from the Loop. The new planters and streetlights have helped the area's appearance and have sparked the first signs of gentrification. The planters also spurred Mayor Daley's craze to put similar adornments on scores of city streets.

Haymarket Riot Monument
On May 4, 1886, striking factory workers held a meeting at Haymarket Square, at Randolph and Desplaines Sts west of the Loop. Toward the end of the meeting a mob of police appeared, things quickly degener-

ated into chaos, and a bomb exploded, killing seven cops. Eight anarchist leaders were convicted of inciting murder, and four were hanged for the crime.

Public sentiment worldwide favored the striking workers, who were demanding an eight-hour workday and were the victims of efforts by the factory owners and their police lackeys to discredit them.

In memory of the seven dead cops, a statue was erected on the spot some years later: a stilted officer standing with arm upraised, commanding peace 'in the name of the people of Illinois.' The statue has since had a history almost more violent than the event it commemorates. Seen as representing anti-labor forces, it was long a focus of protest. Thieves made away with the plaques at its base several times, and shortly after the turn of the 20th century a bus driver rammed it, claiming to be sick of seeing it every day. In 1928 it was moved several blocks west, to Union Park, where it stood peacefully until the uproarious 1960s, when it was blown up twice. Repaired yet again, the statue has found a home in the courtyard of the Chicago Police training center *(1300 W Jackson Blvd)*.

Old St Patrick's Church
A Chicago fire survivor, this 1852 church (☎ 312-782-6171, 700 W Adams St) is the city's oldest and one of its most successful, based on the shrewd strategies of its politically connected pastor, Father Jack Wall. A year-round calendar of social events for single Catholics boosted its membership from the tens to the hundreds in the 1980s. Many of these love-minded members are now married and producing new parishioners.

The domed steeple signifies the Eastern Church; the spire signifies the Western Church. Call to find out when the church is open so you can see the beautifully restored Celtic-patterned interior, which was originally built by parishioners well over a century ago.

Bat Column

No, not the Bat Cave nor the Bat Mobile, it's the...oh, just go see for yourself. This is an excellent example of your federal tax dollars at work in public art. Artist Claes Oldenburg proved himself worthy of every penny of his commission fee with this 100-foot work in front of the regional Social Security office *(600 W Madison St)*.

Chicago Fire Department Academy

Rarely has a public building been placed in a more appropriate place: the fire department's school *(☎ 312-747-7239, 558 W DeKoven St)* stands on the very spot where the 1871 fire began – between Clinton and Jefferson Sts. Although there's no word on whether junk mail still shows up for Mrs O'Leary, the academy trains firefighters so they'll be ready the next time somebody or some critter kicks over a lantern (see the boxed text 'Don't Look at Me – It Was the Cow' in the Facts about Chicago chapter). If you call in advance on weekdays, you might be able to watch some training exercises.

University of Illinois at Chicago

UIC *(☎ 312-996-7000)* used to be a much more interesting place to visit for all the wrong reasons. Noted Chicago architect Walter Netsch created a design that at best can be called eccentric. When the 55-acre campus opened in 1965, it usually provoked extreme protests from those who saw it.

Netsch proclaimed that it was his goal to re-create the sense of wonder one feels when exploring an Italian hill village, but the only emotion he stirred was anger. The area lacks hills, so he designed a double-deck campus with upper-level elevated walkways linking all the buildings. A vast amphitheater area formed the heart of the campus. The looming 28-story administration and faculty building *(601 S Morgan St)* was meant to be the campanile.

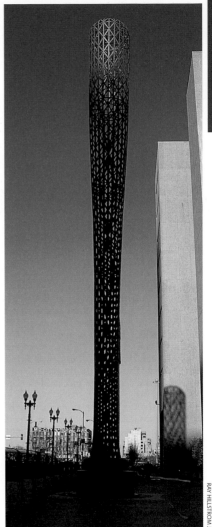

RAY HILLSTROM JR

Claes Oldenburg's Bat Column

The realities of Netsch's design were unremittingly grim. The elevated walkways cast a gloom over the muddy landscape below and the amphitheater became a wind-blown tundra in the winter and a sun-baked desert in the summer. (Netsch lives in Chicago; you'd think he would have known better.)

By the mid-1980s the whole ugly place was falling apart and despised by its 30,000 students and faculty. In 1990 a massive rebuilding program began to eradicate much of Netsch's hill town. His voice of protest was lone.

The **University Center Housing & Commons** *(700 S Halsted St)*, an attractive undergraduate dorm that welcomes people onto the campus, became the first major building to break with the past. In the last decade the campus has become a pleasant place to go to school, but there's no reason to make a special trip there. However, if you don't go to the campus, it might just come to you. It has jumped south of Roosevelt Rd in a big way, in the process gobbling up the historic Maxwell St Market and many other surrounding blocks.

Jane Addams Hull House In 1889, at age 29, Jane Addams founded Hull House *(☎ 312-413-5353, 800 S Halsted St; admission free; open 10am-4pm Mon-Sat, noon-5pm Sun)* in an 1856 home donated by philanthropist Charles Hull. At the time the densely packed neighborhood was filled with recent European immigrants who worked for menial wages and lived in horrific tenements.

With several other women professionals, such as Ellen Gates Starr, Addams provided day-care facilities, a kindergarten, an employment bureau and many other social services to masses of exploited and hopeless people. She also provided space where the burgeoning labor unions could meet.

Addams fought for laws regulating child labor and requiring public education. Also active in the international peace movement, she won the Nobel Peace Prize for her efforts in 1931. She died in 1935, but Hull House continues her work at locations around the city.

UIC has preserved Addams' house, along with the 1905 dining hall where neighborhood residents could come for hot meals. At its peak, the complex contained 13 buildings, which included the city's first public baths, playground, swimming pool, adult-education school and many other service facilities.

A 15-minute slide show on the second floor of the dining hall details Addams' work. Displays document the struggle for social justice waged by Hull House and others in the first half of the 20th century. The 1st floor of the hall has been restored to appear as it did when hundreds found sustenance here daily. The house itself also has been restored to its appearance when Addams and Starr took it over. Many of Addams' possessions, such as her writing desk, are on display. Quiet today, the house served as the social and administrative center for the whole complex at its peak.

Maxwell St Police Station Fans of the TV show *Hill Street Blues* will instantly recognize the exterior of this old police station *(943 W Maxwell St)* – it graced the opening of every episode of the series, which was based on a gritty fictional neighborhood not unlike this one. Long vacant, the structure has been seized by UIC and renovated for use as offices.

Little Italy

The area south of the Eisenhower Expressway to Roosevelt Rd was a thriving Italian community until the 1950s, when several blows almost killed it. The expressway itself was rammed through the most vibrant part of the neighborhood; the surviving commercial area was demolished for the campus of the University of Illinois at Chicago, and several public housing projects were scattered through what was left. Many people still suspect that the old Mayor Daley intended the entire scheme as retribution for the schemes of rival politicians.

Perhaps out of sheer stubbornness, the Italian residents hung on, supporting a commercial district on Taylor St. Meanwhile, professionals drawn to the university and the fast-growing Chicago Medical Center to the west discovered the tree-lined streets of the neighborhood. Beginning in the 1970s, gentrification transformed old homes and added new townhouses. And now that the city has spent vast sums beautifying Taylor St, the neighborhood is set to take off.

The CTA Blue Line serves the northern portion of the neighborhood. The Racine and UIC-Halsted El stops are the most convenient to Little Italy.

Although clearly slated for demolition, the remaining blighted housing projects remain a safety concern; visitors to the area should take care to avoid stretches that go from safe to grim in a block. Be extra careful around the blocks between Racine Ave and Loomis St on Taylor St, and in the areas west of Damen Ave and south of Roosevelt Rd.

Taylor St preserves many old Italian family businesses. See the Places to Eat chapter for restaurant details. As part of the city's beautification campaign, a portion of S Bishop St that meets Taylor St has been converted into **Piazza DiMaggio**, in honor of Joe DiMaggio, the Italian-American baseball star. Never mind that the famously ill-tempered former husband of Marilyn Monroe had nothing to do with Chicago. Directly across the street is the future home of the National Italian American Sports Hall of Fame, which is bound to include more on DiMaggio; there's no opening date set yet.

To the north 6-acre **Arrigo Park**, one block west of Racine Ave and bordered by Cabrini and Loomis Sts, faces the affluent townhouses of the gentrified neighborhood west of the university. To the south it faces the Jane Addams Homes, a 1930s housing project that's as faded as the dreams of its idealistic builders.

The hangar-size **Holy Family Church** (☎ 312-738-4080, 1080 W Roosevelt Rd) received its Catholic dedication in 1860. At times its survival seems to have depended solely on the notoriously strong wills of the Jesuits who run it. Almost demolished a few years ago, it is now being reconstructed – a process that can't happen too quickly, given that the weight of the slate roof has already pushed some of the Gothic pillars out of plumb by 18 inches.

At neighboring St Ignatius Preparatory School, one of the premier Catholic co-

educational high schools in the city, the Jesuits run a very tight ship. The original building opened in 1870.

Cook County Hospital

This huge, gray dinosaur of a hospital (☎ 312-633-6000, 1835 W Harrison St) dates to 1913. Patients whom profit-minded institutions won't accept come to this publicly funded facility. Care varies widely, but the hospital does have one of the best emergency-care programs in the world.

Set up in 1966, the nation's first trauma unit caters to patients critically injured in accidents and violence. Unfortunately, the doctors get all too much practice with victims of shootings and other mayhem. Hundreds of doctors working in emergency rooms worldwide have trained in trauma care at County during the past three decades. More than one famous doctor has told me that if they were ever shot, they'd want to go to here. The hit TV series *ER* is based on County.

Sometime later in 2001 or 2002, a huge new County Hospital is set to open west of the present facility, where Ogden Ave meets Damen Ave.

In the surrounding blocks are several more medical institutions, including two more hospitals and several medical schools. Together the facilities are known as the Chicago Medical Center and comprise the largest collection of health-care facilities in the world.

Farther West

With 4½ acres under glass, the park district's premier **Garfield Park Conservatory** (☎ 312-746-5100, 300 N Central Park Blvd; admission free; open 9am-5pm daily) preserves a significant bit of the tropics on the West Side. Built in 1907, the rambling glass structure houses one of the largest collections of indoor plants in the world. One of the original designers, Jens Jensen, intended for the 5000 palms, ferns and other plants to re-create what Chicago looked like during prehistoric times. Today the effect continues; all that's missing is a rampaging stegosaurus. The Economic House features a fascinating range of plants that are used for food, medicine and shelter.

A spiffy restoration completed in 2000 has made the conservatory better than ever. New halls contain displays of seasonal plants, which are especially spectacular in the weeks before Easter. A children's garden lets kids play with plants that aren't rare or irreplaceable. Watch for special events at night and on weekends.

Transportation links are improving. A new Garfield Park El station on the CTA Green Line is set to open later in 2001. Within sight of the conservatory, it should provide an easy and fairly secure way of reaching the plants. In the meantime, the park district is running a free shuttle from the Loop and Near North; call for hours. If you drive, note that the neighborhood is not the safest.

PILSEN (Map 10)

Pilsen has been the first stop for immigrants to Chicago for more than 100 years. First came the Czechs, who gave the neighborhood its name (Pilsen is the second-biggest town in the Czech Republic). Later it drew Poles, Serbs and Croats. In the 1950s Hispanics began arriving in great numbers, drawn by the low rents for both residential and commercial space, which encouraged small businesses.

Today the streets pulse with the sounds of salsa music, the cries of food vendors with carts and the chatter of a thousand conversations. You'll find the heart of the area on 18th St between Racine Ave and Damen Ave, where you can stop in at scores of *taquerias*, bakeries and small shops selling everything from devotional candles to the latest CDs from Mexico. If you pay more than $1 for a taco, it had better be extra good.

The culture of the neighborhood, rather than specific sites, makes a visit to Pilsen worthwhile. A stroll east on 18th St from the El stop should give you the flavor of Hispanic life here, but expect to see traces of previous residents as well. Beyond the colorful signs and details are traditional Chicago three-flats and storefronts with distinctive Central European details. And

RICK GERHARTER

Pilsen: a modest neighborhood built by immigrants

outside of summer, the weather is unlikely to make you think you're in Mexico or Puerto Rico.

Here you can also see the city's old vaulted sidewalks, especially along 18th Place, where one cottage after another features a front yard several feet below the level of the sidewalks; these homes were built before the streets were raised to allow for the construction of sewers. The sidewalks sit on top of hollow vaults.

Pilsen is easily reached from the Loop. The 18th St El stop on the Cermak branch of the CTA Blue Line puts you in the center of Pilsen. The station itself sets the tone for the neighborhood: every surface has been covered with murals inspired by Mayan, Aztec and modern-day Mexican art.

Mexican Fine Arts Center Museum

Founded in 1982, this vibrant museum (☎ 312-738-1503, 1852 W 19th St; admission free; open 10am-5pm Tues-Sun) occupies a renovated and expanded old field house in Harrison Park. The two large exhibition spaces house temporary exhibits of work by Mexican artists. The museum's high profile in North America means that it draws some of the best paintings, sculpture, textiles and other artwork. A big new addition due to open in 2001 will triple the museum's exhibit space and allow for the installation of permanent exhibits. The museum also sponsors readings by top authors and performances by musicians and artists.

If you are in town during the fall, be sure to check out the exhibits and celebrations relating to November 1, the Day of the Dead, a traditional Mexican holiday that combines the festive with the religious. The events take place for a month on either side of the day.

Other Sights

This 1914 **St Adalbert Church** (1650 W 17th St) features 185-foot steeples that are almost impossible to appreciate, given the narrow streets. This is a good example of the many soaring churches built by Chicago's ethnic populations through thousands of small donations from parishioners, who would cut family budgets to the bone to make their weekly contribution. The rich ornamentation in the interior of this Catholic church glorifies Polish saints and religious figures.

The Poles had St Adalbert's; the Irish had **St Pius Church** (1901 S Ashland Ave), a Romanesque Revival edifice built between 1885 and 1892. Its smooth masonry contrasts with the rough stones of its contemporaries. Catholics of one ethnic group never attended the churches of the others,

RICK GERHARTER

Some of Pilsen's colorful art

which explains why this part of town, with its concentration of Catholic immigrants, is thick with steeples.

The exterior wall of the **José Clemente Orozco Academy** (☎ 773-534-7215, 1645 W 18th Place) is the canvas for a 1990s tile mosaic that shows a diverse range of Mexican images, from a portrait of farmworker advocate Dolores Huerta to the Virgin of Guadalupe. Each summer art students add more panels.

In a neighborhood where most of the structures were built by European immigrants, the **Lozano Public Library** (☎ 312-746-4329, 1805 S Loomis St) celebrates the current population with decorative tile inspired by pre-Columbian buildings in Oaxaca, Mexico. The large branch library occupies a prominent spot at the intersection of 18th St, Blue Island Ave and Loomis St.

Named for the Greek muse of comedy, who casts a bemused gaze from a spot in the arch over the entrance, **Thalia Hall** (1807 S Allport St) brought out the bohemian side of the Czech immigrants, who used it for theater and music productions. The large stone building, which dates from 1893, now houses a row of interesting little stores selling housewares.

SOUTH SIDE (Map 11)

This part of town, south of the Stevenson Expressway and east of the Dan Ryan Expressway, has had a tough time since WWII. Whole neighborhoods have vanished, with crime and blight driving residents away. Among Chicagoans of all colors, the area's reputation is not the best.

The construction of the vast wall of housing projects along the east side of the Dan Ryan created huge impoverished neighborhoods where community ties broke down and gangs held sway. As a result, the Chicago Housing Authority has begun a demolition campaign to try to turn the projects into mixed-income communities. But the news isn't all bad: some parts have remained vital while others are being rediscovered and still others, such as the large area from 26th St south to 31st St, have been successfully redeveloped. Renewed interest in Bronzeville has also brought vigor to that neighborhood.

Illinois Institute of Technology

A world-class leader in technology, industrial design and architecture, IIT (☎ 312-567-3000, 3300 S Federal St) was formed in 1940 by the merger of two earlier institutions. The campus owes much of its world-famous look to legendary architect Ludwig Mies van der Rohe, who fled the Nazis in Germany for Chicago in 1938. From 1940 until his retirement in 1958, Mies designed 22 IIT buildings that all reflect his tenets of architecture, which combine simple metal frames painted black with glass and brick infills. Mies' trademark International Style was endlessly copied throughout the world for the next three decades (see the Architecture special section, earlier in this book, for more information).

The star of the campus and Mies' undisputed masterpiece is **SR Crown Hall** (3360 S State St), appropriately home to the College of Architecture. The building, near the center of campus, appears to be a transparent glass box floating between its translucent base and suspended roof. At night it glows from within like an illuminated jewel.

The 35th/Bronzeville El stop on the CTA Green Line is at the south edge of the campus, which you can best explore by simply wandering around and seeing how all the Mies buildings interrelate. Private police ensure that the campus itself remains safe during the day.

Bronzeville

Once home to Louis Armstrong and other notables, Bronzeville is the semi-official name for the neighborhoods radiating from 35th St and Martin Luther King Jr Dr. From 1920 until 1950 Bronzeville thrived as the vibrant center of black life in the city and boasted economic and cultural strength that matched that of New York's Harlem.

Shifting populations, urban decay and the construction of the wall of public housing along State St – including the Robert Taylor Homes, the worst housing project in the nation – led to Bronzeville's decline. In 1997 attention again focused on the neighborhood when the Black Metropolis Convention and Tourism Council successfully lobbied the city council to designate the neighborhood as a Historic Landmark District. In 2000 the Chicago Housing Authority began demolishing the worst of the Taylor high-rise projects. See the boxed text 'Bronzeville Walk of Fame' for details on sidewalk plaques honoring famous local people.

The same forces that led to the neighborhood's decline can make visiting the area a cautious endeavor. During the daytime it's best to take a friend along. The 35th/Bronzeville Station on the CTA Green Line is on the western edge of the area, which is also bordered by IIT.

Historic Buildings Examples of stylish architecture from the past can be found throughout Bronzeville, but note that some of the buildings listed below are in miserable shape and aren't worthy of more than an inspection of the exterior.

Many of Bronzeville's grand houses have been restored ahead of the commercial districts. In fact, the average purchase price for a home in the area in 1995 was $61,000, but a mere four years later it had soared to $154,000. You can see some fine old homes along two blocks of Calumet Ave between 31st and 33rd Sts, an area known as 'The Gap.' The buildings here include Frank Lloyd Wright's only row houses, the **Robert W Roloson Houses** (3213-3219 S Calumet Ave).

One of scores of Romanesque houses that date from the 1880s, the **Ida B Wells House** (3624 S Martin Luther King Dr) is named for its 1920s resident, a crusading journalist who investigated lynchings and other racial crimes. She coined the famous line: 'Eternal vigilance is the price of liberty.' Another imposing home from the past, the **D Harry Hammer House** (3656 S Martin Luther King Dr) features heavily gabled fronts that look vaguely Dutch.

Gospel music got its start at **Pilgrim Baptist Church** (☎ 312-842-5830, 3301 S Indiana Ave), built as a synagogue from 1890 to 1891. The classic exterior only hints at the vast and opulent interior.

The **Supreme Life Building** (3501 S Martin Luther King Dr), a nondescript 1930s office building, was the spot where John H Johnson Jr, the publishing mogul who founded Ebony magazine, got the idea for his empire, which also includes Jet and other important titles serving African Americans. Behind the porcelain-metal exterior panels lies a classic decorative facade.

In the median at 35th St and Martin Luther King Jr Dr, the **Victory Monument** was erected in 1928 to honor black soldiers who fought in WWI. The figures include a soldier, a mother and Columbia, the mythical figure meant to symbolize the New World.

The long, low **Alco Drugs** building, on the southwest corner of 35th and King, shows the kind of sleek look many of the buildings sported in the 1930s.

The landmark 1915 **Eighth Regiment Armory** (3533 S Giles Ave), a former National Guard building, is both stylish and imposing. It reopened in 1999 as an advanced public high school.

A major milestone in Bronzeville's rejuvenation occurred in 1996, when the Chicago Bee Building reopened as a **public library** (☎ 312-747-6872, 3647 S State St). Restored to all its glory, the 1929 art deco building now houses a large collection of books on African American history.

Bronzeville Walk of Fame

When the city replaced the sidewalks on Martin Luther King Jr Dr between 35th and 25th Sts, it added something extra: 91 bronze plaques celebrating people associated with Bronzeville.

Designed by artist Geraldine McCullough, the plaques incorporate African art and motifs. A central text area describes the person honored, such as Walter T Bailey, the first registered black architect in Illinois. Other Bronzeville luminaries honored include singer Nat King Cole, astronaut Mae Jemison and choreographer Katherine Dunham.

Other Bronzeville buildings included in the historic designation are the **Overton Hygienic/Douglass National Bank Building** *(3619-3627 S State St)*, the **Wabash YMCA** *(3763 S Wabash Ave)*, **Unity Hall** *(3140 S Indiana Ave)* and the **Sunset Cafe/Grand Terrace Cafe** *(315 E 35th St)*, a legendary venue for great entertainers such as Armstrong and Jelly Roll Morton (it's now a hardware store).

Douglas Tomb

Often overlooked, the Douglas Tomb State Historic Site *(☎ 312-225-2620, 636 E 35th St; admission free; open 9am-5pm daily)* is the 96-foot-high memorial and final resting place of Stephen A Douglas. In 1858 a series of famous debates against Abraham Lincoln helped propel Douglas into the US Senate. At the time he lived on part of a 70-acre tract he owned on this location. Later, some of the land was used for Camp Douglas, a notorious Civil War POW camp.

BRIDGEPORT (Map 11)

Bridgeport is more important for its historical role in the city than for its ability to draw tourists. The stockyards were once a major attraction, but they are long closed and their land is being rapidly covered by new warehouses and industry. The traditional home of Chicago's Irish mayors, Bridgeport remains an enclave of descendants of Irish settlers. A few Chinese and Hispanic people have moved in, but many African Americans, who live to the south and east, feel that they're not welcome here. While a number of residents say that Bridgeport is more tolerant now than in its past, it will probably never live down its role in the 1919 race riots, when neighborhood thugs went on a killing spree after a black youth on a raft floated too close to a 'white' beach.

Halsted St from 31st St south to 43rd St is Bridgeport's rather uninteresting main drag. Most of the neighborhood lies west of the huge train embankment that itself is west of Comiskey Park. However, Bridgeport extends north of the park all the way to Chinatown and makes for a good walk after

a game if you're in a group and don't stray east of the Dan Ryan Expressway.

Bridgeport's dearth of concentrated sites makes it best to explore the area by car. Safety depends somewhat on your ethnicity, although the neighborhood is mostly safe during the day.

If you're standing on the litter-strewn bank of **Bubbly Creek** *(37th St at Racine Ave)*, your first thought will be: 'God, I hope I don't fall in.' Little life moves in the stagnant black water, and dead fish rot in the sun, surrounded by murk. Some 90 years ago, Upton Sinclair documented this open sewer of Chicago's stockyards in *The Jungle*. Today the worst section has been covered over and the packing plants that fouled it are long gone. But bubbles still rise from the depths, fed by the tons of waste still rotting on the bottom, a legacy of Chicago's role as 'hog butcher for the world.'

Since 1968 the derelict **International Amphitheater** *(4220 S Halsted St)* has never seen as much action as it did during that year's disastrous Democratic Convention, when Mayor Daley's thugs beat Dan Rather while Walter Cronkite cried foul from the broadcast booth. Another low point came when the mayor openly shouted a racial epithet at liberal Connecticut senator Abe Ribicoff, combining a maternal reference with a vulgar term for sex (12 letters, you figure it out). Ribicoff had just used his nomination speech for George McGovern to condemn the 'Gestapo tactics' of the Chicago police.

A tiny vestige of the stockyards stands just west of the 4100 block of S Halsted St. The **Union Stockyards Gate** *(850 W Exchange Ave)* was once the main entrance to the vast stockyards where millions of cows and almost as many hogs met their ends each year. The value of those slaughtered in 1910 was an enormous $225 million. Sanitary conditions eventually improved from the hideous levels documented by Upton Sinclair, although during WWI American doughboys suffered more casualties because of bad cans of meat from the Chicago packing houses than because of enemy fire. The cow immortalized at the top of the 1879 gate is Sherman, a prize-winning steer.

The most crime-free place in town is the **Richard J Daley House** *(3526 S Lowe Ave)*, where the elder Mayor Daley's widow, 'Sis,' still lives and where son Mayor Richard M Daley grew up. A police car is always outside and a huge station house is just down the block. The block itself, just three blocks east of Halsted St, typifies middle-class blue-collar neighborhoods all over the city.

KENWOOD (Map 12)

The neighborhood just north of Hyde Park is best toured by car. A mix of middle-class and wealthy whites and blacks, including some famous names, make their homes in the many large and imposing mansions.

The **Kehilath Anshe Ma'ariv-Isaiah Israel Temple** *(☎ 773-924-1234, 1100 E Hyde Park Blvd; call for opening times)*, also called 'KAM Synagogue,' is a domed masterpiece in the Byzantine style. Its acoustics are said to be perfect.

A rarity in Chicago, **Madison Park**, east of the 5000 block of Woodlawn Ave, is a refined development set around a private boulevard. Most of the houses date from the 1920s.

Many classic homes old and new line the gracefully shaded Woodlawn Ave, including the **Isidore Heller House** *(5132 S Woodlawn Ave)*, an 1897 Frank Lloyd Wright house with the characteristic side entrance. The house at **4944 S Woodlawn Ave** was once home to Muhammad Ali. The bow-tied guards around the 1971 **Elijah Muhammad House** *(4855 S Woodlawn Ave)* indicate that Nation of Islam leader Louis Farrakhan currently lives here. And **4812 S Woodlawn Ave** is a mostly unaltered 1873 house; before everyone else moved into the neighborhood, it was a lonely country villa.

HYDE PARK (Map 12)

An enclave within the city's South Side, Hyde Park owes much of its existence to the University of Chicago, a school where the graduate students outnumber the under-

grads. The bookish residents give the place an insulated, small-town air that contrasts starkly with the rough neighborhoods to the west and south. A thicket of trees lines the streets, with mature specimens quickly replacing any dead wood.

The major attraction for most visitors is the Museum of Science & Industry, but west of the train tracks the university and the neighborhood itself are also well worth a stroll (see the University of Chicago walking tour, later).

Hyde Park isn't just isolated in spirit; it's isolated transit-wise as well. The best way to get to the center of town is the Metra Electric service from the Loop's Randolph St and Van Buren St Stations. Two trains an hour – one local, one express – serve the neighborhood. The local is slower than the express by just a few minutes, and it serves the convenient 55th-56th-57th St Station. Use the 57th St exit for the most convenient route to the museum and the campus. The express train goes to the 59th St Station; from there it's a 10-minute walk to the museum. Schedules are freely available; nab one so you can plan your return. A one-way trip from the Loop is $1.95.

Promontory Point

Hyde Park's best picnic and view spot, at the end of 55th St and Lake Shore Dr, has a field house designed to look like a lighthouse. In summer neighborhood residents often congregate to sunbathe and swim. Nearby you can still see traces of a 1950s cold war missile battery meant to defend Chicago from Russian bombers.

Museum of Science & Industry

The main building of this vast and confusing place *(☎ 773-684-1414, www.msichicago.org, 5700 S Lake Shore Dr; admission $7/3.50 for adults/children, free Thur; open 9:30am-4pm Mon-Fri, 9:30am-5:30pm Sat & Sun)* was the Palace of Fine Arts at the landmark World's Columbian Exposition in 1893. It was converted to its present use in the 1920s. In 1999 a vast underground parking lot opened and brought with it a cavernous new underground entrance hall. Where once there were rows of cars in front of the museum, there is now a nice expanse of grass.

The MSI has grown into a hodgepodge of huge and small exhibits celebrating the technical aspects of life. Despite the free maps, it's easy to become disoriented as the scores of displays compete for attention. There are two ways people visit the museum: they either wander in, wander around in a daze and emerge hours later squinting into the sun, or they arrive, sit down with the map, plan which exhibits they most want to see and do their darned best to find them. Obviously you should try the latter. (Note that it's dangerous to work up much of an appetite, since the restaurants are lousy.)

Most of the exhibits are the products of joint ventures with industrial groups and companies. For instance, BP Amoco lurks behind the cheery Petroleum Planet display (Fear not, global warming isn't what its cracked up to be!). Some of the many things to see here are up-to-date and fascinating; others have passed their prime. Here's a guide to the most popular and interesting sights.

Omnimax Theater Frequent travelers have probably encountered an Imax movie theater before; they're popping up in tourist attractions all over the world (there's another one at Navy Pier). The films, usually quite stunning, cover everything from nature *(Beavers!)* to space flight *(The Dream Is Alive!)*. If you want to see the movie, head here first to secure tickets, as the showings sell out quickly *(admission $6 extra)*. Near the theater in the Henry Crown Space Center is the Apollo 8 command module, the spacecraft Frank Borman, Jim Lovell and Bill Anders used to become the first humans to travel to the moon and back. Think about spending seven days cooped up in that tiny space and ponder the fact that at one point Borman suffered a fit of vomiting and diarrhea.

U-505 This was the only German submarine to be captured during WWII. A boarding team from the US Navy jumped into the sinking boat, which had been booby-trapped and abandoned by the crew. The navy team closed the sea valves and unhooked the TNT, and the boat ended up here in 1954. Another tight squeeze for humans, the sub

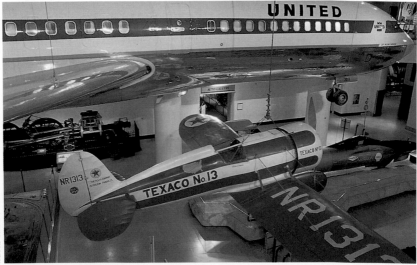

RICHARD CUMMINS

Aviation history on display at the Museum of Science & Industry

housed 60 people in its minuscule spaces for months at a time. (You might want to see the movie *Das Boot* to get a sense of the experience.) This exhibit is always popular, so head here early in the day.

The Coal Mine Visitors ride the same equipment used by miners in a simulated mine where the walls are lined with Illinois coal. Recent additions include a computer control room and displays detailing various types of mining. Kids love the ride in the cage elevator.

Navy: Technology at Sea This is a rah-rah look at the workings of modern ships in the US Navy, including an aircraft carrier, an attack sub and a destroyer. Two F-14 simulators, which always draw mobs, offer thrilling rides that replicate bombing raids, dogfights and carrier landings. The last should give even the most jaded visitors a respect for the pilots who land these things on the stamp-size decks of aircraft carriers in the ocean.

Flight 727 This old United Airlines plane retired to its dramatic perch in the museum after almost 30 years plying America's skies. Its landing gear and flaps rotate through the positions used during flight.

Imaging: The Tools of Science Better than its dry-as-dirt name suggests, this exhibit shows the tools that scientists use to probe the secrets and mysteries of the body and universe.

The Farm This flashy exhibit replaces exhibits that offered an unglamorous yet informative look at what goes into getting food to the average supermarket. Now you get to be a virtual farmer and mow down a field of corn with your combine – not that that doesn't have its thrills.

A chick hatchery shows what happens when an egg incubates to maturity. Should anybody worry, the chicks on display are not on the first stage of a one-way journey to the chicken-finger special in the restaurants downstairs. They're sent north to mature into chickens at Lincoln Park's Farm in the Zoo.

Body Slices In 1943 a dead man and woman were frozen and then sliced up in a manner not unlike deli pastrami. The resulting slices – vertical for the woman, horizontal for the man – show *every* aspect of the human body within their transparent, formaldehyde frames, hanging in the museum's blue stairwell. Dieters will find the exhibit useful before lunch.

Jackson Park

The setting for the 1893 World's Columbian Exposition, Jackson Park moldered for decades. But the overall revitalization of the Chicago Park District has been a boon for Jackson Park. The lagoons have survived from the 1893 fair, of which little remains beyond the heavily rebuilt Museum of Science & Industry.

Another exposition survivor and twice restored, the **Osaka Garden** is a peaceful refuge on an island in the reflecting pond. The most recent restoration in 1981 gave it a new teahouse. Take time to inspect the characteristic intricacy of the rocks, hills, plants, lanterns and bridges. The surrounding island has become a nature sanctuary.

In the middle of the park, *The Republic (Hayes Ave at Richards Dr)* is a smaller replica of a statue that celebrated 400 years of post-Columbus civilization at the 1893 fair. Its blinding brilliance arises from a 1992 restoration.

The simple wooden details and shingles of a former **Coast Guard station** would make this charming building much more at home in a rural setting. It sits on the yacht harbor, a quarter-mile north of where Lake Shore Dr – formally called Coast Guard Dr at this point – meets Marquette Dr. The station now holds a restaurant.

University of Chicago

Some universities collect football championships. The University of Chicago (☎ 773-702-1234, 5801 S Ellis Ave) collects Nobel Prizes – 73 through 2000. In particular, the economics department has been a regular

RICK GERHARTER

Rockefeller Memorial Chapel

Walking Tour This tour covers the campus' highlights and lowlights. It takes about an hour unless you dawdle along the way. When viewing the classic old buildings, keep looking up for the stone menageries of critters, fairies, monsters and other creatures that are carved into cornices, rooftops, entrances and windows. Follow the path on the accompanying map.

Start at Robie House (for details on Robie House, see the separate heading, later). Walk a half-block south down Woodlawn Ave to **Ida Noyes Hall**. Built as a women's dormitory in 1916, it is now the student center. Note the woman's head carved into the entry arch. Inside, the lobby, lounge and library are richly detailed.

Cross Woodlawn Ave to **Rockefeller Memorial Chapel**. University officials sent themselves off on junkets to England to ensure the authenticity of the main campus chapel, which was completed in 1928. Sculpture lovers will be in heaven: the outside features 24 life-size and 53 smaller religious figures, with even more inside.

winner, with faculty and former students pulling in 22 prizes since the first Nobel for economics was awarded in 1969. Merton Miller, a U of C economics faculty member and a Nobel winner, explained the string of wins to the *Sun-Times:* 'It must be the water; it certainly can't be the coffee.'

The university's classes first met on October 1, 1892. John D Rockefeller was a major contributor to the institution, donating more than $35 million, which he called 'the best investment I ever made in my life.' The original campus was constructed in an English Gothic style. Since WWII modern architects have made use of a cacophony of styles, many quite ugly. A new master plan unveiled in 2000 calls for numerous changes to improve the campus, including a beautification of the long-ignored Midway Plaisance that would include canals.

Turn west (right) on 59th St, then turn right again into the courtyard just past Foster Hall. **Foster, Kelly, Green & Beecher Halls**, the first women's halls, were built in 1893 and 1899. Foster Hall features a pack of gargoyles on the turret overlooking the midway.

Continue north, walking between the Walker Museum (actually used for classrooms), on the left, and Pick Hall, on the right. Cross the Main Quad to reach **Eckhart Hall**. One of the last Gothic buildings built on campus, it was completed in 1930. The carved details honor the resident physics, astronomy and mathematics departments.

Pass into Hutchinson Court through the arched entrance to the left of Eckhart, and you'll reach the **Tower Group**. Dominated by Mitchell Tower, which is modeled after Oxford's Magdalen College, these four 1903 buildings are linked by interior cloisters. The tower, which was the first purely aesthetic building at the university, contains 10 bells, whose cacophonous chimes delight some and annoy others.

Exit Hutchinson Court by walking to the west, then turn right into **Hull Court**. This area includes (in clockwise order starting at Culver Hall, on the left) the 1897 Anatomy, Zoology and Biology Buildings. Look for the griffins atop Zoology. The pond was once stocked with exotic fish.

Continue north through **Cobb Gate**. A university architect actually felt his style

was cramped on campus, so he donated this ceremonial entryway in 1900 and let loose with his ornamental passions. The gargoyles struggling on the climb to the top are said to represent undergraduate students.

Turn west (left) and face north to see the **Joseph Regenstein Library**. Walter Netsch, the architect whose notions of an Italian hill village led to some perverse creations at the University of Illinois at Chicago, brought brutalism to the U of C in 1970. The vertical grooves and slit windows are supposed to help the library fit in with the classic structures to the south. The result actually fits in

UNIVERSITY OF CHICAGO WALKING TOUR

about as much as the proverbial turd fits into the proverbial punch bowl.

From here, walk west along 57th St to Ellis Ave, turn right and walk a half-block north to the 1967 bronze sculpture *Nuclear Energy*. A human skull and a mushroom cloud come together in this work, which sits on the exact spot where Enrico Fermi and company started the nuclear age (see the boxed text 'A Bomb Is Born').

Turn back south and go to the corner of 57th St and Ellis Ave, where you'll come to **Charles Hitchcock Hall**. The usual ornamental English posies are dispensed with on this 1902 men's dormitory, in favor of corncobs and other prairie flora.

Continue south to where 58th St ends, on your right; turn right and walk a half-block west to the **Cummings Life Science Center**. A huge brick-and-limestone building and the tallest on campus, this 1973 structure features 40 brick chimneys climbing the walls to provide ventilation for the many labs within.

A Bomb Is Born

At 3:53pm on December 2, 1942, Enrico Fermi looked at a small crowd of men around him and said, 'The reaction is self-sustaining.' The scene was a dank squash court under the abandoned football stadium in the heart of the University of Chicago. With great secrecy, the gathered scientists had just achieved the world's first controlled release of nuclear energy. More than one sigh of relief was heard amid the ensuing rounds of congratulations. The nuclear reactor was supposed to have been built in a remote corner of a forest preserve 20 miles away, but a labor strike had stopped work. The impatient scientists went ahead on campus, despite the objections of many who thought the thing might blow up and take a good part of the city with it. Places such as Los Alamos, New Mexico, and Hiroshima and Nagasaki, in Japan, are more closely linked to the nuclear era, but Chicago is where it began.

Walk back to the corner of 58th St and Ellis Ave. At the **University Bookstore**, you can buy a T-shirt to remember your visit forever.

Across the street stands the **Administration Building**. The fact that no donor wants to be associated with this dud tells you all you need to know. Hand-wringing over the 'appropriateness' of Gothic architecture after WWII resulted in this unspectacular building, which the university's own public relations literature sums up by saying that it allows you to better appreciate its neighbors.

Next door you'll find **Cobb Hall**, the university's oldest building, which opened its classrooms and offices in 1892. The architect, Henry Ives Cobb, designed the next 18 buildings constructed on campus. The 4th-floor Renaissance Society holds frequent art shows.

Walk diagonally southeast through the cloister joining Swift Hall and **Bond Chapel**. Built in 1926, this exquisite 300-seat chapel is the harmonious creation of the architects, sculptors, woodcarvers and glassmakers who worked together on the project. Look for the lute player on the cornice.

Exit the chapel and turn right into the courtyard. The **Classics Quadrangle** includes (in counterclockwise order starting at Cobb Hall) Gates-Blake and Goodspeed Halls (1892), the Classics Building (1915), Wieboldt Hall (1928) and Frederick Haskell Hall (1896). Characters from Aesop's fables decorate the Classics Building, while images of noted authors adorn Wieboldt.

Pass through the archway between Wieboldt and Haskell to get to the **William Rainey Harper Memorial Library**. The massive 1912 twin-towered building presents a grand facade both to the campus and the midway. The long row of arched, two-story windows bathe the 3rd-floor reading room with light.

To the right of Harper Library you'll see **Harold Leonard Stuart Hall**. The 1904 law school building features the original lawgiver on the roof. This Moses doesn't look like Charlton Heston.

Walk north to **Swift Hall**, the 1926 home of the Divinity School. Its prominent position on campus signifies the importance of religion in education. In the basement there's a decent coffee shop.

Continue north to the center of the traffic circle; turn east (right) and walk along 58th St to the **Chicago Theological Seminary**, on your left. The redbrick 1926 buildings provide a Tudor contrast to the university. The cloisters invite contemplation, and the beautiful Hilton Memorial Chapel invites prayer.

Across the street stands the **Oriental Institute**. See the separate heading, later, for information on the institute's museum.

Continue west to Robie House to complete the campus tour.

Robie House The ultimate expression of Frank Lloyd Wright's Prairie School style is embodied in this masterpiece (☎ 773-834-1847, 5757 S Woodlawn Ave; admission $9/7 for adults/children; tours 11am, 1pm & 3pm weekdays, continuous 11am-3:30pm weekends), which makes the otherwise charming surrounding houses look like so many dowdy old aunts.

The long, thin Roman bricks and limestone trim mirror the same basic shape of the entire house. The dominant feature on the prominent south side is the long row of carefully detailed windows on the 1st floor. The long and low lines, which reflect Midwest topography, are ornamented solely by the exquisite stained- and leaded-glass doors and windows.

The materials used to construct the house were as revolutionary as the design. Poured concrete forms the basis of many of the floors and balconies, while steel beams support the massively overhanging roof – a radical concept for residential construction.

The Robie family, for whom the house was built in 1909, lived there only until 1911, when the family bicycle business died right along with the couple's marriage. The Chicago Theological Seminary turned the house into a dorm, and conditions soon became hellish. By 1957 what the students hadn't destroyed

RICK GERHARTER

Robie House: a masterful example of Prairie School architecture was ready to be demolished. Designated a National Historic Landmark in 1963, the house was taken over by the U of C, which allowed it to molder further until 1993. Since then, a joint agreement between the university and the Oak Park–based Frank Lloyd Wright Home and Studio Foundation has set the stage for a massive multiyear restoration. One look at some of the critical exterior details, such as the foundation, will hint at the urgency of this work.

Tours of the interior take in only the central living and dining room. But it's worth paying admission to see the sweep of the space, broken into its components by the fireplace. Note that Wright, a control freak if there ever was one, used built-in furniture, windows and other details to prevent the owners from messing with his interior design vision.

A gift shop with books and other mementos operates in the garage.

Oriental Institute Museum This fascinating museum (☎ 773-702-9507, 1155 E 58th St; admission free; open 10am-4pm Tues-Sat, until 8:30pm Wed, noon-4pm Sun), in the heart of campus, contains artifacts from Egypt, Mesopotamia and other ancient cultures. The 'Oriental' in the name refers to the Near East, where University of Chicago archaeological work has been under way since 1919. In the museum's early years the exploits of its original curators were a bit like those of Indiana Jones. Today the museum continues work in Israel, Egypt, Jordan and Syria.

The often overlooked collection received some new displays in 1998, but overall it still has the feel of a place in need of a benefactor. Take some time to examine the almost 3000-year-old carved stone reliefs that once adorned the Assyrian city of Khorsabad when Sargon II was king. Other objects come from the Achaemenid palace complex in Persepolis, which ill-mannered Alexander the Great sacked in 331 BC.

David & Alfred Smart Museum Named after the founders of *Esquire* magazine, who contributed the money to get it started, the

official fine arts museum of the university (☎ 773-702-0200, 5550 S Greenwood Ave; admission free; open 10am-4pm Tues-Fri, until 9pm Thur, noon-6pm Sat & Sun) opened in 1974 and expanded in 1999. The 8000 items in the collection include some excellent works from ancient China and Japan and a colorful and detailed Syrian mosaic from about AD 600.

The strength of the collection lies in paintings and sculpture contemporary to the university's existence. Auguste Rodin's *Thinker* occupies a thoughtful place (hey, it's a Smart museum), as do works by Arthur Davies, Jean Arp, Henry Moore and many others. The freakish 1929 painting *Four Arts Ball*, by Guy Pène Du Bois, has become something of a museum icon. As you study the groundbreaking Robie House dining-room set by Frank Lloyd Wright, you might wonder why it's not back in the original house three blocks away.

Washington Park

Designed in 1871, this classic lakeside park is linked to Jackson Park by the Midway Plaisance. The *Fountain of Time*, a 1922 concrete Lorado Taft sculpture that commemorates 100 years of peace between the US and England, sits at the junction of the Midway Plaisance and Washington Park. Its original meaning all but lost, the statue is in dire need of repair. But the hooded figure of Time continues to watch over the rising and falling waves of humanity, inspired by the phrase 'Time goes, you say? Ah no! Alas, Time stays we go…' One of the city's most moving monuments, this is well worth seeking out.

In a peaceful part of Washington Park, the **DuSable Museum of African American History** (☎ 773-947-0600, 740 E 56th Place; admission $3/2 for adults/children, free Sun; open 10am-5pm Mon-Sat, noon-5pm Sun) features more than 100 works of African American art and permanent exhibits such as Up from Slavery, which covers African Americans' experiences from slavery through the Civil Rights movement. A new exhibit, Harold Washington in Office, re-creates the mayoral office of the charismatic

Washington, who was elected in 1983 and 1987 and died on November 25, 1987. The museum, housed in a 1910 building, takes its name from Chicago's first permanent settler, Jean Baptiste Point du Sable, a French-Canadian of Haitian descent (see the History section of Facts about Chicago).

FARTHER SOUTH
Pullman

George Pullman's dream community turned into a nightmare when idealism ran headlong into capitalism in 1894. The millionaire railroad car manufacturer started his namesake town in 1880 in order to provide his workers with homes in a clean and wholesome environment. He built houses, apartments, stores, a hotel and churches, all of which were meant to return 6% on his investment.

Pullman earned kudos from both industrialists and social activists. The town's careful design was based on French models and featured an aesthetic that was unknown in workers' housing then or now. But the 1893 depression hit Pullman's luxury railcar business hard. The firm laid off some workers and cut the pay of others. Rents and prices in Pullman's town stayed high, however, to ensure that 6%.

Worker resentment grew and resulted in the Pullman strike of 1894. Violent clashes between the strikers and thugs hired by Pullman were finally settled when federal troops were sent in to force the strikers back to work. It was another turning point for the American labor movement, which had been fueled by the 1886 Haymarket Riot (see the Facts about Chicago chapter for more information on Chicago history).

Pullman died a bitter man in 1897. The following year, the Illinois Supreme Court ordered the company to sell the town except for the factories. The sale of the town's properties was completed by 1907, and the neighborhood has experienced ups and downs since then. The last part of the complex finally closed for good in 1981.

The southern part of Pullman, where the higher-paid craftsmen and managers lived, has been largely bought up by people determined to preserve it. North Pullman, with simpler housing for laborers, is only now being appreciated for its underlying architectural qualities.

Visit Pullman in the daytime so you can appreciate the buildings. Start with the **Hotel Florence** (☎ 773-785-8181, 11111 S Forrestville Ave), a striking Queen Anne building that closed in 2000 for 'restoration.'

RICK GERHARTER

Washington Park's *Fountain of Time*

Owned by the state, the Hotel Florence needs new mechanical systems. Unfortunately, the state hasn't said how long work will take, which has caused many to worry that things will drag on forever, given the state's dubious record in this arena.

The **Colonnade Apartments** *(112th St at Champlain Ave)*, four matching curved 1892 apartment buildings, surround the former market hall. The tiny bachelors' apartments upstairs were obviously not intended for men who expected company.

A rambling complex with varied rooflines, the **Pullman Administration Building and Clock Tower** *(111th St at Cottage Grove Ave)* is solidly French in conception. A fire in 1998 nearly destroyed the building. The state of Illinois is moving forward – albeit at a glacial pace – with plans to restore the complex and create a railroad museum.

Pullman lies 13 miles south of the Loop; Metra Electric trains run here from the Randolph St Station. Get off at the 111th St Station, which is right in the heart of the most scenic section. The fare is $2.75 one-way. A side note: the double-decker Metra Electric trains were among the last passenger trains built by Pullman in Chicago.

If you're driving, take I-94 south to the 111th St exit. Pullman is a half-mile west. The Historic Pullman Foundation (☎ 773-785-8901, 11141 S Cottage Grove Ave) offers information on walking tours. Call for their hours.

ACTIVITIES

If you are staying at a hotel, definitely check with the concierge or front desk about arrangements the hotel may have with private clubs for any of the sports listed here. Many hotels can get you discounted indoor tennis time, health club access or day passes for pools or other facilities the hotel doesn't have.

Bicycling

Chicago is well suited for biking. The very popular lakefront path covers 18½ miles from Hollywood Beach to the South Shore Country Club, at 71st St. Every July, progressive rock station WXRT (☎ 773-777-1700) hosts a midnight bike ride that starts

Fun in the sun on the shore of Lake Michigan

at Buckingham Fountain and winds its way through the city all night long. It's a fun event, and survivors are treated to breakfast at the finish line. Check with the station for exact dates.

See the Getting Around chapter for details on bike rental.

Bowling

Once called 'the opiate of the masses,' bowling is a distinctly Midwestern activity. People of all shapes, sizes and ages gather in boisterous groups to send balls crashing into pins. Talent is not a prerequisite, but the willingness to consume copious pitchers of cheap beer is. The lanes draw the most crowds during the cold months, when bowling is a great indoor sport (although the preponderance of beer bellies should tell you everything you need to know about how athletic this so-called sport is).

The following are big, cheap bowling alleys open way past midnight; they rent any equipment you'll need and feature bright 1970s vinyl decor.

Diversey-River Bowl (☎ 773-227-5800, 2211 W Diversey Parkway)

Marigold Arcade (☎ 773-935-8183, 828 W Grace St; Map 7)

Waveland Bowl (☎ 773-472-5900, 3700 N Western Ave)

For bowling with charm, try Wrigleyville's Southport Lanes (☎ 773-472-1601, 3325 N Southport Ave; Map 7). This 75-year-old bar has four lanes with hand-set pins in the basement.

Canoeing

Retrace the route of French trapper Louis Jolliet while you have an urban adventure by canoeing. Besides urban sprawl, you'll see deer, red foxes, beavers and birds. You'll also see parks and houses being built, which shows that Chicago has finally discovered that the river can serve a better purpose as a scenic backdrop than as a sewer. Chicagoland Canoe Base (☎ 773-777-1498, 4019 N Narragansett Ave) will rent you a canoe for about $40 plus deposit, and owner Vic Hurtowy will give you tips on where to paddle. And fear not, the Chicago River is a lot cleaner than it used to be. Many species of fish have returned, and none have more than one head.

Golf

Chicago golfers stretch the season as far as possible in both directions. There's a certain macho pride in playing with neon-colored balls in the snow. Most courses are open from April to November. If it's a nice day outside of those months, phone the courses – they might be open.

The Chicago Park District has turned management of the courses over to Kemper Golf (☎ 312-245-0909), whose automated phone line offers information about the courses, tee times, costs, directions and opening dates and will accept reservations.

Public Courses The district operates the Sydney R Marovitz Course (☎ 773-868-4113, Irving Park Rd in Lincoln Park; Map 7). Commonly known as 'Waveland,' the nine-hole course enjoys sweeping views of the lake and skyline. Its 1932 Gothic field house contains a clock tower with chimes for the hours. Sadly, neighbors across Lake Shore Dr complained about the noise, and the chimes have been turned off. Obviously, they preferred the sonorous roar of traffic.

The course is very popular, and in order to secure a tee time, golfers cheerfully arrive at 5:30am. You can avoid that sort of lunacy by spending a few dollars extra to get a

Lakefront Parks & Beaches

The lakefront parks and beaches are certainly Chicago's most democratic institutions. On the same day you might find extended African American families holding huge reunion barbecues under one tree, while a white yuppie couple fusses over their perfect baby in a pricey stroller under another and a Hispanic amateur soccer club competes on the grass.

The notable parks along Chicago's lakefront (eg, Grant and Lincoln Parks) are covered separately in their corresponding neighborhood sections; see those headings for detailed information.

Chicago's beaches stretch like a string of pearls along the lake, making the city the Miami of the Midwest, if only for a few months each year. The wide array of beaches ranges from vast, steamy meat markets to quiet secluded coves. People from every one of Chicago's ethnic groups, rich and poor alike, flock to the cooling waters of Lake Michigan on hot summer weekends. All of Chicago's beaches are free, in contrast to those in some nearby suburbs.

From late May until early September, the Chicago Park District (☎ 312-747-2200) provides lifeguards. However, a usual amount of prudence is all that's really required for safe swimming, since the Lake Michigan surf can usually be measured by the inch. Take note: the water temperature can vary dramatically, depending on a variety of factors; one day it will be in the 80s, the next in the 50s.

The drinking-water fountains always run because it would cost too much to turn them on and off each year, and this way their pipes don't freeze. Besides, the lake threatens to engulf the lakefront every few years, so every bit drained away helps.

The city's best beaches include the following, from north to south:

Loyola Beach, which stretches for more than eight blocks from North Shore Ave to Touhy Ave, features one of those upscale wooden playgrounds for kids. It's fairly close to the Chicago International Hostel and the Loyola El stop.

Montrose Beach is a great wide beach with a curving breakwater. The Montrose Harbor bait shop sells ice for coolers. There's ample parking, but the walks to the beach can be long. To get there by bus, take No 146 or No 151.

---

reservation. Fees vary widely through the year, from $7 to $15, with extra charges for nonresidents and reservations. You can also rent clubs here.

The district's only 18-hole course is the Jackson Park Golf Course (☎ 773-493-7085, E 63rd St at S Stoney Island Ave), considered moderately challenging. Fees range from $7 to $15. Reservations are recommended.

At the South Shore Country Club (☎ 312-747-2536, S Lake Shore Dr at E 71st St), the public course has a mere nine holes. It's right on the lake, and crowds aren't bad. And this is a favored course for cops, so crime is very low. Enter through the police stables at S Lake Shore Dr and E 71st St.

If you just want to knock a bucket of balls, the Diversey Driving Range (☎ 312- 281-5722; open 7am-10pm daily; Map 7), in Lincoln Park where Diversey Parkway meets the lake, will let you whack away to your heart's content. Rental clubs are available, and a bucket is about $6. A reconstruction of the building has won kudos for its creative design.

Private Courses In an inspired move, acres of vacant tracts of Illinois Center land have been turned into a golf course just east of the Loop. Family Golf Center (☎ 312-616- 1234, 221 N Columbus Dr; Map 3) features a driving range, nine short holes with a complex green, chipping greens and a bar and restaurant. You can make reservations to get a round in ($15) before or after a big meeting. But finding your way to the course

Lakefront Parks & Beaches

It isn't really a beach, but **Belmont Rocks** *(Map 7)* is a popular gathering point for gays from nearby Lake View. It's just south of Belmont Harbor at Belmont Ave.

Zoo day-trippers and Lincoln Parkers fill **Fullerton Beach** *(Map 6)*. The narrow beach can get jammed on weekends, but a five-minute walk south from Fullerton yields uncrowded vistas.

The closest thing Chicago has to a Southern California beach is **North Ave Beach** *(Map 6)*. Countless volleyball nets draw scores of beautiful people wearing the latest skimpy, neon-hued togs. The steamship-inspired beach house, nicely renovated in 1999, now contains a seasonal café. In summer you can sit on the upper deck and sip a beer. Nice. A short walk out on the curving breakwater anytime of the year yields postcard views of the city from a spot that seems almost a world apart.

Fabled **Oak St Beach** *(Map 5)* lies at the north end of Michigan Ave, less than five minutes from the Water Tower. The hulking Lake Shore Dr condos cast shadows in the afternoon, but this beach remains the place to go for those who spend the winter at the health club and in the tanning booth, preparing for summer.

Nestled between Lake Shore Dr and Navy Pier, **Ohio St Beach** *(Map 3)* is convenient for those who want a quick dip or a chance to feel some sand between sweaty toes.

12th St Beach *(Map 4)*, hidden east of Meigs Field and south of the Adler Planetarium, makes a great break from the myriad sights of the Museum Campus. Its out-of-the-way location gives the narrow enclave an exclusive feel.

Just across Lake Shore Dr from the Museum of Science & Industry, **57th St Beach** *(Map 12)* features an expanse of clean, golden sand. A bit farther south, **Jackson Park Beach** *(Map 12)* contains a stately, recently restored beach house with dramatic breezeways. This beach, next to the yacht harbor, has a charm lacking at the beaches with more modern – and mundane – facilities.

Venture behind the golf course and the elegant South Shore Cultural Center (71st Ave at South Shore Dr) and you find a hidden treasure: **South Shore Beach**. The medium-size beach is set in a cove with trees along one side.

can be a tougher challenge than making par from a trap: its address is Columbus Dr, but Columbus is actually about 50 feet above the ground where the course is. From the Loop, you can get there by cutting through Randolph St Station; from River North, take Columbus Dr over the river and then climb down every flight of stairs you can find out of the Illinois Center morass to the ground below. When you're chipping away, imagine that the faces of the Illinois Center architects are on every ball.

Health Clubs

Hotels almost always have either their own facilities or agreements with nearby clubs. Otherwise, Lakeshore Athletic Clubs offer pools, full equipment, jogging tracks and more in two convenient locations: River North (☎ 312-644-4880, 441 N Wabash Ave; Map 3) and Lincoln Park (☎ 773-477-9888, 1320 W Fullerton Ave; Map 6). Day-use rates average $18 and don't include tennis.

Avoid the ubiquitous Bally Total Fitness Clubs, where commission-paid drones will dog you during your visit with increasingly desperate membership pleas, even if you're from out of town.

Ice Skating

The ice-skating season is depressingly long for sunbathers and even skaters. Skate on State (☎ 312-744-3315; admission free; open 9am-7pm daily, Nov-Mar; Map 3), across from Marshall Field's on the vacant Block 37, offers winter skating. You can rent skates and drink hot chocolate. Note that if work *finally* begins on the long-delayed shopping complex here, the skating will just skate away.

The Chicago Park District operates a first-class winter rink at Grant Park's Daley Bicentennial Plaza (☎ 312-742-7650, on the south side of the 300 block of E Randolph St; admission free; call for hours; Map 3). You can rent skates here.

In-Line Skating

At all the places you'd ride a bike, you can in-line skate. Many businesses, however, have clamped down on customers who try to act oh so cool by skating, say, to the bar for a beer or to the frozen foods section for a Lean Cuisine. Sources of rental skates include Windward Sports (☎ 773-472-6868, 3317 N Clark St; Map 7) and Bike Chicago (☎ 312-944-2337, 800-915-2453, Navy Pier, 600 E Grand Ave; Map 3). Be prepared to pay a large deposit and rates of about $20 a day.

Running

As with biking, Chicago is well suited for running. The lakefront and Lincoln and Grant Parks are all popular with runners throughout the day. For information on organized races, try the Chicago Area Runners Association (☎ 312-666-9836).

Swimming

Lakefront beaches have lifeguards from late in May through early September. However, you can swim at your own risk whenever you want, depending on what you think of the temperature. The water in August is usually in the 70s Fahrenheit.

In the summer the public pool at Holstein Park (☎ 312-742-7554, 2200 N Oakley Ave; admission free; open during daylight hours), in the heart of Bucktown, is large and refreshing. You can rent a suit and leave your sweaty duds in a locker. Best of all, the pool has frequent adult-only hours, when squealing kids are sent packing.

Tennis

Some public tennis courts require reservations and charge fees, while others are free and players queue for their turns on the court. Place your racket by the net and you're next in line. The season runs from mid-April to mid-October.

At Grant Park's Daley Bicentennial Plaza (☎ 312-742-7650, on the south side of the 300 block of Randolph St; Map 3), you can pay a fee to use 12 lighted courts.

Waveland Tennis Courts (☎ 312-868-4132, on the east side of N Lake Shore Dr where Waveland Ave meets Lincoln Park; Map 7) charges fees for its 20 lighted courts.

Runners and skaters take to the road in Lincoln Park.

Lake Shore Park (☎ 312-742-7891, 808 N Lake Shore Dr; Map 5), near the lake, features two very popular (and free) lighted courts.

In Grant Park (900 S Columbus Dr near E Balbo Dr; Map 4) you'll find several courts. No reservations are taken, but fees are charged at peak times.

Though it's privately owned (and usually only open to dues-paying members), the Lakeshore Athletic Club (☎ 312-644-4880, 441 N Wabash Ave; Map 3) in River North might offer day passes to its indoor courts during off-peak hours.

Offbeat Activities

When you've seen enough pigeons, call the Chicago Audubon Society (☎ 773-539-6793). The group organizes frequent and free **birdwatching** expeditions all around the area, and novices are encouraged to come along. Chicago is host to hundreds of bird species, from eagles to the rare white-breasted nuthatch, as well as Canadian geese .

You can go **windsurfing** on Lake Michigan (this *is* the Windy City) at Montrose Beach (see the boxed text 'Lakefront Parks & Beaches'). Windward Sports (☎ 773-472-6868, 3317 N Clark St; Map 7) rents boards for about $35 a day. Call to see if the company is operating its on-site summer rental hut at the beach.

For an even bigger blow, try **sailing**. Bill Gladstone's Chicago Sailing Club (☎ 773-871-7245, at Belmont Harbor where W Belmont Ave meets the lake; Map 7) rents boats in several sizes and prices. You leave from Belmont Harbor, the scenic haven on the North Side for hundreds of sailboats. If you don't know your jib from a poop deck, you can take lessons. Call for details.

The many forest preserves surrounding the city have miles of trails for **horseback riding**. Glen Grove Equestrian Center (☎ 847-966-8032, 9453 Central Ave, Morton Grove) rents horses by the hour, starting at $40 an hour. The center also offers organized rides in the woods.

Places to Stay

The myriad lodging choices in Chicago range from world-class five-star hotels on N Michigan Ave to hostels far from the center. Your budget and your choice of neighborhood in which to lay your head should help you decide among them.

HOSTELS

As in many towns, here you'll find that the greatest number of hostel rooms are available in summer, when students leave town and universities rent out some of their rooms. No hostels are in the heart of the Near North action, but several are in attractive locations. Best of all is the new hostel right in the Loop.

Hostelling International–Chicago (☎ 312-360-0300, 800-909-4776, fax 312-360-0313, reserve@hichicago.org, www.hichicago.org, 24 E Congress Pkwy at Wabash Ave; postal address: PO Box 0452, Chicago, IL 60690; Map 3) Bed in separate-sex dorm with six to 10 beds per room $17.50; private rooms not currently available. Open 24 hours; check-in after 2pm. Visa and MasterCard accepted.

This big new hostel opened in fall 2000 and occupies a renovated Queen Anne industrial building in the Loop Retail Historic District. It offers 250 beds during the academic year and 500 beds in summer. Amenities include a kitchen and a large student center providing insider information on the best things to see and do in the city.

Chicago International Hostel (☎ 773-262-1011, fax 773-262-3673, chicagohostel@hotmail.com, 6318 N Winthrop) Bed in three- to six-bed dorm $15, private double $35 with shared bath, $40 with private bath. Check-in times 7am-10am and 4pm-midnight. No credit cards.

Near Loyola University, this major year-round hostel housed in a 1960s building lies three blocks south of the Loyola El stop on Sheridan, then two blocks east. Though the location is safe enough, you're far from the action. The El takes at least 35 minutes to get you to Chicago Ave.

Arlington House (☎ 773-929-5380, 800-467-8355, fax 773-665-5485, mitch@arlingtonhouse.com, www.arlingtonhouse.com,

When the sun sets, you'll find plenty of places to spend the night.

616 W Arlington Place; Map 6) Bed in four, six- or seven-bed dorm $17 for HI cardholders, $20 for others. Private rooms (by reservation) $48 with shared bath, $55 with private bath. Open year-round, 24 hours a day. Visa and MasterCard accepted.

Arlington House occupies an excellent location in the heart of Lincoln Park, one block west of Clark St. The new managers, who took over recently, claim to have tossed out some of the less-than-salubrious former residents. The rooms in the classic brick building are purely adequate, but try not to get one of the less-than-ideal basement rooms.

Eleanor Residence *(☎ 312-932-2000 or 664-8245, 888-393-1898, fax 312-664-0888, information@eleanorresidence.com, www .eleanorresidence.com, 1550 N Dearborn St; Map 5)* Singles $65 (including breakfast and dinner, except Sun).

It's not quite a cloistered existence, but life at the women-only Eleanor Residence, just south of Lincoln Park, is tightly regulated, with no men allowed in the rooms. The included meals make the place an excellent value – if you qualify in the gender department.

Three Arts Club of Chicago *(☎ 312-944-6250, fax 312-944-6284, info@threearts.org, www.threearts.org, 1300 N Dearborn St; Map 5)* Nightly/weekly/monthly rates are $45/250/810 per person (including breakfast and dinner); long-term monthly rates of $550-690 for stays of four months or longer. All major credit cards except American Express accepted.

Artistic women should take note: since 1912, the Three Arts Club of Chicago has tried to assist emerging women artists by providing inexpensive housing while they study in Chicago. For nine months of the year female students or practicing artists can stay here. During the summer the place goes coed and gets a lot less picky about artistic and educational credentials.

B&BS

Chicago has finally caught on to the bed-and-breakfast concept. ***Bed & Breakfast Chicago*** *(☎ 773-248-0005, 800-375-7084, fax 773-248-7090, stays@chicago-bed-breakfast.com,* www.chicago-bed-breakfast.com, PO Box 14088, Chicago, IL 60614)*, a booking service, ha dles rooms at more than 60 places throughout the city, most of them in the Gold Coast, Old Town and Lincoln Park areas. The units run the gamut, from bedrooms in upscale old graystones to whole apartments where you're left to your own devices. This is an excellent way to experience life in the more interesting neighborhoods. The service provides you with a list of places based on your desires for price, location and proximity of the owners. Rates for singles and doubles range anywhere from about $85 to over $300. The minimum stay at most of the places is two or three nights.

Gold Coast Guest House *(☎ 312-337-0361, ☎/fax 312-337-0362, sally@bbchicago.com, www.bbchicago.com, 113 W Elm St near Clark St; Map 5)* Doubles $129-199.

Visitors from abroad will be especially welcomed by innkeeper Sally Baker at the Gold Coast Guest House. Baker has been steadily refining her 1873 classic three-flat for 12 years. Her experience as a travel guide based in London helps her understand the needs of travelers new to the US or to Chicago. Each of the four guest rooms includes a private bath and individual air-conditioning controls. Guests receive a bounteous breakfast and can help themselves to sodas, beer and snacks in the refrigerator at other times. The walled-in garden out back makes a pleasant escape from the city.

House of Two Urns Bed & Breakfast *(☎ 312-810-2466, fax 773-235-1410, www .twourns.com, 1239 N Greenview Ave; Map 6)* Rooms $80-160.

Not a far walk from the diverse charms of Wicker Park, this B&B sits on a classic Chicago residential street. Inside the typical former two-flat brownstone, you'll find a long list of amenities like VCRs, free local calls, a laundry and a great roof deck. Owner Kapra Fleming can chat you up in German, Spanish and French (and Anglaise, oui).

HOTELS

As the most popular convention city in the US, Chicago abounds with hotels. In the Loop and North Side more than a hundred

10 Great Hotels

You'll find details for all of the following in this chapter.

Best Central Cheap Place Cass Hotel (Near North)

Best Convention Giant Sheraton Chicago Hotel and Towers (Near North)

Best Family Hotel Embassy Suites Chicago–Downtown (Near North)

Best Grand Experience The Drake (Gold Coast)

Best No Expense Spared Four Seasons Hotel (Gold Coast)

Best Place to Check in with No Questions Asked Days Inn Gold Coast (Lincoln Park)

Best Place to Collapse after Shopping Park Hyatt (Gold Coast)

Best Place to Have an Edifice Complex Hotel Burnham (Loop)

Best Pool Hotel Inter-Continental Chicago (Near North)

Best Proximity to Nightlife City Suites Hotel (Lake View)

hotels of all types offer more than 25,000 rooms. The conventions can attract tens of thousands of visitors, who fill up even the most remote locations and pay top dollar for the chance to do so. During one of the major shows (see the boxed text 'Bad Dates' in the Facts for the Visitor chapter) it might be better to skip Chicago entirely: the best restaurants and hotels will be packed.

Not so long ago, you could usually count on great lodging deals when conventions weren't in town and hotels were scrambling to fill their rooms at almost any cost. Sadly, though, Chicago's popularity means that this is no longer the case. The average room rate in 1996 was $118, but by 2000 it had soared to $152. Still, it's worthwhile to look for any deals – especially on weekends. During non-holiday weekends in the dead of winter, the best hotels sometimes offer rooms for $99 a night, or even less. Package deals may include in-room treats such as champagne, as well as free theater tickets and parking. The latter can shave $20 a night off your bill.

Unless otherwise specified, the rates listed in this chapter are the average prices a hotel charges. Use them for comparison purposes only, since they can vary so widely. Weekend or special rates are listed when the hotel offers them fairly regularly. Call and see what deals are available for the dates you want to visit. Frequently you can do better by calling chain-affiliated hotels directly than by calling their national toll-free numbers. Families should note that suite hotels can be a good deal; the kids can be exiled to the sofa bed while the adults take refuge in the real bed behind a closed door.

Beware of a nasty surprise you will find on your bill: the hotel tax is a gnarly 14.9%. Also, the more a hotel charges per night, the more likely it is to levy some sort of ridiculous fee on local calls. These can run $1.25 or more per call, so if you have a lot of business to conduct and you're paying your own bill, ask about these charges when making reservations.

Finally, in a city bursting with splendid food and drink options, it rarely makes sense to eat or drink in your hotel. Most have restaurants and bars that are somnolent in quality and nightmarish in price. If a hotel features a worthwhile dining option, I've noted it below.

The Loop (Map 3)

Loop hotels are convenient to Grant Park, the museums and the central business and financial districts. They are usually no more than a 15-minute walk away from River North and N Michigan Ave (and for those near the river, much less). But despite several promising signs, such as the development of the theater district, the area is still a few years away from having its own hopping nightlife.

Mid-Range *Hotel Allegro* (☎ *312-236-0123, 800-643-1500, fax 312-236-0917, www.allegrochicago.com, 171 W Randolph St)* Singles and doubles $135-260.

Located in what was once the Bismarck Hotel, the Allegro has a notorious past to live down. For years it was home to various Chicago political organizations, and its hallways and rooms were the scene of all manner of dubious dealings. Now, however, its hip makeover has chased out the pinky-ring-clad political fat cats. Bright primary colors dominate the public spaces and the rooms, which vary widely in size. Try not to get one overlooking another building.

Hotel Burnham (☎ *312-782-1111, 877-294-9712, fax 312-782-0899, www .burnhamhotel.com, 1 W Washington St)* Singles and doubles $150-270.

Architecture buffs might have a hard time going to sleep in one of the most historic buildings in Chicago. Built as the Reliance Building in the early 1890s, this one languished in recent decades as tenants shunned its small floors. However, small floors proved perfect for a hotel, and it's been lavishly restored and reopened as the Hotel Burnham, in honor of one of its architects (for more details, see the Loop Architecture Walking Tour in the Architecture special section). The rooms all feature period-inspired decor to lavish and elegant effects. The hotel's Atwood Café gets good reviews from some of my pickier friends.

Silversmith (☎ *312-372-7696, 800-227-6963, fax 312-372-7320, www.crowneplaza .com/chi-silversmith, 10 S Wabash Ave)* Singles and doubles $150-250; weekend specials as low as $119.

Another Loop architectural gem that has been converted into a hotel, the Silversmith was built in 1894. Although the exterior was designed by Daniel Burnham's firm, the hotel's interior recalls Frank Lloyd Wright. The rooms are big, and the furniture has a distinct Prairie-style charm. Try to get one of the rooms that doesn't look right into another building.

Top End *W Chicago City Center* (☎ *312-332-1200, 800-621-2360, fax 312-332-5909, www .midlandhotelchicago.com, 172 W Adams St)* Singles $249-309, doubles $274-334.

By the time you show up here, the European-style Midland Hotel will have been rechristened as the contemporary-chic W Chicago City Center, a new link in the upscale W hotel chain (☎ 877-946-8357, www.whotels.com). The conversion will likely bring higher rates. Look for good deals on weekends, when the moneyed neighborhood folks working at the surrounding financial district have gone home and you can expect to find a tumbleweed or two rolling up the street.

Palmer House Hilton (☎ *312-726-7500, 800-445-8667, fax 312-917-1707, www.hilton .com, 17 E Monroe St at State St)* Singles normally $159-279, doubles $184-304; weekend deals in Dec and Jan as low as $99.

PLACES TO STAY

RICK GERHARTER

The Hotel Burnham has transformed the Reliance Building.

Built in 1927, the Palmer House hotel has gone through three incarnations in 125 years. As in many hotels of its era, the Hilton's 1640 rooms vary greatly in size, so ask for a big one when you check in. Let those too mesmerized by the 21 murals on the lobby ceiling take the dinky, dark rooms. Up one flight on an escalator, the lobby is the stunning feature of the place, with enough gilding to cover several lesser establishments.

Fairmont (☎ *312-565-8000, 800-527-4727, fax 312-946-5311, chicago@fairmont.com, www.fairmont.com, 200 N Columbus Dr)* Doubles $179-349; weekend deals as low as $129.

Overall, the Fairmont would rank among the elite of Chicago hotels if it weren't lost in the depths of the otherwise odious Illinois Center. Tall people will be thrilled with the extra-long beds, and less lofty-heighted souls will enjoy the spacious rooms, well-equipped work areas, opulent bathrooms and other luxuries provided by this San Francisco–based company. Rooms near the top of the hotel's 45 stories can enjoy excellent views if they face the park or lake. The public spaces are equally grand, and the hotel is convenient to the museums and Grant Park.

Renaissance Chicago Hotel (☎ *312-372-7200, 800-468-3571, fax 312-372-0834, www.renaissancehotels.com, 1 W Wacker Dr at N State St)* Singles $279-439, doubles $299-459.

This modern luxury hotel, next to the offices of advertising giant Leo Burnett, is lavish in its decor and amenities. The public spaces are actually much nicer than the somewhat bland exterior would suggest, with ornate tapestries and other elegant touches. The rooms are large and include sitting areas, which will be appreciated by those who don't want to spend all their time in their room in bed. Bay windows offer good views of the skyline and the river. All rooms contain modem ports, and the business traveler rooms come with fax machines and printers. In addition, a 24-hour Kinko's business-service facility is on the premises. The hotel offers packages that include tickets to shows in Loop theaters.

Hyatt Regency Chicago (☎ *312-565-1234, 800-233-1234, fax 312-565-2966, www.chicago.hyatt.com, 151 E Wacker Dr, one*

The ornate lobby of the Palmer House Hilton

block east of Michigan Ave) Singles $225-295, doubles $225-315.

A vast convention hotel with 2019 rooms, the Hyatt Regency is best at being big. The slew of restaurants are okay, and so are the bars. But there's really no reason to seek the place out unless you want to be close to your meeting at the Illinois Center or you want to collect Hyatt frequent-stayer points. The hotel doesn't even have a pool. Lots of specials keep all those rooms filled in off-peak times.

Swissôtel Chicago *(☎ 312-565-0565, 800-654-7263, fax 312-565-0540, www.swissotel .com, 323 E Wacker Dr)* Rack rates $400-650; with reservations, singles $189-359, doubles $229-429. Weekend and package rates as low as $149.

On the eastern frontier of Illinois Center, the Swissôtel – in a striking triangular mirrored-glass high-rise – is easy to spot. The 632 large rooms offer the expected good views from their individual sitting areas. Separate showers and bathtubs mean that one can douse while the other dunks. The casual Cafe Suisse bakes its own bread and pastries, and the Palm is a notable steak house. Anyone wandering through can lay waste to the huge bowl of mini Swiss chocolates on the concierge counter.

Near North (Map 3)
North of the river you can't go a block in any direction without finding a hotel. If you want to be near the center of Chicago's tourist action, stay here and enjoy all the eating, drinking, shopping and entertainment you could possibly desire.

Budget *Ohio House Motel (☎ 312-943-6000, 600 N LaSalle Dr at Ohio St)* Singles/ doubles starting at $85.

Make your reservations quick at the Ohio House, before developers turn it into a trendy restaurant. This throwback auto-court motel, with its cement-block detailing, has remained resolutely unchanged since JFK was president.

Cass Hotel *(☎ 312-787-4030, 800-227-7850, fax 312-787-8544, 640 N Wabash Ave)* Singles/doubles starting at $74/79.

Not much to look at inside or outside, the Cass won't give you much to look at in the bill department either. Rooms are very simple and rather small; in some the TV sits on a shelf at an angle hard to see from the beds. The location, however, is excellent.

Hotel Wacker *(☎ 312-787-1386, 111 W Huron St)* Singles/doubles $55/60.

If you've ever wondered what it would be like to stay on Mediterranean Ave in the Monopoly game, this place comes close. Actually, it's probably more like Baltic Ave. Rooms are clean and include TVs and air-conditioning, but you need to leave a $5 deposit for linen and your key. And note: budget motels and American slang notwithstanding, the hotel is named for Charles H Wacker, a great local brewer and preserver of the lakefront. So there.

Howard Johnson Inn *(☎ 312-664-8100, 800-446-4656, fax 312-664-2365, www.hojo .com, 720 N LaSalle Dr at Superior St)* Doubles $88-115.

Straight out of your old family vacation in the minivan (or station wagon, if you have gray hair), the HoJo offers free parking in a lot surrounded by a classic American motel. The only thing missing is a pool with a slide.

Mid-Range *House of Blues Hotel (☎ 312-245-0333, 800-235-6397, fax 312-923-2444, www.loewshotels.com/houseofblueshome .html, 333 N Dearborn St)* Rooms $130-180.

Once upon a time, this concrete building was the grim office component of the noted Marina City complex (see the Loop Architecture Walking Tour in the Architecture special section). However, it's been reborn in a big way as the hotel component of the adjacent House of Blues club (see the Entertainment chapter). You need look no further than the huge gold Buddha near the door to get a sense of the over-the-top decor. If you get a room with a view (many have none), you might just be distracted from the many goofy and colorful details. Expect to luxuriate in the huge bathrooms.

Hampton Inn & Suites–Chicago River North *(☎ 312-832-0330, 800-426-7866, fax 312-832-0333, www.hamptoninn-suites.com,*

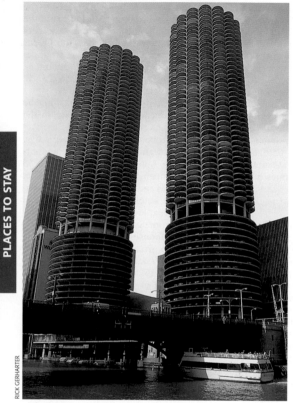

RICK GERHARTER

The Marina City complex, home to the House of Blues Hotel

you can't beat the location. It's a favorite with tour groups, so hold your breath as you pass all the buses idling outside.

Holiday Inn–Chicago City Centre (☎ 312-787-6100, 800-465-4329, fax 312-787-6259, info@chicc.com, www .basshotels.com, 300 E Ohio St) Doubles $150-180; look for deals.

Though nearly generic, this hotel is better than many of its namesake brethren, but it's still unremarkable in most respects. Views aren't bad, and you do get access to a health club in the same complex.

Hilton Garden Inn (☎ 312-595-0000, 800-445-8667, fax 312-595-0955, www .hilton.com/hiltongardeninn/ hotels/CHIDNGI, at 10 E Grand Ave) Singles/doubles $120-270; weekend specials $99 if booked well ahead of time.

This 23-story hotel opened in 2000 as part of the vast North Bridge development. Rather bland, it does feature bright, good-size rooms that boast microwaves. There's a small pool and the usual – for this price range – business and fitness centers. The small restaurant is one of the bleakest I've seen. Don't linger for a minute.

Embassy Suites Chicago–Downtown (☎ 312-943-3800, 800-362-2779, fax 312-943-5979, www.embassy-suites.com, 600 N State St between Ohio and Ontario Sts) Doubles $229-309, with frequent weekend and holiday deals.

A good deal for families, this chain hotel offers all the expected suite features, including the two-room layout with beds in one room and a sofa bed in the other. The kitchenette has a microwave, which means you can nuke up some sort of popcorn and pizza horror for the kids and then head down to

33 W Illinois St at Dearborn St) Doubles $129-199.

The relatively new Hampton features 230 rooms (including 100 suites, some with full kitchen), an indoor pool, hot tub, sauna, exercise room, free continental breakfast buffet, a guest coin laundry and a 24-hour business center. It's fairly generic, but the location is good.

Best Western Inn of Chicago (☎ 312-787-3100, 800-557-2378, fax 312-573-3136, www .bestwestern.com, 162 E Ohio St near Michigan Ave) Doubles $89-189.

One of the neighborhood's best values, the Best Western Inn of Chicago offers less-than-fancy rooms in an older building, but

Papagus, the excellent Greek restaurant on the ground floor. Not hungry? Work up an appetite at the indoor pool or in the coin laundry. You can feast on a free full – not continental – breakfast served in the lobby each morning.

Lenox Suites (☎ 312-337-1000, 800-445-3669, fax 312-337-7217, www.lenoxsuites .com, 616 N Rush St between Ohio and Ontario Sts) Singles $129-199, doubles $159-299.

While none of the rooms are striking (sometimes the beds fold down from the wall), the location and prices of the Lenox are hard to beat. Some of the suites are barely bigger than one room, but others are fairly sizable. Your free breakfast is delivered to your room.

Motel 6 (☎ 312-787-3580, 800-466-8356, fax 312-787-1299, www.motel6.com, 162 E Ontario St) Singles/doubles starting at $91/101.

Those accustomed to the tatty roadside outlets of Motel 6 will be surprised at the budget hotel chain's Chicago offering. Once a French-style hotel in a building from the 1930s, it features trappings you wouldn't normally expect, such as flowers in the lobby. But loyalists should fear not: any trace of the property's roots has been resolutely eliminated from the utilitarian rooms.

Radisson Hotel & Suites (☎ 312-787-2900, 800-333-3333, fax 312-787-5158, radchgo@ix.netcom.com, www.radisson .com, 160 E Huron St near Michigan Ave) Discount and package rates as low as $130.

Newly renovated, this Radisson is an excellent value. Many of the rooms come with microwaves and refrigerators, and the hotel contains a small heated pool and sun deck. The furniture has a vague institutional feel, but it's too new to have any cigarette burns yet.

Top End **Westin River North** (☎ 312-744-1900, 800-228-3000 or 800-937-8461, fax 312-527-2664, www.westinrivernorth.com, 320 N Dearborn St) Weekday doubles $249-469; weekend rates starting at $159.

On the north bank of the river, the former Hotel Nikko continues to reflect its Asian roots; the rock garden, for example, is still carefully raked each day. But fans of the Westin chain can now rest easily in a hotel that's much better than its odious older sibling farther north. Rooms are large, views are good, and the service is splendid. The lobby bar, with its clubby leather seats, makes an excellent place for a meeting.

Sheraton Chicago Hotel and Towers (☎ 312-464-1000, 877-242-2558 or 800-325-3535, fax 312-329-7045, sheratonchicago@ sheraton.com, www.sheratonchicago.com, 301 E North Water St) Singles/doubles starting at $199/219; deals usually available.

The best of the monster convention hotels contains 1204 rooms, all with excellent views, especially those on the river. The vast public spaces feature huge plate-glass walls and fountains made with black granite, while the room decorations are typical of corporate hotels: nice but nothing special. The lower level lies on the bucolic River Esplanade, which runs east from Michigan Ave. The hotel's bizarre address means it is just behind the NBC Tower, one block east of Michigan Ave along Columbus Dr.

Hotel Inter-Continental Chicago (☎ 312-944-4100, 800-628-2112 or 800-327-0200, fax 312-944-1320, chicago@interconti.com, www .interconti.com, 505 N Michigan Ave) Doubles $229-429.

The Inter-Continental has a split personality. The older portion, on the south side, dates from 1929 and underwent a careful restoration a few years ago. Once a health club for rich men, it holds such classic details as a beautifully mosaicked indoor swimming pool in a setting worthy of William Randolph Hearst. The rooms got the same treatment and have become both elegant and convenient, with all the facilities business travelers expect. Just north, the cheesy aluminum addition used to house the Inter-Con's budget chain, now dead. When reserving and checking in, be sure to go for the classic side. Swimmers should note that the pool is the largest inside any hotel in the city.

Courtyard by Marriott Chicago Downtown (☎ 312-329-2500, 800-321-2211, fax 312-329-0293, www.courtyard.com, 30 E Hubbard St at State St) Doubles $189-299.

Don't be fooled by the fact that this hotel is part of a chain known for its moderate prices. This outpost charges rates that fall at the high end of the moderate range. However, unlike at its hulking corporate brother a few blocks away on Michigan Ave, here you get what you pay for. Rooms on the high floors in the fairly new building enjoy excellent views, and all contain good work areas for travelers needing to pound away at the laptop. There's also a sun deck, whirlpool and indoor lap pool. The management has cut deals with several nearby restaurants, so you can charge your meals at those places to your room account.

Chicago Marriott Hotel (☎ *312-836-0100, 800-228-9290, fax 312-836-6139, www.marriotthotels.com, 540 N Michigan Ave*) Doubles starting at $189.

Barring a good deal, there's little reason to stay here. Several nicer places lie within a two-block radius. Long one of Chicago's ugliest hotels, the Marriott now sports new exterior cladding that does nothing more than cover up the old cladding. The inside isn't much better, with gloomy public spaces and so-so restaurants. The cracker-box rooms on the high floors of this 46-story behemoth enjoy good views. The car entrance is off Rush St.

W Chicago–Lakeshore (☎ *312-943-9200, 877-946-8357, www.whotels.com, 644 N Lake Shore Dr*).

By the time you read this, the long-in-the-tooth Days Inn should have been magically (and they're going to need a lot of magic!) transformed into a hip and trendy new W Chicago–Lakeshore. Rates will then likely start at $150. The hotel's location, on the inner access road away from other high-rises, means that the rooms are sunny and the views of either the lake and Navy Pier or the city aren't bad. Low rooms on the Lake Shore Dr side suffer from traffic noise. It's a hike west to Michigan Ave.

Omni Chicago Hotel (☎ *312-944-6664, 800-843-6664, fax 312-266-3015, www.omnihotels.com, 676 N Michigan Ave*) Doubles $229-319 (a good deal); weekend rates usually lower.

One of the nicest properties on Michigan Ave (the entrance is just west on Huron St),

the modern all-suite Omni rises high above a retail and office building. The rooms are decked out in rich colors and cherry wood. The living room of each of the 347 units features an excellent work area with a two-line phone – perfect for leaving the boss on hold on one while you talk nice-nice to a loved one on the other. Other amenities include an indoor pool, whirlpools and an exercise room.

The Peninsula (☎ *312-337-2888, 866-288-8889, fax 312-932-9529, www.peninsula.com, 108 E Superior St at N Michigan Ave*) Rooms starting at $425.

Scheduled to open in mid-2001, The Peninsula will be the local outpost for arguably the world's most luxurious hotel chain. The large rooms will feature control centers for a host of electronic marvels. The roof will boast a glass-enclosed health club, and the hotel will include a pool and various expensive bars and restaurants. If nothing else, it will be fun to watch The Peninsula do battle with the equally upscale and new Park Hyatt just across Chicago Ave.

South Loop & Near South Side (Map 4)

Places in this area offer convenient access to the Museum Campus and McCormick Place but are far from the North Side action.

Mid-Range *Best Western Grant Park Inn* (☎ *312-922-2900, 800-472-6875, fax 312-922-8812, 1100 S Michigan Ave*) Doubles $159-189; frequent specials.

This hotel is not much to look at inside or out, though it does feature a great view. The neighborhood is still in transition – it's not bad, just dead – but the hotel lies close to the Museum Campus, only about a mile from McCormick Place and three blocks from the Roosevelt El stop. At night there's not much going on except at the Chicago police headquarters, a half-block away. If you plan on getting into trouble, you'll have a short walk home from the pokey.

Essex Inn (☎ *312-939-2800, 800-621-6909, fax 312-939-0526, 800 S Michigan Ave*) Doubles $89-149.

Once down at the heels, the Essex has recently been spruced up a bit, although its

1964-vintage-motel roots are very apparent. Still, it's a fine place to rest your head and even a good value if you can get a room under $90. Try for a park view.

Congress Plaza Hotel (☎ 312-427-3800, 800-635-1666, fax 312-427-3972, www .congressplazahotel.com, 520 S Michigan Ave) Doubles $119-165; higher-priced rooms and suites available.

If you're on a group tour and you're reading this, don't despair if you're booked into the Congress Plaza; you can spend lots of hours out of your room. Those not booked here may not want to penetrate the legions of tour buses stationed outside to find out what a dump the place has become. The downward slide seems to have started when the hotel opened in 1893, though some refurbishing in 1998 helped things a bit. While working on the earlier edition of this book, I ran into a couple morosely staring into their beers at the Billy Goat Tavern and desperately trying to find *any* other place where they could stay on a fully booked convention weekend. I had to assure them repeatedly that I did not write the guidebook that had steered them there.

Top End *Chicago Hilton & Towers* (☎ 312-922-4400, 800-445-8667, fax 912-917-1707, www.hilton.com, 720 S Michigan Ave) Singles $119-294, doubles $144-319.

When it was built in 1927, this was the largest hotel in the world, with close to 2000 rooms. A $225-million renovation in the mid-1980s brought that total down to a still huge 1543. Some of the resulting rooms now have two bathrooms, perfect if one member of a party locks him- or herself away for hours of ablutions. The public spaces are exquisitely grand, reaching a crescendo in the gilded ballroom, which is modeled after one at Versailles. Even if you're not staying here, it's worth a peek. The lobby bar that overlooks Michigan Ave at the north end of the block-size building also played a minor role in history: Chicago police tossed protesters through the plate-glass windows here at the height of the riots during the 1968 Democratic National Convention. The only riots today are in Kitty O'Shea's, the

faux Irish pub at the south end of the ground floor: people get a $6 tab for a Guinness and scream in horror.

Hyatt on Printer's Row (☎ 312-986-1234, 800-233-1234, fax 312-939-2468, 500 S Dearborn St) Doubles $200-250.

With nice-size rooms and good amenities, this is the pick of the South Loop litter. On weekends, when the streets are tranquil (read: dead), it's an even better deal. The resident restaurant, Prairie, is a worthy destination in itself (see the Places to Eat chapter). The rates vary widely depending on what's going on in town. On weekends you might get a double here in the $100-200 range, but when occupancy is high, rates can climb to $300 or more.

Hyatt Regency McCormick Place (☎ 312-567-1234, 800-233-1234, fax 312-528-4189, www.hyatt.com, 2233 S Martin Luther King Jr Dr) Singles and doubles $200-300 during conventions, $90-150 other times.

If you're manning a booth at McCormick Place during a show, this is the most convenient place imaginable; after a short walk you can pass out in bed with memories of a day spent glad-handing dolts – er, potential clients – dancing in your head. The 800 rooms come with all the usual conveniences and boast good views of the Loop, more than 2 miles north. Of course, if you're not doing anything at McCormick Place, then there's no reason to stay down here, so far from most of the city's action.

Gold Coast (Map 5)

Home to many of the city's best hotels, the Gold Coast also has a few moderately priced gems.

Mid-Range *Raphael Hotel* (☎ 312-943-5000, 800-983-7870, fax 312-943-9483, 201 E Delaware Place) Doubles $199-360.

The Raphael is one of several boutique hotels in older buildings in this neighborhood near Water Tower Place. You won't find many amenities in the building itself, but the rooms are spacious, and many also have sitting rooms. The hotel serves a continental breakfast in the morning, and at night you can unwind in the quaint little bar

PLACES TO STAY

RICHARD I'ANSON

Pricey hotels abound on the Gold Coast.

downstairs or with the in-room honor bars. The Raphael has a very loyal following.

The Seneca (☎ *312-787-8900, 800-800-6261, fax 312-988-4438, www.senecahotel .com, 200 E Chestnut St)* Doubles $199-279; discounts and occasional promotions as low as $125.

Another boutique hotel, the Seneca is popular with people who want a nice room but don't need all the accouterments of a major hotel. The place has the feel of a well-maintained older apartment complex from the 1920s. Accommodations include voice mail, coffeemakers and refrigerators and range in size from one room to large suites.

Claridge Hotel (☎ *312-787-4980, 800-245-1258, fax 312-266-0978, tnewmark@ claridgehotel.com, www.claridgehotel.com, 1244 N Dearborn St)* Doubles $180-250; package deals plentiful during slack times.

A nicely renovated neighborhood hotel in the heart of the Gold Coast, the Claridge features rooms that range from tiny to spacious, so inquire carefully when you make your reservation and again at check-in.

Parks, the lake and nightlife are all short strolls away. Amenities include complimentary continental breakfast and newspaper, as well as complimentary morning limo shuttles around the immediate neighborhood.

Top End *Park Hyatt* (☎ *312-335-1234, 800-233-1234, fax 312-239-4000, www.hyatt.com, 800 N Michigan Ave)* Rooms $350-500, suites much higher.

This new flagship of the locally based Hyatt chain replaces an ugly predecessor of the same name. No expense has been spared, from the flat-screen TVs to the DVD players to the oodles of phones in every one of the 203 rooms. For once, the word 'stunning' adequately describes the NoMI restaurant and bar, with its views over Michigan Ave and the Water Tower, plus a nice outdoor area looking west. The hotel's amenities include a pool and concierges ready and willing to jump at your request. Suites come with balconies and cost the moon. Of course not everything is always perfect: my friend Ted stayed here as part of a story for *Esquire* and found that the fruit in his bowl was rotten. No doubt someone was shot for that oversight.

Ritz-Carlton (☎ *312-266-1000, 800-621-6906, fax 312-266-9498, www.fshr.com, 160 E Pearson St near Michigan Ave*) Doubles $340-965; specials and packages available.

A tad less opulent in every way than its corporate sibling, the Four Seasons (see below), the Ritz-Carlton is perhaps a tad more discreet. One of the city's finest hotels, it occupies 32 stories above Water Tower Place. The lobby, mostly understated, bursts with stunning floral arrangements. The large rooms embody refinement, with antique armoires and floral prints. The concierges have earned a reputation for being able to conjure up the answer to any guest's demand. The well-equipped health club includes an indoor pool. The eponymous Dining Room is an excellent French restaurant serving prix-fixe and degustation menus, including vegetarian options. The well-staffed kitchen rises to the challenge of special requests.

The Tremont (☎ *312-751-1900, 800-621-8133, fax 312-751-8691, 100 E Chestnut St near Michigan Ave*) Doubles $179-349.

The priciest of the neighborhood boutique hotels, The Tremont boasts fully wired rooms with fax machines, VCRs, CD players and more. The decor – sort of whimsical European – is fairly bright for an older, somewhat staid building like this one. The clientele leans toward the tasseled-loafer lawyer set, who enjoy the speaker phones in the rooms. Off the lobby is Mike Ditka's Restaurant, which lures in the unwary fans of 'Da Coach.' He don't spend much time here.

Four Seasons Hotel (☎ *312-280-8800, 800-332-3442, fax 312-280-9184, www.fourseasons .com, 120 E Delaware Place*) Singles $375-975, doubles $415-975; weekend rates a little lower.

If your name regularly appears in the newspaper in bold type, you are a typical guest of the Four Seasons. Rising high above the 900 N Michigan Ave mall, the hotel is often considered the best in Chicago. It pampers its guests and firmly believes in the old maxim 'your wish is our command.' For instance, room service will endeavor to rustle up whatever you desire, whether it's

on the menu or not, 24 hours a day. Each of the 343 rooms is unique, thanks to the handmade rugs and other decor. Needless to say, the amenities include an indoor pool, health club, whirlpool, sauna and just about anything else spa-related short of a mud bath. (On the other hand, if you wanted one…) Seasons restaurant serves superb American cuisine in a plush setting. The casual café is good as well, and the commodious bar overlooking Michigan Ave makes an excellent meeting place. The hotel avoids being stuffy through clever touches such as the statue of the man hailing a taxi near the entrance.

Westin Hotel, Chicago (☎ *312-943-7200, 800-228-3000, fax 312-649-7456, www .westinmichiganave.com, 909 N Michigan Ave*) Rack rates $429-489; doubles more typically $269-359.

Let the record show that I've usually enjoyed excellent stays at Westin hotels the world over, but I would be hard-pressed to repeat the experience at this one. This 751-room beast from the 1960s lacks any trace of charm. The rooms, though big, usually stare out at another building, which makes them very dark. Because of the steady stream of groups plodding through, the staff tend to be abruptly expeditious. The parking garage attendants have been known to lose cars for hours. And to ensure business, management has cut deals with most visiting professional sports teams, leaving the lobby often thronged with groupies. Note that the hotel entrance is well east of Michigan Ave, on Delaware Place.

DoubleTree Guest Suites Hotel (☎ *312-664-1100, 800-222-8733, fax 312-664-9881, www.doubletreehotels.com, 198 E Delaware Place at Seneca St*) Doubles $269-384; weekends generally lower than weekdays.

Dysfunctional couples love the Double-Tree: each room includes two TVs, two phones and other amenities in pairs, including the freshly baked chocolate chip cookies. There's only one indoor pool, however. The striking modern lobby rises a few notches above the usual hotel entry. The Park Ave Cafe and its casual cousin at street level, Mrs Park's Tavern, are excellent outlets of the famous parent restaurant in New York.

The Drake (☎ 312-787-2200, 800-553-7253, fax 312-787-1431, www.hilton.com, 140 E Walton St) Doubles $275-450, suites more.

The ageless Drake is Chicago's grandest hotel. Listed on the National Register of Historic Places, the hotel has hosted the likes of Gloria Swanson, Queen Elizabeth, Bill Murray and other glitterati, as well as heavyweight politicians such as Helmut Kohl and Ted Kennedy, since opening in 1920. It enjoys a commanding location at the head of Michigan Ave and offers convenient access to Oak St Beach, a short stroll through the pedestrian tunnel under Lake Shore Dr. In fact, the Drake is really Chicago's undiscovered beach hotel. The very quiet rooms are built like bank vaults, with heavy old doors and marble baths. The suitably grand public places include restaurants and bars that are many notches above the norm. The Cape Cod Room serves excellent seafood, and the casual Oak Terrace prepares excellent Bookbinder soup, which my friend John ate every day for lunch when he worked across the street as an ad exec. Coq d'Or is one of the classiest bars in town.

Sutton Place Hotel (☎ 312-266-2100, 800-606-8188, fax 312-266-2103 res@chi.suttonplace.com, www.suttonplace.com, 21 E Bellevue Place at Rush St) Doubles $260-295.

This hotel works hard at staying true to its European roots; built as a German-owned Kempinski Hotel in the mid-1980s, it was bought by the French chain Le Meridian in the early 1990s before adopting its rather anonymous name now. Electronics freaks will enjoy the rooms, which all come with CD players, VCRs and stereo TVs. When not exercising your finger on the remotes, you can work out at the nearby health club or check in to the 'Aerobics Suite' and feel the burn. The contemporary decor is accented by Robert Mapplethorpe's lush floral photos (the controversial stuff is over at the Museum of Contemporary Art). Gaunt models haunt the Whisky Bar, off the lobby (see the Entertainment chapter).

Ambassador West (☎ 312-787-3700, 800-300-9378, fax 312-640-2999, www.wyndham.com, 1300 N State St at Goethe St) Rack rates $314/334 single/double; weekend specials as low as $145 single or double.

Less famous than its former partner across the street (see the Ambassador East, below), the Ambassador West is a good choice if the hotel is running a special deal. The public areas are meant to evoke an old, woodsy English manor. The rooms are equally traditional, if a bit dark because of the small windows.

Ambassador East (☎ 312-787-7200, 800-843-6664, fax 312-787-4760, www.omnihotels.com, 1301 N State St) Rack rates around $289-319 single or double; with advance reservations $199-239; weekend specials and promotional rates around $165.

In Hitchcock's *North by Northwest*, Cary Grant gets to hang out at the Ambassador East with Eva Marie Saint before he meets that crop-duster in the Indiana cornfield. Your stay may lack the same glamour or

Elaborate detail at The Drake

RICK GERHARTER

danger, but you will still be in swank surroundings that include the famous Pump Room off the lobby (see the Places to Eat chapter). Grand touches abound, from the marble floors to the heavy woodwork. Rooms vary widely in size and style, with some seemingly untouched since Grant and Saint made eye contact. Aim for one of the large, bright ones. To reflect its chain affiliation, the hotel has added 'Omni' in front of its name.

Old Town & Lincoln Park (Map 6)
These hotels and inns, often cheaper than the big ones downtown, place you near a lot of the city's best nightlife. Daytime pleasures at the museums and in the Loop and Near North are a short El or bus ride away.

Days Inn Gold Coast *(☎ 312-664-3040, 800-325-2525 or 800-544-8313, fax 312-664-3048, www.daysinn.com, 1816 N Clark St)* Rates starting at $89 on weekdays, $119 (two-night minimum) on weekends.

Once a flophouse called the Hotel Lincoln, this place has been upgraded to the low standards of Days Inn. However, it's clean, and the furniture is much younger than you are. The best feature, besides the rate, is the excellent location across from the zoo and in the midst of Old Town. You can easily walk to many of the top destinations on the North Side from here.

Days Inn Lincoln Park North *(☎ 773-525-7010, 800-325-2525 or 800-544-8313, fax 773-525-6998, www.daysinn.com, 644 W Diversey Parkway)* Singles/doubles starting at $96/126; weekend rates usually about $5 more; low-price specials sometimes offered.

With 122 rooms near the busy intersection of Clark St, Diversey and Broadway, this good-size hotel occupies a prime location. Otherwise, it's not the most charming place, situated in an old retail building above one of the North Side's four gazillion coffee bars. The free breakfasts include bagels.

Comfort Inn of Lincoln Park *(☎ 773-348-2810, fax 773-348-1912, www.choicehotels.com, 601 W Diversey Parkway)* Singles $85-145, doubles $90-155.

A motel with parking! In the city! And it's not a dive! The Comfort Inn sits right on enjoyable Diversey Parkway, east of Clark St, and about five minutes' walk from Lincoln Park and the lake. Built in 1918, the building was modernized in the 1980s, bringing it up to true anonymous Comfort Inn standards. Amenities include free continental breakfast. Some rooms come with king beds, and a couple feature whirlpool tubs. If you pay one of the lower rates here, you'll get a good deal.

Lake View & Wrigleyville (Map 7)
These places all lie near great nightlife spots and away from the tourist bustle of N Michigan Ave.

City Suites Hotel *(☎ 773-404-3400, 800-248-9108, fax 773-404-3405, www.cityinns.com, 933 W Belmont Ave)* Singles $129-229, doubles $139-239; promotional rates as low as $99.

Location, location, location: the City Suites Hotel, between Clark St and the El, definitely has it. You won't go hungry or thirsty or get bored in this stylish little place, full of brightly redone rooms (not all of which are suites). This is one of my top recommendations in the city; it reminds me of the kind of place and neighborhood where I like to stay when I'm traveling in Europe. The same company, Neighborhood Inns of Chicago, also operates the following two North Side hotels. All serve Ann Sather's cinnamon rolls for breakfast.

Willows Hotel *(☎ 773-528-8400, 800-787-3108, fax 773-528-8483, www.cityinns.com, 555 W Surf St near Broadway)* Singles/doubles starting at $109/119.

The architectural pick of the Neighborhood Inns of Chicago trio, the Willows puts up an ornate terra-cotta facade on a very narrow strip of property. Built in 1925, the hotel contains a small lobby but big rooms with traditional decor.

Majestic Hotel *(☎ 773-404-3499, 800-727-5108, fax 773-404-3495, www.cityinns.com, 528 W Brompton Ave)* Singles/doubles starting at $139/149.

The Majestic, one block south of Addison St, lies close to Wrigley Field and the Halsted St gay scene. The inside has a bit of a Laura Ashley feel.

Best Western Hawthorne Terrace (☎ 773-244-3434, 888-675-2378, fax 773-244-3435, www.hawthorneterrace.com, 3434 N Broadway) Rooms $100-150.

Another good North Side option, this hotel in a 1920s residential building features in-room fridges, microwaves and speakerphones (so you can sound like an annoying big shot). At the $100 rate, it's a very good value, especially if business brings you to this area.

West Side (Map 10)

Unless you have a compelling reason to stay on the West Side, your Chicago stay will be much more enjoyable at one of the places that's more central.

Holiday Inn–Chicago Downtown (☎ 312-957-9100, 877-779-7789, fax 312-957-0474, www.basshotels.com/holiday-inn, 506 W Harrison St) Rooms starting at $89-150.

On the west side of the river, this Holiday Inn offers convenient access to such exciting attractions as Union Station, the bus station and the post office (!). Its location is a bit bleak but okay if you don't plan to hang around. Amenities include a small rooftop pool with a good view of the Sears Tower, a guest laundry and a business center.

Hyatt at University Village (☎ 312-491-1234, 800-233-1234, fax 312-529-6080, www.hyatt.com, 625 S Ashland Ave at Harrison St) Singles $190-240, doubles $215-265; specials $140-165, single or double.

This Hyatt is in the middle of the vast medical center complex and the University of Illinois at Chicago campus. Rooms are large and rather posh.

Hyde Park (Map 12)

Ramada Inn Lake Shore (☎ 773-288-5800, 800-228-2828 or 800-272-6232, fax 773-288-5745, www.ramada.com, 4900 S Lake Shore Dr) Singles $85-130, doubles $85-140; weekend deals $70-85.

You won't hear the sound of the lake at this faded former Hilton on the inner access road. You will hear the sound of traffic. The whole place needs an overhaul. Only stay here if you really need to be in Hyde Park.

Near O'Hare International Airport

Hotels near the airport don't offer any price advantage over those downtown, and you're stuck in the suburbs around O'Hare – places that might be nice for raising a family but are hardly of interest to visitors.

Most of the hotels in Rosemont are linked to an enclosed pedestrian walkway that leads to the Rosemont Convention Center, a growing collection of buildings hosting trade shows and fairs for collectors of limited-edition plates and the like. If you're stuck at one of these places, you're probably within walking distance of the Rosemont CTA station for the 30-minute ride to downtown.

The airport hotels may come in handy if you have a very early flight. But remember, the same traffic that plagues the expressways around O'Hare will swallow up your hotel shuttle bus; many people instead use the CTA for its five-minute ride to O'Hare from Rosemont. If bad weather hits O'Hare – thunderstorms in the summer, snow in the winter – and you notice more and more flights being canceled, it can't hurt to call one of these hotels fast and secure a room. Otherwise, you might end up bedding down in the concourses and being the subject of chirpy TV news reports about 'chaos at O'Hare.'

All the following places offer free shuttle service to and from O'Hare.

Budget ***Excel Inn of O'Hare*** (☎ 847-803-9400, 800-367-3935, fax 847-803-9771, 2881 Touhy Ave, Elk Grove Village) Doubles starting at $78, including continental breakfast.

A favorite dumping ground for airline passengers whom the airlines don't like (ie, nonfrequent fliers with dirt-cheap tickets) but who still have to be put up for the night, the Excel is a simple motel in a town that claims to be America's largest industrial park. All rooms include coffeemakers, ironing boards and other useful touches.

Chicago O'Hare Rosemont Travelodge (☎ 847-296-5541, 800-578-7878, fax 847-803-1984, www.travelodge.com, 3003 Mannheim Rd, Des Plaines) Singles $79-99, doubles $84-99; discounts available.

The sleepy bear comes alive at this Travelodge – the aggressive management provides free incoming fax service, cable TV, newspapers, coffee and more. The place looks like a throwback, but the staff really do aim to please. It's also the closest cheap hotel to the airport.

Mid-Range & Top End *Clarion Hotel Barcelo* (☎ 773-693-5800, 800-252-7466, fax 773-693-0881, www.choicehotels.com, 5615 N Cumberland Ave, Chicago) Singles $195-205, doubles $205-295.

Pop-culture buffs will be keen to stay at the Clarion, where OJ Simpson checked in after his flight from California on the night of his ex-wife's murder. The broken glass and other memorabilia are long gone, as is the name of the place: in 1994 it was the O'Hare Plaza. Now this rather undistinguished hotel only begs the question: Why did OJ opt to stay here in the first place?

Holiday Inn O'Hare International (☎ 847-671-6350, 888-642-7344 or 800-465-4329, fax 847-671-5406, hiohare@enteract .com, www.basshotels.com, 5440 N River Rd, Rosemont) Doubles $89-249.

When I was a kid, the thought of a Holidome at a Holiday Inn – with an enclosed swimming pool and amenities such as the ever-challenging shuffleboard – was enough to make me want to run away from home. The Holiday Inn O'Hare International features a Holidome and a whole bunch of other delights: an indoor pool, whirlpools, arcade games and more. Best of all, it maintains an ambience unchanged since my childhood, when Richard Nixon was president.

O'Hare Hilton (☎ 773-686-8000, 800-445-8667, fax 773-601-2873, www.hilton.com) Singles $159-259, doubles $174-275; weekend rates usually $99 single, $114 double.

If you want a real airport hotel, you can't get closer than the Hilton – it's right in the middle of the airport, across from Terminals 1, 2 and 3. Underground tunnels link the hotel with the terminals, the shuttle tram and the CTA. The rooms are large and soundproof. Amenities include an indoor pool, a sauna, whirlpool and exercise center. The restaurants aren't bad, either – definitely better than what you'll find in the terminals.

Hyatt Regency O'Hare (☎ 847-696-1234, 800-233-1234, fax 847-698-0139, www.hyatt .com, 9300 W Bryn Mawr Ave, Rosemont) Singles/doubles $225/250; $119 single or double on weekends.

This ever-expanding property contains 1099 rooms, many with views of the expressway or the enclosed parking garage. It's across from the convention center and a short walk away from the El.

Hotel Sofitel (☎ 847-678-4488, 800-763-4835, fax 847-678-4244, H0894@accor-hotels .com, www.sofitel.com, 5550 N River Rd, Rosemont) Doubles $235-255; weekend specials as low as $99.

The pick of the O'Hare litter is the Sofitel, member of the friendly French chain of the same name; the hotel even makes especially flaky croissants in its own bakery. The large rooms include a number of amenities.

O'Hare Marriott (☎ 773-693-4444, 800-228-9290, fax 773-693-3164, www.marriott .com, 8535 W Higgins Rd, Chicago) Rack rates around $229/244 single/double; discounts and weekend rates as low as $89.

This Marriott often becomes a temporary home for bumped passengers. It's big and has a big parking lot, but it's otherwise unremarkable.

Marriott Suites Chicago O'Hare (☎ 847-696-4400, 800-228-9290, fax 847-696-2122, www.marriott.com, 6155 N River, Rosemont) Singles $189-269, doubles $204-284; weekend specials as low as $99.

Compared to the O'Hare Marriott listed above, this one offers much bigger rooms in a much newer building.

LONG STAYS

Hotels often offer very attractive rates for stays of a week or longer, so you can start your hunt for a long-term stay with them. You can also look in the Yellow Pages under 'Apartments': several of the large management companies run advertisements of their furnished apartments, geared toward corporate clients.

Residence Inn by Marriott *(☎ 312-943-9800, 800-331-3131, fax 312-943-8579, www.residenceinn.com, 201 E Walton St; Map 5)* Doubles (studios) $109-199.

The Residence Inn offers apartment-size units, each with a full kitchen. The hotel also provides breakfast every day, as well as a free buffet (with beer and wine) in the lobby on Monday to Thursday evenings – a perk that seems more suited to the sterile suburban corporate neighborhoods where this chain usually operates than the bustling Gold Coast neighborhood just north of Water Tower Place. Rooms in the fairly new building are bigger than typical hotel rooms and make good homes for the person stuck on the road. There's even a laundry room where you can wash your dirty duds.

Habitat Corporate Suites Network *(☎ 312-902-2090, 800-833-0331, info@ habitat.com, www.habitatcsn.com)* Rates on 30-day rentals $70-120 per day.

The Habitat Company manages many of the city's upscale high-rises in the Near North. The fully equipped rental units come with cable TV and voice mail, and they enjoy good locations, in buildings with door attendants. One note of caution: unless you want to be in a dull part of the West Loop, avoid the Presidential Towers property.

Places to Eat

Visitors to Chicago regularly cite its restaurants as the city's top draw, ahead of other virtues such as museums or shopping. And these people aren't dumb: some of the most innovative chefs in the US are working in Chicago kitchens. You'll find a breathtaking array of dining options, with excellent food available at all prices.

Best of all, you can have a memorable experience whether you wish to spend $5 or $150. The sheer numbers of restaurants in town create ruthless competition to attract diners' dollars. Places that coast on their laurels, offer sloppy or indifferent service, charge outlandish prices or commit other crimes soon fade from existence. This competition also ensures that the staff at the restaurants – often recent college grads waiting for their break in a creative pursuit like acting – have become compulsive in their efforts to satisfy customers and garner those critical tips.

However, one development in recent years has slightly dulled the Chicago restaurant scene, and that's the actual lack of development. With rents and costs higher than ever, local restaurateurs have shifted away from innovation in favor of tried-and-true formulas in order to maximize profits while the economic boom lasts. Once upon a time, several new and unusual places would open every week, but the debuts of late have tended to replicate what already exists. Local institutions such as Leona's are becoming chains in their own right. For years Bar Louie had been a one-location café on Chicago Ave, but its offspring are now opening quicker than gas stations did in the 1950s. To see the most dramatic example of this trend, stroll down N Clark St near Wrigley Field (see the boxed text 'Chicago as a Theme Park').

Although interesting new places still pop up here and there, for the most part the Chicago restaurant scene has been coasting. What the town definitely doesn't need is one more high-priced steak house; the half-dozen that operated in Chicago 15 years ago have become more than two dozen today – and counting.

The restaurants in this chapter were selected both for their qualities and their 'Chicago-ness.' I've tried to eschew national chains, except where the local venue is especially notable or has become a major destination in its own right, such as the tourist-mobbed theme joints in River North. I've also done my best to ignore the hugely expensive national chains that have blotted the North Side in search of expense account dollars (see the boxed text 'The Chain Gang').

Reservations are always a good idea at more expensive places, although not all places accept them. If you are staying in a hotel with a concierge, ask him or her to make your reservations for you. Concierges can often get you a table at fully booked restaurants or secure reservations at places that don't 'officially' accept them.

Some of the restaurant listings in this chapter have been broken into price categories based on the cost of a typical meal with drinks: budget spots run less than $15 per person; mid-range, $15 to $40 per person; top end, $40 and up per person. Elsewhere, we have arranged the recommendations by neighborhood, with listings in ascending order of price.

For more information on all of the neighborhoods covered in this chapter, see the Things to See & Do chapter.

FOOD

Classic American food like the ubiquitous steak or hamburger can be found all over the city. If you really want to sample the culinary delight of the common person, seek out a Chicago hot dog (see the boxed text 'Gone to the Dogs').

Ribs – a Chicago specialty – owe their roots to African American culture on the South Side. The preferred variation, slabs of pork baby-back ribs, get the long, slow treatment in an oven, usually with lots of smoke.

The sauce is sweet, tangy and copious. Another popular variation is rib tips, the cheap bits of pork chopped away near the ribs. These meaty pieces can be a real mess to eat but are usually excellent.

Chicago-style pizza is absolutely nothing like any pizza that was ever tossed in Italy; lofting one of these deep-dish leviathans in the air could actually hurt someone. To prepare their mammoth pies, pizza chefs line a special pan – not unlike a frying pan without a handle – with dough and then pile on the toppings. These must include a red sauce, chopped plum tomatoes and a mountain of shredded American-style (read: yellow) mozzarella cheese. Optional extras include Italian-style herb sausage (actually almost mandatory), onions, mushrooms, green bell peppers, pepperoni, black olives and more. Although Pizzeria Uno likes to claim that it invented Chicago-style pizza in the 1940s, some of its rivals also vie for credit.

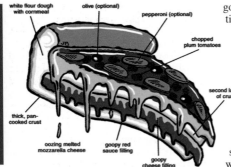

white flour dough with cornmeal

olive (optional)

pepperoni (optional)

chopped plum tomatoes

second layer of crust

thick, pan-cooked crust

oozing melted mozzarella cheese

goopy red sauce filling

goopy cheese filling

You'll find a good representation of regional American cuisine throughout the city, with Cajun and soul cooking readily available. Many restaurants defy easy categorization; they serve their own interpretation of fusion cuisine, mixing ingredients and recipes from a number of regions and cultures.

But it's in purely ethnic cuisine where Chicago excels. The waves of immigrants who populated the city have created restaurants devoted to scores of cultures. Italian remains the most common variety by far, with pasta joints in every corner of the city. The breadth of cuisine served there ranges from northern Italian to Sicilian, plus everything in between and plenty of local interpretations as well. Chicago's improvised 'Italian' dishes include garlicky chicken Vesuvio (sautéed chicken with potatoes and peas) and Italian beef sandwiches.

Other cultures with their fair share of restaurants include, but are by no means limited to, Mexican, French, German, Greek, Turkish, Indian, Vietnamese, Japanese and Chinese in its many forms.

DRINK

Drinking is a big part of life in Chicago. Maybe it's those long, cold winters or those long, hot summers or those couple of weeks in between, but something's driving legions of Chicagoans to seek out the consolation of spirits and each other's company. See the Entertainment chapter for a selection of bars good for a drink or three.

A few years ago Chicago had several good microbreweries. But the evil competition in this business has emptied the kegs on most of them. Goose Island makes several pretty tasty brews, including a beer that's widely available at a multitude of locations beyond its namesake's microbrewery. Beyond Goose Island, look for regional beers by the likes of Three Floyds from Indiana or New Glarus from Wisconsin.

Otherwise, there's no drink in particular that's really unique to the city. The same trends that influence drinking elsewhere also prevail here, whether it's the martini craze or the sudden popularity of Japanese sake. Good wines come here from all directions, but definitely not from Illinois.

The drinking age in Chicago, like the rest of the US, is 21, and that's pretty strictly enforced.

FARMERS' MARKETS

Chicago's city government has begun an aggressive program to sponsor farmers' markets throughout the city from June through October. The markets attract growers from around the region and offer excellent opportunities to try some of the wonderful Midwestern produce that seems to lose something – say, flavor – on its way to the huge supermarkets. Strawberries in June and tomatoes in August are just two of the treats.

The market schedule is rather complex, but there is an information line (☎ 312-744-9187) that will tell you about times and locations convenient for you. In the Loop a market takes place from 7am to 3pm on Tuesday in the Federal Plaza, bounded by Adams and Dearborn Sts.

SUPERMARKETS

Supermarkets abound throughout Chicago. The following three are especially useful.

Whole Foods (☎ *312-932-9600, 50 W Huron St; Map 3*) One of several Chicago lo-cations of this national chain, this huge place sells both mainstream and organic items in vast quantity. The deli areas offer plenty of supplies for great picnics, and you can get ready-made food to go from the café.

Treasure Island (☎ *312-664-0400, 680 N Lake Shore Dr; Map 3*) This outlet of the local chain of gourmet grocers carries a large assortment of interesting and ready-to-eat items. Since this location shares a building with *Playboy* magazine, you might see future playmates squeezing the melons.

Sherwyn's Health Food (☎ *773-477-1934, 645 W Diversey Parkway; Map 6*) A huge health-food store with every kind of potion and lotion imaginable, this market features an unusual food selection that includes in-numerable types of sprouts, weird tropical

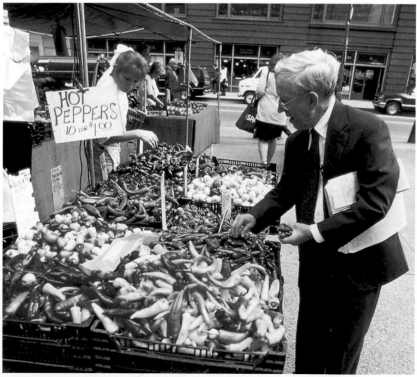

Bring on the heat.

RICK GERHARTER

PLACES TO EAT

fruits and juices made from things that you thought should be composted.

THE LOOP (Map 3)

Most Loop eateries cater to the lunch crowds of office workers, but given the burgeoning nightlife and residential character of the area, more and more places serve diners well into the night. If your desires lean toward fast food, you'll find scores of chain outlets dotting every block. You'll have no trouble finding 'extra value meals' wherever you wander. However, there are many more choices that are either homegrown, cheap, especially good or all three. These are noted below.

The Theater District has finally taken off and promises to spark the opening of quite a few new places, plus persuade others to stay open at night. Already, famous local restaurateur Rich Melman has announced that a branch of his ubiquitous *Corner Bakery* chain

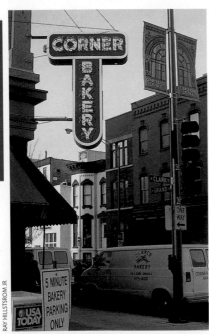

RAY HILLSTROM JR

Corner Bakeries have popped up everywhere.

of upscale bakeries and cafés will open at the northwest corner of Randolph and Dearborn Sts, right by the new location of the Goodman Theatre. More exciting are his plans to open a place called *Peterino's*. Melman hopes that this will become a local version of New York's Sardi's, which used to draw packs of Broadway stars every night in its heyday.

Budget

Pockets (☎ 312-922-9255, 329 S Franklin St) Lunch $4-6. Right in the shadow of the Sears Tower, this outlet of the local chain serves up veggie and meaty sandwiches stuffed into pita-like bread. It's small but fast and cheap.

Burrito Buggy (☎ 312-362-0199, 206 W Van Buren St) Lunch $5. Once one of those trucks that park in spots convenient for lunching workers, this place has grown into a storefront operation, on the strength of its big burritos alone. Choose from a range of fillings while your burrito is assembled on the spot.

Jacobs Bros Bagels (☎ 312-922-2245, 53 W Jackson Blvd at S Dearborn St) Bagels $1. The bagels are almost as substantial as the surrounding 6-foot-thick walls of the Monadnock Building, one of Chicago's first skyscrapers. Many people, my wife Sara enthusiastically included, think these are the best bagels in town. They come in a myriad of flavors. I prefer garlic with a slathering of cream cheese.

European Sunny Cafe (☎ 312-663-6020, 304 S Wells St) Lunch $4-6. Closed Sun. For a taste of Warsaw, try this optimistically named simple lunchroom with pierogi-size prices. A plate of homemade stuffed cabbage is only $4, and daily specials are even cheaper. The charming owners will cheerfully tell you, in heavily accented English, how they fled the old country for Chicago.

Heartwise Express (☎ 312-419-1329, 10 S LaSalle St) Lunch $5. Closed Sun. LaSalle St bankers can try to lower their blood pressure at this very slick operation with all the trappings – but not the unhealthy cuisine – of a fast-food joint. The menu offers veggie burgers, bags of carrot sticks and more non-animal items, with the fat content of every option listed. Enter off Madison St.

Artist's Snack Shop (☎ *312-939-7855, in the Fine Arts Building at 410 S Michigan Ave*) Meals $5-11. The sign surrounded by light bulbs may be the best feature of this updated diner, which offers a better-than-usual selection of coffee and beer.

Boudin Bakery (☎ *312-332-1849, 20 N Michigan Ave*) Lunch $5-8. At its excellent location right on Michigan Ave, this California chain serves sandwiches on San Francisco–style sourdough bread. The clam chowder comes in hollowed-out round loaves ($4.50). When you're done with your soup, you eat the bowl. White-chocolate-chip cookies cost $1.50. The outside tables are perfectly situated for people-watching. The menu offers several veggie options.

Sopraffina (☎ *312-984-0044, 10 N Dearborn St*) Lunch $6-10. Open until 4pm, closed Sun. Fast-food Italian with panache, the fresh cuisine here includes a bevy of salads such as chickpea, wheat berry and portobello mushroom and *giardiniera* (hot peppers). Sample your choice of three with focaccia for $7. You can also order sandwiches, pasta and super-thin-crust pizza. Eat in or take out.

Heaven on Seven (☎ *312-263-6443, on the 7th floor – surprise! – of the Garland Building, 111 N Wabash Ave*). Lunch $6-14. Open 9am-4pm, closed Sun. Jimmy Bannos has carved out a busy empire by faithfully cooking up the classics of the Big Easy. Louisiana shrimp po' boys, jambalaya, sweet potato pie and more feed mobs of people at every lunch hour. One of the most gratifying sights is the vast array of hot sauces lining the walls and tables. To get a seat without joining the besuited minions in line, drop by before 11:45am or after 1:30pm. Two other locations in Near North and Wrigleyville are open for dinner (see the Near North section, later in the chapter).

Mid-Range

Russian Tea Time (☎ *312-360-0000, 77 E Adams St*) Lunch & dinner $15-35. You've got to like a place where the menu starts with detailed, seven-step instructions on how to drink a shot of vodka properly. (Step 6: Say 'Oh Khorosho!' – 'It feels good!' Step 7: Repeat process in 10 to 15 minutes.) Clearly there's more than tea flowing here. The czar-

---

10 Great Restaurants

This was tough to do. Only 10! But here goes.

Best Bargain Le Bouchon (Bucktown)

Best Breakfast Lou Mitchell's (West Side)

Best Burrito Tecalitlan (West Side)

Best Creative Kitchen
Topolobampo (Near North)

Best Family Italian
Tufano's Vernon Park Tap (Little Italy)

Best for Groups
Brasserie Jo (Near North)

Best Historical Atmosphere
The Berghoff (Loop)

Best Inventive Asian
Yoshi's Cafe (Lake View)

Best Pizza Leona's (Lake View)

Best Vegetarian
Chicago Diner (Lake View)

---

worthy menu includes borscht, *pelmeni* (dumplings), beef stroganoff and more. Russian folk songs complete the mood.

The Berghoff (☎ *312-427-3170, 17 W Adams St*) Lunch $10-25, dinner $12-30. Closed Sun. The building and this historic restaurant both date from 1898. (Outside, check out the reprinted menu from the 1890s posted in a window.) The first place in Chicago to serve a legal drink at the end of Prohibition, the Berghoff is currently the only restaurant in town with its own carpentry shop that employs full-time workers who maintain the antique woodwork and furniture. The menu carries old-world classics such as sauerbraten and schnitzel, but it also features modern treats such as swordfish Caesar salad. The creamed spinach is good for you and just plain good. The quick and efficient waiters serve a huge crowd of regulars, plus day-trippers from the 'bur... adjoining *Stand Up Bar* has chang... a century, although women ha... mitted for the past 35 years. S...

PLACES TO EAT

are served from a buffet line at lunch, and frosty mugs of Berghoff beer, direct from the Wisconsin brewery, still line the bar. Look carefully toward the rear for federal judges from the courthouse next door.

Miller's Pub (☎ *312-645-5377, 134 S Wabash Ave*) Meals $7-25. Open until 1am. A photo of your favorite dead celebrity can probably be found somewhere on the walls at this Loop institution next to the Palmer House – though some of the photos are of celebrities you only *thought* were dead. (See if you can count how many times Phyllis Diller appears.) Miller's has been serving remarkably tender and candy-sweet ribs for decades. The rest of the menu includes the usual salads, burgers and the like. The pub

draws a post-theater crowd and some office trolls who are burning the midnight oil.

Italian Village (☎ *312-332-7005, 71 W Monroe St*) Meals $12-50. Village open Sun, others closed. There are three restaurants under one roof here. The namesake **Village** looks a bit like a Disney set, with twinkling lights and storefronts that evoke the feeling of a southern Italian hill town. The very traditional red-sauce menu includes old-style cuisine such as *mostaccioli* with sausage. If you're part of a couple, you can cozy up in the private booths, but you can't reserve these in advance so you'll have to hope your timing is right. **La Cantina Enoteca** is a casual supper club that serves regional specialties such as cannelloni and seafood. A few distinctly American steaks make the cut here as well. **Vivere,** at the high end of the Village in both price and cuisine, boasts more than 1500 bottles in its wine cellar. The menu features high-minded interpretations of standards such as veal scaloppini, joined by unusual numbers such as bass-filled squid-ink pasta. And the restaurant's interior is a high-concept jumble of baroque design elements.

Top End

The Grillroom (☎ *312-960-0000, 33 W Monroe St*) Dinner starting at $45. Still another steak place, albeit a very classy one, the Grillroom is right across from the Shubert Theater and is within walking distance or many other theaters. It's a good choice if you want some meat before or after the show.

Palm (☎ *312-616-1000, 323 E Wacker Dr in the Swissôtel Chicago*) Dinner starting at $40. Not picking up the check tonight? Then head to here for the best lobster you've ever had (about $20 a pound). Given that these crustaceans average about 5lb, you can see why you'll want to be sitting on your wallet and

ff: a Chicago institution

brimming with thanks at check time. Equally costly New York strip steaks are also about the best ever. Company accountant lax with expense reports? Have the surf and turf.

Everest (☎ *312-663-8920, 40th floor of One Financial Plaza, 440 S LaSalle St)* Dinner starting at $75. Closed Sun. Masters of the Universe ride up two elevators to congregate at this temple of power and consumption. Corporate tigers can strut across the leopard-skin-patterned carpet while surveying their next conquest. You expect to find Gordon Gekko holding court in one of the private dining rooms. The views and prices are both spectacular. The food is French, with a slant toward the Alsace region, home of chef Jean Joho, who is also chef at Brasserie Jo (see the Near North section, below).

NEAR NORTH (Map 3)

The area north from the river to Chicago is generally known as River North or Near North. Either way you're always near food, as literally hundreds of restaurants dot the area. From family-run snack bars to over-hyped international theme cafés, from cheap vegetarian to haute cuisine, you can find it all here. However, beware of the onslaught of chains – from downscale to upscale.

Budget

Gold Coast Dogs (☎ *312-527-1222, 418 N State St)* Meals $5-8. Ambience is at a minimum and calories at a maximum at this prime example of a Chicago hot dog and burger joint. Dogs come boiled or char-grilled (I prefer the latter). Few places have relish any brighter green. High-brows can opt for the fine grilled tuna sandwich.

Rock & Roll McDonald's (☎ *312-664-7940, 600 N Clark St between Ohio & Ontario Sts)* Meals $3-5. Open 24 hours. Like the Hamburgler on a feeding frenzy, this uncommon outlet of the common chain has gobbled up its entire block. Inside the ever-expanding, mansard-roofed burgery you'll find a rollicking museum of rock music from the 1950s and '60s. Album covers, posters and a life-size plaster re-creation of the Beatles' *Abbey Road* album cover are just some of the artifacts on display. Otherwise, this Mc-

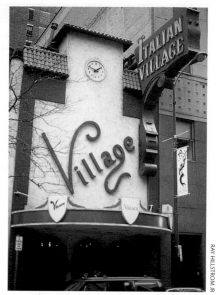
Italian Village: three restaurants in one

RAY HILLSTROM JR

Donald's holds no surprises, with harried parents carting away plastic trays of Happy Meals by the score. But there is a gift shop for those besotted with the golden arches.

Mr Beef (☎ *312-337-8500, 660 N Orleans St).* Meals $5-7. A local classic, the $4 Italian beef sandwiches come with long, spongy white buns that rapidly go soggy after a load of the spicy beef and cooking juices has been ladled on. Expect the juice to run down your arms. If you're not ready to ask for hot peppers, don't bother coming. Those not willing to bite into cow will enjoy the recent addition of deli sandwiches, including a roasted-red-pepper sub for $4. Past a sign marked 'Classy Dining Room,' you'll find a decidedly unclassy porch with picnic tables and an odd selection of movie posters on the wall. The pictures of Jay Leno aren't fake – he regularly appears and eats two or three beef sandwiches.

Pita Pavilion (☎ *312-335-9018, 8th floor of Chicago Place, 700 N Michigan Ave)* Lunch $5-10. On crummy days the atrium winter garden atop Chicago Place can be one of the

PLACES TO EAT

Gone to the Dogs

Nobody knows how the classic Chicago hot dog evolved, but it's definitely become a unique creation you won't find anywhere else in the US. More than just a wiener and a bun, a Chicago dog contains a vast array of condiments and flavorings. When done right, it should defy easy consumption, with various ingredients flopping out all over the place and juices and sauces oozing in all directions.

For the record, a Chicago hot dog begins with an all-beef hot dog, preferably a local Vienna brand. Some places steam them, others boil and a few grill. Which method is best is a matter of great debate. However cooked, the 'tube steak' is then laid into a fresh poppy-seed bun. Now the fun begins. A traditional dog will have all of the following toppings, although local variations exist:

- Diced onions, white or yellow
- Diced tomatoes
- Sliced cucumbers, possibly slightly pickled
- Shredded iceberg lettuce
- Diced green bell pepper
- Peperoncini (Italian hot and pickled peppers)
- Sweet relish, usually a virulent shade of green
- Bright yellow mustard
- Catsup (although some would say 'never!')
- Celery salt

The result? Part salad, part hot dog. It's not hard to find a good Chicago hot dog; several hundred joints throughout the city peddle different varieties. Start by looking for the big Vienna Beef signs. You'll know you've found a promising spot if it contains a few distinctly un-fancy Formica tables and a long counter for ordering. The following three places are all recommended (see the neighborhood sections for details):

Gold Coast Dogs (Near North)
Demon Dogs (Lincoln Park)
Wiener Circle (Lincoln Park)

brightest places to eat lunch, amid palm trees and burbling fountains, with a great view up and down the Magnificent Mile. The pick of the food court here has to be the Pita Pavilion, which serves a great falafel pita sandwich for $4. The other cuisine choices are mall food-court standards. To get to the atrium, be sure to take the express elevator off Rush St; using the escalators will expose you to depressing, shop-free floors.

Pockets (☎ *312-664-4808, 75 W Chicago Ave*) Lunch $4-6. Scores of posters explain why the doughy *chapati* bread here is not a pita. But whatever they call it, the veggie, turkey and tuna sandwiches are delicious, and the hearty calzones are guaranteed to thwart any hope of a productive afternoon back at the office. This was the first branch of this local chain.

Mike's Rainbow Restaurant *(☎ 312-787-4499, 708 N Clark St)* Meals starting at $3.50. Open 5am to 1am every day. Big portions and small prices are the hallmark at this classic Midwestern diner, which is *the* hot spot for cops and cabbies. Huge breakfasts come with real hash brown potatoes. Act enthusiastic and you'll get a shot of *ouzo*. Now that's the hair of the dog!

Boston Blackies *(☎ 312-938-8700, 164 E Grand Ave)* Lunch & dinner $7-20. The gregarious old guys playing dollar poker up front (you use dollar bills as the playing cards, betting on the serial numbers) set the tone at Blackies, one of the best of the usually excellent Greek-owned coffee shops. Platters of burgers and sandwiches are made with top-notch ingredients. The cheddar oozes out like volcanic magma under the chives and bacon bits on the potato skins ($6).

O'Neil's Bar & Grill *(☎ 312-787-5269, 152 E Ontario St)* Meals $10. Open 11am-midnight. The bar at O'Neil's – which used to be known as Howard's until Howard passed on to the great tavern in the sky – remains about the narrowest in town. The $7 cheeseburgers and other sandwiches, all served with potato chips, come on paper plates, which make them perfect for eating on the hidden patio with picnic tables.

Thai Star *(☎ 312-951-1196, 660 N State St)* Lunch & dinner $7-15. This survivor sparked the affordable Thai food rage of the early 1980s. Now its legions of competitors have closed, and it continues to soldier on with excellent and inexpensive food served on plywood tables in a charmless corner location. Palate-scorching curries are the specialty; none cost more than $5. Once your eyes are watering, you're less likely to notice the lack of decor.

Big Bowl *(☎ 312-787-8297, 159 W Erie St & ☎ 312-951-1888, 60 E Ohio St)* Lunch & dinner $10-20. You won't find any cheeseburgers or gift stores at this rapidly expanding local chain that's part of the Rich Melman

empire. What it does have are big bowls of Asian noodles – more than 30 varieties at last count, all of them fresh, hot and different from anything else you've had. The choices include wheat noodles with shrimp, black beans and snow peas and barbecued chicken and noodles in broth. The original location on Erie St feels like an upscale diner. The Ohio St branch is stylish, with huge booths in the shape of – you guessed it – big bowls.

Pizzeria Uno *(☎ 312-321-1000, 29 E Ohio St at Wabash Ave)* Meals $8-15. Ike Sewell supposedly invented Chicago-style pizza here on Dec 3, 1943, although his claim to fame is hotly disputed by other claimants. This well-worn building has been gussied up to resemble the franchised branches, but the pizza still tastes best here. A light, flaky crust holds piles of cheese and an herb-laced tomato sauce. The pizzas take awhile, but stick to the pitchers of beer and cheap red wine to kill time and avoid the salad and

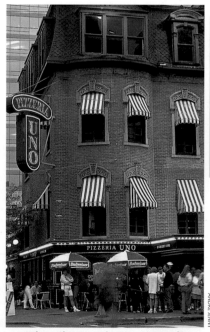

Where Chicago-style pizza originated?

other distractions, so you can save room for the main event. The $14 classic lands on the table with a resounding thud and can feed a family of four.

Gino's East (☎ *312-943-1124, 633 N Wells St)* Meals $8-15. The pizza at this institution somehow tasted better before the concept was franchised in upscale malls from coast to coast. Long located on Superior St, Gino's East was booted out for still another upscale apartment complex. But then opportunity knocked in the form of the failed Planet Hollywood. With minimal redecoration, Arnie's out and pizzas are in. In the old tradition, every surface (except for the actual food) is rapidly being covered with graffiti by patrons who cheerfully endure waits of up to 45 minutes, first for a table and then for the pizza. The classic stuffed cheese and sausage pizza oozes countless pounds of cheese over its crispy cornmeal crust. At $15, it's a bargain, since it can feed two very hungry folks.

Giordano's (☎ *312-951-0747, 730 N Rush St)* Meals $8-20. The stuffed-pizza special stuffs two people for $14 at this spot run by another of the classic purveyors of Chicago-style pizza. Each pizza contains sausage, green peppers, mushrooms and onions. Although the hard-working journalists at *Business Insurance* magazine, right above, must live with the aromas wafting up all day, don't let guilt stop you from eating away.

Mid-Range

Spectators (☎ *312-464-1000, 301 E North Water St in the Sheraton Chicago Hotel and Towers)* Meals $12-25. Rarely in Chicago should you bother with a hotel restaurant, but this one is a find, because the hotel's location, on a slight bend in the Chicago River, offers splendid views right out to Lake Michigan through the huge windows. Enjoy snacks, burgers and salads in a relaxed, barlike setting.

Green Door Tavern (☎ *312-664-5496, 678 N Orleans St)* Meals $10-20. Kitchen open until 10pm, bar 1am. This veteran bar and grill is approaching the century mark; the gobs of old paraphernalia lining the walls prove it. The tavern stops just short of being a parody of itself, and the hordes of upscale patrons enjoy the burgers, salads and pasta.

Heaven on Seven (☎ *312-280-7774, 600 N Rush St at Ohio St in the 600 N Michigan building)* Meals $14-30. The Loop's classic Cajun and Creole restaurant has spawned a much more stylish and fancy outlet here. For food details, see the Loop listing, earlier, but be forewarned that the prices here are a bit higher. Unlike its Loop counterpart, this Heaven on Seven stays open for dinner. The decor is hot: one wall is full of nothing but colorful bottles of Louisiana hot pepper sauces.

Bandera (☎ *312-644-3524, 535 N Michigan Ave)* Lunch & dinner $15-40. Closed Sun.

RAY HILLSTROM JR

A casual meal at the Green Door Tavern

One of the few restaurants on the Mag Mile itself, Bandera offers reasonably priced American classics such as fried chicken platters, meat loaf and grilled fish. If it's winter, the mound of mashed potatoes served with entrées will insulate you from the foul winds outside. Of course, you could always do what Richard Dreyfus did in *Close Encounters of the Third Kind* and make a sculpture.

Shaw's Crab House (☎ *312-527-2722, 21 E Hubbard St*) Lunch & dinner $20-50. My favorite fish place in Chicago is vaguely modeled on a Maryland seafood restaurant; the noisy, woodsy dining area wends its way through several rooms. To find out what's best and freshest, ask one of the friendly and efficient servers. They'll steer you to some can't-miss choices. The crab-cake appetizer and the key lime pie make good bookends to the meal. The adjoining **Blue Crab Lounge** serves oysters on the half-shell in an open and appealing bar area.

Hudson Club (☎ *312-467-1947, 504 N Wells St*) Dinner $25-40. Kitchen open until 10pm, bar until 2am, closed Sun. The burnished aluminum and smooth lines of 1930s aviation is overlaid upon the elegance of a supper club from the same era at Hudson Club. The menu is long and diverse with numerous steak and seafood choices. 'Flights' of wines and beer are offered; these include up to 20 different samples. The youngish crowd is in the highest tax bracket and is possibly fonder of their cell phones than of each other.

Carson's – The Place for Ribs (☎ *312-280-9200, 612 N Wells St*) Meals $18-30. Huge piles of fall-off-the-bone baby-back pork ribs are the specialty at this Chicago classic, a potential gold mine for cardiologists with cash-flow problems; the doctors can practically camp outside and wait for the clogged arteries to come their way. The decor here is dated, but you'll be gazing at your sauce-covered fingers anyway. Cole slaw, fries and rolls accompany the main attraction, which costs $20. Fish swim at the bottom of the menu; leave them there.

Blackhawk Lodge (☎ *312-280-4080, 41 E Superior St*) Lunch & dinner $18-38. Can't get to one of those rustic supper clubs in the woods of Wisconsin this trip? Don't bother – Blackhawk Lodge is prettier and offers much better food. The hickory smoke wafting from the kitchen tells you that good things are in store. Smoky corn chowder is a signature item; other choices vary with the season. I always enjoy the smoked trout as a starter. Try the microbrewed beer sampler, and you might just think you're in the backwoods.

Wildfire (☎ *312-787-9000, 159 W Erie St*) Lunch & dinner $20-40. A huge grill, rotisserie and wood-burning oven roast shrimp, prime rib, steak and ribs at this haven for barbecuers with snow-covered grills. Prices for the generous portions average about $18 – not bad for this comfortable and welcoming place. Hot fudge figures in several of the desserts. In the best tradition of Chicago smoke-filled rooms (where dubious political deals are cut), you'll emerge smelling of smoke, but at least it's barbecue rather than cigar.

Ed Debevic's (☎ *312-664-1707, 640 N Wells St*) Meals $10-25. The battle for the suburban prepubescent dollar is a tough one in River North, and there's nobody tougher than the actress/waitresses here. A local fave 15 years ago, Ed's received plaudits for its 'comfort' food but now merely milks the tourist dollar. It's become a parody of a place that was a parody of a 1950s diner. The quip-snorting waitresses don't seem to have quite the same sense of fun anymore either. The menu is as long as the runs in their nylons and features not-so-cheap burgers, chili, grilled cheese sandwiches and stalwarts such as meat loaf.

Hard Rock Cafe (☎ *312-943-2252, 63 W Ontario St*) Meals $14-30. Tourists and suburbanites flock through the doors as fast as the $18 T-shirts fly out of the newly expanded gift shop. Filled to the rafters with rock and roll memorabilia of varying importance, the two-level café serves a variety of moderately priced burgers, sandwiches and veggie offerings. Through numerous environmental messages adorning the menu, management urges patrons to think green. Cynics, noting the $230 bomber jackets, might suspect that management's green thoughts are more monetary than conservationist. A telling

PLACES TO EAT

moment came a few years ago, when the Hard Rock chopped down a tree out front to build a bigger sign.

Rainforest Cafe (☎ *312-787-1501, 605 N Clark St*) Meals $15-30. This big-concept, big-event eatery/gift store/theme park takes the mall underpinnings of the theme-restaurant craze to new highs – or lows. Keep the following quote from one of its managers in mind as you enter: 'The restaurant drives traffic and the retail drives revenue.' That revenue comes from potions, lotions, T-shirts and stuffed vanishing species (Cha!Cha! the tree frog, Tuki the elephant, etc), all showing what happens when an endangered ecosystem becomes a marketing concept. Through shopping? The menu items include the pan-continental 'Rainforest Pita Quesadillas' and the 'Maya Mixed Grill,' which includes 'Wild Waffle fries.' Robot animals prowl the plaster boulders, and every 20 minutes an electrical storm lights up the fake trees. A family of four can easily drop $100 here.

Dao (☎ *312-337-0000, 230 E Ohio St*) Lunch & dinner $10-25. A classic Thai restaurant in an area that could use a few more eateries, Dao is popular with lunching local workers. Service at all times is quick and cheerful. Head here if you get a sudden craving for satay with peanut sauce.

Hatsuhana (☎ *312-280-8808, 160 E Ontario St*) Meals $20-40. Closed Sun. A suitably hushed atmosphere prevails at this simple temple for sushi and sashimi, one of the city's original Japanese restaurants and a perpetually popular spot. Natural wood, white walls, lanterns and paintings complement the long sushi bar, where chefs carefully prepare the food.

Ben Pao (☎ *312-222-1888, 52 W Illinois St at Dearborn St*) Meals $20-40. Chinese food reaches new heights under the inspiration of Rich Melman; the high-ceilinged, dark interior, with its circular bar, is one of the most chic Asian restaurants in town. The menu features many twists, including five-spice

PLACES TO EAT

RICHARD CUMMINS

Rainforest Cafe: restaurant or theme park?

shrimp satay, lemon-crusted chicken and Hong Kong spicy eggplant.

Cyrano's Bistrot *(☎ 312-467-0546, 546 N Wells St)* Lunch & dinner $15-35. Closed Sun. This popular casual French restaurant is named for the famous Cyrano of Bergerac, the hometown shared by chef and owner Didier Durand. Not quite cheap but very cheerful, Cyrano serves a menu of southern French favorites, including numerous roasted meats (and, in a bow to local culinary obsessions, a few pasta dishes as well). A few tables line the street and make a good place to sip one of the many wines while watching the after-work hordes march home. The $12 lunch special is a four-course marvel that's served all at once.

Brasserie Jo *(☎ 312-595-0800, 59 W Hubbard St)* Lunch & dinner $25-45. The extended Ver Berkmoes family was once lured from our usual favorite (see Bistro 110, in the Gold Coast section) to this huge, open place that serves wonderful food from Alsace, the French region near Germany where owner Jean Joho was born. We were beguiled. From the signature beer specially brewed by a local microbrewery to the hot and fresh baguettes, all the details are right. Try the great *choucroute* (smoked meats and sausages on sauerkraut) or the shrimp in a bag. The service is as bright and cheery as the decor.

Leona's *(☎ 312-867-0101, 646 N Franklin St)* Meals $10-26. There's an outpost of the reliable local Leona's chain right under the El tracks and near the many River North galleries. See the Leona's listing in the Lake View section for full details.

Harry Caray's *(☎ 312-828-0966, 33 W Kinzie St)* Lunch & Dinner $15-40. Harry's gone, but his name lives on in this fairly standard Chicago-style Italian steakhouse, which serves an especially garlicky chicken Vesuvio and some good steaks. Not a bad place, but it survives more on the enduring afterlife charm of the beloved Cubs announcer. Note to Budweiser: do you really want a dead man hawking your beer? (There's a huge mural of Harry doing just that.)

Trattoria Parma *(☎ 312-245-9933, 400 N Clark St)* Lunch & dinner $22-35. Paul LoDuca has created one of the city's best Italian restaurants in a neighborhood where prices often outpace quality. Here, however, prepare for a treat of well-prepared classics like eggplant parmigiana. My favorite is the chicken *saltimbocca*, an updated version of the great old veal dish with flavorings of ham and fresh sage. The decor is a delightful Italian pastiche.

Frontera Grill *(☎ 312-661-1434, 445 N Clark St)* Lunch & dinner $15-40. Closed Sun. Once you've eaten here, you'll never be able to look at the slop most places pass off as Mexican food again. Chef-owner Rick Bayless has achieved celebrity status with his fresh variations inspired by south-of-the-border fare. His unusual pepper sauces are worth rolling around your palate like a fine wine. Hot tortillas made near the entrance hold *tacos al carbón*, which are filled with charred beef and grilled green onions. *Chiles rellenos* await converts to their succulent richness. The place is always mobbed, so expect to wait; reservations are only taken for five or more. See also the listing for Topolobampo under Top End, later.

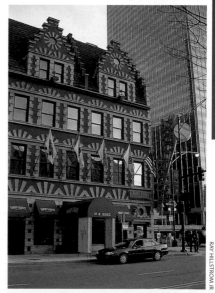

RAY HILLSTROM JR

PLACES TO EAT

Harry Caray lives on at his namesake restaurant.

Sun-dappled dining at the Frontera Grill

RAY HILLSTROM JR

PLACES TO EAT

Cafe Iberico (☎ 312-573-1510, 737 N LaSalle St) Meals $18-30. Happy diners look like kids in a candy store as they ponder their little plates of tapas here. Among the choices: *salpicon de marisco* (seafood salad with shrimp, octopus and squid), *croquetas de pollo* (chicken and ham puffs with garlic sauce) and *vieiras a la plancha* (grilled scallops with saffron). Finish it off with flan. Most of the small dishes average $4-6. The large wine list includes several $16 Riojas. The sherries run the gamut, from dry to rich cream. Tables sprawl through several tiled rooms.

Pasha (☎ 312-397-0100, 642 N Clark St) Dinner $20-35. Kitchen open until 1am, bar until 4am. Pasha is a pastiche of opulent styles from Russia, the Middle East and Italy. The open kitchen serves up eclectic fare like risottos and pâtés. On most nights there's dancing; Wednesday is samba night. Shake your heels or settle back into the pillow-covered seats and observe.

Papagus (☎ 312-642-8450, 620 N State St in the Embassy Suites Hotel) Meals $22-35. You'll find moderate prices and excellent service at this *House & Garden* version of a Grecian taverna. Old faves like *taramasalata* (cod roe spread), *spanakopita* (spinach and feta cheese in phyllo) and *saganaki* (the flaming cheese of 'Opaa!' fame) breathe new life, thanks to a fresh touch in the kitchen.

Top End

Joe's Steak & Stone Crab (☎ 312-379-5637, 60 E Grand Ave) Lunch & dinner $30-55. A Chicago restaurateur imported Joe's Stone Crab from Miami Beach and gave it a distinctly local spin, not the least of which is the 'Steak &' in the name. Few restaurants dare to chase the local dining dollar without steaks and/or pastas on the menu, but the signature item here is the stone crabs, succulent claws of shellfish that may be unavailable in summer months. Note that the menu mentions that stone crab prices vary, so brace yourself. Expect dinner to be mobbed at this see-and-be-seen place. Reservations are taken, but many tables are held for walk-ins.

Gene and Georgetti (☎ 312-527-3718, 500 N Franklin St) Lunch & dinner $35-60. Closed Sun. For once, a place touting itself as one of Frank Sinatra's favorite restaurants can back up the claim, which should tell you everything you need to know about this classic steak house, more than half a century old. Out of place in the city, the wooden building looks like it would be more comfortable on a two-lane road in some farm town. Old-timers, politicos and crusty regulars are seated downstairs. New-timers, conventioneers and – eek! – tourists are seated upstairs. The steaks are the same on both levels: thick, well aged and well priced. Wear a pinky ring (this advice is for men) and act like a big shot and you may get better service. On the other hand, you might get mistaken for an alderman and served with a subpoena.

Erie Cafe (☎ 312-266-2300, 536 W Erie St) Lunch & dinner $30-55. Steaks bigger than the plate are the sizable feature at this spot, housed in a renovated meat-packing plant that's almost on the north branch of the Chicago River. The menu is heavy (and we mean heavy) with T-bones, filet mignons and lamb chops. The Chicago-Italian selections include a volcanic chicken Vesuvio erupting with garlic, as well as that old standby: calamari.

Bice (☎ 312-664-1474, 158 E Ontario St) Lunch & dinner $28-50. This import from Milan provides an excellent chance to savor the delicately spiced foods of northern Italy without the jet lag. Risottos are superb, as are the creamy pastas. At the outdoor tables you can keep your eyes on the sidewalk crowd and ignite the jealousy of the passing rabble by letting your tongue linger on the housemade gelato. Inside, the stylish art deco decor makes a good backdrop for the stylish patrons.

Rosebud on Rush (☎ 312-266-6444, 720 N Rush St) Lunch & dinner $30-55. Huge portions of familiar Italian standards dominate the tables at this outpost of the Rosebud empire (see the Little Italy section, later). The prices, quality and weight of the doggie bags are all high. Specialties include veal in its many forms. You'll be unlikely to find enough energy to sing 'Chicago' as you and a companion attempt to plow your way through the Festivale di Sinatra con Amore, a massive meal for two that seems to include half the menu.

Topolobampo (☎ 312-661-1434, 445 N Clark St) Lunch & dinner $35-55. Closed Sun. Part of the same operation as Frontera Grill, this is where chef Rick Bayless lets his creativity flow unfettered by cost restrictions. Compared to its rollicking neighbor, Topolobampo's mood seems downright serious, as diners sample combinations of flavors most people never knew existed. The menu changes almost nightly; be prepared for a memorable experience. Reservations are required here.

Spago (☎ 312-527-3700, 520 N Dearborn St) Lunch & dinner $30-55. Closed Sun. Like so many other trendy places in River North, Spago isn't unique to Chicago. Nevertheless, the local edition of celebrity chef Wolfgang Puck's Hollywood original is thronged with the glitterati every night; a horde of paparazzi would make the atmosphere com-

plete. The entrées – as pricey as the coifs on the patrons' heads – come from the California fusion palette, which blends techniques and cuisines from every continent.

Zinfandel (☎ 312-527-1818, 59 W Grand Ave) Lunch & dinner $35-50. The menu changes often to reflect the seasons at this innovative and classy Near North favorite. Flavors from Asia, the Europe and the Americas combine to insure that your meal is never predictable. Special regional American menus are always a treat. The friendly service matches the bright decor, and you can expect expert help with the long wine list (which, not surprisingly, features many zinfandels).

Tru (☎ 312-202-0001, www.leye.com/restaurants/tru, 676 N St Clair St) Dinner $90-160. Closed Sun. Gale Grand and Rick

Tramonto, a married pair of chefs, have opened one of the city's best restaurants in years with the backing of Rich Melman. The food is French but with a sense of humor. If this seems a contradiction in terms – or, worse, conjures up some sort of image of Jerry Lewis – fear not. Starters include a trademark staircase of caviar, with a variety of the little fish eggs waltzing down the steps. The eclectic and ever-changing menu also features a cheese course that's one of the best in the US and renowned deserts, such as the heavenly roasted pineapple carpaccio. Expect flawless service in the all-white dining room. Menus include an all-vegetable version ($75) and a chef's special collection ($125). After eating here, one can only wonder how long it will take Grand and Tramonto to reach the celebrity status of arch-competitor Charlie Trotter (see the boxed text 'Charlie Trotter's' for details on him).

NAVY PIER (Map 3)

The none-too-great dining options at Navy Pier include an assortment of contrived theme restaurants as well as chains like Mc-Donald's. If you're planning a sojourn here, save your eating for spots farther west, although kids will no doubt be satisfied with the offerings.

Riva (☎ 312-644-7482, 700 E Grand Ave) Lunch & dinner $20-45. The high-class option for Navy Pier victuals, Riva combines the ever-popular Italian with seafood. The latter is fitting, given Lake Michigan laps a few feet away. Needless to say, the menu features plenty of calamari and various fresh grilled fish dishes. The high prices make a big splash but buy great views of the lake and city skyline.

SOUTH LOOP (Map 4)

Edwardo's (☎ 312-939-3366, 521 S Dearborn St) Meals $10-20. Edwardo's, a Chicago-based chain, serves justifiably famous stuffed spinach pizza, as well as thin-crust models, sandwiches and salads. Everything is fresh and cheap.

Prairie (☎ 312-663-1143, Hyatt on Printer's Row, 500 S Dearborn St) Lunch starting at $15, dinner $25-50. The name here reflects this restaurant's celebration of Midwestern food and ingredients. The dining room, in a prominent ground-floor corner of the Hyatt, has the studied mannerism of Frank Lloyd Wright, with oak chairs that replicate some of Wright's best-known designs. Featured menu items include baby coho salmon, whitefish from Lake Superior and other fishy denizens of the Great Lakes. Corn figures in many dishes, from the chowder to the muffins.

Printer's Row (☎ 312-461-0780, 550 S Dearborn St) Meals $40-60. Lunch weekdays, dinner Mon-Sat. When he opened this restaurant almost 20 years ago, Michael Foley was ahead of two trends: the resurgence of traditional American foods and the revitalization of his Printer's Row neighborhood. Both have long since come to pass, but Foley's restaurant still provides fresh pairings of primarily Midwestern foods. The menu changes with the seasons, but venison direct from the woods and fish direct from the rivers are featured nightly. The smoothly professional service is just what one would expect from a restaurant that has matured without losing an ounce of vitality.

NEAR SOUTH SIDE (Map 4)

White Castle (☎ 312-949-0717, 2134 S Wabash Ave at Cermak Rd) Meals $2-5. This fairly new branch of the legendary Midwest-based fast-food chain serves the well-known fly-weight burgers somewhat affectionately known as 'sliders.' A cheese-less version, cooked with steamed onions, costs 44¢; you literally 'buy 'em by the bagful,' as the ad copy suggests. Midwesterners transplanted to parts of the US not graced by White Castle have been known to sate their cravings by ordering shipments of frozen sliders.

Firehouse (☎ 312-786-1401, 1401 S Michigan Ave) Lunch & dinner $25-40. An old firehouse that's been beautifully restored, this place offers the kind of traditional tasty fare that would light up the face of any firefighter, albeit at prices that might force the firefighter to take a second job. Ribs and steaks headline the show here, although they're pushed out of the spotlight when local resident Mayor Richard M Daley stops by.

Chinatown 229

A restored fire department on the South Side houses the Firehouse restaurant.

RAY HILLSTROM JR

Gioco (☎ *312-939-3870, 1312 S Wabash Ave*) Meals $22-50. Lunch weekdays, dinner nightly. Restaurateurs Jerry Kleiner and Howard Davis made Randolph St on the West Side one of Chicago's hottest dining areas in the 1990s. Now they've opened a whimsical Italian restaurant in a desolate stretch of the Near South Side that hasn't seen this much action since the 1930s, when almost every building was a speakeasy (including, they'd contend, the home of Gioco). A menu laden with classic Chicago-Italian dishes includes delicate pizzas from a wood-burning oven. Surprises abound, such as the tasty lobster gnocchi.

CHINATOWN (Map 4)

Chinatown is easily reached by the El – ride the Red Line to the Cermak stop and you're one block east of Wentworth Ave, the traditional heart of the neighborhood. Chinatown includes scores more restaurants than the ones listed here. If you wander the streets, you'll reap the reward of discovering little noodle shops seemingly transplanted from China. New places crop up weekly in the Chinatown Square development, southwest of Wentworth along Archer Ave.

Hong Min (☎ *312-842-5026, 221 W Cermak Rd*) Meals $12-25. Bring your reading glasses to study Hong Min's menu, as it's an encyclopedia of Cantonese cooking. Tired standbys such as chow mein and sweet and sour dishes come back to life here. If it crawled, swam, quacked or mooed, you can probably order its culinary incarnation. The moody decor makes you think skullduggery is afoot – Hong Min would make a good movie set.

Three Happiness (☎ *312-791-1228, 2130 S Wentworth Ave*) Meals $10-25. Open 10am-10pm daily. Between 10am and 3pm, sit back as cart after cart bursts from the kitchen carrying steaming arrays of little dim sum treats. The staff may or may not be ready to help you choose, so plunge in and pick a plate. Savvy nibblers angle for tables near the kitchen, where they can get first dibs on the emerging bounty. Everything is tallied on little cards; the meal will rarely add up to more than about $10 a head. Three Happiness also does dinner, but that's not the

PLACES TO EAT

point. Sunday is the most popular dim sum day – be prepared to line up.

Seven Treasures *(312-225-2668, 2312 S Wentworth Ave)* Lunch & dinner $14-25. Open until 2am daily. The ducks in the window aren't going anywhere, but the frenetic cooks at the woks in the kitchen, which overlooks the sidewalk, compensate for the ducks' inactivity. Who needs a TV food show when you can watch these Cantonese masters slicing, dicing and stir-frying up a storm? When you're tired of just looking, or you're just too hungry, step inside this steamy, bustling family restaurant. All the usual items are here – choose what looked especially good from the street.

Phoenix (☎ *312-328-0848, 2131 S Archer Ave)* Meals $14-30. This popular spot rises above the old veterans of Chinatown with excellent, fresh food prepared by chefs direct from Hong Kong. Midday sees an endless parade of dim sum issuing forth on trolleys from the kitchen. On Sunday the parade is lengthier yet. Cuisine-wise, Phoenix is about as close as you can get to the former British colony in Chicago without the 15-hour flight.

Emperor's Choice (☎ *312-225-8800, 2238 S Wentworth Ave)* Lunch & dinner $14-35. This local veteran has earned a reputation for excellent seafood and service to match. Lobster — the center of the menu — stars in several prix-fixe meals that average $26 per person. The ginger scallops are just as succulent as the name suggests. Feel like some snake? Ask for the special menu for more adventurous diners. But fear not, it doesn't list anything you'd typically call the exterminators for.

GOLD COAST (Map 5)

Loads of restaurants crowd the streets of this affluent neighborhood, which is the first primarily residential neighborhood on the North Side as you head away from the Loop. Although some of the city's toniest addresses are here, many of the eateries and bars are still living off the area's nightlife reputation of 25 years ago and seem dated. However, as the Gold Coast becomes less of a destination and more of a neighborhood, restaurants are springing up to serve its upscale denizens.

Budget

Ghirardelli Soda Fountain (☎ *312-337-9330, 118 E Pearson St)* Sundaes $7. The San Francisco–based chocolate company serves a calorie-counter's nightmare of elaborate and tasty ice-cream creations in an 1890s marble-and-wood setting. The hot chocolate will chase away any winter chills pronto.

McDonald's (☎ *312-649-9262, 10 E Chicago Ave)* Meals $3-6. Finding a Golden Arches in Chicago is about as hard as finding a fire hydrant if you're a dog. But this one

RICK GERHARTER

Restaurant lineup in Chinatown

bears mention for its history. In the early 1980s Burger King ran an operation right next door. Never were the burger wars so fiercely fought. One night McDonald's founder Ray Kroc passed by and decided he'd had enough. Getting some spray paint, he tagged BK with a nice, simple 'Burger King Sucks.' Well, actually, billionaire Kroc had his chauffeur do the spraying; his reputation remained unsullied until the colorful tale emerged after his death.

Lo-Cal Zone (☎ *312-943-9060, 912 N Rush St*) Meals $5-8. A budget haven in the midst of the Gold Coast's ritziest shopping, this spot offers twists on its namesake calzones, as well as veggie burgers, funky burritos (try the Cajun with turkey sausage and red beans and rice) and the creamiest, chocolatiest frozen yogurt anywhere. Lo-Cal Zone occupies a tiny, tatty building that will last only until the next real estate speculator happens by.

Boudin Bakery (☎ *312-649-3570, 5th level of the 900 N Michigan mall*) Meals $5-8. Here you can take a break from shopping or stock up on picnic provisions on your way to nearby Oak St Beach. See the listing in the Loop section, earlier, for food details.

Johnny Rockets (☎ *312-337-3900, 901 N Rush St*) Meals $8-14. This faux '50s diner, on the back side of the vast 900 N Michigan mall, features a kitchen, eating area and servers all clad in white. Kids like the spot, though the nostalgic schtick is getting a bit time-worn. Folks rave about the burgers.

Tempo Cafe (☎ *312-943-3929, 6 E Chestnut St*) Meals $6-15. Open 24 hours daily. Here you'll pay moderate prices for tasty omelets, BLTs, soups, salads and more. A new stylish location right across from the old stylish location is definitely a few cuts above the usual all-night coffee shop.

Mid-Range

Foodlife (☎ *312-335-3663, mezzanine level of Water Tower Place, 835 N Michigan Ave*) Lunch $12-20. At this high concept cafeteria (although they'd shoot me for calling it that), you pick up a magnetic card on the way in, and the staff reserve you a table. Then you wander around and choose items from the stir-fry, Mediterranean, Mexican, salad or rotisserie bars. Unfortunately, most portions are too large for you to sample lots of different cuisines. Your meal gets tallied up on the card, and you pay on the way out – probably more than you expected, because of the above-average prices and the service charge for the deserving, cheerful staff – but Foodlife is still a fun refuge from the Water Tower shopping hordes.

PLACES TO EAT

Settle in for a spell at one of Chicago's classic diners.

RAY HILLSTROM JR

Puck's at the MCA (☎ 312-397-4034, 220 E Chicago Ave) Lunch $8-20. Located in the Museum of Contemporary Art, this outlet of the irrepressible Wolfgang Puck features strictly contemporary cooking, with dishes that fuse Asian and Mediterranean cuisine. The changing menu features lots of marinated seafood and salads, as well as a few hot items. A deli counter offers sandwiches and more to go. In summer, dine out back on the MCA's patio, one of the city's great hidden gems.

Wolfgang Puck

Cru Cafe & Wine Bar (☎ 312-337-4078, 888 N Wabash Ave) Meals $10-25. Open until 1am daily. Choose among no less than 400 bottles at this sleek wine bar. The well-dressed patrons speak in lots of European accents, some of them even authentic. In summer you can idle away hours people-watching from the outdoor tables. In winter you can gather with a full-bodied red around the roaring fireplace inside. The food ranges from sandwiches to salads to quiche, none of it cheap; a club sandwich is $16. The late-night cheese platters seem a world removed from the late-night weenies you can get elsewhere.

Signature Room at the 95th (☎ 312-787-9596, John Hancock Center, 875 N Michigan Ave) Lunch $10-20, dinner $25-50. Near the top of the Hancock Center – no points for guessing the correct floor – this large room offers stunning views on clear days. (But remember, the prices don't diminish when the weather diminishes the view, so pick your day carefully.) Given that diners spend more time looking out the windows than looking at their plates, you'd think the kitchen wouldn't trouble itself over the food, but the meals are quite good. The lunch buffet ($12) can be a fine deal, especially if you satisfy your view cravings here as opposed to buying a ticket to the Hancock observation deck. Families come for the Sunday brunch.

Jilly's (☎ 312-664-2100, 1007 N Rush St) Dinner $25-45. The slogan out front, credited to Frank Sinatra, says: 'My favorite bistro.' Though one would assume that Frank meant this place, those in the know will note that Frank was quite dead when Jilly's opened. Oh well – the ghoulish and/or Rat Pack fanatics will still thrill to the woodsy interior, which features no shortage of pictures of Dean Martin (dead), Sammy Davis Jr (dead) and many of their pals (probably dead). Jilly (dead) is up there too; he was Frank's bodyguard – as if the pugilistic crooner needed one. You can feast on steaks and Italian fare and smoke cigars and pipes in the bar – all of which should put you in a position to join Frank, Jilly and company very soon.

Three restaurants in a row near the corner of State and Division Sts serve the thirty- and fortysomething singles who live in the area.

PJ Clarke's (☎ 312-664-1650, 1204 N State St) Meals $18-25. Kitchen open until 1am. This always-crowded pub is named after the classic Third Ave bar in New York City. That's where the resemblance ends. It's not a bad place, and the burgers are quite good, but don't expect to make a lot of eye contact here – everybody's watching everyone else. After all, the grass is always greener…

Yvette (☎ 312-280-1700, 1206 N State St) Meals $28-45. Kitchen open until midnight. Once people have met their match at Clarke's (above), they can go next door for their first date. Yvette features a jazzy piano player most nights and a dance trio that plays on weekends. The new owners have injected some needed pizzazz into the competent French bistro food, but the prices might still seem too high.

Dining at the Ambassador East hotel: perfect for an expense-account lunch

The State Room (☎ 312-951-1212, 1212 N State St) Dinner $25-50. Kitchen open until 1am daily. The third place on this stretch is where you go with your trophy spouse after you've made it. Local nightlife maestro Demetri Alexander owns a share of this place, and his sterling connections guarantee that the politically connected can be found gabbing after a hard day of grabbing. Order a drink from the long glass bar – a dream of blue light – then settle into one of the comfortable booths in the main dining room. The food is pure upscale Chicago: steaks and pasta.

Top End

Bistro 110 (☎ 312-266-3110, 110 E Pearson St) Lunch & dinner $20-50. Although my mother always wants to try a new place every time she visits Chicago, she's usually drawn back to this bright and bustling brasserie across from the Water Tower. She's got good reason. Shortly after you sit down, you're given a sliced baguette, accompanied by roasted heads of garlic to spread on it. The roasted vegetable plate, a heavily herbed selection, holds surprises such as wild mushrooms – it's a big hit with my vegetarian sister. Dad likes the spicy pepper steak with *frites* (french fries). As for dessert, it's hard to tell who moans with delight more loudly between mouthfuls of the crème brûlée: me or my wife. The Sunday jazz brunch may make you moan with delight.

Le Colonial (☎ 312-255-0088, 937 N Rush St) Lunch & dinner $30-50. A colonial outpost of the New York original, Le Colonial re-creates the feel of a swank Vietnamese restaurant during the French era of the 1950s. Fortunately, there's no malaria, and the food shows more imagination than the French exhibited during their rule. The delicately seasoned offerings include warm salads and several seafood and duck dishes. The upstairs bar and the rest of the interior achieve an evocative faded charm that will have you reaching for a tonic.

Gibson's (☎ 312-266-8999, 1028 N Rush St) Dinner $40-70. It's a scene seven nights a week at this local original. Politicians, movers, shakers and the shaken-down compete for prime table space in the buzzing dining area. The bar is a prime stalking place for available millionaires –

said one 40-year-old friend: 'I haven't felt like such a piece of meat in 20 years.' As for the meat on the plates, the steaks are as good as they come, and the seafood is fresh and expensive.

Morton's (☎ *312-266-4820, 1050 N State St)* Dinner $50-75. With a clubby ambience and prime service, Morton's has remained Chicago's premier steak house long enough for scores of competitors to arrive on the scene. The meat here is aged to perfection and displayed tableside before cooking. See that half a cow? It's the 48oz double porterhouse. Smaller – but still quite dangerous if dropped on your toe – are the filets, strip steaks and other cuts. The immense baked potatoes could prop up church foundations. Try the hash browns, superb versions of a side dish all too often ignored. Expensive reds anchor the wine list.

Pump Room (☎ *312-266-0360, 1301 N State St in the Ambassador East hotel)* Lunch $25-45, dinner $35-70. Book yourself into Booth One at this legendary spot and you'll have something in common with the pantheon of celebrity customers whose photos line the walls. Famous since the 1940s, this Pump Room continues its tradition of understated elegance. Real VIPs, or just lucky poseurs, sit in Booth One, a see-and-be-seen throwback to a previous, glamorous era. There's a dress code, which means you'll be well-attired for the cheek-to-cheek dancing that takes places most nights after dinner. Prime rib and roast duck head up the American menu.

OLD TOWN (Map 6)

Trendy in the '70s, Old Town fell on hard times in the '80s as trends moved elsewhere. In the '90s the pleasant neighborhood centered on Wells St north of Division St has stabilized and now contains a nice assortment of enjoyable eateries that mix old and new. They're a decent stroll – or a $5 cab ride – away from River North.

A textbook table setting at the Pump Room

Fresh Choice (☎ *312-664-7065, 1534 N Wells St)* Meals $5-8. Here you can recharge your body with a glass of the fresh-squeezed juices of carrots, beets, celery, cucumbers, spinach and parsley. A 12oz shot ($4) is probably the healthiest thing you'll ingest in Chicago, especially after a rigorous sampling of hot dogs, pizza and Italian beef. Purists can choose less complex combinations and add more roughage to their diets at the salad bar.

Fireplace Inn (☎ *312-664-5264, 1448 N Wells St)* Lunch & dinner $18-35. Kitchen open until midnight. This local classic has been serving up Chicago-style baby-back ribs for almost 35 years. Steaks, burgers and seafood round out the menu. The steak fries are perfectly crisp on the outside and tender on the inside. Blue-cheese lovers will want to spring for the extra charge for that dressing on the side salad. The two-level dining room is heavy with wood – almost as much as the namesake fireplace burns up in a night. When the snow is blowing off the lake and the sidewalks are piling up with drifts, you can warm your cockles here. (But you can also air them out in summer at the garden tables.)

Twin Anchors (☎ *312-266-1616, 1655 N Sedgwick St)* Meals $22-28. My brother-in-law Danny swears by the baby-back ribs here, and you will too; the meat drops from the ribs as soon as you lift them. Choose among fries, onion rings and baked potatoes for sides. This spot doesn't take reservations, so you'll have to wait outside or around the neon-lit 1950s bar, which sets the tone for the whole place. An almost-all Sinatra jukebox completes the '50s supper-club ambience. (Actually, the restaurant itself dates from 1932.) To avoid a really long wait, drop by midweek.

¡Salpicón! (☎ *312-988-7811, 1252 N Wells St)* Meals $22-40. Closed Sun. The linguistically aware will immediately suspect that this place is a Mexican restaurant. But don't bother coming here if all you want is the Holy Trinity of T's – tacos, tostadas and tamales – this menu gets a lot more creative than that. The *ceviche* (raw fish marinated in lime juice) includes versions made with lobster. *Chiles rellenos* (stuffed poblano peppers that are batter-fried) have been raised to an art. Many other items come slathered in heavenly mole. The festive interior features high ceilings and bold colors. Create bright colors in your head by trying some of the 60 tequilas, including some rare, oak-barrel-aged numbers.

Topo Gigio (☎ *312-266-9355, 1516 N Wells St)* Lunch & dinner $25-40. Roasted peppers and grilled zucchini on the antipasto table are just some of the treats that await at this faithful adaptation of a Roman trattoria, an excellent choice for a relaxing evening of delicious Italian food. The linguini Cinque Terre isn't just named for one of my favorite regions of Italy; it's also a good deal when you consider the mound of shrimp that comes with it.

Bistrot Margot (☎ *312-587-3660, 1437 N Wells St)* Dinner $25-40. A visit to Bistrot Margot is like a visit to a little Parisian corner bistro in one of the remoter districts. Roast chicken, steak and frites, mussels and other coastal shellfish highlight the classic menu. The interior mixes dark wood with bright tiles and red booths, and the busy crowd adds to the atmosphere. It's a good idea to make reservations for the popular Sunday brunch and for dinner most nights.

O'Briens (☎ *312-787-3131, 1528 N Wells St)* Lunch & dinner $18-50. Clouds of cigar smoke waft away from the sizable outdoor garden at this Old Town institution. O'Briens' upscale clientele puffs away on hand-rolled specials that each cost dollars rather than cents. The faces behind the cigars frequently belong to aging politicos reliving their days in smoke-filled rooms. The interior, which thankfully boasts high-powered ventilation, is dark and clubby. The food is old-boy American: steaks, chops, a passle of burgers and the highly trumpeted (at least by the establishment itself) 'liver O'Brien.'

Tanzy (☎ *312-202-0302, 215 W North Ave)* Dinner $25-50. American regional classics get a thorough and appealing update in memorable preparations that are simple yet vigorously spiced. Think of it as comfort food for those who don't want to be complacent. Look for seafood such as crab, salmon and various whitefish. Meat here includes lamb,

PLACES TO EAT

chicken and the usual range of beef. Like the menu, the interior is simple but bright; in nice weather, be sure to sit on the outside patio.

LINCOLN PARK (Map 6)

Chicago's most pleasant and popular neighborhood teems with restaurants. A stroll down any of the commercial streets will yield a bounty of choices. The Fullerton El stop is only about a 20-minute (or shorter) stroll away from most of the places listed here. Cruising cabs are plentiful, parking is frightful and the streets are generally safe. See the Entertainment chapter for clubs and bars for post-meal joy.

Establishments in this section are listed by geographic grouping and in ascending order of price.

Halsted St

Nookies, too (☎ *773-327-1400, 2114 N Halsted St*) Meals $6-12. Open 7am-11pm, 24 hours Fri & Sat. You can cleanse your previous night's sins with the oat-bran pancakes at this popular brunch spot or choose from a full complement of eggs, waffles and sandwiches. The fresh-squeezed orange juice is pricey but worth it if your taste buds are already awake.

O'Famé (☎ *773-929-5111, 750 W Webster Ave*) Meals $12-25. Just one door west of Halsted St, O'Famé is a booming carry-out and delivery business, but you can also try one of these gourmet treats while seated inside. Popular selections include sandwiches, salads and pasta, with basil and roasted red pepper joining the usual ingredients. You can get picnic versions of anything from the gleaming white-tile deli area and enjoy them at Oz Park, across the street.

Tilli's (☎ *773-325-0044, 1952 N Halsted St*) Meals $12-25. On weekends this huge, noisy place attracts crowds of yuppies whose growing salaries far outpace their ages and beautiful people who are too young for their first facelift. The menu bounces from Italy to Asia, with food such as goat-cheese pizza by the slice and chicken satay. Prices are moderate, which means you can keep saving for that first Chanel suit. Lately a number of the customers have spawned, and you'll see many a couple showing off their progeny to insincere acclaim from groups of dear friends.

King Crab (☎ *312-280-8990, 1816 N Halsted St*) Dinner $18-35. The prices and the sartorial demands on the customers are modest at this simple place that's popular

Drinks before dinner at The Berghoff in the Loop

with people seeing shows at the nearby Steppenwolf and Royal George theaters. The generous portions of seafood include treats such as grilled prawns, blackened tuna and oysters from the notable raw bar. The restaurant's namesake is always available, but the price varies with the market.

Vinci (☎ 312-266-1199, 1732 N Halsted St) Dinner $20-38. This popular and upscale neighborhood Italian restaurant is also popular with the crowds hitting the local theaters. The simple yet stylish dining room features a decent amount of space between the tables. The menu holds no stunning surprises but is solid and reliable.

Cafe Ba-Ba-Reeba! (☎ 773-935-5000, 2024 N Halsted St) Meals $22-35. If you plan on kissing anyone after dinner, make certain they've dined with you at this trendsetting, delightfully ersatz tapas joint where the garlic-laced sauces are worth licking the dishes for. The menu changes daily but always includes some spicy meats, marinated fish and a potato salad that will forever have you lambasting the gloppy American version. Plates cost about $6 apiece. If you want a main event, order one of the nine paellas ($10 a person) as soon as you get seated in one of the many rooms – they take awhile to prepare.

Cafe Bernard (☎ 773-871-2100, 2100 N Halsted St) Lunch & dinner $25-38. This fun veteran has been peddling simple French food for decades – since the times when this was a solid blue-collar neighborhood and French meant something you tried on a date. The tables are intimate, the atmosphere romantic and the French bistro classics well prepared. Try the pork loin *au poivre* (with pepper). Out back is the Red Rooster Cafe & Wine Bar – a great post-meal stop (see the Entertainment chapter for more details).

Louisiana Kitchen (☎ 773 529-1666, 2666 N Halsted St) Dinner $25-38. Closed Mon. This is probably the best place to have a great N'Awlins Cajun and Creole chow without a trip to the French Quarter. Chef and owner John Moultrie uses recipes handed down from his grandmother Mama Bazzell and spares no seasonings on the jambalaya, blackened pork chops, red beans and rice and other classic items. Be sure to reserve early for the very popular Sunday brunch and try to get a seat in the adjoining garden.

Armitage Ave

Armitage Ave west of Halsted St to Sheffield Ave was once a wonderful microcosm of the North Side, with a range of great places. Sadly it's now Exhibit A of the malaise found in many corners of the Chicago dining scene. Huge rent increases killed almost every restaurant that was thriving only a few years ago. The notable exception – and boy, what a notable exception – is Charlie Trotter's (see the boxed text of the same name). CTA Brown Line trains stop at the Armitage Station, but only until about 9:30pm. Cabs abound.

Chicago Bagel Authority (☎ 773-248-9606, 953 W Armitage Ave) Meals $3-10. This lively little spot makes a good stop for a fast breakfast and lunch. The bagels are fine plain or holding a sandwich.

Lincoln Ave

Chipotle Mexican Grill (☎ 773-935-6744, 2256-58 N Orchard Ave) Meals $6-8. Fast-food Mexican in a minimalist setting is the formula at this local chain. The meats are marinated and grilled, then served with a range of interesting accompaniments such as tomatillo–red chili salsa. Drink choices include numerous beers.

John Barleycorn Memorial Pub (☎ 773-348-8899, 658 W Belden Ave at Lincoln Ave) Meals $10-20. Discovered about every 10 years by another generation, this windowless tavern that dates from the 1890s stays perpetually young. Amid the hubbub, a continuous-loop slide projector shows classic Western art, while somewhere under the buzz classical music plays. Model ships garnered over the years from romantic ports of call in Asia adorn shelves along the walls. The vast comfort-food menu offers burgers, tuna melts, potato skins and the like. Outdoor seating started in the side garden and has spread right around to the front. The beer selection is good, but this is

Charlie Trotter's

I was standing on Armitage Ave, admiring the grape leaves growing over the arbors next to the entrance to **Charlie Trotter's Restaurant** (☎ *773-248-6228, www.charlietrotters.com, 816 W Armitage Ave; Map 6*) when one of the valet parkers appeared at my elbow and asked me if I would like a menu. 'Sure,' I said. A short time later, the valet returned with a creamy sheet of paper listing the night's lineup. 'Please,' he said with a gentle and sincere smile, 'enjoy your evening.'

Despite the utter lack of evidence that I, a grubby guidebook writer lurking on the sidewalk, would ever have the means to spend an evening in Charlie Trotter's rarefied air (roughly $150 per person), a valet had anticipated my needs and sought out what I desired. Menu in hand, I departed with a big smile on my face.

Making people smile – that's the goal of the thirtysomething Trotter, who modestly says his dream is to run the finest restaurant in the world. It's a

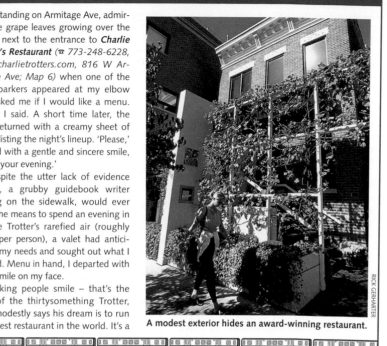

RICK GERHARTER

A modest exterior hides an award-winning restaurant.

really more eatery than bar. Note: avoid the oversize poseur in Wrigleyville (see the boxed text 'Chicago As Theme Park').

Bacino's (☎ *773-472-7400, 2204 N Lincoln Ave*) Meals $12-20. This local chain specializes in the stuffed variation of Chicago-style pizza. A very thin layer of crust on the top allows still another layer of cheese to be piled on even higher. The stuffed spinach model – the most popular choice – contains plenty of useful iron to fuel your grueling tourism schedule.

Lindo Mexico (☎ *773-871-4832, 2642 N Lincoln Ave*) Meals $14-22. This old standard cleverly rode the Mexican food trend through the '80s with big margaritas, 'El Chow' (cheap and tasty) and a staff that would clear out of the kitchen and surround

the table of any birthday celebrant, singing appropriate songs. Each year the empire spread through adjoining properties, an expansion that's culminated in a hacienda-style backyard patio that's a great spot for a summer meal with friends.

Clark St

Wiener Circle (☎ *773-477-7444, 2622 N Clark St*) Meals $4-7. Open 24 hours daily. 'Order now or get the f*** out!' screams the apron-clad man behind the counter while an addled patron tries to comply. It's 4:30am at this Lincoln Park equivalent of a roadhouse, and the scene has reached its frenetic peak. Mobs of patrons displaced from closed bars are clamoring for cheap char-burgers and char-dogs to satisfy their munchies. The veteran

Charlie Trotter's

goal he's meeting: he's won a slew of culinary honors, including French ones and the Grand Award from the *Wine Spectator,* which named Charlie Trotter's the 'Best Restaurant in the United States' in 2000.

Part of the allure is the surprise that awaits each night. There is no regular menu, no signature dish. Rather, an ever-changing lineup of offerings varies according to the seasons and the ingenuity of Trotter and his artful staff. The kitchen's creations cater to the eye as much as the palate. Architects could learn a thing or two from the complex constructions of food and sauces.

Diners choose between the $90 prix-fixe vegetarian menu and the $110 grand menu. The wine selection spans a 45-page list and a 40,000-bottle cellar. A Grand Menu in late 2000 read as follows:

Grilled hamachi with water chestnuts, horseradish and an assortment of clams: littleneck, cockles and geoduck; Amish capon breast poached in buttermilk with cumin-scented carrot and black truffle emulsion; roasted Maine monkfish with Swiss chard and braised pork cheek tortellini, caramelized salsify and red wine–foie gras sauce; Broken Arrow Ranch black buck rack and loin with braised Savoy cabbage, adzuki beans, lentils and French lentils; quince broth with caramel-apple sorbet and quince-apple pavé; chocolate-coconut cake with caramel ice cream

On better-dressed days I've had some splendid meals at Charlie Trotter's. For each meal I booked weeks in advance, and you should, too. Make that months in advance, if you want the kitchen table, where four people can enjoy a ground-zero view of the action.

Should you not dine at the restaurant, you can always partake of some other part of the growing Trotter empire. Trotter has put out a long list of cookbooks and started the PBS series *The Kitchen Sessions with Charlie Trotter.* But as proof that sometimes even a master can overdo things, Trotter is still smarting from a disastrous deal with United Airlines whereby he created dishes for business-class and 1st-class passengers. Despite his gourmet intentions his airline meals, when served at 35,000 feet, tasted just like, well, airline meals served at 35,000 feet.

staff gleefully take full advantage of their boozy delirium. A young woman clad in condiment-smeared sweats grills a cross-eyed woman in a cocktail dress about her preferences: 'Catsupmustardcelerysaltrelishpickles?' It's a sobriety test more devious than any traffic cop could devise. The woman, her senses well beyond overload, casts her eyes wildly about and proclaims, 'Huh?'

Pasta Bowl (☎ 773-525-2695, *2434 N Clark St*) Meals starting at $10. At this neighborhood joint the pasta comes in big bowls and rarely costs more than $7. Sauces are top-notch: the pesto reeks of garlic and the Bolognese is redolent with basil. The decor and the menu length are both minimalist.

My π (☎ 773-929-3380, *2417 N Clark St*) Meals $12-20. Open until midnight. This wood-paneled pizza joint is another local vet with a huge loyal following. The deep-dish pizzas, enormous salad bar and the decor itself have changed little since the early 1970s. Parents dealing with their own offspring's tuition bills will be transported back to a time when their parents worried about theirs.

Lincoln Park West

RJ Grunts (☎ 773-929-5363, *2056 N Lincoln Park West*) Lunch $8-14. The vintage pictures of waitresses that line the walls here will take you right back to the swinging '70s, when Lincoln Park emerged as the young singles' neighborhood of choice. Famed restaurateur Rich Melman got his start at RJ Grunts in 1971. Now, as then, the huge fruit and vegetable bar and the burgers are the mainstays.

Don't even think for a second about the fact that some of the original customers are now grandparents.

Ambria (☎ 773-472-5959, 2300 N Lincoln Park West) Dinner $65-90. Closed Sun. Ambria occupies a large corner off the lobby of the Belden-Stratford, a classic grande dame of an apartment building overlooking the park. The restaurant is oh-so-fittingly elegant, the cooking is careful and imaginative and the service refined and unobtrusive, in keeping with the quiet location away from the city's bustle. Various multicourse degustations go for $55 to $75. Plenty of vintage wines rest comfortably in the wine cellar.

Elsewhere in the Neighborhood

Demon Dogs (☎ 773-281-2001, 944 W Fullerton Ave) Meals $4-7. The Schiavarelli Brothers, ward politicians and record promoters, have turned this classic hot dog joint under the El tracks into a shrine for their buddies in the band Chicago. The strains of 'Saturday, in the park…' can be heard almost around the clock. The short menu celebrates another local institution, the Chicago-style hot dog (see the boxed text 'Gone to the Dogs').

Charlie's Ale House (☎ 773-871-1440, 1224 W Webster Ave) Meals $14-22. This classic Lincoln Park tavern offers good burgers, sandwiches and other bar chow. The beer selection lives up to the bar's name, and the beer garden is a good place to have a bite and sip or two or three or…

LAKE VIEW & WRIGLEYVILLE (Map 7)

Another restaurant-rich part of town, this area of the North Side contains a huge variety of eateries whose quality – but not prices – match that found closer to the center of town. The Belmont El stop is central to much of the area. For other transit options, see the individual geographic designations, below.

Belmont Ave Area

Dunkin' Donuts (☎ 773-477-3636, 3200 N Clark St at Belmont Ave) Meals $2-5. Open 24 hours. An infamous outlet of the not justifiably famous chain, this joint is a gather-ing place for Goths, runaways, bums, cops and all sorts of assorted other life. On weekends the crowd above is joined by religious fanatics trying to save one and all. If you hate your car, park it in the small lot; it will be towed the second you step off the premises.

Pat's Pizzeria (773-248-0168, 3114 N Sheffield Ave) Meals $12-20. Thyme is a key ingredient of the sausage here, and combined with a few other toppings, it makes for a great thin-crust combo pizza. A frequent winner of *Chicago Tribune* competitions (which means that the *Sun-Times* regularly dumps on it), Pat's is a family place that still seems a bit overwhelmed by the huge changes in the neighborhood. If you're not here for a thin-crust, skip it.

Ann Sather (☎ 773-348-2378, 929 W Belmont Ave) Meals $8-20. In the early 1980s local marketing genius Tom Tunney took a longtime neighborhood coffee shop and gave it a trendy and quirky ad campaign that emphasized its good, basic food. Young professionals now flock here for platefuls of reasonably priced chow served in stylishly friendly surroundings. At night Swedish standards such as meatballs and potato sausage join American classics like salmon and meat loaf. Famous for breakfast are Ann Sather's warm and gooey cinnamon rolls, worth a trip in themselves.

Moti Mahal (☎ 773-348-4392, 1031 W Belmont Ave) Meals $9-16. It doesn't look like much from the outside and actually looks worse inside, but it serves excellent Indian food. Everybody working here learned to cook in India, and it shows. The various legume curries are spiced just right. The 'Big Mix' combines a lot of everything – curries, tikkas and more – and tops the price list at $15. You'll find it next to impossible to spend more per person. The drink selection is BYOB, which gives you infinite choice (1000 Liquors, a quirky late-night liquor store/bar, is across the street) and keeps the costs down even more.

Leona's (☎ 773-327-8861, 3215 N Sheffield Ave) Meals $12-25. Once I had a bad meal at Leona's and wrote a letter to the owner. He called me up shortly thereafter. Soon pizzas were being delivered to my door for free, and my wife and I were summoned to the restaurant to eat and drink ourselves silly. This place takes customer service very, very seriously, and it pays off. From this original location, outlets have spread all over town. Leona's packs crowds in because it serves tasty food at tasty prices. Sandwiches, salads and various entrées are huge. The justifiably famous pizzeria supports a full-time delivery staff of 250. A medium for two costs less than $14. Oh, and if there's a lengthy wait when you arrive, you'll get lots of red wine to help pass the time.

Halsted St

The heart of Chicago's gay community, Halsted St north of Belmont Ave contains many restaurants catering to all tastes and preferences. There may be a few more men than average, but the crowds are very mixed. Ride to the CTA's Belmont stop to reach the south end of this area, Addison to get to the north.

Chicago Diner (☎ 773-935-6696, 3411 N Halsted St) Meals $8-20. Obviously, with a slogan like 'Love animals, don't eat them,' this spot doesn't attract people looking for a steak – despite how much it looks like a traditional diner, with counter stools and booths. Choose among large portions of fresh vegetarian food, including salads, egg dishes and grilled sandwiches. Breakfast tofu omelets are a hit. At night, entrées feature varying amounts of grains and veggies. Vegans take note: even the pesto for the pasta can be had without a lick of cheese.

Arcos de Cuchilleros (☎ 773-296-6046, 3445 N Halsted St) Dinner $15-25. Closed Mon. This comfy place avoids the upscale hype of some of the other tapas joints. The owners come from Madrid, and they have faithfully replicated one of that city's family cafés, with a long bar, narrow room and dark wood furniture. Small plates of classics such as sautéed lima beans, chickpea croquettes and *tortilla española* (a cold egg and potato omelet) average $5 each. Don't keep track of how many pitchers of tangy sangria you drink; just keep ordering.

Oo-La-La (☎ 773-935-7708, 3335 N Halsted St) Dinner $22-32. The menu here straddles the sinuous border of Italy and France, adding a dose of humor and flair to standards like calamari and veal piccata. A local joint that reflects the spirit of its neighborhood, Oo-La-La makes a good spot for Sunday brunch. The interior decor is stark, the patio out back shady.

Tarasca's (☎ 773-281-5510, 3324 N Halsted St) Dinner $22-35. A Mexican-flavored bistro in an inviting corner location, Tarasca's features a simple and spare dining room that takes its elegance from the white tablecloths. The food, a few levels above the usual burrito fare, includes an array of interesting items such as spicy pork tenderloin with pineapple salsa.

Jack's on Halsted (☎ 773-244-9191, 3201 N Halsted St) Dinner $27-36. Special of the day? It's always fun food served in an eclectic dining room by highly personable staff. The menu hops around the world, stopping off for American classics like steak or Cajun and then moving on for Italian, French and Asian, with a number of good vegetarian choices along the way. You can wash down every course with the many fine American wines. Be sure to save room for dessert. Sunday brunch is worthy of special occasions.

Yoshi's Cafe (☎ 773-248-6160, 3257 N Halsted St) Dinner $25-42. Closed Mon. Yoshi and Nobuko Katsumura preside over one of the most innovative casual places in town. The changing menu focuses on low-fat dishes with a Japanese flair. The kitchen treats all ingredients with the utmost respect, from the salmon and other seafood options to the tofu in the vegetarian dishes. Try to save room for the group dessert, which includes a little bit of everything on the menu. The service is every bit as good as the food.

Erwin (☎ 773-528-7200, 2925 N Halsted St) Meals $27-45. Closed Mon. 'Comfort food' is the trendy term for the kind of rib-sticking fare that Midwestern moms have served for decades. When Mom's not around to heat up the stove, your average Joe might resort to the supermarket's frozen food section for his comfort. High-class Joes – or at least those with sophisticated palates – resort to Erwin. Dishes on the ever-changing menu feature American ingredients but combine food styles from around the world in imaginative ways. Bring Mom (especially to the delightful Sunday brunch).

Clark St

Scores of moderate and budget-priced eateries serve food from around the world on Clark St, roughly from Belmont Ave to a little north of Wrigley Field. Some aim their menus squarely at the undiscriminating tastes of suburban day-trippers. Others offer imaginative food at excellent prices, including those listed below. The CTA Belmont and Addison stops are close to either end of the strip.

Penny's Noodle Shop (☎ 773-281-8222, 3400 N Sheffield Ave just west of Clark St) Meals $7-14. Despite several other excellent Asian choices within a few blocks, this place attracts crowds most hours of the day and night; you'll see people waiting outside in all weather, good and bad. Maybe these hapless hordes are drawn by the place's minimalist decor, low prices or – no doubt – the cheap, tasty noodle soups ($5 average). If you get tired of waiting, you can always head north a few blocks to several equally good but less crowded places. Penny's is BYOB, so stock up on drinks before you get here.

Duke of Perth (☎ 773-477-1741, 2913 N Clark St just north of Diversey Parkway) Meals $8-18. This genuine Scottish pub offers various Scottish delights like haggis, which may well drive you to drink any of the vast number of single-malts on offer. However, punters from all around drop in for the excellent fish and chips (all-you-can-eat for $6.95 Wednesday and Friday). The beer garden is a good refuge.

El Jardín (☎ 773-528-6775, 3335 N Clark St) and **El Jardín Cafe** (☎ 773-935-8133, 3401 N Clark St) Meals starting at $10. The Mexican food is only so-so at these siblings, but if you're looking for a raucous evening that revolves around tequila, then these are the places for you. One sight I won't soon forget involves a patron who put his complementary sombrero to use as a receptacle for overindulgence.

Andalous (☎ 773-281-6885, 3307 N Clark St) Lunch & dinner $12-20. There's much than couscous on the menu at this cheerful Moroccan bistro, which offers numerous veggie options. The *meknes tagine* is a charming concoction of lemony chicken sautéed in onions.

Texas Star Fajita Bar (☎ 773-975-8188, 3365 N Clark St at Roscoe St) Meals $12-20. The food might not attract much notice (nor should it), but the restaurant's doorway, under the El tracks, has starred in a movie: it's famous as the location used for the explosion that killed the little girl at the beginning of *The Untouchables*.

Addis Abeba (☎ 773-929-9383, 3521 N Clark St) Dinner starting at $12. A nice change from the fare at the mobs of sports bars in the area, the heaping portions of Ethiopian food here include lots of legumes, grains, spices and vegetables. Everything comes atop *injera*, large and spongy flat bread good for virtually all purposes except paying the bill.

Ethiopian Village (☎ 773-929-8300, 3462 N Clark St) Meals starting at $12. It seems every Clark St restaurant has at least one twin, and this is no exception. Addis Abeba (above) too crowded? Drop in on this cheery joint and dig your fingers into the piles of tasty stews and flat breads.

A one-block thicket of densely packed Asian eateries includes the following: **Pad Thai** (3466 N Clark St), the Vietnamese **La Paillotte** (3470 N Clark St), the brightly lit Japanese **Nagano** (3475 N Clark St) and the dark sushi café **Sanko** (3485 N Clark St) Meals at all places cost $12-22.

Matsuya (☎ 773-248-2677, 3469 N Clark St) Meals $18-25. The wooden boat in the window hints at the sushi-dominated menu here, one of the best values on the Japanese dining scene. The sushi offerings include standards such as California rolls on down to the square-shaped Osaka-style sushi. The rest of the menu plumbs unusual depths (sample item: octopus marinated in bean paste). Less adventurous types will be

PLACES TO EAT

happy with the teriyaki-marinated grilled fish.

Tomodachi (☎ 773-296-0857, *3468 N Clark St*) Meals $14-22. This place is a good alternative to Matsuya (above) if that spot gets too crowded. Sushi neophytes will enjoy the full-color place mats that describe and show pictures of the offerings.

PS Bangkok (☎ 773-871-7777, *3345 N Clark St*) Lunch & dinner $16-25. Closed Mon. The shrimp curries burst with hot, plump shrimp at this spot, one of Chicago's best Thai restaurants. The various fish tanks hint at the long list of seafood dishes, many of them the elaborate kind found at banquets in Thailand. The chicken satay, which leads the lengthy menu, comes with an excellent peanut sauce. Buried deep on the menu but worth requesting is the spinach oozing with garlic. Simple dishes average about $9, but prices escalate rapidly for the seafood creations. Can't bear a poached egg awash in Hollandaise sauce? Try Sunday brunch here.

Thai Classic (☎ 773-404-2000, *3332 N Clark St*) Meals $13-20. If PS Bangkok is jammed – it often is – try this alternative right across the street. The menu is shorter and simpler, but the food is still quite good.

Le Loup (☎ 773-248-1830, *3348 N Sheffield Ave just west of Clark St*) Meals $18-28. Locals have made this casual and friendly French bistro a popular spot. The name means 'the wolf,' and you'll happily wolf down classics such as the $7 blue cheese salad and the $11 cassoulet, made with white beans, duck and sausage. The dining area is small and intimate. The adjoining garden, lushly planted with flowers and trees, comes alive in the summer.

Raw Bar & Grill (☎ 773-348-7291, *3720 N Clark St*) Meals $20-35. A big tank of doomed live lobsters sits near the door here – a fitting accessory in a place that attracts lots of tanked Cubs fans doomed to cheering for a bad team. Fresh seafood is not one of Chicago's strengths, given the dearth of local seas, but what you get here isn't bad. After a game those boozy fans boisterously slurping raw oysters make quite a show all by themselves.

Chicago As Theme Park

In the area around Wrigley Field auto repair shops once stood next to cop bars, which stood next to greasy spoon diners. But so much for gritty authenticity – that world is rapidly dying as the neighborhood devotes itself to milking visiting Cubs fans for all they're worth (maybe they feel that any people who devote their energies to cheering for the Cubs' losing efforts make easy marks). In a disturbing recent trend famous Chicago restaurants have been opening up branches – often the size of hangars – entirely lacking in the charms that made the originals the institutions they are.

Consider the following, all within the length of a poorly hit fly ball of each other (all on Map 7):

Heaven on Seven (☎ 773-477-7818, *3478 N Clark St*) The concept has strayed pretty far from the Loop original here.

Billy Goat (☎ 773-327-4361, *3516 N Clark St*) There is no hope of this coming within a Cheezburger's thickness of the original (see the boxed text 'Cheezburger! Cheezburger!' in the Entertainment chapter). Here you'll find no decor, no regulars and no Jeff behind the bar.

John Barleycorn (☎ 773-549-6000, *3524 N Clark St*) About the only thing this barn-like restaurant has in common with the Lincoln Park original is the name. The entertainment includes, of all things, techno dancing upstairs on weekends (the original plays classical).

Goose Island Brewpub (☎ 773-832-9040, *3535 N Clark St*) This is also a cavernous imitation of a Lincoln Park original.

Bar Louie (☎ 773-296-2500, *3545 N Clark St*) This location of the local chain just lays in wait for the hapless crowds torn between barnlike copies and characterless imitations.

PLACES TO EAT

Outpost (☎ *773-244-1166, 3438 N Clark St*) Dinner $25-35. During the 1930s the China Clipper flying boats of Pan American World Airways linked the world to the US on routes spanning the globe. Journeys were made in segments, stopping at company outposts in the Pacific and the Atlantic. Ted Cizma, the son of one of Pan Am's former flight attendants, has teamed up with his partners to create a warm, casual and chic restaurant that draws inspiration from the clippers' many ports of call. Dishes offered on the always-changing menu have included plantain fritters and grilled tuna and New Zealand venison. The room is decorated with maps showing the clipper routes (which date from a time when travelers had to make due without *Lonely Planet* guides; how'd they do it?).

Mia Francesca (☎ *773-281-3310, 3311 N Clark, St*) Dinner $25-35. Diners jam the large room at one of the most popular small, family-run Italian bistros in the city. A buzz of energy swirls among the closely spaced tables, topped with white tablecloths, and the arrangements of fresh flowers. The kitchen is open on one side, allowing full view of your food's preparation. The frequently changing handwritten menu features earthy standards with aggressive seasoning from southern Italy. Other treats include wafer-thin pizzas and the often-overlooked staple of Italian kitchens: polenta. Service can be harried because of the clamoring crowds.

Jezebel (☎ *773-929-4000, 3517 N Clark St*) Meals $25-40. This artful restaurant is a cut above the budget nature of the strip. The richly decorated black-and-gold fixtures match the black-and-gold fettucine. The Italian menu spans that country. Have some pasta shaped like little ears: *orecchiette* with seasonal vegetables.

Tuscany (☎ *773-404-7700, 3700 N Clark St*) Dinner $28-40. A branch of the well-known original on Taylor St in Little Italy, this Tuscany has a wood-burning pizza oven and a real grill to prepare the various steaks on the menu. The menu draws its inspiration

Outdoor tables sprout throughout the city in warm weather.

from northern Italy; look for creamy risottos and rosemary-flavored grilled meats. Although rather hoity-toity by Clark St standards, this place is still very casual.

Southport Ave

In 1987 I lived near Southport Ave. It had a couple of bars, a few markets and no decent place to eat. Then word of its cheap rents, tree-lined streets and easy El access got out. In 1991 a Starbucks opened, and that was the beginning of the end of its mild-mannered days. The stretch of Southport from Belmont Ave north to Irving Park Rd has become one of the hottest neighborhoods for nightlife in the city. Take the CTA Brown Line to the Southport stop to put yourself in the heart of the action.

Chinalite (☎ 773-244-0300, 3457 N Southport Ave) Meals $12-20. The health-conscious concerns of Wrigleyville's young and affluent residents have prompted several restaurants like this one to incorporate the marketing moniker 'lite' into their names. The menu here promises all the standards without all the fat. Szechuan string beans and rice noodles with asparagus in a black bean sauce set the tone. You'll have to decide if the pork fried rice is in keeping with the theme.

Still Lite Cafe (☎ 773-929-5090, 3647 N Southport Ave) Meals $12-20. The antifat theme continues here, where brown rice in various forms is both the main attraction and a principal sideshow. The menu changes often. Look for the sesame-cilantro sandwich, a regular feature. A slew of outdoor tables line the sidewalk.

Banana Leaf (☎ 773-883-8683, 3811 N Southport Ave) Meals $12-20. Inside a suitably leafy and lush room you choose from a lengthy Thai menu that is refreshingly free of the designer touches now commonplace elsewhere. Thai noodles, curries and basil dishes run about $8. At dessert bananas come fried, roasted or steamed.

Hi Ricky (☎ 773-388-0000, 3730 N Southport Ave) Meals $12-22. The long, inexpensive menu travels through Vietnam, Indonesia, Thailand and China. Satays are the stars and come with prawn chips and an array of sauces. A sampler of all seven satay

varieties is only $6. Other items include noodles, soups and stir-fries, all served in a bright and cheerful setting.

Dish (☎ 773-549-8614, 3651 N Southport Ave) Lunch & dinner $16-28. Dish is as small as the dress sizes of its well-buffed clientele. The imaginative Southwestern menu features items such as portobello mushroom fajitas and vegetarian burritos. It's a boisterous and cozy spot all winter long. In summer tables stretch across the uncommonly wide Southport sidewalk.

Cullen's (☎ 773-975-0600, 3741 N Southport Ave) Meals $14-30. Upscale bar chow predominates at this welcoming tavern connected to the Mercury Theatre. Lots of wood and tile attempt to evoke a classic Chicago watering hole, though this place dates from more recent times and owes its existence to entrepreneur Michael Cullen, who has earned a fortune at what was once a humdrum haberdashery where I used to buy cheap underwear. Baked artichoke appetizers, marinated tuna sandwiches and juicy burgers are typical of the fare. The beer list is long and interesting.

Strega Nona (☎ 773-244-0990, 3747 N Southport Ave) Lunch & dinner $18-30. That hallmark of late-20th-century restaurant design – exposed brick – is the dominant element of the dining room here, which opens onto the street. Locals twirl the typical Italian fare around their forks with glee. The name comes from a witch in Italian children's stories.

Bistrot Zinc (☎ 773-281-3443, 3443 N Southport Ave) Lunch & dinner $15-40. The namesake metal covers the bar at this fun French bistro, where classic French comes in fair-size portions at fair prices. Just thinking about the lunchtime quiche has me ready to stop typing right….Okay, I'm back. Needless to say, the menu finishes with a full range of splendid desserts. If you find something smoother to put in your mouth than the chocolate mousse, don't tell me. Decorum wouldn't allow it.

Tango Sur (☎ 773-477-5466, 3763 N Southport Ave) Meals $20-30. This Argentine steak house smells great and serves classic skirt steaks and other beefy options. Not in the

PLACES TO EAT

Sample the flavors of France at Bistrot Zinc.

RAY HILLSTROM JR

mood for steak? Then kidneys await. Not in the mood for meat? Go elsewhere. Tables outside expand the seating from the very small and spare interior. This may be the only smoke-free steak place in town.

Deleece (☎ *773-325-1710, 4004 N Southport Ave*) Dinner $20-30. At this upscale café that was once a grocery you can still catch a whiff of five decades' worth of ripening fruit. But now the predominant aromas come from the ever-popular fusion of foods. Poblano peppers and cilantro add a Mexican touch, ginger chimes in for Asia and olive oil speaks for the Mediterranean. Prices reflect the grocery-store roots, but the soup is definitely not canned. The staff get praise for being able and affable. Deleece has become a popular Sunday brunch spot.

Elsewhere in the Neighborhood

Village Tap (☎ *773-883-0817, 2055 W Roscoe St*) Meals $6-12. This neighborhood tavern does everything well: food, drink and atmosphere. And that's the problem – it can get crowded on Friday and Saturday night. Otherwise, it's a real winner. The friendly bartenders give out free samples of the ever-changing and carefully chosen lineup of Midwestern microbrews. The kitchen turns out some great burgers, veggie burgers and chicken sandwiches, and the spiced pita chips are a nice touch. Out back the beer garden contains a fountain; inside the tables enjoy good views of the TVs for ball games. There are board games available so you and your friends can make your own fun.

Brother Jimmy's BBQ (☎ *773-528-0888, 2909 N Sheffield Ave*) Meals $15-25. Pork ribs come in a variety of styles drawn from various regions of the US. I like the tangy Southern recipe, which is vinegar-based. The Northern version is sweet and tomatoey. Several combo plates give you the chance to sample all the offerings. The main room looks like an old warehouse that might appear in a beer ad. On some nights it gets converted to a blues club, with decent bands taking the low stage. Many of the boisterous patrons still smell of their former frat-house lodgings.

ANDERSONVILLE (Map 8)

Centered on Clark St, the neighborhood stretches from a block south of Foster Ave to about five blocks north. It's a 10-minute walk west from the Berwyn El stop on the Red Line.

Swedish Bakery (☎ 773-561-8919, 5348 N Clark St) Snacks $1. You get free coffee in amazingly small cups here, but that's the only thing minimalist about the place, with its butter-laden breads, cookies and pastries. The coffeecakes will make you want to (a) buy one and (b) go get a real cup of coffee.

Kopi, A Traveler's Cafe (☎ 773-989-5674, 5317 N Clark St) Meals $5-10. If you're reading this book at Kopi, then you'd better have paid for it! An extremely casual coffeehouse with a pile of pillows on the floor in the window, Kopi stocks a large range of travel books. However, lest a java catastrophe lay waste to the inventory, you're supposed to buy the books before you read them. Feeling cheap? The café carries piles of some of the most esoteric free weeklies in town, as well as travel magazines and brochures galore. On the bulletin board you'll find ads from people looking for trekking partners for Kazakhstan and the like. You can order various sandwiches and desserts here, although at times the help seems to be on a trip of their own.

Ann Sather (☎ 773-271-6677, 5207 N Clark St) Meals $8-20. Although it looks old and authentic, this branch of the Lake View original (see the Lake View section, earlier) actually opened in 1987. It's just as popular as its Belmont Ave parent, and its cinnamon rolls are just as deliciously decadent.

Cousin's (☎ 773-334-4553, 5203 N Clark St) Meals $12-20. Lots of vegetarian options populate the menu here, along with chicken kebabs and roasted lamb. You can make a great meal of warm pita bread, hummus and baba ghanoush. Lots of Chicago's finest stop by for the lunch deals – the presence of cops is considered the ultimate endorsement at Windy City restaurants.

Dellwood Pickle (☎ 773-271-7728, 1475 W Balmoral Ave just east of Clark St) Meals $9-20. Closed Mon. The side-street location doesn't keep the hordes from seeking out their ultimate comfort food at prices that might make you think you're back in Des Moines. Meat loaf and mashed potatoes come together in a New Orleans shepherd's pie, while salmon and fresh pasta meet beneath surprising sauces. Fresh muffins and breads adorn the Sunday brunch, when the lines are long. Just sit back in a crumbling easy chair or browse other patrons' art for sale on the walls. This spot is BYOB, so come with your own alcohol.

Andie's (☎ 773-784-8616, 5253 N Clark St) Meals $10-26. The larger Reza's next door may draw the yuppie hordes, but discerning Andersonville locals flock to Andie's for smooth, garlicky hummus and more. A recent remodeling has turned the dining room into a Mediterranean showplace. The cooking occurs in an open kitchen, and smells of grilling meat, eggplant and the world's best lentil soup fill the air. If you somehow manage to spend $20 a person, you'll either be drunk, bloated or both.

Fireside Restaurant & Lounge (☎ 773-878-5942, 5739 N Ravenswood Ave) Meals $10-26. This pub-cum-restaurant serves excellent American food, such as Cajun burgers and ribs, that you can linger over in the large and sunny beer garden. The bar offers a vast selection of microbrews, and on many Saturdays some actual brew masters lead tastings at the 'Brewmaster's Dinner.' Bite back the dog that bit you at the Sunday brunch's 'build your own Bloody Mary' bar.

La Donna (☎ 773-561-9400, 5146 N Clark St) Dinner $20-30. This casual, imaginative Italian place packs locals in for fresh pastas and risotto. The Italian staff help set the right mood. Dishes (about $11) might include linguini with clams, pumpkin ravioli or the capellini puttanesca, a spicy concoction of tomatoes, capers, olives and garlic. Don't get too stuffed to try one of the marvelous microbrews next door at the Hop Leaf (see the Entertainment chapter for details).

Tomboy (☎ 773-907-0636, 5402 N Clark St) Dinner $22-30. You might wonder about the name here until you realize that Andersonville is a favorite neighborhood of Chicago's lesbian community. A good spot for vegetarians, Tomboy prepares artful and filling dishes, including a number of meat-free pasta dishes, plus carnivorous items like grilled pork chops with Gorgonzola-topped potatoes. Entrées average $17, and this place can be a real gourmet bargain because it's BYOB. Buy your alcohol from the liquor store three blocks south, at Foster and Clark – but watch your change. Inside the restaurant white tablecloths offer a stark counterpoint to the natural-brick walls.

Calo (☎ 773-271-7725, 5343 N Clark St) Meals $12-28. Open until 2am. You'll keep looking for your parents, or maybe your grandparents, at this old-time red-sauce Italian joint. Calo was selling out of its wheel-size, tomato-stuffed focaccia when few people outside of Genoa had heard of the stuff. Today middle-aged and older folks chow down on pasta, ribs and chicken cacciatore while catching the news or the Bulls game in the windowless den. Surf & turf is still a throwback at $24.95.

Finestra (☎ 773-334-4525, 5341 N Clark St) Dinner $20-35. Closed Mon. The Calo kids have opened a counterpoint to their folks' place next door. The stylish dining room is all brushed metal and exposed brick. The food is modern Italian, which means that you can't buy frozen versions at the supermarket just yet. Among the tasty options you'll find the signature *gnocchetti dello chef*, a mixture of spinach and gnocchi bathed in a cheesy sauce that includes Gorgonzola.

Argyle St

Even the Argyle El Station sports an Asian motif in this neighborhood full of restaurants and shops run by people from Southeast Asia. Families in search of the American dream are always opening someplace new on Argyle. The same holds true on the adjoining blocks of Broadway and Sheridan Rd (three blocks east of Broadway).

Nha Trang (☎ 773-989-0712, 1007 W Argyle St) Meals $10-20. The children of the charming husband-and-wife owners of Nha Trang used to sit quietly in the corner and play cards with decks they'd made out of newspaper coupons. Older now, the kids have taken up official duties, serving excellent Vietnamese specialties at this very inexpensive and simple storefront. Various dishes come covered in fresh cilantro and are meant to be wrapped in sheets of rice paper. Regu-

lars often order multiple portions of the sweet and crunchy sesame chicken.

WICKER PARK & BUCKTOWN (Map 9)

Wicker Park and Bucktown symbolized hip Chicago in the 1990s. Lots of twentysomethings were drawn to the cheap rents and eclectic bars, wild eateries and funky shops. Things have calmed down a bit, and the now-thirtysomethings support a string of comfort-food houses where trendsetting restaurants once thrived. Fortunately, even these joints retain some of the neighborhood's edge.

Ground zero for Bucktown is the six-way intersection of Damen, North and Milwaukee Aves. The Blue Line El stop at Damen will put you right in the heart of the action. Farther north along Damen, public transportation is more problematic, since the CTA's Damen bus runs every half hour at best. A cab ride from River North costs about $6.

Milwaukee Ave

El Chino (☎ 773-772-1905, 1505 N Milwaukee Ave) Meals $3-10. The $1.25 tacos rank among the best bargains in this part of town. Choose among eight varieties and eat them in the Formica-clad dining area while listening to Bruce Springsteen blare from the speakers.

Local Grind (☎ 773-489-3490, 1585 N Milwaukee Ave) Meals $6-10. Open 6am-1am weekdays, to 3am weekends. Avoid the Starbucks juggernaut at this popular local coffeehouse. The sandwiches range from hummus to tuna; most are veggie. The weekend brunch buffet features lots of fresh fruit and the antithesis of such: Fruit Loops.

PaPa Jin (☎ 773-384-9600, 1551 N Milwaukee Ave) Meals $12-20. This neighborhood Asian favorite is low-key in its decor and menu. The fairly inexpensive offerings include hot Mongolian shrimp for $8.

Sinibar (☎ 773-278-7797, 1540 N Milwaukee Ave) Meals $15-25. Kitchen open 7pm-1am, closed Mon; lounge open until 2am daily. It's like a trip to a fantasy casbah at Sinibar, which is the work of John Bubala and Joe Russo. Walk through the dark and

PLACES TO EAT

heavily curtained entrance to find a multi-level space where DJs spin a range of music from funk to reggae to house. The Mediterranean items on the moderately priced menu range from Moroccan to Italian. Try the steak frites with a tangy mustard sauce; they're proving to be a fave.

Soul Kitchen (☎ 773-342-9742, 1576 N Milwaukee Ave) Meals $20-35. The tangerine and olive walls and leopard-skin motif set the mood at this hipster hangout. Big, bright dishes drawn from the South come to the table with plenty of spices and eclectic accents. The Jamaican jerk chicken skewers are fiery, while the pecan-coated catfish is sweet and crunchy. Other interesting touches include the collard greens seasoned with cilantro and barbecued lamb with mango sauce. Wrap everything up with cinnamon-spiced coffee. This highly recommended corner spot doesn't take reservations, so be prepared to, like, chill.

Damen Ave

Miko's (☎ 773-645-9665, 1846 N Damen Ave) Treats $1.50. Pause on a hot day for some cool homemade Italian ice at this seasonal fave. You can sit under the large oak tree in front and enjoy fruit flavors such as lemon, raspberry and peach.

Pontiac Cafe (☎ 773-252-7767, 1531 N Damen Ave) Meals $6-15. The perfect slacker diner for the neighborhood, this café resides in an old gas station that's been converted (sort of). Its mismatched booths occupy the old garage section, where the management hasn't quite gotten around to removing all the mechanic's stuff. The young and pierced crowd is served (sort of) by an equally young and pierced staff. Sample conversation between a dazed and confused customer and a dazed and confused employee: 'Hey, like, are we gonna get our food someday?' 'Oh wow, sorry. What did you order?' Long pause. 'Hmmm… Like, I don't know.' If you do get your food, expect interesting sandwiches on panini and good whole-grain salads.

Toast (☎ 773-772-5600, 2046 N Damen Ave) Meals $7-15. In the old days these kind of places were called diners and served lots of fried breakfast foods like omelets. At Toast, a local chain with outlets in trendy neighborhoods, you get diner food but pay a couple of dollars more for it. Maybe you're paying for the trendy logo?

Silver Cloud (☎ 773-489-6212, 1700 N Damen Ave) Meals $9-17. This bar/café takes itself seriously, perhaps too much so. The sloppy joes cost $7. They're good, but the price seems a bit steep for a trip back in time to your grade-school cafeteria. Still, the corner location offers a good vantage point for people-watching, and the sidewalk tables are usually jammed.

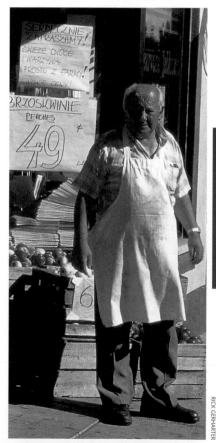

Do-it-yourself cuisine at a Polish grocery

PLACES TO EAT

Commune (☎ *773-772-7100, 1616 N Damen Ave)* Meals $6-22. Open 7am-1am. This upscale diner/bar serves comfort food from a menu that changes through the day. Early on breakfast burritos and the like predominate, while lunch sees the addition of salads; at night meaty entrées with lots of mashed potatoes or pasta take over. In good weather you can eat in the nice outdoor area.

Northside (☎ *773-384-3555, 1635 N Damen Ave)* Meals $10-18. This bar features a large adjoining dining room, the front of which is an atrium. The menu favors grazers, with finger-food classics such as nachos and hummus. Beware of rich guys on Harleys trying to act cool, however. In fact, attitude comes in ample portions here.

Rinconcito Sudamericano (☎ *773-489-3126, 1954 W Armitage Ave at Damen Ave)* Dinner $15-25. More than 100 kinds of potatoes are grown in Peru. You won't find that many on the menu here, but you will find some wonderful mashed potatoes with ground meat. Other moderately priced Peruvian treats include ceviche (a very popular fresh fish appetizer) and grilled beef heart (eek!) with spicy salsa. Enough art and artifacts fill the place to keep your eyes wandering for hours.

Lou Lou (☎ *773-782-9700, 2145 N Damen Ave)* Meals $12-30. Open 11am-1am. A variation on the local Bar Louie empire, Lou Lou offers a comfort food menu with the accent on Italian. This means you can order things like a single-serving artichoke and asparagus pizza for $11. Other draws here include the sharp service and commodious bar.

Le Bouchon (☎ *773-862-6600, 1958 N Damen Ave)* Dinner $20-35. Closed Sun. Classic French food at nonclassic prices makes for a winning combination at this quaint little spot that flies the tricolor over the street. Neighborhood types who know a good deal when they see it often pack Le Bouchon to feast on all the standards from France. The pepper steak and frites are *très bons*. The Lyonnaise salade is a winner. Other faves on the short menu range from escargot to chocolate mousse. Want to see the tiny kitchen? Head to the bathroom – it's on the way.

Meritage Cafe & Wine Bar (☎ *773-235-6434, 2118 N Damen Ave)* Dinner $30-50. The wine list is almost as long as the gaze down the nose you get from the haughty help at this ode to the Pacific Northwest. But if you're ready for this kind of scene, you'll be rewarded with some really good regional American food featuring lots of fish like salmon, plus mushrooms and game from the forest and various Asian influences. The former corner bar has been renovated just enough to let the light in while still preserving the Victorian character of the building. The covered and heated patio allows you to eat outside in all but the worst weather.

Elsewhere in the Neighborhood

Soju (☎ *773-782-9000, 1745 W North Ave)* Dinner $15-25. Open until 1am, closed Sun. If the crowds at Soju are any indication, Korean may well be the next big trend. Black-clad folk chopstick their kimchi (pickled vegetables) and reek of garlic. The menu stays faithful to many Korean standards, right down to those Korean M&Ms: candied soy beans.

WEST SIDE (Map 10)

Good restaurants are scattered throughout the West Side. The best way to reach them is by cab. Note that you'll want to call one from the restaurant when you're ready to go, or you'll be waiting a long time on the sidewalk for one to happen along.

Establishments in this section are listed by geographic grouping and in ascending order of price.

Ukrainian Village

More diverse than the name implies, this neighborhood has become a refuge for lots of creative types fleeing the soaring rents of Wicker Park and Bucktown.

Cleo's (☎ *312-243-5600, 1935 W Chicago Ave)* Meals $8-15. Open until 2am. A typical storefront masks this fun little bar/café on a rapidly burgeoning stretch of Chicago Ave. The menu includes interesting sandwiches and other upscale chow. Candles and comfy booths set the mood here, helped by a lovely long bar, good jazz on the sound system and a pool table out back. Regulars consider it one-stop joy. Sunday brunch is popular.

Smoke Daddy Rhythm & Bar-B-Que (☎ 773-772-6656, 1804 W Division St) Meals $15-25. Open until 1am daily. This is a great example of the bar/restaurant/club fusion places that are opening in some of the hipper parts of town. Top-notch ribs emerge from the huge wood-fired pit. The sweet-potato fries on the side win raves, and non-carnivores can enjoy barbecued veggies. Live blues and jazz acts play on a small stage every night. Watch for blues singer Lenny Linn. You can hang onto the bar as you ponder the interesting aprons hanging on the wall.

Randolph St Area

Where vendors once hawked zucchinis and cucumbers, some of the most innovative restaurants in town have set up shop. This area is a $5 cab ride from River North.

Wishbone (☎ 312-850-2663, 1001 W Washington St) Meals $8-12. Breakfast & lunch daily, dinner Tue-Sat. Chicago's often mediocre Southern cooking makes good – very good – here. The perfect corn muffins set the tone for a menu featuring spicy classics such as blackened catfish, fried chicken and baked ham. A big choice of sides includes sweet potatoes that should be a lesson to all the cooks who kill these veggies every Thanksgiving. Breakfasts come with hot, fresh buttermilk rolls. At lunch you can opt for the speedy cafeteria line. Oprah's Harpo studios are just down the street.

Red Light (☎ 312-733-8880, 820 W Randolph St) Meals $30-40. Red Light serves up fare that isn't anything like the fortune-cookie standard. In fact, mention 'sweet and sour pork' to the waiters and their already inscrutable attitudes might just freeze you right out the door. Roasted duck and rock shrimp are a few of the stars amid the fresh ingredients. Whole Taiwanese crispy catfish has emerged as a signature item. The entire restaurant glows like a lit-up jewel box at night; this is one beautiful space.

Thyme (☎ 312-226-4300, 464 N Halsted St) Meals $35-45. Thyme's chef-owner John Bubala moved just a few blocks north from his former kitchen at the noted Marché and opened up this spot in a neighborhood where you once went to sell your blood. The food is just as inventive as at Marché, with the menu nabbing ideas and influences from around the globe. On weekends you may have to dine early or late to find a table in the heaving dining room. Better yet, hope for a warm summer night and dine in the verdant garden.

Millennium (☎ 312-455-1400, 832 W Randolph St) Dinner $35-48. Closed Sun. Stylish, chic and casual, Millennium is a modern steak house for the new…oh you get it. Anyway, first-rate steaks and seafood at top-drawer prices attract diners. Other draws include a cigar lounge and a range of unusual victuals behind the bar. There aren't any surprises on the menu, but that's not the point. Be sure to get some of the superb horseradish sauce to go with your meat.

Marché (☎ 312-226-8399, 833 W Randolph St) Dinner $36-48. Lunch weekdays, dinner nightly. Them that are cool are dining on fine French-ish fare inside this hip stalwart; those that aren't (or those whose car has been towed) stand outside with their noses pressed against the windows overlooking the open kitchen. The menu is wide-ranging, the ingredients top-notch and the service highly proficient. The chocolate trio for dessert defies a description that won't leave you drooling.

Greek Town

The immigrants moving in now are yuppies in search of lofts rather than Greeks in search of a new life, but a string of authentic restaurants keeps Greek Town true to its name. Prices are uniformly cheap and the crowds uniformly lively, preserving elements that have kept this neighborhood, centered on Halsted St right across the expressway from the Loop, popular for generations.

Mr Greek Gyros (☎ 312-906-8731, 234 S Halsted St) Meals $4-7. Open 24 hours daily. Although there's no sign of Mrs, Ms or Mr Greek, 'the Mr' is a classic gyros joint with good prices. While the fluorescent lighting and plastic decor may be lacking in charm, the gyros have a beauty of their own.

Artopolis Bakery & Cafe (☎ 312-559-9000, 306 S Halsted St) Meals $6-14. Like a good Greek salad, this one has many ingredients: one of the city's top bakeries (many of the nearby Randolph St joints get their bread here), which sells oozing baklava for $1.50; a café/bar that opens onto the street, with tables along the front; and a food bar with classics like spinach pie, which you can eat in or take out. A lot of art by local artists hangs on the walls – thus the name.

Greek Islands (☎ *312-782-9855, 200 S Halsted St*) Meals $15-27. Kitchen open until midnight. Seemingly bigger than any one island, this stalwart of the Greek Town strip can accommodate groups of up to a few hundred. The blue-checked tablecloths may be the best part of the noisy place, which always seems to be hosting a table full of accountants in the corner. Beady-eyed waiters – less fun here than waiters elsewhere – serve all the standards: moussaka, gyros and company.

Parthenon (☎ *312-726-2407, 314 S Halsted St*) Meals $16-24. Kitchen open until midnight. This vet has anchored Greek Town for three decades. The amount of saganaki set ablaze here may be a principal factor in global warming. The yelps of 'Opaa!' as the cheese ignites reverberate off the walls of the small dining area. Greeks returning to the city from their suburban retreats have made this place a favorite. All the usual suspects are present, and the lamb comes in many forms.

Santorini (☎ *312-829-8820, 800 W Adams St*) Meals $20-35. Kitchen open until midnight. Fish, both shelled and finned, honor the legacies of Greek fishermen at this popular spot, where fresh whole fish is prepared and served in a tableside display. The boisterous room manages to seem cozy, thanks in part to the large Aegean fireplace. Everything, from the bread to the baklava, goes down swimmingly. Portions are huge, which encourages convivial sharing.

Elsewhere on the West Side

Jim's Original (*1300 S Halsted St*) Meals $3. Open 24 hours daily. Since it opened for business in 1939, Jim's has never closed. Perhaps that's why this corner of the old Maxwell St Market reeks so deeply of grilled onions. The half-life of the smell has got to be about 58 years. The University of Illinois has chased away every other bit of character in the neighborhood, leaving only Jim's and the many characters who sell quirky goods like those little dogs with bobbing heads for the back window of your car. Your food choices are the classic Chicago Polish sausage sandwich or the classic Chicago pork chop sandwich, both always served with free fries.

Lou Mitchell's (☎ *312-939-3111, 565 W Jackson Blvd*) Meals $5-9. Open 6am-3pm daily. Immediately west of the Loop and close to Union Station, this great coffee shop draws hordes who line up to eat elbow to elbow. What draws them? Breakfast dishes that are tops in town. Whether it's omelets hanging off the plates, fluffy flapjacks, crisp waffles or anything else on the long menu (most items are $4 to $7), you can expect perfect preparation with premium ingredients. Cups of coffee ($1.25) are bottomless, just like the charm of the staff, who hand out free treats to young and old alike.

Tecalitlan (☎ *312-384-4285, 1814 W Chicago Ave*) Meals $7-15. The best burrito in the world is here; weighing more than a pound and costing less than $5, the *carne asada* burrito with cheese is not just one of the city's best food values, it's one of the city's best foods. Add the optional avocado, and you'll have a full day's worth of food groups wrapped in a huge flour tortilla. For a tasty, greasy change, ask to mix the carne asada with pork. The many other Mexican staples on the menu are all cheap and good.

You can't miss Jim's: look for the signs.

I've been known to stop here on my way into town from the airport.

Jaks Tap (☎ *312-666-1700, 901 W Jackson Blvd) Meals $9-14. Great outside in the garden when it's nice, fine inside the other nine months of the year, Jaks can keep you occupied for a long time, with 40 beers on tap, 30 of them from Midwestern microbreweries. If Solsun from Michigan is available, clear your day's agenda and start ordering. Can't decide? They'll give you samples. A clever extrapolation of the usual bar food, the fare here includes burgers with guacamole or hummus and quesadillas with a smoky salsa. Jaks is run by the same smart people who operate the Village Tap (see the Lake View & Wrigleyville section, earlier in the chapter).

LITTLE ITALY (Map 10)

Taylor St is the focus of this vibrant neighborhood just southwest of the Loop. The University of Illinois at Chicago helped stabilize the area, but the public housing project right in the middle of the area makes safety a bit of an issue. Take a cab to any of the places below to play it safe. All offer valet parking.

Mario's *(1068 W Taylor St)* Treats $1.50. Open May-Oct. Super Italian ice keeps the crowds coming in the months when there's no ice on the streets.

Conte di Savoia (☎ *312-666-3471, 1438 W Taylor St)* Lunch $5-8. This large grocery sells everything an Italian cook could hope for, including scores of imported rarities and fine wines. The deli counter will make real *paisani* swoon and sells various lunch items you can eat at simple tables inside and out.

Jamoch's Cafe (☎ *312-226-7666, 1066 W Taylor St)* Meals $5-9. Open 7am-9pm, closed Sun. Breakfast is served all day here, which is good for some of the cramming U of I students, who may not even know what time it is. The long sandwich and snack menu offers veggie options. Those not studying can enjoy stacks of games and magazines.

Tufano's Vernon Park Tap (☎ *312-733-3393, 1073 W Vernon Park)* Dinner $15-25. Still family-run after three generations (it opened in 1930), Tufano's serves up the kind of old-fashioned Italian food that has become trendy again. Spaghetti and meatballs and other rib-sticking classics are good, filling and cheap. The blackboards carry a long list of daily specials, which can include such wonderful items as pasta with garlic-crusted broccoli. Amid the usual celebrity photos on the wall you'll see some really nice shots of Joey Di Buono and his family and their patrons through the decades. The surrounding, leafy neighborhood has changed little over the years. Oddly, nearby Vernon Park has been renamed Arrigo Park.

Rosebud (☎ *312-942-1117, 1500 W Taylor St)* Dinner $25-37. Rosebud is not only the beginning of a movie but also the beginning of an empire of Italian restaurants in the city. Massive piles of prime pasta, such as lip-shaped *cavatelli*, come with one of the finest red sauces in town. The high-quality cuisine means that even those with reservations can wait an hour or more. So what's the problem? Have some good red wine and settle in for some people-watching – you're bound to see several folks who regularly turn up in bold type in the local gossip pages.

PILSEN (Map 10)

During the months when the weather is not miserably cold, Pilsen could be a side street in Mexico City. Blaring signs in Spanish all but obscure the architecture of this neighborhood, which derives its name from the Czechs who originally lived here 100 years ago. Vendors sell ice cream and especially good rice-pudding pops from carts. Others sell corn on the cob that, once bought, is dipped in melted butter and then rolled in spices. Mariachi music bursts out of stores and apartments. The whole scene makes for good strolling, and the innumerable restaurants make for good eating. The 18th St stop on the CTA Blue Line puts you at the west end of the strip.

Panadería Laredo (☎ *312-733-9293, 1540 W 18th St*) Snacks $1. Closed Sun. At this great Mexican bakery (one of the best in Chicago), you grab a pair of tongs and a tray as you enter and pick and choose from the cases to your stomach's content. Your selections, which should definitely include some of the cinnamon-encrusted buns, are tallied up at the cash register – and they won't cost much. Panadería Laredo specializes in whipped-cream cakes, such as the lavish First Communion models on display, complete with little statues of devout children.

Cafe Jumping Bean (☎ *312-455-0019, 1439 W 18th St*) Meals $5-9. Pilsen's bohemian roots merge with its contemporary reality here. Neighborhood artists lounge around on the castoff furniture, awaiting the inspiration for their next creation. A long list of coffees –

many with a Mexican flavor – leads an eclectic menu of snacks, focaccia sandwiches, baked goods and other treats, all priced cheap. There's usually a chess game going on at one of the tables. Dominoes are big, too.

Los Comales #3 (☎ *312-666-2251, 1544 W 18th St*) Meals $4-10. Open 8am-1am, until 4am weekends. The big bowls of marinated vegetables on the tables set the tone at this bustling Mexican coffee shop. Like everything else the *tortas* (soft buns filled with standard taco fare) are fresh and tasty.

Playa Azul (☎ *312-421-2552, 1514 W 18th St*) Meals $6-12. The blond mermaid on the sign is the symbol for this seafood restaurant, which serves various choices of whole fish, such as red snapper, as well as classic Mexican coastal appetizers, such as ceviche. Get the broiled shrimp with extra garlic for an extra-good and tasty meal.

Nuevo Leon (☎ *312-421-1517, 1515 W 18th St*) Meals $6-14. This popular place in a beautifully painted three-flat looks like it belongs in Mexico City. Behind the wrought iron on the windows lies a brightly lit gem that offers superlative versions of all the usual suspects – tacos, tamales, enchiladas, etc. In addition, you can enjoy the *menudo* (tripe soup), chicken mole and steaks grilled up with onions, tomatoes and jalapeño peppers. The soft corn tortillas are hot and just as fresh as everything else. Prices are peso-size.

SOUTH SIDE (Map 11)

Interesting places to eat are scattered about the South Side, but it can be difficult to get to them unless you have a car.

Bronzeville & Around

Bronzeville is a bit of a walk east of the 35th St Station on the CTA Red and Green Lines.

Jazz & Java (☎ *312-791-1300, 3428 S Martin Luther King Jr Dr*) Snacks $2-5. Open at 9am, closing times vary; call. This upscale joint serves up good coffee and snacks to chess players, jazz musicians, poets and passersby. It's a good place to pick up the neighborhood vibe.

Gladys' Luncheonette (☎ *773-548-6848, 4527 S Indiana Ave*) Meals $5-10. Open

Slow times in the tamales trade

RAY HILLSTROM JR

PLACES TO EAT

RICK GERHARTER

Dressing up Nuevo Leon

7am-10pm, closed Mon. Mamma Gladys and her daughter Gladys have been serving the notable and the common for more than 50 years. The white-aproned waitresses are ageless and their service timeless. The menu bursts with inexpensive soul food and other American standards. You'll find traditional fare at breakfast, but lunch mixes sandwiches with soul food and dinner sees a more extensive soul menu, with items like baked turkey necks and fried catfish.

Bridgeport

Both of these places can be reached on the No 8 Halsted bus.

Healthy Food Lithuanian Restaurant (☎ 312-326-2724, 3236 S Halsted St) Meals $8-15. Don't take the name of this place too seriously. You're not any more likely to find tofu and sprouts on the menu now than you were when this spot opened in 1938. The

kugelis (meat-filled dumplings) are fried in good, honest bacon fat; the *blinis* (pancakes) are filled with sour cream; and the cakes are made with real butter. But at least the food is homemade with fresh ingredients. Hey – Grandma would have called it healthy.

Hickory Pit Restaurant (☎ 312-842-7600, 2801 S Halsted St) Meals $15-26. The giant parking lot fills up after Sox games at this old favorite. Here you can feast on super-tender ribs in a mild sauce at the scores of Formica tables beneath the transparent ceiling. Be sure to have some fries.

HYDE PARK (Map 12)

Ride the Metra Electric Line from the Randolph St Station to Hyde Park. You can exit at the 53rd, 55th-56th-57th or 59th St Stations. Alternatively, the drive south on Lake Shore Dr offers nice views of the lake and the Loop.

Within the environs of the University of Chicago, you'll find a true college-town atmosphere. The people at the table next to yours may well be debating whether a butterfly flapping its wings in Indonesia really is responsible for global warming.

SU4 (☎ 773-684-3532, 1331 E 57th St) Meals $5-8. Open until 3am daily. This coffeehouse serves good deli sandwiches and contains a few computers with Internet access, as well as Ethernet connections for those with their own laptops.

Valois (☎ 773-667-0647, 1518 E 53rd St) Meals $5-8. Feel like you're in the midst of one of those atmospheric National Public Radio segments at this cafeteria where the motto is 'See your food.' Author Michael Dunier based his best-selling book *Slim's Table* on Valois customers, who run the gamut of Chicago denizens, from number-crunching Nobel Prize–winners to rock-crunching ditch diggers. They've been feasting on the large and tasty portions here for more than 70 years. The standards include long-steamed vegetables, hot beef

PLACES TO EAT

sandwiches, casseroles and good, fresh biscuits, all of it cheap and hearty.

Cocorico Rotisserie (☎ *773-684-8085, 5428 S Lake Park Ave*) Meals $6-10. Open 9am-7pm daily. Smells of roasting meat waft through this small café and carry-out spot. Buy yourself a picnic or settle in for a great burger or turkey with dressing.

Medici (☎ *773-667-7394, 1327 E 57th St*) Meals $9-19. The world's woes have been solved several times over here, chiefly in the form of thin-crust pizza, sandwiches and salads. Burgers come in myriad choices, with optional toppings such as blue cheese and olives. Vegetarians can seek refuge in the veggie sandwich. For breakfast, try the 'eggs espresso,' made by steaming eggs in an espresso machine. After your meal, check out the vast bulletin board out front. It's the perfect place to size up the character of the community and possibly find the complete works of John Maynard Keynes for sale cheap.

Edwardo's (☎ *773-241-7960, 1321 E 57th St*) Meals $10-20. This branch of the good local pizza chain (see the South Loop section, earlier, for details) attracts plenty of students to its prime location, right off campus.

Caffè Florian (☎ *773-752-4100, 1450 E 57th St*) Meals $9-20. The menu here traces its heritage back to the original Caffè Florian, which opened in Venice in 1720 and became a meeting place for 'the intelligentsia, with patrons including the most celebrated artists, poets, dramatists, actors, musicians and philosophers of the time,' according to the menu here. The humbler modern version serves lesser mortals, and much of the fare (black bean nachos, fish and chips) has never graced a tabletop in Venice. But a few Italian items do make the menu, which covers much of the world.

Calypso Cafe (☎ *773-955-0229, 5211C S Harper Ave*) Lunch & dinner $14-26. Jerk chicken leads the spicy menu at this Caribbean restaurant. Forget Chicago's nine-month chill in the atmospheric dining room with its corrugated metal walls and roof. Tropical drinks add to the mood, and the vaunted pineapple upside-down cake completes it.

Leon's: home to some of the best ribs in town

Dixie Kitchen & Bait Shop (☎ 773-363-4943, 5225 S Harper Ave) Lunch & dinner $15-24. Given Chicago's geographic obsession with 'sides,' be they North, West, South, or a combination thereof, it gladdens the heart to find a restaurant that applies such logic to the menu. The 'south sides' here are soulful standards such as sweet potatoes and black-eyed peas. The main events reflect both uptown and downtown tastes: shrimp in garlic, blackened catfish and country-fried steak. Prices are as cheap as the faux rummage-sale interior. Try some of the good gumbo or the luscious oyster po' boys.

ELSEWHERE IN CHICAGO
Far North
India meets Israel along Devon Ave west of Western Ave. The two cultures coexist in a short four-block stretch. Shops selling saris alternate with kosher butchers. An influx of Russian shops and cafés has also started to shape the street's culture. The El doesn't come close to this area, so you'll have to drive, take a cab or ride the El to the Red Line's Morse Ave stop and transfer to the No 155 Morse Ave bus.

Indian Garden (☎ 773-338-2929, 2548 W Devon Ave) Meals $15-22. Items not found on most South Asian menus dominate here. The cooks use wok-like pans and simple iron griddles to prepare a lot of the items. Vegetables go beyond the soggy cauliflower in goopy sauces found at other, less inspired places. Wash it all down with a mango shake.

Viceroy of India (☎ 773-743-4100, 2516 W Devon Ave) Meals $14-25. Devon Ave's premier Indian choice includes a casual takeout side and a more formal white-tablecloth side. The menu comprises such common standards as tandooris and curries,

all prepared with care. The $8 lunch buffet is a bargain; it makes a good break spot if you're exploring the street.

The Jewish businesses observe strict opening hours, so keep that in mind if you'd like to visit. *Kosher Karry* (☎ 773-973-4355, 2828 W Devon Ave) and *Tel-Aviv Kosher Bakery* (☎ 773-764-8877, 2944 W Devon Ave) sell smoked fish, baked goods and other items ready to eat.

Far South
Getting to these places can be dicey without a car.

Army & Lou's (☎ 773-483-3100, 422 E 75th St near Martin Luther King Dr) Meals $10-20. Open 7am-9pm, closed Tue. If you've never had soul food, start at this warm and welcoming Chicago classic, which rises above the crowd of similar local establishments, many of which are little more than storefronts serving takeout buckets of wings, rib tips and macaroni and cheese. Here you can order fried chicken, catfish, collard greens, sweet-potato pie and all the other classics at prices that are good for your soul. Don't be surprised if you see a few famous black politicians, led by Jesse Jackson. And don't be surprised if some white politician shows up for a photo op.

Leon's Bar-B-Q (☎ 773-731-1454, 1640 E 79th St) Meals $10-20. Since there's no seating inside, you'd better arrive by car and use your vehicle as your dining room. The big slabs of ribs – some of the best in town – come with your choice of sauce, from mild to hot. I prefer hot so I can grow some hair on my chest while I fill my belly. Just watch your upholstery or, better yet, take a rental car and let Mr Hertz or Ms Avis worry about theirs.

PLACES TO EAT

Entertainment

THEATER

After exploding locally in the early 1980s, Chicago theater imploded later in the decade, as too many companies chased too few ticket buyers. Things have stabilized since then, and the surge in the economy during the 1990s began the vital flow of corporate dollars. In 2000 the long-talked-about 'Theater District' in the Loop helped to bring the local theater scene back to life; see the boxed text for details.

An excellent theater town, Chicago attracts young talent drawn to its well-established world of companies and acting schools. The fact that many go on to much bigger things in New York and LA is all the more inducement.

Some theater groups have their own venues; others don't. Throughout this chapter we've noted the addresses of those that have regular homes and just the phone numbers of those that don't; the listings here give just a small idea of what's being staged. As always, check the local press – especially the *Reader* – to find out what's hot.

Buying Tickets

Ticket prices for shows range from $10 for small shows to $40 or more for main companies like Steppenwolf. Most average $15 to $25. However, there are a variety of ways to beat these costs.

In fact, buying a theater ticket can be like shopping for a bargain airfare, with plenty of discounts available to those willing to seek them out. The League of Chicago Theaters operates **Hot Tix** booths, where same-day tickets to participating shows are sold at half-price. The lineup varies every day; it's usually best early in the week. Hot Tix now sells weekend tickets beginning on Friday, and the booths also offer regular full-price tickets. To find out what's available, go to the Internet site www.hottix.com, which is updated daily, or simply stop by one of the booths.

Hot Tix operates three city locations: in the Loop (78 W Randolph St; Map 3), at the Chicago Visitor Center (163 E Pearson St; Map 5) and at Tower Records (2301 N Clark St; Map 6).

Also, students, children, senior citizens, the disabled, groups and even actors may qualify for special prices from the theaters themselves. Plus, some places offer low-cost preview shows before the official premiere and last-minute deals right before curtain time. The moral of this story? Always check with the box office for any and all deals before plunking down your bucks – even at Hot Tix.

Major Companies

Goodman Theatre (☎ *312-443-3800, 170 N Dearborn St; Map 3)* The city's oldest professional theater group celebrated 2000 in a big way by moving into a huge new space that sports the facade from the historic Selwyn and Harris Theaters. The main Albert Ivar Goodman Theatre seats 830, while the Owen Bruner Goodman Theatre is a 400-seat flexible space. The Goodman specializes in new and classic American theater. Its annual production of *A Christmas Carol* has become a local family tradition.

Chicago Shakespeare Theater (☎ *312-595-5600, Navy Pier, 800 E Grand Ave; Map 3)* This long-established theater enjoys a beautiful new home out on Navy Pier. As the name implies, the productions are usually adaptations of the Bard's work.

Steppenwolf Theater (☎ *312-335-1650, 1650 N Halsted St; Map 6)* This legendary ensemble group helped put Chicago theater on the map when it won a Tony Award in 1985 for regional theater excellence. Among the actors who have starred here and then gone on to fame and fortune (and who regularly come back to perform) are John Malkovich, Terry Kinney, Gary Sinise and John Mahoney, the crotchety old coot on *Frasier*. The troupe celebrates its 25th anniversary in 2001.

Victory Gardens Theater (☎ *773-871-3000, 2257 N Lincoln Ave; Map 6)* Long-established and playwright-friendly, Victory

Gardens specializes in world premieres of plays by Chicago authors.

Court Theatre *(☎ 773-753-4472, 5535 S Ellis Ave; Map 12)* A classical company hosted by the University of Chicago, the Court focuses on great works from the Greeks to Shakespeare, as well as various international plays not often performed in the US.

Small Companies

Noble Fool Theater Company *(☎ 773-202-8843; Map 3)* Renowned for its biting and satirical shows, this itinerant troupe once staged *Flanagan's Wake*, a brutal – and of course true – look at an Irish wake that featured audience members. The company will move to a new permanent home in the Loop Theater District at 16 W Randolph St in late 2001.

About Face Theatre *(☎ 773-549-7943, Jane Addams Center Hull House, 3212 N Broadway; Map 7)* This group primarily stages serious plays dealing with gay and lesbian themes and issues.

Live Bait Theater *(☎ 773-871-1212, 3914 N Clark St; Map 7)* Actors who hoped to lure audiences with the 'bait' of their talent founded this renowned theater in 1987. They've been reeling them in ever since. Mostly the group mounts productions by founders Sharon Evans, Catherine Evans and John Ragir. You'll find a casual restaurant and bar in the same building.

Strawdog Theatre *(☎ 773-528-9696, 3829 N Broadway; Map 7)* This company performs quirky works of their own devising in a highly inventive and fun style.

Black Ensemble Theatre *(☎ 773-769-4451, Uptown Center Hull House, 4520 N Beacon St; Map 8)* This established group performs original works about the lives of African Americans. Its 2000 production of *The Jackie Wilson Story* won huge plaudits. The theater

RICHARD CUMMINS

A modern home for the Bard's work

is not far from the Wilson El stop on the CTA Red Line.

Griffin Theatre Company *(☎ 773-769-2228, 5404 N Clark St; Map 8)* This Andersonville troupe is known for its fun adaptations of children's books.

Puppet Parlor *(☎ 773-774-2919, 1922 W Montrose Ave)* True marionette magic staged by experts distinguishes these shows, which are usually based on classic fairy tales such as *Beauty and the Beast*. The Puppet Parlor is not far from the Montrose El stop on the CTA Brown Line.

ENTERTAINMENT

Loop Theater District

Talked about for longer than a four-act play, the Loop Theater District finally opened for what's hoped will be a long run in 2000.

It's a combination of several new and renovated theaters that include the renovated Cadillac Palace Theater, the Chicago Theater and the Ford Center/Oriental Theater as well as the new Goodman Theatre, Gallery 37 and the Noble Fool Theater Company. Details on all of these can be found in the Theater section of this chapter.

The Theater District has been a pet project of the Daley administration, which hopes the Loop will again see the kind of vibrant nightlife that it hasn't had in 40 years. Time will tell, but the addition of the Gene Siskel Film Center (see the Cinemas section in this chapter) and the prospect of some new high-profile restaurants (see the Places to Eat chapter) mean that perhaps Mayor Daley's dreams will come true.

RICHARD CUMMINS

Famous Door Theatre Company (☎ 773-404-8283) This group presents a long-running production of Will Kern's *Hellcab*, which features an uncomfortably accurate portrayal of a crazed taxi driver.

Free Associates (☎ 773-975-7171) This comedy improv group is responsible for works such as *BS*, a much-needed skewering of the TV show *ER*. When not laying waste to pop culture, the group also does a send-up of Shakespeare. It's about time.

TimeLine Theatre Company (☎ 312-409-8463) In 2000 TimeLine emerged as one of the most promising new companies with its production of *Not About Nightingales*, which got rave reviews.

Venues

The Loop (Map 3) *Auditorium Theater* (☎ 312-902-1500, 50 E Congress Parkway) This huge and beautiful old theater is worth the price of admission even if the performance stinks. It usually hosts short runs performed by traveling companies.

Cadillac Palace Theater (☎ 312-902-1500, 151 W Randolph St) Part of the Hotel Allegro, the Palace is quite swank.

Chicago Theater (☎ 312-443-1130, 175 N State St) The grandest of the grand old movie palaces, the Chicago was restored in 1986. Now run by the Disney organization, it features a rotating lineup of stage versions of Disney classics.

Ford Center/Oriental Theater (☎ 312-902-1400, 24 W Randolph St) Grandly restored in 1998, this old classic usually hosts big-name shows.

Shubert Theater (☎ 312-977-1700, 22 W Monroe St) This is the place to go for traveling Broadway productions.

Other Locations *Gallery 37* (☎ 312-744-8925, 66 E Randolph St; Map 3) This mixed-use city facility includes some space for performances.

Arie Crown Theater (☎ 312-791-6190, East Building at McCormick Place, 23rd St & Lake Shore Dr; Map 4) This enormous, 4300-seat theater is almost lost in the far more enormous convention center. It books more concerts than stage productions,

ENTERTAINMENT

though it does host the *Nutcracker* every year.

Tommy Gun's Garage (☎ 312-728-2828, 1239 S State St; Map 4) This theater has chosen a phone number thoroughly in keeping with its name; converted into letters, the numbers 728-2828 spell out 'rat-a-tat.' Though the offerings at this dinner theater vary between painfully hokey and downright stupid, the performers – beginning with the guy at the door, who talks with lots of 'de's' and 'dems' – have an infectious energy that comes from not taking the material too seriously. Soon the large numbers of bus tour groups are singing right along.

Apollo Theater (☎ 773-935-6100, 2540 N Lincoln Ave; Map 6) One after another, the high-energy productions here pay tribute to the music of the 1950s.

Royal George Theatre (☎ 312-988-9000, 1641 N Halsted St; Map 6) The Royal George is three theaters in one building. The cabaret venue presents long-running mainstream productions such as *Forever Plaid*, a send-up of all-male singing groups. The main stage presents works with big-name stars, and the gallery hosts various improv and minor works performed by small troupes.

Trap Door Theatre (☎ 773-384-0494, 1655 W Cortland St; Map 6) Depending on the production, you might feel like you've fallen through a trap door at this nearly anarchist operation, where the out-there productions showcase works by writers far from the mainstream.

Athenaeum Theatre (☎ 773-935-6860, 2936 N Southport Ave; Map 7) One of the many small theater spaces in Lake View, the Athenaeum often hosts productions by some of the itinerant troupes mentioned under Small Companies, earlier.

Bailiwick Arts Center (☎ 773-883-1090, 1229 W Belmont Ave; Map 7) This facility boasts two stages that see a constant stream of productions, many of them gay-oriented and many by the resident Bailiwick Repertory.

Briar Street Theatre (☎ 773-348-4000, 3133 N Halsted St; Map 7) This facility usually stages major theatrical works that often turn into movies later, as *Six Degrees of Separation* did.

Mercury Theatre (☎ 773-325-1700, 3745 N Southport Ave; Map 7) Michael Cullen, owner of the adjoining bar of the same name, has created a fast-rising star among North Side theaters with this classy space.

Theatre Building (☎ 773-327-5252, 1225 W Belmont Ave; Map 7) Lots of small troupes present shows in this flexible space.

WNEP Theater (☎ 773-755-1693, 3209 N Halsted St; Map 7) This well-located space hosts a variety of productions, including many experimental ones late at night.

Chicago Dramatists (☎ 312-633-0630, 1105 W Chicago Ave; Map 10) This new West Side theater is home to several interesting companies. One worth noting is the Congo Square Theatre Company, an African American troupe that has won plaudits since its first production in 2000.

New Regal Theatre (☎ 773-721-9230, 1645 E 79th St) A community-based African American theater, the South Side–based New Regal books touring national acts. Built in 1927, the theater features a grand lobby with a ceiling that replicates an Oriental rug in tile.

COMEDY CLUBS

After a burst of club openings in the 1980s, Chicago comedy has shrunk back to its roots, which are dominated by Second City and Zanies. Cover charges vary; call to find out.

Second City (☎ 312-337-3992, 1616 N Wells St; Map 6) A Chicago must-see, this club is best symbolized by John Belushi, who emerged from the suburbs in 1970 and earned a place with the Second City improvisational troupe with his creative, manic, no-holds-barred style. Soon Belushi had moved up to the main stage, and then it was on to *Saturday Night Live* and fame and fortune.

Since its founding in 1959, Second City has staged more than 90 revues, usually sharp and biting commentaries on life, politics, love and anything else that falls in the cross hairs of their comedians' rapid-fire, hard-hitting wit. Other famous alums include Bill Murray, Gilda Radner, Rick Moranis, Dan Aykroyd and Elaine May.

Purists point out that the quality of the performances dipped in the mid 1980s, when the stage was flooded with legions of Shelly Hack wannabes. Try to guess which cast members will be the next to ride the train of celebrity and success.

Second City ETC *(☎ 312-642-8189, 1608 N Wells St in the Pipers Alley complex; Map 6)* Second City's second company often presents more daring work, as actors try to get noticed and make the main stage. Both theaters offer the city's best comedy value after the last show most nights, when the comics present free improv performances to keep everybody's wit sharp.

Zanies *(☎ 312-337-4027, 1548 N Wells St; Map 6)* The city's main stand-up comedy venue was also its premier club long before a wave of closings sharply reduced competition. Zanies regularly books big-name national acts familiar to anyone with a TV and also frequently invites comics you're *about* to hear about on TV. The shows last less than two hours and usually include the efforts of a couple of up-and-comers before the main act. The ceiling is low and the seating is cramped, which only adds to the good cheer.

Improv & Other Comedy

The mere presence of Second City fuels the dreams of would-be comedians all over the city. Improvisational clubs litter the North Side like the broken dreams of funny people doomed to no greater fate than cutting up for their coworkers forever. The quality of the talent varies from uproarious to cute to stupid, with everybody competing to be the one in a million who hits the big time.

Tony and Tina's Wedding *(☎ 312-664-8844, 230 W North Ave in the Pipers Alley complex; Map 6)* I hate weddings (except my own, of course), but if they all were as much fun as this I might drag myself to more of them. The performers string together the worst moments of every Catholic wedding you've ever attended and take them to high levels of parody. The audience members play the guests and get to participate in the ceremony and reception. The results, which vary with the crowd, are usually hilarious. Admission includes the show and basic Italian chow.

ComedySportz *(☎ 773-549-8080, 2851 N Halsted St; Map 7)* The gimmick here is that two improv teams compete with deadly seriousness to make you laugh hysterically. The audience benefits from this comic capitalism.

ImprovOlympic *(☎ 773-880-0199, 3541 N Clark St; Map 7)* First among the improvs, this comic veteran actually pays its professional performers (but some shows feature improv students who haven't quite achieved the status of 'professional' yet), and they earn every dime. Sketches hinge heavily on audience suggestions, and each turn can run 40 minutes or longer. If you're thoroughly motivated by what you see, ImprovOlympic offers a range of courses to suit every temp's budget. The same stage also hosts various improv groups composed of the talented alums.

CINEMAS

The daily papers publish all the listings for the first-run places. Check out the *Reader* or *New City* for the more offbeat choices.

Each October the Chicago Film Festival brings a score of films from around the world to town for two weeks. Check with the festival (☎ 312-644-3456) for each year's schedule.

First Run

There are good and bad choices if you want to see the latest Hollywood blockbuster. Here's a guide.

IMAX Theater *(☎ 312-595-0090, 600 E Grand Ave at Navy Pier; Map 3)* One of the ubiquitous mega-screen theaters is out on the pier.

McClurg Court Theaters *(☎ 312-642-0723, 330 E Ohio St; Map 3)* If your movie is playing in the main theater here, you're in for a treat: it's one of the city's largest screens. The other two theaters were once the balcony, and they should have stayed that way.

600 N Michigan Theaters *(☎ 312-255-9340; Map 3)* Despite the name, the entrance to these theaters is off Rush St. This comfortable complex features six screens of various sizes, plus a café and concessions

Windy City Television

You don't have to go to Hollywood or New York to land in the audience of a national TV talk show; three are based in Chicago, all of them named after their hosts. If you reserve tickets in advance, you can sit in the audience and watch episodes being taped. Afterward, you may get to meet the hosts and their guests, although in the case of the latter two, you may not want to.

The charismatic ratings leader of syndicated talk shows, **Oprah Winfrey** is also a local celebrity. From her own production facility in the West Loop – Harpo Studios (wondering about the name? Spell it backward) – she tapes her wildly popular show, which features celebrities, the occasional serious news investigation and discussions of issues as diverse as racial prejudice and whom to invite to your third wedding. (Expect plenty of swooning over the likes of Ivana Trump and other notables.)

For tickets, call ☎ 312-591-9595 at least a month in advance. Harpo Studios is at 1050 W Washington Blvd (Map 10).

If Oprah is the class act of daytime TV, the following two hosts mud-wrestle for the title at the opposite end of the spectrum. They invite the kind of guests whose intimate lives could involve hedgehogs. Their programs post good ratings (a measure of how many people are watching), which just goes to show that you should never overestimate the intelligence of the viewers. Joining the audience can be a raucous or sickening experience.

A former stand-up comedian, **Jenny Jones** has become her own unintentional joke. Her monthly firings of hapless stylists unable to breathe life into her chemically damaged hair have been gleefully followed in the *Tribune*'s Inc. column.

Jones specializes in tawdry topics that involve unconventional sexual pairings. Guests for whom the chance to fly to Chicago and stay in a cheap hotel represents the high point of their lives cheerfully bare every last detail of their low-jinx. But lest we joke too much, these antics can have grim consequences. Several years ago, a heterosexual man killed a gay man a few days after the latter revealed that he had a crush on him on Jenny Jones' show. For tickets, call ☎ 312-836-9485.

The third local talk-show host, **Jerry Springer** disingenuously admits that his guests are vile but that he's really trying to communicate valid moral messages. Yeah, right. At the end of each episode Springer delivers a pious sermon that's a laugh in itself. During ratings periods he heroically books neo-Nazis whom he then throws out of the studio for being Nazis. For tickets, call ☎ 312-321-5365.

The latter two shows are taped at the NBC Tower (454 N Columbus Dr, east of Michigan Ave; Map 3). A friend who works in the building told me that security had to be increased after various 'guests' were found attempting petty crimes.

ENTERTAINMENT

stand on each of its three floors. The views of Michigan Ave from inside are great.

Burnham Plaza Theaters *(☎ 312-922-1090, 826 S Wabash St; Map 4)* Though sorely needed, this multiplex serving the South Side is not a terribly great facility.

Esquire Theaters *(☎ 312-280-0101, 58 E Oak St; Map 5)* This once-grand theater got chopped up into five small ones with predictably unfortunate results.

900 N Michigan Theaters *(☎ 312-787-1988; Map 5)* Oddly, a decent modern theater with two sizable screens hides in the basement of the mall of the same name.

Village Theater *(☎ 312-642-2403, 1548 N Clark St; Map 5)* This is a cool old theater broken up into several smaller ones. It shows quirky new releases and second runs at good prices.

Webster Place *(☎ 773-327-3100, 1471 W Webster Ave; Map 6)* This seven-screen multiplex is really nothing special.

Pipers Alley *(☎ 312-642-7500, North Ave at Wells St; Map 6)* Located in the complex of the same name, this is a pretty decent multiplex with good sight lines.

Landmark's Century Centre *(☎ 773-248-7744, 2828 N Clark St; Map 7)* This is a useful neighborhood multiplex.

Meridien Theaters *(☎ 312-444-3456, 5238 S Harper Ave; Map 12)* This multiplex in the heart of Hyde Park is worthwhile only if you're already in the neighborhood.

Rep Houses

Many of the following theaters show different films every night.

Fine Arts Theaters *(☎ 312-939-3700, 418 S Michigan Ave; Map 3)* The facilities here are a bit worn and the carpeting can be sticky, but what do you want from a facility that saw its first performance in 1898? The old and grand main theater contains a huge screen. The three smaller theaters are just

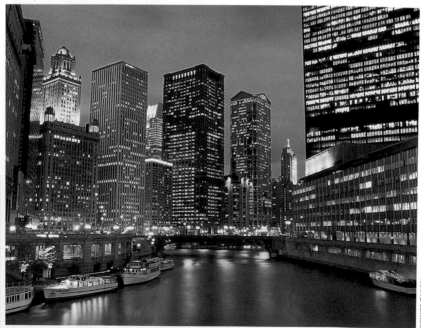

Chicago stays alive late into the night.

that – small. This is the principal venue for 'serious' movies in the city; look for the latest Merchant-Ivory production here.

Gene Siskel Film Center (☎ 312-443-3733, 164 N State St; Map 3) The former Film Center of the Art Institute was renamed for the late *Chicago Tribune* film critic Gene Siskel in 2000. Late in the year it also moved to a grand new space that boasts two theaters. It shows everything from dreck by students who should hang onto their day jobs to wonderful but unsung gems by Estonian directors. The monthly schedule includes theme nights of forgotten American classics.

Facets Multimedia (☎ 773-281-4114, 1517 W Fullerton Ave; Map 6) Facets shows interesting obscure movies that would never get booked elsewhere. This is the place to find the denizens of Chicago's film community between Hollywood contracts.

Three Penny Cinema (☎ 773-935-5744, 2424 N Lincoln Ave; Map 6) The floors creak at this ramshackle, family-run complex of tiny theaters in Lincoln Park. But what the family saves in maintenance expenses, you save in admission. Tickets are cheap for major releases that have passed their prime and for a good selection of the better minor films.

Brew & View (☎ 312-618-8439, Vic Theater, 3145 N Sheffield Ave; Map 7) Even the worst film gets better when you've got a pizza in front of you and a pitcher of beer at your side. As you watch second-run Hollywood releases here, you can behave as badly as you would at home – in fact, the staff encourage it.

Music Box Theater (☎ 773-871-6604, 3733 N Southport Ave; Map 7) No matter what's showing, it's worth going to the Music Box just to see the place. This perfectly restored theater dates from 1929 and looks like a Moorish fantasy. Clouds float across the ceiling, which has twinkling stars. The film programs are always first-rate. A second, small and serviceable theater shows held-over films that have proved more popular than expected.

CLASSICAL MUSIC

You can find classical music performances throughout the year. In the summer they move outside, under the stars and amid the mosquitoes.

Performances of the Chicago Symphony Orchestra are sold out each year to subscribers. However, even the most devout fans don't make every performance. Check with the box office, or hang around about 30 minutes before curtain; more often than not, some besuited swell will offer you a pair of tickets, and in my experience these people got class – they would sooner cough during a solo than gouge you. Check the *Reader* or *Chicago* magazine to see what's being performed when you're in town.

Chicago Symphony Orchestra (☎ 312-294-3333) The CSO enjoys lavish support locally. The group makes its home in the Symphony Center (220 S Michigan Ave; Map 3), which underwent a major reconstruction in the late 1990s. The late Sir George Solti was music director from 1969 to '92 and is credited with propelling the CSO to the very front ranks of world symphony orchestras. The current director, Daniel Barenboim, had the classic big pair of shoes to fill and has done so masterfully. He has molded the group with his personality, and the acclaim continues. He celebrated 50 years of performing in 2000. The CSO season runs from September to May. In the summer, when the orchestra isn't wowing some European capital, it often performs at Ravinia (see separate heading, later).

Civic Orchestra of Chicago The training branch of the CSO has carved out a fine reputation as well. Visiting conductors and musicians often work with the group, which also performs in the Symphony Center. And their tickets are free!

Apollo Chorus of Chicago (☎ 630-960-2251) A vocal group founded by a group of men in 1872, the Apollo usually performs at the Symphony Center, though it's based in suburban Downer's Grove. Tickets for the chorus' Christmas performance of Handel's *Messiah* sell out every year.

Chicago Chamber Musicians (☎ 312-225-5226) This 14-member group has dedicated itself to spreading the sound of chamber music by performing the classics, as well as initiating numerous outreach programs to the community.

ENTERTAINMENT

His Majestie's Clerkes (☎ 312-461-0723)
This a cappella group, named after the
'clerkes' who sang in 16th-century England,
produces a clear and haunting sound. Most
of their performances take place in the city's
grand churches.

Music of the Baroque (☎ 312-551-1415)
One of the largest choral and orchestra
groups of its kind in the US, MoB brings the
music of the Middle Ages and Renaissance
to life. Its Christmas brass and choral concerts are huge successes.

Chicago Sinfonietta (☎ 312-857-1062)
This group of notable young musicians, led
by the locally well-known Paul Freeman,
performs classics as well as adventurous
modern works by the likes of Thelonious
Monk.

Grant Park Musical Festival

Classical music for the masses is performed
four nights a week for most of the summer at
the Petrillo Music Shell, in Grant Park at
Jackson and Columbus Sts between the Art
Institute and the lake. Under the auspices of
the Chicago Park District, the **Grant Park
Symphony Orchestra** (☎ 312-742-7638) gives
free (read: free!) concerts, usually on
Wednesday, Friday, Saturday and Sunday
evenings, although events such as the jazz
festival can alter the schedule. At present
Chicago is the only city in the US to boast a
free symphony orchestra. The classical orchestra's solid performances span several
genres, from opera to Broadway and 'pop.'
New conductors Carlos Kalmar and James
Paul have received critical acclaim.

The amphitheater seating in front of the
stage is first-come, first-served, although
members of the Grant Park Musical Festival get reserved seats. Anybody who doesn't
get a seat can spread out on the vast Grant
Park grasslands. Viewing is problematic
from the park – often some lout comes and
puts his blanket right in front of yours. But
the sound is good. You can bring a picnic or
buy food from the growing number of
vendors who set up along Jackson St. This is
a classic Chicago experience and a great
way to relax for an hour or the whole show.

Ravinia Festival

In the summer the CSO and other classical,
jazz, folk, ethnic and pop groups perform at
Ravinia (☎ 847-266-5100), a vast open-air
festival in Highland Park (Green Bay and
Lake Cook Rds), on the North Shore. The
main pavilion contains seating for several
hundred in a bowl-like setting with a good
view of the stage and the performers. But
these tickets sell quickly, and most people
end up sitting on the acres of lawn. Here's
the catch: you can't see the performers from
the lawn, nor can you hear them, except
from the huge speakers hanging in the trees.

So for about $10 (pavilion seats cost much,
much more), you get to sit on grass and listen
to music from a speaker. Some people revel
in the experience, bringing baskets of designer picnic ware, gourmet edibles and fine
bubbly. They lie back, stare at the stars and let
the music send their blood pressure plum-
meting. Others just can't see the point of all
the bother (count me in this churlish lot).
Bathroom lines can be long, parking can be
bad and traffic after the show can negate any
calming influence. You'll have to decide this
one for yourself – look in the mirror and say,
'Am I type A? Or am I type B?'

If you do go, avoid the traffic and take the
45-minute Metra/Union Pacific North Line
train from Ogilvie Transportation Center to
Ravinia Station ($3.50). Trains stop before
and after the concerts right in front of the
gates. Food and expensive drink are available
at the park.

OPERA

Like the Chicago Symphony Orchestra, the
Lyric Opera of Chicago sells out its tickets
to subscribers each year. See Classical
Music, above, for tips on getting tickets to
fully booked performances.

Lyric Opera of Chicago (☎ 312-332-
2244) One of the top opera companies in
the US performs in the grand old Civic
Opera House (20 N Wacker Dr; Map 3), on
the south branch of the river. The Lyric's
repertoire is a shrewd mix of old classics
and much more modern and daring work.
You can catch the *Mikado* one week and

some totally new but emotionally stunning piece the next.

The company has had excellent luck luring top international names, such as Placido Domingo. It also has joined the international trend of projecting translations of the lyrics onto a screen above the proscenium. Purists shudder with horror; others, whose Italian or German isn't what it could be, sit back and happily read away.

Gregarious Andrew Davis, former music director of the BBC Symphony, took the helm of the Lyric in 2000 to good reviews. Also watch for promising new soprano Jonita Lattimore. The season runs from September to March.

Chicago Opera Theater (☎ *312-704-8420*) This innovative group stages contemporary and popular works during the summer. Under general director Brian Dickie, COT has scored some artistic success. It concentrates on little performed 17th- and 18th-century classics as well as contemporary American works. Check local listings for performance venues.

DANCE

Dance and ballet can seem to have fallen through the cracks of the Chicago cultural scene. Several excellent companies perform here, and they do receive some support, but the lack of a main performing venue has kept the groups continually striving for recognition. However, developments at the Joffrey and at Columbia College (see below) could change this finally. The Chicago Dance Coalition (☎ 312-419-8384) can tell you when and where performances are being staged. Check the *Reader* also.

Major Companies

Hubbard St Dance Chicago (☎ *312-850-9744*). Hubbard St is the preeminent dance group in the city, with an international reputation to match. The group has become known for energetic and technically virtuoso performances under the direction of the best choreographers in the world, including founder Lou Conte. In 2000 Hubbard received raves for a season directed by Jim

Vincent and Lucas Crandall. The troupe really needs a permanent performance facility. If you have a few spare millions, give them a call.

Joffrey Ballet of Chicago (☎ *312-739-0120*) This famous group has flourished since it relocated from New York in 1995. Noted for its energetic work, the company frequently travels the world and boasts an impressive storehouse of pieces it regularly performs. In 2000 the Joffrey announced plans for its first permanent home in Chicago. Under a $24 million scheme, an old building at 6 E Lake St in the Loop will be transformed into a performance and administrative center. No completion date has been given, however.

Other Companies

Ballet Chicago (☎ *312-251-8838*) This home-grown troupe has received much acclaim for its precision and skill performing classical ballet works.

Chicago Moving Co (☎ *773-880-5402*) This exciting group was founded by Nana Shineflug, one of the pioneers of modern dance in Chicago. The works and performers are all local.

Dance Center at Columbia College (☎ *312-344-8300, 1306 S Michigan Ave; Map 4*) More than an academic institution, the Dance Center has carved out a fine reputation by presenting top local and international talent. The center's new state-of-the-art facility within Columbia College should help to continue attracting quality dance.

Muntu Dance Theater of Chicago (☎ *773-602-1135*) The word 'muntu' means 'the essence of humanity' in Bantu, and this company performs African and American dances that draw on ancient and contemporary movement.

River North Dance Company (☎ *312-944-2888*) This vibrant young company brings elements of punk, house, hip-hop, mime and more to modern dance.

LIVE MUSIC

There's more music being played any night of the week in Chicago than you could ever listen to, even if you had a year. Obviously, given the city's blues and jazz roots, you can hear world-class performances in those genres. You can also catch plenty of live rock, by everyone from garage bands to revival groups to cutting-edge names. And with the wealth of ethnic enclaves, you're sure to hear just about anything else you desire. When it comes to finding out what's happening on the live-music scene during your visit, check the *Reader* – its listings and reviews are voluminous.

Cover charges vary widely depending on the venue, the day of the week, the musicians playing, etc. Small places presenting relative unknowns might charge nothing on a Sunday night, while larger venues with top names on the weekend will demand $15 or more.

Jazz & Blues

In a city that has played a pivotal role not just in jazz and blues but in the genres they have engendered (such as rock), it would be foolish not to sample some of this vibrant scene. Some clubs book only jazz, some only blues and some both. Whatever your preference is, myriad venues devote themselves to blues or jazz any night of the week. Aficionados can find well-regarded players all over town.

Near North (Map 3)

Andy's (☎ 312-642-6805, 11 E Hubbard St) This veteran jazz and blues bar/restaurant doesn't charge a cover for its lunchtime shows. Some workers come at lunch and never quite make it back to the office.

Blue Chicago (☎ 312-642-6261, 736 N Clark St) The talent lives up to the club's name at this mainstream blues club. If you're staying

in the neighborhood and don't feel like hitting the road, you won't go wrong here.

Blue Chicago on Clark (☎ 312-661-0100, 536 N Clark St) This is a smaller and cleaner version of the club above. Horror of horrors, it has a gift shop.

House of Blues (☎ 312-923-2000, Marina City, 329 N Dearborn St) Blues Brother Dan Aykroyd invested in this spot, virtually guaranteeing that the House of Blues would make a big splash in Chicago. On the main floor – a casual eatery in a broken-down bayou setting – video monitors show diners what's happening upstairs in the large and open music venue. You can sometimes hear blues here, but more often it's something else. Some nights aging rockers like Ted Nugent perform; other nights a salsa band

takes over. The Sunday gospel brunch features soul-stirring Chicago groups and Cajun chow. Reserve early – it's usually mobbed. Oh, and try not to notice the gift shop near the door.

Jazz Showcase (☎ *312-670-2473, 59 W Grand Ave*) Owner Joe Segal presides over an elegant club that caters to jazz purists. Nobody's yelling 'Hey gimme anudda pitcha!' here.

South Loop (Map 4) *Buddy Guy's Legends* (☎ *312-427-0333, 754 S Wabash Ave*) You're likely to find the namesake here, although instead of playing, Buddy will probably be giving the crowd a circumspect gaze as he adds up a stack of receipts. Look for top national and local blues groups in this no-nonsense, cavernous space.

HotHouse (☎ *312-362-9707, 31 E Balbo Dr*) Not far from Grant Park and the Loop, the jazz club HotHouse has been called 'indispensable' by *Tribune* critic Howard Reich. It regularly draws top artists from as far as South Africa and Japan. Look for the great local saxophonist Ernest Dawkins.

Koko Taylor's Celebrity (☎ *312-566-0555, 1233 S Wabash Ave*) Local blues legend Koko Taylor owns this top-notch venue and often performs here herself.

Velvet Lounge (☎ *312-791-9050, 2128½ S Indiana Ave*) Tenor saxophonist Fred Anderson owns the Velvet, near the South Side. Visiting jazz musicians often hang out here late at night. The tiny place rocks during frequent impromptu jam sessions.

Lincoln Park (Map 6) *Blues* (☎ *773-528-1012, 2519 N Halsted St*) Long, narrow and crowded, this veteran club crackles with electric moments where the crowd shares in the music. Look for names like Big James & the Chicago Playboys.

Green Dolphin Street (☎ *773-395-0066, 2200 N Ashland Ave at Webster Ave*) This classy venue combines excellent and inventive cuisine with good jazz. It's hard to

Buddy Guy

imagine that this riverside club, which looks like it's been around since the 1940s, used to be a junk-auto dealer before the renovation.

Kingston Mines (☎ *773-477-4646, 2548 N Halsted St*) It's so hot and sweaty here that the blues neophytes in the audience will feel like they're having a genuine experience – sort of like a gritty theme park. Two stages mean that somebody's always on. The club's popularity means that it attracts big names.

Lilly's (☎ *773-525-2422, 2513 N Lincoln Ave*) Lilly's routinely presents excellent local blues acts inside a club with an odd Mexican air. The largely ignored balcony offers good views on crowded nights.

Elsewhere in Chicago *Back Room* (☎ *312-751-2433, 1007 N Rush St; Map 5*) In this tiny place you view the jazz musicians via a mirror. If you're on the small main floor, you might find the intimacy reminiscent of a concert held in your own bedroom.

ENTERTAINMENT

Mill (☎ 773-878-5552, 4802 N
away; Map 8) You can sit in Al
one's booth at the timeless Green Mill, a
rue cocktail lounge complete with curved
leather booths. Little has changed in 70
years – the club still books top local and national jazz acts. On Sunday night it hosts a
nationally known poetry slam where would-
be poets try out their best work on the
openly skeptical crowd.

New Checkerboard Lounge (☎ 773-624-
3240, 423 E 43rd St; Map 11) This is just what
you would expect from one of the most well-
known blues clubs in town. People from
around the world and just down the street
gather on the mismatched furniture to hear
some of the greats. The friendly staff contrast with the rough edges of the decor and
the neighborhood – they'll even get you a
cab when you leave.

Rosa's Lounge (☎ 773-342-0452, 3420 W
Armitage Ave) This is hardcore blues. Top
local talents perform at this unadorned West
Side club in a neighborhood that's still a few
decades away from attracting developers.
Take a cab.

New Apartment Lounge (☎ 773-483-7728,
504 E 75th St) Talk around the oval bar
centers on jazz at this far South Side place, a
simple storefront venue where the crowds
are friendly and saxophonist Von Freeman
jams on Tuesday nights.

Rock

Hog Head McDunna's (☎ 773-929-0944,
1505 W Fullerton Ave; Map 6) By day this is
a large bar with good burgers. At night it's a
showcase for good local rock bands, the
better products of Chicago's garages.

Cubby Bear (☎ 773-327-1662, 1059 W
Addison St; Map 7) Absolutely lacking in
charm when there isn't a band playing *(don't
go after a Cubs game)*, the sprawling Cubby
Bear sometimes books decent bands, especially when it isn't baseball season.

Metro (☎ 773-549-3604, 3730 N Clark St;
Map 7) Acts on the verge of superstardom
regularly play this former classic theater.
Some of the big names have included the
Smashing Pumpkins, who held their farewell
concerts here in 2000. Fans flock in from all

over the Midwest to hear the latest in rock.
After the show, or even if you don't have
tickets, the *Smart Bar*, in the basement,
offers dancing until dawn.

Shuba's (☎ 773-525-2508, 3159 N Southport Ave; Map 7) Time was when the big
breweries owned their own corner bars all
over town. Shuba's is one; look for the big
Schlitz globe carved in limestone over the
door. Fortunately, that bad beer and its
brewers are long gone. Good local bands
and vocalists regularly play the back room,
which looks like something out of a Catholic
grade school when the lights are on.

Double Door (☎ 773-489-3160, 1572 N
Milwaukee Ave; Map 9) Hard-edged,
cutting-edge rock echoes off the walls in this
former liquor store, which still has its original sign out front. The bouncer will steer you
less than carefully to the proper door. On
some nights you'll hear punk while on
others you can join various fetish nights
(proper attire required).

The Note (☎ 312-489-0011, 1565 N Milwaukee Ave; Map 9) This is a dive – and not in an
atmospheric way. The stage in this rather un-
comfortable spot can be hard to see; however,
the many samba nights draw crowds, and the
place also hosts dance competitions. Look for
local rock bands here as well.

Empty Bottle (☎ 773-276-3600, 1035 N
Western Ave; Map 10) This creative place
always seems to hit on all cylinders. The
music spans the styles from funk to punk.
The progressive, hip bands reflect the crowd.
Check out the goofy decor, which includes a
door from a cop car. No word on how it was
obtained.

Phyllis' Musical Inn (☎ 773-486-9862,
1800 W Division St; Map 10) This classic
Chicago rock bar features bands who want
to be the next Smashing Pumpkins or, better
yet, their replacements. Bored with the
band? Shoot hoops in the beer garden.

Folk & World Music

Exedus II (☎ 773-348-3998, 3477 N Clark St;
Map 7) This narrow bar fills with smoke and
the sounds of good reggae, performed by
acts often on their way to or from the place
listed next.

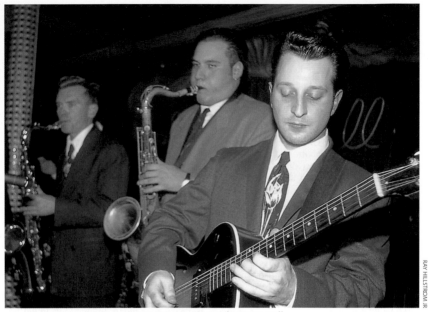

A swinging time at the Green Mill

Wild Hare and Singing Armadillo Frog Sanctuary (☎ 773-327-4273, 3530 N Clark St; Map 7) Dreadlocks meet capitalism at this modern reggae club run by guys from Jamaica but financed by local venture capitalists. It books top touring acts. Beware after Cubs games, when the baseball caps outnumber the dreadlocks by a factor of 10.

Old Town School of Folk Music (☎ 773-728-6000, 4544 N Lincoln Ave) You can hear the call of the banjos from the street outside this venue, where major national and local acts like the Lonesome River Band play regularly. If you want to join in, you can take classes. Legend Steve Earle offered an amazing two-month seminar on songwriting in 2000. The school isn't too far from the Montrose stop on the El Brown Line. Its original location (☎ 773-525-7793, 909 W Armitage Ave; Map 6) offers programs aimed at children.

Abbey Pub (☎ 773-478-4408, 3420 W Grace St at Elston) The closest you can come to a major venue for Irish music in Chicago, the Abbey features a vast music area with second-level tables that let you gaze down on all the red hair below. An adjoining pub is smoky and crowded. This club is located far from the city center, on the northwest side. It's about a $15 cab ride from River North.

Lounge

Coq d'Or (☎ 312-787-2200, The Drake, 140 E Walton St; Map 5) Cole Porter, Frank Sinatra and others are part of the repertoire of the highly talented piano players and singers who rotate through this stately lounge.

Zebra Lounge (☎ 312-642-5140, 1220 N State St; Map 5) For a funky night dating back to the days before colorization, try this small, smoky joint decorated entirely in black and white. The piano can get as scratchy as the voices of the crowd, which consists mainly of older people who like to sing along. Regular ivory-stroker Tom Oman is a veteran who knows his stuff.

RAY HILLSTROM JR

ENTERTAINMENT

Davenport's Piano Bar & Cabaret
(☎ 773-278-1830, 1383 N Milwaukee Ave;
Map 9) Old standards get new interpretations and new songs get heard for the first time at this swank place on an up-and-coming stretch of Milwaukee Ave. A changing lineup of great vocalists and piano players performs.

BARS

As I said in the introduction to my book, the *Official Chicago Bar Guide*, this city boasts the best selection of bars in the US. The drawn-out winters mean that for decades Chicagoans have pursued their social lives indoors – which in turn means that bars have sprung up to suit every mood and personality. The descriptions run the gamut: classy, fun, loud, sports-oriented, quiet, literary, young, old, cozy, romantic, smoky – you name it. The selection here is just a smattering of the best. (Other places are listed in the Live Music section, as well as in the Places to Stay and Places to Eat chapters.)

Though bars draw a lot of patrons in the dead of winter, summer also makes a good bar season, as many pubs boast beer gardens and outdoor seating.

Note, too, that although the usual closing time is 2am, many bars stay open until 4am weekdays and 5am Saturday.

The Loop & Near North (Map 3)

Although the following bars – with one notable exception – aren't bad, be prepared to head farther north for the best ones.

Berghoff Stand Up Bar (☎ 312-427-3170, 17 W Adams St) Adjoining the restaurant, this bar has changed little in a century, although women have been admitted for the past 35 years.

Brehon Pub (☎ 312-642-1071, 731 N Wells St) Forget the Hollywood crap, forget the thespian waiters and all the other gimmicks found in neighboring blocks, and experience the real Chicago at this fine example of the corner saloons that once dotted the city. The Brehon purveys draft beer in frosted glasses to neighborhood crowds perched on the high stools. And there's no hideous gift shop at the entrance.

Celtic Crossing (☎ 312-337-1005, 751 N Clark St) In this neighborhood where everything is faux and for sale, word of a new Irish bar sparks fears of high-concept Blarney. But fear not: this bar is owned by real Irish people and employs actual Irish bartenders. Barely a year old, it already feels like it has been here for years. Best of all, the pints of Guinness come in *imperial* pints. That's a little over 3oz more!

Clark St Ale House (☎ 312-642-9253, 742 N Clark St) Come here for the neighborhood's best beer selection, which includes a rotating selection of tap beer from some of the best Midwestern microbreweries. Work up a thirst on the free pretzels and cool off in the beer garden out back.

Dick's Last Resort (☎ 312-836-7870, River East Plaza, 435 E Illinois St) I include this dump only to warn people away. By virtue of being a national chain that runs lots of ads in in-flight magazines, Dick's has installed itself on the map. If you're in a group and

ENTERTAINMENT

someone insists on going here, opt for a different taxi.

ESPNZone (☎ *312-644-3776, 43 E Ohio St*) The Disney Corporation has opened an outlet for another one of its brands: ESPN. Here you'll find a collection of bars and video games aimed at the same couch potatoes who watch the cable sports channel. For those able to make it off the Barcalounger, the place is open from 11am until after midnight daily.

Green Door Tavern (☎ *312-664-5496, 678 N Orleans St*) See the Places to Eat chapter for details on this good bar.

Hudson Club (☎ *312-467-1947, 504 N Wells St*) See the Places to Eat chapter for details on this stylish bar with an excellent selection of beer.

Tavern on the Pier (☎ *312-321-8090, River East Plaza, 455 E Illinois St*) A survivor in the corpse of what was once called North Pier Terminal, this mellow pub is a great spot in the summer, when you can sit at one of the outdoor tables along Ogden Slip, a popular docking place for boaters.

Gold Coast (Map 5)

Dave & Buster's (☎ *312-943-5151, 1030 N Clark St*) This 60,000-sq-foot drinking, dining and entertainment bazaar is a playground for young single guys with too much disposable income and few obligations. The Chicago branch of this national chain features a sports bar, bowling, pool, shuffleboard, electronic golf, 3-D interactive games and a whole lot more.

Gibson's (☎ *312-266-8999, 1028 N Rush St*) See the Places to Eat chapter for all the details on the lively bar here.

The Lodge (☎ *312-642-4406, 21 W Division St*) A survivor of the days when this bit of Division St was one big singles bar, the Lodge is beloved by thirty-, forty- and fiftysomethings with failed marriages, failed social lives or both.

Whisky Bar (☎ *312-266-2100, Sutton Place Hotel, 21 E Bellevue Place*) This Chicago hotel bar has become inexplicably popular with models – of both sexes. The bar is minimalist and stylish, and the patrons (who only show up after 10pm) are, too.

Beer Riots

Chicago has always had a taste for beer. The roots of this passion go all the way back to the beer riots of 1855. Back in the 19th century a group of xenophobes from the appropriately named Know-Nothing political party tried to stanch the flow of German and Irish immigrants into the city by banning beer sales on Sunday and raising license fees to a then-outrageous $300 per year. These rules, however, did not apply to saloons that sold the more expensive whiskey, the drink of choice for the Know-Nothings.

Riots broke out as Germans from the North Side and Irish from the South Side made their anger and beverage preferences known. Mobs roamed the city, fighting with the police and 'liberating' kegs from bars. The two ethnic groups discovered a long-term solution to the problem when they registered to vote en masse and seized control of City Hall for the next 120 years.

Old Town (Map 6)

Marge's (☎ *312-944-9775, 1758 N Sedgwick St*) A typical neighborhood bar, Marge's is a friendly corner pub that has survived unscathed the ravages of the neighborhood's rapid climb up the property value ladder.

Olde Town Ale House (☎ *312-944-7020, 219 W North Ave*) One of my favorite bars, the Ale House caters to winners, losers and everyone in between. A neighborhood staple from the days before this was a neighborhood, it has been the scene of delusionary late-night musings since the 1960s – the last time paint was applied. Grab a front-window table and settle in for a few hours but never before 11pm. To complete the scene, drop a quarter into the jukebox for Nat King Cole's 'Too Young.'

Weed's (☎ *312-943-7815, 1555 N Dayton St*) The bras hanging from the ceiling like animal pelts set the tone at this bar where beatnik meets bohemia. The tables sport candles in old wine bottles, and anarchist or profane slogans cover the bathroom walls.

ENTERTAINMENT

Owner Sergio Mayora – whose name has motivated him to run most unsuccessfully for mayor – keeps spirits loose with frequent shots of tequila on the house.

Lincoln Park (Map 6)

It's hard to find a really bad bar in this neighborhood. They all got chased away by picky residents.

Goose Island Brewery (☎ 773-915-0071, *1800 N Clybourn Ave*) This original brewpub spawned the Goose Island empire. The six or so beers on tap change by the season. You can wash them down with the acceptable pub grub, then head for the pool tables or watch a game on one of the many TVs. The outdoor area is a must in summer.

Kelly's (☎ 773-281-0656, *949 W Webster Ave*) DePaul students and fans gather at this classic Chicago bar right under the El – hold onto your glass when a train goes by. Since 1933 the same family has been welcoming all comers with tasty burgers and booze.

Kincade's (☎ 773-348-0010, *950 W Armitage Ave*) A true singles bar for people in their 20s (although any bar can be a singles bar if you have personality), Kincade's is filled with people looking over your shoulder as they talk to you, in case somebody more appealing walks in the door.

Louie on the Park (☎ *312-337-9800, 1800 N Wells St*) Stop in at this branch of the Bar Louie chain if you need some reviving after a brisk walk in Lincoln Park.

Lush (☎ *773-871-8123, 948 W Armitage Ave*) This dark joint that's almost under the El tracks is exactly what it looks like: an unadorned, youthful pub.

McGee's (☎ *773-871-4272, 950 W Webster Ave*) Another DePaul bar in the heart of Lincoln Park, this lively place attracts undergrads and recent grads alike. Stop here if you're feeling nostalgic for your college days.

Red Rooster Cafe & Wine Bar (☎ *773-871-2100, 2100 N Halsted St*) Connected to Cafe Bernard (see the Places to Eat chapter), this funky little wine bar makes a great stop before or after meals or the theater. Choose among oodles of wines by the glass.

Lincoln Ave Starting at Armitage, you can head north on Lincoln through Wrightwood Ave, hopping from pub to pub if your constitution holds out.

Several bars in the 2200 block of Lincoln are similar to one another: lots of old wood, plenty of beer and hygienic standards that fall short of strict. On Friday the after-work yuppie crowd jams these spots, which include

Cheezburger! Cheezburger!

Only the dimmest of rubes tries to order fries at the ***Billy Goat Tavern*** (☎ *312-222-1525, lower level of 430 N Michigan Ave; Map 3)*, a cathedral of grease, smoke and rousing conversations that also qualifies as a tourist attraction. John Belushi brought national fame to this place with his skit on *Saturday Night Live*. Among the memorable lines: 'No fries – chips!' and 'No Coke – Pepsi!'

Local fame stems from its subterranean position between the *Sun-Times* and *Tribune*. Legions of photos of dead writers and columnists line the walls; any link between their demises and a steady diet of beer, burgers and cigarettes must be coincidental. Some of the legendary patrons have included Mike Royko. On weekdays a few families attired in Cubs clothing sometimes visit, but they're soon chased away by the after-work hordes of drunken journalists, carousing ad execs and no-nonsense laborers. It warms the heart to see a suburban family cowering next to some beer-swilling, smoke-blowing galoot. But beware: the tourists get their revenge on the weekends, when they own the place. Prices are dirt cheap, but if you like your burger to have the distinctive taste of meat, order a double. Note: when I'm in town, you can find me on Friday after work at the corner table on the far left as you enter.

ENTERTAINMENT

Kelsey's (☎ *773-348-1666, 2265 Lincoln Ave*), **Waterloo** (☎ *773-929-1300, 2270 Lincoln Ave*) and **Jerry's** (☎ *773-929-8188, 2274 Lincoln Ave*).

Sterch's (☎ *773-281-2653, 2238 N Lincoln Ave*) A genial older crowd of writers and would-be poets hangs out at this convivial bar where there's never a shortage of conversation, some of it even sensible. If you're lucky, you'll visit on 'bag night' and find out for yourself what that means.

John Barleycorn Memorial Pub (☎ *773-348-8899, 658 W Belden Ave at Lincoln Ave*) See the Places to Eat chapter for all the details of this timeless charmer.

Red Lion Pub (☎ *773-348-2695, 2446 N Lincoln Ave*) A British-style pub run by real Brits, this cozy spot features plenty of UK brews and the best onion rings in the city ($4). Definitely better than Spotted Dick.

Gin Mill (☎ *773-549-3232, 2462 N Lincoln Ave*) The slogan here is: 'We drink our share and sell the rest.' They're very friendly about it, too, with remarkable $2-pint specials on microbrews some nights.

Lucille's (☎ *773-929-0660, 2470 N Lincoln Ave*) A rarity: the food is as good as the music (classic rock, some of it live). Instead of stale pretzels and day-old popcorn, how do munchies like bruschetta and prosciutto sound? The alcoholic offerings include an excellent selection of wines by the glass.

Deja Vu (☎ *773-871-0205, 2624 N Lincoln Ave*) A lively 4am bar, the Vu sometimes books bands but at the very least makes sure that good rock is belting from the sound system.

Lake View & Wrigleyville (Map 7)

There's a bar for every taste in these popular neighborhoods. See the Gay & Lesbian Venues section for listings of the many gay bars along Halsted St and elsewhere. In Wrigleyville, Clark St north of Belmont Ave is chock-a-block with bars. Many come and go with passing fancy. Start at one end of the strip and work your way to the other. See the boxed text 'Chicago As Theme Park' in the Places to Eat chapter for several places not listed in this section.

Duke of Perth (☎ *773-477-1741, 2913 N Clark St*) See the Places to Eat chapter for all the details about this excellent pub and beer garden.

Pops for Champagne (☎ *773-472-1000, 2934 N Sheffield Ave*) This refined and classy place makes a perfect spot for a post-theater drink, a celebratory toast or a romantic tête-à-tête. You can choose among 12 champagnes by the glass, 140 more by the bottle and scores of excellent wines as well. The snacks are suitably chichi – pâté and the like – and Pops features live jazz some nights.

Cullen's (☎ *773-975-0600, 3741 N Southport Ave*) See the Places to Eat chapter for the details on this fine tavern that's connected to the Mercury Theatre.

Ginger Man (☎ *773-549-2050, 3740 N Clark St*) A splendid place to pass an evening, this spot features a huge and eclectic beer selection that's enjoyed by theater types and other creative folks. The G-Man, as it is often called, avoids the overamped Cubs mania of the rest of the strip by playing classical music when the Cubs play at home. There are numerous pool tables in back.

Guthrie's (☎ *773-477-2900, 1300 W Addison St*) A local institution and the perfect neighborhood hangout, Guthrie's remains true to its mellow roots even as the neighborhood goes manic around it. The glassed-in back porch is fittingly furnished with patio chairs. Most tables sport a box of Trivial Pursuit cards.

Southport Lanes (☎ *773-472-6600, 3325 N Southport Ave*) This old-fashioned local bar with a good beer selection has undergone a renaissance under the thoughtful management of some upscale types, who oversee the bar itself and an annex with four hand-set bowling lanes. The main bar features an inspirational old mural of cavorting nymphs. Lots of tables populate the sidewalk in summer.

Yak-zies (☎ *773-525-9200, 3710 N Clark St*) Relive college here with lots of young people wearing sweats and working quickly through pitchers of beer. The TVs show plenty of college sports action, while the frat crowd digs into plates of the popular Buffalo wings and unique parsley-crust pizza.

ENTERTAINMENT

Andersonville (Map 8)

Hop Leaf (☎ 773-334-9851, 5148 N Clark St) Owner Michael Roper has created one of Chicago's best bars using the name of the national beer from his ancestral Malta. Highlights here include an intricate original tin ceiling and a good selection of wines. The beers are artfully selected by Roper, with an emphasis on American, Belgian and German brews.

Simon's (☎ 773-878-0894, 5210 N Clark St) Artsy folk, people who wear only black clothes and creative types who have sold out to ad agencies have replaced the old Swedes at this old neighborhood tavern. The long bar is right out of the '50s, long before the twentysomething patrons saw daylight. Former owner Simon Lundberg installed the portholes in the facade to remind him of the ship that carried him to America from Sweden.

Wicker Park & Bucktown (Map 9)

Funky and relaxed bars litter these two neighborhoods.

The Charleston (☎ 773-489-4757, 2076 N Hoyne Ave) The resident cats will curl up on your lap at this thoroughly laid-back Bucktown hangout.

Danny's (☎ 773-489-6457, 1951 W Dickens Ave) This old house has been converted into a funhouse. Tables, chairs and old sofas litter the many rooms on the many floors. People feel so much at home they forget where their own is.

Holiday Club (☎ 773-486-0686, 1471 N Milwaukee Ave) You'll find a little bit of everything, including attitude, here: live music, sidewalk tables and enough kitschy crap from the '50s to stock a bad thrift shop.

Lemmings (☎ 773-862-1688, 1850 N Damen Ave) This mellow bar features a pool table, pinball machine, good beers on tap and a sign in the window telling local artists how they can get their work displayed in the bar. Keep an eye out for the archaic Schlitz sign.

Mad Bar (☎ 773-227-2277, 1640 N Damen Ave) Part club, part neighborhood hangout, Mad Bar packs 'em in most nights, thanks to good drinks and even better sound. Though it's not enormous, tables and chairs abound, many of them full of friends who come here to engage in the old pastimes of drinking and dancing.

Map Room (☎ 773-252-7636, 1949 N Hoyne Ave) Drink locally and think globally at this friendly corner bar where globes line the walls and a huge map of the world covers the back wall and ceiling. Gaze at the map from the overstuffed furniture and try to find some place Lonely Planet doesn't cover. The Map Room features lots of local brews and games for whiling away cold winter days.

Nick's (☎ 312-252-1155, 1516 N Milwaukee Ave) Free of attitude and blessed with friendliness, this big joint offers good beer and good conversation. If the roar of the El excites you, hop out to the beer garden in back.

Quenchers (☎ 773-276-9730, Fullerton Ave at Western Ave) At the north end of Bucktown, Quenchers is one of my favorite bars. With over 200 beers from more than 40 nations, it offers ample opportunities to find that certain something missing from the swill peddled by the US brewery giants: flavor. Locals, artisans, laborers and visiting brew masters enjoy Earle Miller's hospitality. The prices are the cheapest in town.

West Side (Map 10)

Cleo's (☎ *312-243-5600, 1935 W Chicago Ave)* See the Places to Eat chapter for all the details on this bar and café.

Hawkeye's (☎ *312-226-3951, 1458 W Taylor St)* This Little Italy institution is popular with locals and Blackhawks fans who stop by after the game. Its virtues include a good burger-based menu and fine seasonal tables outside.

Mirai Sushi (☎ *773-862-8500, 2020 W Division St)* This stylish and trendy bar and café does for sake what wine bars did for vino two decades ago. The Japanese rice wine comes in myriad forms. Try the vast variety and cushion your tasting with some prime raw fish.

Tuman's Alcohol Abuse Center (*2201 W Chicago Ave)* The lack of a phone at this Ukrainian Village place dates from the days when this bar was filled with folks who didn't want to be tracked down. Nowadays this barely retro old spot attracts everyone from frustrated artists to bike messengers trying to drown their annoyance at those damn pedestrians who clog up the sidewalks. The abuse of alcohol is encouraged by the cheap prices: a pint of Guinness is $2.50.

South Side (Map 11)

Puffer's (☎ *773-927-6073, 3356 S Halsted St)* A cool pub in staid old Bridgeport, Puffer's boasts a bright orange facade and the neighborhood's most amiable clientele, with folks hanging out, talking and sampling from the excellent beer selection. A good choice after a Sox game, it's a 15-minute walk west from Comiskey Park.

Gerri's Palm Tavern (☎ *773-373-6292, 446 E 47th St)* Since 1933 this Kenwood neighborhood classic has entertained the likes of Joe Lewis, Langston Hughes and other notable African Americans. Photos of many of them hang on the walls. Gerri's hosts occasional live jazz, blues and poetry readings.

Hyde Park (Map 12)

Jimmy's Woodlawn Tap (☎ *773-643-5516, 1172 E 55th St)* 'Why?' It's a question I wrote thousands of words about on my college philosophy final, and it's a question eternally debated here. U of C types debate even weightier questions in this intellect-rich but bar-poor neighborhood.

DANCE CLUBS

Chicago clubs range from hip, snooty places where admittance is at the whim of some dullard at the door to casual joints where all you do is dance.

Cover charges vary widely depending on the venue or the day of the week. They can be as much as $20 or as little as nothing at all. Your best bet is to call and find out what the charge will be on the night you'd like to go. Most of the places below are open until 4am weekdays and 5am Saturday night.

Near North (Map 3)

Excalibur (☎ *312-266-1944, 632 N Dearborn St)* Despite its elegant exterior (the building once housed the Chicago Historical Society), Excalibur is really the strip mall of clubs. On one dance floor DJs spin classics that would do any wedding reception proud. In a soaring space by the door called 'the Dome Room,' you can hear edgier rock bands more often found in Wicker Park. Other areas in this three-floor funhouse include jukeboxes, electronic games, pool and more. The touristy and suburban crowd loves every minute.

Pasha (☎ *312-397-0100, 642 N Clark St)* See the Places to Eat chapter for details on this club where there's dancing most nights.

Voyeur (☎ *312-832-1717, 151 W Ohio St)* The shtick here is just what the name implies: clubgoers enjoy all manner of ways of spying on each other. Those using the bathrooms might be so entertained (or repelled) by what they see on monitors from the other sex's facilities that they'll forget why they went. The decor is sort of industrial bare. The music revolves around house, which is aimed at the River North masses.

Lincoln Park (Map 6)

Crobar (☎ *312-413-7000, 1543 N Kingsbury St)* The postindustrial music matches the neighborhood at this huge club, whose cavernous interior is a stylish mix of materials intercepted on their way to the metal recycler. The crowd consists of yuppies gone punk for the night and punks who will never go yuppie. On many nights tattoo artists are on call for emergency skin art.

Exit (☎ *773-395-2700, 1315 W North Ave)* Despite the name, there are few exits from the caged dance floor at this punk club where you'll want to be wearing leather for self-protection if nothing else.

Katacomb (☎ *312-337-4040, 1916 N Lincoln Park West)* This underground bar looks like what the name implies. DJs spin hip-hop, funk and trip-hop. It's open until 4am nightly.

Neo (☎ *773-528-2622, 2350 N Clark St)* This crusty veteran (and we're not talking about the bartender) dates from the time that Lincoln Park was the city's hottest neighborhood. Though the streets have gone quiet and upscale, this gritty dance club holds its own, having long since shed its trendy attitude.

Paparazzi (☎ *312-335-0081, 826 W Blackhawk St)* This hidden champagne bar barely has a neighborhood and definitely doesn't have a sign. Everything feels illicit about the place except for the DJs, who are explicitly cool.

Lake View & Wrigleyville (Map 7)

Berlin (☎ *773-348-4975, 954 W Belmont Ave)* Feeling lost, lonely, antisocial? Berlin caters to virtually everyone. The crowd is as mixed as the music, so you're bound to find a friend. Funky and bizarre videos alternate with MTV tracks on the scores of TV screens.

Club Eden (☎ *773-327-4646, 3407 N Clark St)* This big club features DJs spinning on two levels. Most nights it's hip-hop and soul, with the odd salsa night tossed in.

Wicker Park & Bucktown (Map 9)

Red Dog Supreme Funk Parlor (☎ *773-278-1009, 1958 W North Ave at Damen Ave)* Some of the hottest DJs in town work weekends and Monday in this kitschy old warehouse, which pulses with funk, hip-hop and house. The lively crowd is as mixed as you can get sexually and ethnically.

Sinibar (☎ *773-278-7797, 1540 N Milwaukee Ave)* See the Places to Eat chapter for all the details on this restaurant and club where DJs spin a range of music from funk to reggae to house.

Subterranean (☎ *773-278-6600, 2011 W North Ave)* DJs spin hip-hop and other styles to a way-stylish crowd at this place, which looks slick inside and out. The cabaret room upstairs draws some inventive singers whose styles defy immediate categorization.

West Side (Map 10)

Nocturnal (☎ *312-491-1931, 1111 W Lake St)* Rich guys and gals get VIP service at this exclusive and small club right by the El. The music is alternative and trance, the perfect background noise as you settle into one of the VIP booths.

rednofive (☎ *312-733-6699, 440 N Halsted St)* The DJs play house, acid jazz, funk and more at this cross between a bare-bones rock club and a salsa dance club.

Slick's Lounge (☎ *312-932-0006, 1115 N North Branch St)* This super-hip dance club caters to upscale African Americans. The DJs spin house, soul, hip-hop, acid jazz and more; all the music reverberates off the nearby waters of the north branch of the Chicago River.

Elsewhere in Chicago

Cotton Club (☎ *312-341-9787, 1710 S Michigan Ave; Map 4)* A dose of funk mixes with jazz and lounge music at this swank place near the South Side. The patrons tend to dress sharply to match the elegant surroundings. Some nights you can catch good live jazz at the piano bar out front.

Pump Room (☎ *312-266-0360, Ambassador East hotel, 1301 N State St; Map 5)* A certain timelessness prevails at this Gold Coast classic, where jazz and dance trios and vocalists provide slow-dance swing every night. The black they insist you wear here should be formal, not grunge. See the Places to Eat chapter for details on the exquisite food.

GAY & LESBIAN VENUES

Halsted St north of Belmont Ave in Lake View is the heart of Chicago's vibrant gay neighborhood, although you can find venues elsewhere in the city as well.

Lake View (Map 7)

Bucks (☎ 773-525-1125, 3439 N Halsted St) Scoping is the pastime here. But if you feel a pair of eyes on you in this relaxed bar, it may actually be the stuffed deer looking down from the wall.

Closet (☎ 773-477-8533, 3325 N Broadway) This fun and lively bar attracts a gay and lesbian crowd. The videos may leave you transfixed or otherwise stirred.

Cocktail (☎ 773-477-1420, 3359 N Halsted St) This classic corner tavern attracts a merry crowd.

Gentry (☎ 773-348-1053, 3320 N Halsted St) Local acting sensation and diva Alexandra Billings gives regular Sunday night performances here.

Manhole (☎ 773-975-9244, 3458 N Halsted St) It's as hardcore as you can get at this gay club where the porn films on the TVs are mere precursors of things to come. DJs spin dance tunes with a heavy dose of disco every night but Tuesday.

Roscoes (☎ 773-281-3355, 3354 N Halsted St) This is the kind of gay bar you could take your straight brother to. A very friendly corner pub, Roscoes features a tasty menu, a beer garden and dancing.

Sidetrack (☎ 773-477-9189, 3349 N Halsted St) This expansive, elegant club has a lovely shaded area out front. In summer you'll love it; in winter you'll wish you and Sidetrack were someplace warm.

Elsewhere in Chicago

The Baton (☎ 312-644-5269, 436 N Clark St; Map 3) The boobs are as fake as the big hair at this legendary venue for female impersonators. Three shows happen nightly, and the cost is quite reasonable: $10 per person plus two drinks.

Gentry (☎ 312-836-0933, 440 N State St; Map 3) A brethren of the Gentry on Halsted St, this bar for older and richer gay men fea-

tures a good wine list, fireplace and nightly piano music.

Madrigal's (☎ 773-334-3033, 5316 N Clark St; Map 8) This Andersonville bar caters to both gays and lesbians, drawing in customers with a good menu of snacks and a fine beer garden out back.

SPECTATOR SPORTS

Chicagoans are deeply loyal to their sports teams, despite the teams' mixed results in competition. Attending a game is a real part of life in the city. Each of the teams, their stadiums and their fans has a unique tradition that enriches the experience. Don't miss the chance to take part.

Baseball

Winning is not a tradition in Chicago baseball. The Cubs last won the World Series in 1908, the Sox in 1917. The Sox tend to have a better record, but it's still nothing that will prompt you to reserve postseason tickets. Regardless, local baseball enjoys a big following thanks to the teams' longevity in town. Traditionally, Cubs and Sox fans engage in a great rivalry, but in reality it tends to be rather one-sided: when the Sox lose, the mellow Cubs fans shrug their shoulders, but when the Cubs lose, the grittier Sox fans, on the South Side, are jubilant.

Both teams' stadiums are easily accessible via the El, an excellent way to avoid extortionist parking fees, long traffic jams and concerns over beer consumption and driving. At both places buy your peanuts from the vendors outside the park; they're much cheaper. The baseball season runs from early April, when both stadiums can be very cold, to early October.

Chicago Cubs (☎ 773-404-2827, www .cubs.com, Wrigley Field, 1060 W Addison St; Map 7) The Cubs defy logic: they are a losing team playing in an old stadium with one of the best attendance records in baseball. The Cubs have been dropping games at the corner of Addison and Clark for more than 80 years, while filling their stadium and the neighborhood with fans.

RAY HILLSTROM JR

The friendly confines of Wrigley Field

ENTERTAINMENT

Much of the team's charm comes from intangibles such as the famous ivy that covers the outfield wall. Outfielders fear running into its hard, gnarled branches, but who can argue with this gorgeous greenery? Planted in 1937 under the orders of chewing gum baron and team owner Philip K Wrigley, the ivy is but one of his legacies. The other is losing. Wrigley never made it a secret that he wanted Wrigley Field to be a nice place to watch a game. He didn't care if the team lost – a tradition its present owner, the Tribune Company, has had little luck reversing.

With little to celebrate on the field, fans have instead celebrated the field itself. Known as 'the friendly confines,' Wrigley Field dates from 1916. Although often changed through the years, it retains its historic charm and remains the smallest and most intimate field in Major League Baseball. Popular new stadiums in other cities, such as Baltimore and Denver, have borrowed heavily from its charm.

Few experiences in Chicago can equal an afternoon at Wrigley: the clatter of the El, the closeness of the seats, the spectators on the rooftops, the derisive return of the opposing team's home run balls, the often-friendly folks around you and, yes, the green leaves of the ivy glistening in the sun. Whether it's riding the El to the Addison stop, grabbing a pre-game beer on the patio at Bernie's (see the boxed text 'Bar Stools & Ball Games') or going a little nuts in the bleachers, each Cubs fan has his or her own rituals that make a day at Wrigley not a spectator sport but an almost religious experience.

Because of the good attendance, Cubs tickets can be hard to find for night games and on Fridays, weekends and holidays. Scalping is illegal, and you'll feel like you're doing a drug deal if you try to buy tickets on the street.

Wrigley Field is one block west of the Addison El stop on the CTA Red Line. Parking stinks (it's mostly reserved for neighborhood residents with permits), so take the El or walk.

Chicago White Sox (☎ 312-674-1000, www.chisox.com, Comiskey Park, 333 W 35th St; Map 11) Timing is everything, and the Sox's timing sucks. By threatening to move to Florida in 1990, the team extorted a new stadium out of the state. Unfortunately, that happened right before the Baltimore Orioles moved into their own park, which is a re-creation and celebration of the stadiums of old (in fact, it's a lot like Wrigley Field). So the Sox now have the misfortune of playing in Comiskey Park, a 1991 big bowl with the dubious honor of being the last of the antiseptic stadiums to be built. The old Comiskey Park was rough around the edges, but it was a memorable place to see a game.

The team itself labors under one of the least popular owners in baseball, Jerry Reinsdorf (who also owns the Bulls), a perplexing man who makes no effort to win any popularity contests. His legendary cheapness means that he regularly trades away popular players who might ask for a raise. The 2000 season was a classic by cynical Chicago sports standards: the Sox had the best record in baseball right into the first round of the playoffs, when they promptly lost all their games.

As is the case with many ballparks, the best reason to go to Comiskey is the fans. They love the team despite the stadium and owner, and they direct many creatively profane slogans toward the latter. And the

Bar Stools & Ball Games

A great Chicago tradition takes place after nearly every baseball game: dissecting the team's latest loss while nursing beers at a corner tavern. The following two bars attract downtrodden crowds from the nearby stadiums and boast a diehard clientele of fans who pronounce their 'th's' like d's, as in 'da Cubs' and 'da Sox.'

Bernie's Tavern (☎ 773-525-1898, 3664 N Clark St; Map 6) This Wrigleyville stalwart doesn't jack up its prices on game days to fleece unsuspecting fans, as the many upscale joints in the neighborhood do. The side yard filled with cheap patio furniture is one of the nicest places before, during and after a Cubs game.

Jimbo's (☎ 312-326-3253, 3258 S Princeton Ave; Map 11) In the far shadow of Comisky Park, Jimbo's is as unimpressive outside as it is inside. But its charm lies in its crowd: people who prefer their beer out of cans, since bottles are for special occasions like weddings and funerals. For an advanced lesson in profanity, ask them what they think of the Sox's owners.

food isn't bad either – the tasty burritos for sale on the mall-like concourse are only part of a long list of good and greasy choices. Finally, there's the fireworks – if the Sox hit a home run at night, plumes of color shoot into the air.

Tickets are pretty easy to come by, although it's still worth calling ahead to make certain they're available. Whatever you do, don't buy seats in the infamous 'nosebleed' upper deck, where the sharply inclined aisles are best scaled with rope and piton.

The stadium is a short walk from the Sox-35th Station on the CTA Red Line and the 35th-Bronzeville-IIT Station on the CTA Green Line. The slightly suspect neighborhood is safe on game days, when it's flooded with cops. Since the city tore down several blocks for the new stadium, parking is plentiful.

ENTERTAINMENT

Basketball

Chicago Bulls *(☎ 312-559-1212, www.nba
.com/bulls, United Center, 1901 W Madison
St; Map 10)* Try to remember when the Bulls
won a game, and you have to reach back to
the 1997–98 season, when Michael Jordan
was still with the team. Since then the Bulls
have stunk. The bonehead owner Jerry
Reinsdorf allowed Jordan, coach Phil
Jackson, Scottie Pippin and other key parts
of the Bulls juggernaut to leave after that
championship year. His bonehead buddy,
general manager Jerry Krause, had always
said that it was his managerial prowess that
led to the six championships. Well, under
Reinsdorf's ownership and Krause's inspired management, the Bulls have been
the worst team in the NBA since 1998.
Prospects don't look good any time soon.

The Bulls play on the West Side in the
huge United Center, which replaced the
beloved Chicago Stadium in 1995. To com-
pensate for the bad results on the court, the
Bulls resort to an indoor blimp, lasers, floor
games and more to keep the crowd engaged
during the interminable timeouts for TV
commercials.

The CTA runs special buses to the games,
mostly from the Loop; call the information
line ☎ 836-7000, preceded by the area code
of the area of town you're in (312, 708, 847,
630 or 773) for information. Cab rides are
cheap from the Loop and Near North – $4
to $5 – and parking is plentiful. The neigh-
borhood is improving but still not really safe
enough to do much walking, so don't stray
far from the United Center. The basketball
season runs from September to May.

Football

Chicago Bears *(☎ 312-559-1212, www
.chicagobears.com, Soldier Field, 425 E
McFetridge Dr at S Lake Shore Dr; Map 4)*
Once upon a time the Chicago Bears were
one of the most revered franchises in the National Football League. Owner and coach
George Halas epitomized the team's no-
nonsense, take-no-prisoners approach.

The tradition continued with players
such as Walter Payton, Dick Butkus and
Mike Singleterry and coach Mike Ditka. In
1986 the Bears won the Super Bowl with a
splendid collection of misfits and characters, such as Jim McMahon and William

The Bulls take to the court at the United Center.

Air Jordan

Day in and day out, Chicagoans need to bless Michael Jordan not only for supplanting Al Capone as the most famous Windy City resident worldwide but also for finally giving at least one of the professional sports teams a winning tradition.

In 1984 Jordan arrived in Chicago from his home state of North Carolina, a mostly ignored draft pick for the Bulls. He couldn't even find the ride that had supposedly been sent to O'Hare to pick him up, and he ended up arranging his own.

As his skills perked up the previously somnolent play of the Bulls, his local reputation grew. In the 1986–87 season the 6-foot, 6-inch Jordan lead the National Basketball Association in scoring for the first of eight times through 1996. In 1988 he was named the NBA's most valuable player for the first of four times through 1996.

His local celebrity exploded nationally in 1991, when he led the Bulls to the first of three successive championships. His affable demeanor combined well with his sheer determination on the court. Advertising and movie contracts have followed, most notably his huge deal for athletic wear with Nike.

Unlike some other sports figures, Jordan kept his private life private, although public tragedy struck in 1993, when his father, James, was murdered. Jordan's interest in basketball waned, and he shocked the town by announcing his retirement and undertaking a professional baseball career with a minor league team connected to the Chicago White Sox.

The little white ball proved entirely different from the big orange one, however. After 18 months of lackluster performance Jordan returned to the Bulls, who had gone adrift in his absence, not even coming close to the championship in the 1993–94 season.

Near the end of the 1994–95 season an electrifying rumor swept the city: Jordan wanted to come back to the Bulls. If any Chicagoans doubted how deeply Jordan had entrenched himself in the city's psyche, they must have been convinced by the crowd that spontaneously blocked off the street in front of his agent's office, hoping for word of his return.

He did return, playing the remaining 17 games of the season. It was too late to lift the Bulls to the championship that year, but no one cared. The next three seasons, 1995–96, 1996–97 and 1997–98, Jordan led the Bulls to an amazing three more championships. After the last championship, Jordan retired, which sent Chicago into a collective funk that persists to this day. During his retirement Jordan has gotten involved in managing the NBA Washington Wizards. The Bulls, meanwhile, have posted some of the worst records of any NBA team ever.

ENTERTAINMENT

RAY HILLSTROM JR

Chicagoans turn out in full force for sporting events.

'the Refrigerator' Perry, who enthralled and charmed the entire city.

As they say, that was then and this is now. Over 15 years of mediocrity have taxed all but the most loyal fan's allegiance. Tickets, once a hot commodity, now sell for just a little cold cash. But Chicagoans still cling to that 1985–86 season, as Ditka maintains his hold over the Chicago psyche. Though he's gone many other places since leaving the Bears, fans still long for his return. In response to the popular demand, he's opened restaurants bearing his name and collected the fans' cash in his absence.

Despite the team's lack of wins on the field, the Bears have won in the Illinois state legislature. Late in 2000 legislators unveiled a nearly $600-million deal to transform Soldier Field into a modern stadium with lots of extra-cost seating. The new place should open in 2003 and will thankfully still be open-air. Oh, and who's picking up the bill? You! A large portion of this money will come from the various taxes Chicago slaps on hotel rooms, restaurant meals and rental cars.

Soldier Field is a nice autumn-day walk and a really miserable winter-day forced march. Metra trains from Randolph St Station stop at nearby 12th St Station ($1.75), and the Roosevelt Road El stops

are a half-mile stroll away. The greatest joy for Bears fans of late has been their elaborate tailgate feasts in the parking lots before the games. The football season runs from August to December, when you can get snowed on while you watch.

Hockey

Chicago Blackhawks (☎ 312-455-7000, www.chiblackhawks.com, United Center, 1901 W Madison St; Map 10) Almost every year, the Chicago Blackhawks make the National Hockey League playoffs. Of course, in the NHL, almost every team can make the same boast. The Stanley Cup last came to Chicago in 1961, but the Hawks win enough games every year to keep their rabid fans frothing at the mouth.

The fans' fervor is a show in itself, though it never quite reaches the bloodletting antics of the players on the ice. Games against the Detroit Redwings and the New York Rangers call for extra amounts of screaming, and the crowd always seems to come with bottomless reserves of lung power. The action starts with the traditional singing of the national anthem, which here becomes a crowd performance of raw emotion.

Hawks tickets are often sold out, but brokers and concierges can usually obtain them for a minimal markup. Transportation and parking information is the same as for the Bulls (see Basketball, earlier). The hockey season runs October to April.

Soccer

Chicago Fire (☎ 312-705-7200, www. chicago-fire.com, Soldier Field, 425 E McFetridge Dr at S Lake Shore Dr; Map 4) The Fire have been attracting a growing fan base in Chicago thanks to the fact that they're not bad. The team has made Major League Soccer playoffs a few tin. in recent years and won the championship in 1998. And the many people living in Chicago who originally came from countries where soccer is *the* national sport boost ticket sales greatly.

The Fire play at Soldier Field. Transportation information is the same as that for the Bears (see Football, earlier). The soccer season runs from April to September.

Y

Needless to say, you can buy anything you want in Chicago, and lots more things you didn't think you wanted but have to have once you've seen them. You'll have your pick of a wide range of items, from the standard mugs and T-shirts to handmade jewelry and unusual antiques.

Antiques

Chicago is a magnet for the best antiques and collectibles between the two coasts. Serious shoppers can easily make a week of it. Casual collectors or browsers will enjoy

the many antique malls that bring scores of dealers together under one roof. You will find clusters of them in the blocks around the Merchandise Mart and Kinzie St in River North, along the stretch of Lincoln Ave north from Diversey Parkway to Irving Park Rd and along Belmont Ave west from Ashland Ave to Western Ave. Cruising that last strip is like driving along a country road laced with antique stores without ever leaving the city.

The standard advice to call and check business hours before venturing out is doubly important when it comes to antique malls, whose hours can be as quirky as the dealers themselves.

Antiquarians Building *(☎ 312-527-0533, 159 W Kinzie St; Map 3)* Look for rare items from five continents in 22 shops.

Antiques Centre at Kinzie Square *(☎ 312-464-1946, 220 W Kinzie St; Map 3)* Twenty dealers peddle high-end pieces from the 18th and 19th centuries here.

Jay Robert's Antique Warehouse *(☎ 312-222-0167, 149 W Kinzie St; Map 3)* This vast place boasts more than 60,000 square feet of furniture and clocks.

Rita Bucheit Ltd *(☎ 312-527-4080, 449 N Wells St; Map 3)* One of my favorites, this dark and classy store specializes in Vienna Secession and art deco works.

Chicago Antique Mall *(☎ 773-252-6900, 1934 W North Ave; Map 9)* More than 30 dealers offer goods that range from curios to clocks to couches at this large warehouse.

Books

The following are just a few of the hundreds of bookstores found in the city. Check the Yellow Pages for complete listings of special-interest stores for everything from religion to socialism.

The Magnificent Mile: a premier shopping area

ANN CECIL

General *Brent Books & Cards (☎ 312-363-0126, 309 W Washington St; Map 3)* This busy store has good business, art and travel sections.

Marshall Field's (☎ 312-781-4284, 111 N State St; Map 3) Tucked away in the basement of the State St store is an excellent all-around book department. Besides the selection, its absolute best feature is the staff: these people have been working in the department for decades. They know their selections inside and out and offer wonderful suggestions.

Sandmeyer's Bookstore (☎ 312-922-2104, 714 S Dearborn St; Map 4) Suitably located in the heart of Printer's Row, Sandmeyer's holds a special place in my heart, because it's where I bought my books for my first trip to Europe many years ago. Besides a good selection on travel, the family-run store emphasizes fiction and architecture.

Barbara's Bookstore (☎ 312-642-5044, 1350 N Wells St; Map 6) For serious fiction, you can't touch this locally owned store. The staff have read what they sell, and touring authors regularly give readings. There's another location near the entrance to Navy Pier *(☎ 312-222-0890; Map 3)*.

57th Street Books (☎ 773-684-1300, 1301 E 57th St; Map 12) A vast selection of general-interest titles here fills the basements of two buildings. The travel section features a commendable choice of Lonely Planet guides, a table and chairs for careful choosing and a chilled water dispenser to cool the sweaty tourist.

Rand McNally (☎ 312-321-1751, 444 N Michigan Ave) Rand McNally, the map publisher, operates this small travel book and map store. The friendly staff will help you find what you want on the densely packed shelves. In addition to books, you can pick up other travel necessities, like that electrical converter you forgot. See the N Michigan Ave & Oak St Shopping map in this chapter.

The following mass-market bookstores offer the same array of material that they carry in all of their branches throughout the US.

Super Crown (☎ 312-782-7667, 105 S Wabash Ave; Map 3) This discount bookseller carries a little bit of everything, but don't come here for the ambience.

Borders Books & Music (☎ 312-573-0564, 830 N Michigan Ave) This huge Borders, right across from the Water Tower, is always crowded. Thousands of books, spread over four floors in the bright and airy place, include lots of special-interest titles. You'll find a good selection of magazines and newspapers near the main entrance. See the N Michigan Ave & Oak St Shopping map in this chapter for the store's exact location. Borders had also opened a much-needed branch in the Loop *(☎ 312-606-0750, 150 N State St at Randolph St; Map 3)* and a less attractive store in Lake View *(☎ 773-935-3909, 2817 N Clark St; Map 7)*.

Barnes & Noble (☎ 773-871-9004, 659 W Diversey Parkway; Map 6) This bustling location draws crowds every day of the week and has become a prime meeting place for Lincoln Park yuppies. Listen for lines like: 'Do you prefer your books hardback or softback?' echoing down the aisles. There's also a Gold Coast location *(☎ 312-280-8155, 1130 N State St; Map 5)*.

Special Interest *Abraham Lincoln Book Shop (☎ 312-944-3085, 357 W Chicago Ave; Map 3)* In the 'Land of Lincoln' this delightful store is a natural. It carries new, used and antiquarian books about the 16th president, the Civil War and the presidency in general. The knowledgeable staff regularly hold open round-table discussions with Civil War scholars.

Afrocentric Bookstore (☎ 312-939-1956, DePaul Center, 333 S State St; Map 3) 'Seeing the world through an Afrikan point of view' is the slogan at this store, where many big-name black authors give regular readings.

Prairie Avenue Bookshop (☎ 312-922-8311, 418 S Wabash Ave; Map 3) This is easily the classiest and most lavishly decorated bookstore in the city. The beautiful architectural tomes – including many hard-to-find titles – rest on hardwood shelves, and the thick carpet muffles the noise of customers. Soon you'll want to find a smoking jacket, take up pipe smoking and curl up in a corner leather chair.

Savvy Traveller (☎ 312-913-9800, 310 S Michigan Ave; Map 3) The goal here is to carry every travel-related title in print, which means that you'll find plenty of obscure tomes tucked in among the comprehensive selection of Lonely Planet guides. If you can't locate something among the big selection, ask the staffers – who are all travel enthusiasts between vacations – and they'll order it for you. You can also buy gadgets such as electricity converters, luggage and atlases.

US Government Bookstore (☎ 312-353-5133, 401 S State St; Map 3) Here's where you can buy the complete series of the excellent National Park Service publications. Among the other titles – some obviously more popular than others – are *Bankruptcy Basics* ($4) and *A Vision for a New IRS* ($20).

Act 1 (☎ 773-348-6757, 2632 N Lincoln Ave; Map 6) What would a great theater town be without a great bookstore? Act 1 takes its bow in this category with plays, anthologies, works by local authors and a large area devoted to production and the often ignored business end of theater. I particularly like the section devoted to combating stage fright – but why are all those people looking at me?

Chicago Historical Society Store (☎ 312-642-4600, 1601 N Clark St; Map 6) The museum shop boasts an excellent selection of books devoted to local history, many of which are hard to find elsewhere.

Hit the Road (☎ 773-388-8338, 3758 N Southport Ave; Map 7) This little shop is jam-packed with books and stuff related to travel. Not only can you find maps and guides, but the shop also carries a huge selection of road games, novelties and other stuff related to travel.

Women & Children First (☎ 773-769-9299, 5233 N Clark St; Map 8) Much of the selection inside this expanding feminist and children's bookstore is actually fairly mainstream, with an excellent collection of fiction by women authors. Some famous names, such as Sara Paretsky, give readings.

Myopic Books (☎ 773-862-4882, 1468 N Milwaukee Ave; Map 9) An eclectic used book store, Myopic contains large sections for special interests such as lesbian, gay, geek and more.

Not surprisingly, the neighborhood around the University of Chicago boasts several good bookstores, including the following:

O'Gara & Wilson Ltd (☎ 773-363-0993, 1448 E 57th St; Map 12) The tone here is set by the leaded glass in the oaken door. Ladders run on tracks along the walls amid the used and obscure titles, which lean toward American and English literary criticism.

Powell's (☎ 773-955-7780, 1501 E 57th St; Map 12) The leading local used bookstore can get you just about any book ever published – for a price. Another location is near Lake View (☎ 773-248-1444, 2850 N Lincoln Ave; Map 7). Both stores are all very well arranged.

Seminary Cooperative Bookstore (☎ 773-752-1959, 5757 S University Ave; Map 12) This is the bookstore of choice for several University of Chicago Nobel Prize winners, including Robert Fogel, who says, 'For a scholar, it's one of the great bookstores of the world.' The store carries more than 100,000 academic and general titles.

University of Chicago Bookstore (☎ 773-702-7712, 970 E 58th St; Map 12) Gussied up under the management of Barnes & Noble, the campus bookstore still stocks textbooks on everything you can imagine (the color titles in the medical section will put you off smoking, drinking, meat and perhaps even life itself), plus many more titles penned by faculty and students. On the 2nd floor you'll find a souvenir and paraphernalia section.

Newspapers & Magazines Just outside the 24-hour Walgreens pharmacy, a ***24-hour newsstand*** (*southeast corner of N Michigan Ave and E Chicago Ave; Map 3*) offers reading materials that range from the inspirational to the perspirational. You won't find a wider selection anywhere at 4am, when all the morning newspapers start to arrive.

Europa Books (☎ 312-335-9677, 832 N State St; Map 5) As the name promises, this store carries newspapers, magazines and books, primarily in European languages.

Crafts

Illinois Artisans Shop (☎ 312-814-5321, 2nd level, James R Thompson State of Illinois Center, Randolph & Clark Sts; Map 3) One of those rare government bureaucracies that makes you say 'cool' is this small shop run by the Illinois Department of Natural Resources. The best works of artisans throughout the state are sold here, including ceramics, glass, wood, fiber, toys and more, at prices that verge on the cheap. The enthusiastic staff will tell you all about the people who created the pieces; artists are chosen by a twice-yearly jury. The Illinois Art Gallery, immediately next door, sells paintings and sculptures under the same arrangement.

Orca Aart (☎ 312-245-5245, 812 N Franklin St; Map 3) This interesting store sells unusual works in stone, seal hide and other traditional materials by Eskimo, Inuit and other Northwest-coast artisans.

Fine Art

In the 1980s, Chicago's galleries were concentrated in the gallery district of River North. But climbing rents there fragmented the scene. River North still contains a concentration of big-name places, but you can also find scores of galleries in Wicker Park and Bucktown (and even here rents are driving some galleries farther afield). The South and West Loop areas are up and coming, as artists are drawn to enormous warehouses that have been chopped up into very ungentrified lofts.

Openings take place on Friday evening – usually the first Friday of the month – with the first Friday after Labor Day being the start of the season. Galleries hold open receptions on these days, and you can wander around River North drinking more cheap white wine out of plastic cups than health would generally allow.

To try to make sense of the Chicago art scene, which is worth its own book, consult the excellent free *Chicago Gallery News*, which you can usually find near the door of galleries.

River North Gallery District (Map 3)

Perhaps the best way to approach this district is just to wander the blocks along Huron and Superior Sts west from LaSalle

RICK GERHARTER

Chicago's Merchandise Mart, home to retail stores and decorator showrooms

St. The number of galleries in the neighborhood hovers around 60.

Akainyah (☎ 312-654-0333, 357 W Erie St) African-influenced contemporary art is creatively displayed here.

Carol Ehlers Gallery (☎ 312-642-8611, 750 N Orleans St) Vintage and contemporary works by top photographers are the focus.

Douglas Dawson Gallery (☎ 312-751-1961, 222 W Huron St) The namesake owner is an internationally recognized expert in Asian, African and American textile art. You'll always find some prime examples on display.

Jean Albano Gallery (☎ 312-440-0770, 215 W Superior St) The artists featured here create three-dimensional pieces out of unusual materials. The gallery also often shows interesting textile paintings.

Robert Henry Adams Fine Art (☎ 312-642-8700, 715 N Franklin St) This large gallery shows works by pre-WWII 'American impressionist, regionalist and modernist painters.

Zolla-Lieberman Gallery (☎ 312-944-1990, 325 W Huron St) In 1975, when the neighborhood was still a dump, this became the first gallery with acclaimed work for sale. It's noted for nurturing and enriching the careers of many young artists.

Michigan Ave & Around As you'd expect, Michigan Ave and its environs are home to some of the priciest galleries in the city.

Billy Hork Gallery (☎ 312-337-1199, 109 E Oak St) This Oak St veteran displays a wide range of contemporary works. See the N Michigan Ave & Oak St Shopping map in this chapter.

Richard Gray Gallery (☎ 312-642-8877, John Hancock Center, 875 N Michigan Ave, Suite 2503; Map 5) Here you can find works by 20th-century greats from Miró to Nancy Graves.

RS Johnson Fine Art (☎ 312-943-1661, 645 N Michigan Ave, entrance off Erie St) This family-run gallery sells the kinds of works you find in museums – old masters, recently dead masters such as Picasso, and other A-level works – at prices only a museum or a really rich person can afford. But the gallery makes an impressive effort to reach out to the masses through its educational programs. See the N Michigan Ave & Oak St Shopping map in this chapter.

Wally Findly Galleries (☎ 312-649-1500, 188 E Walton St; Map 5) This branch of the international gallery sells pieces from a select range of contemporary American and European artists.

Wicker Park & Bucktown (Map 9) Galleries in this area open and close with a frequency dictated by the terms of one-year leases. This constantly shifting mélange defies easy categorization. However, the following are a couple of good places to start:

The historic *Flat Iron Building* (1579 N Milwaukee Ave) plays host to exhibits by neighborhood artists. You can never be sure what space may have been rented out by whom. The best thing to do is stop by if you're cruising past and see what's up. Check the entrance for fliers for local shows.

Gallery 1633 (☎ 773-384-4441, 1633 N Damen Ave) Local artists who may be in the process of being discovered show their art at this slick little gallery. Many of the paintings are definitely sofa-size.

Jewelry

A number of jewelers practice their craft in The Loop. See the Wabash Ave section under Where to Shop, later in this chapter.

Music

New Recordings For current CDs, you can't beat the prices at Best Buy. See details under Photography & Video in the Facts for the Visitor chapter. The gift shop of the Chicago Symphony Orchestra is an excellent place for classical music; see the Souvenirs section, later.

Rock Records (☎ 312-346-3489, 175 W Washington St; Map 3) This place stocks a huge selection of music by local and offbeat artists.

Tower Records (☎ 773-477-5994, 2301 N Clark St; Map 6) Besides all types of mainstream music, this large store sells books and concert tickets, plus an excellent selection of 'zines and products from the alternative press. There's another Tower location in the Loop (☎ 312-663-0660, 214 S Wabash Ave; Map 3).

Second-Hand Recordings *Jazz Record Mart* (☎ 312-222-1467, 444 N Wabash Ave; Map 3) Musicians, serious jazz and blues aficionados and vintage album collectors flock here. Bob Koester and his dedicated staff can find just about anything, no matter how obscure. This is the place to go to complete your Bix Biederbecke collection.

You'll find a string of second-hand recording shops on a short stretch of N Clark St near Diversey Parkway.

Djangos 2nd Hand Tunes (☎ 773-929-6325, 2602 N Clark St; Map 6) Buy both music and videos in this large store spanning two storefronts.

HiFi Records (☎ 773-880-1002, 2570 N Clark St; Map 6) Another large and varied store, this one carries a plethora of CDs and albums.

Video Beat (☎ 773-871-6667, 2616 N Clark St; Map 6) Choose among a large selection of music videos on tape as well as funky recordings. I was fascinated and horrified by *Ronald Reagan's Favorite Ballads*.

Earwax (☎ 773-772-4019, 1564 N Milwaukee Ave; Map 9) This popular store offers a polyglot selection of music from around the world, experimental stuff and thousands of other CDs that would never make the racks of mainstream places. Exhausted by the choices? Refuel at the café.

Instruments & Sheet Music The 'Music Mart' is the name given to the first few levels of the *DePaul Center* (☎ 312-362-6700, 1 E Jackson Blvd; Map 3). This collection of specialty shops sells obscure CDs, drums, concert pianos, stringed instruments and more.

Carl Fischer (☎ 312-427-6652, DePaul Center, 333 S State St; Map 3) This shop sells sheet music for just about every song ever written. Scores and arrangements for individual instruments, choral groups, bands and orchestras are filed away *someplace* in this old classic, where one employee or another will be able to find even the most obscure request.

Guitar Center (☎ 773-327-5687, 2633 N Halsted St; Map 6) This large store caters to the instrument needs of bands from all over Chicagoland – some of which are actually good.

Chicago Music Exchange (☎ 773-477-0830, 3264 N Clark St; Map 7) This is the place for vintage and classic guitars and other instruments. Watch out for the drool left by garage-band hopefuls.

Outdoor Gear

Uncle Dan's (☎ 773-477-1918, 2440 N Lincoln Ave; Map 6) The smell of leather hits you in the face as you walk into this former army surplus store, which offers a big selection of hiking boots and gear, plus camping supplies and many brands of backpacks. It's a very relaxed place to buy outdoor equipment without the derisive looks of lurking sales dudes who consider anything less than a frontal assault on K-2 to be for wimps.

Active Endeavors (☎ 773-281-8100, 935 W Armitage Ave; Map 6) Prices are high here, but so is the quality. If you need lots of personal help choosing top-end outdoor gear, come here.

Army Navy Surplus USA (☎ 773-348-8930, 3100 N Lincoln Ave; Map 7) The merchandise area here would send a drill sergeant into a conniption. The place is a huge mess. But among the torn boxes and shambles of merchandise are actual military surplus items of the highest quality the taxpayer can afford. I bought some wool socks in designer olive drab for a ludicrously low price, and they still look almost brand new after lots of seasons of keeping my smelly feet warm.

North Face (☎ 312-337-7200, John Hancock Center, 875 N Michigan Ave) This well-known brand operates a large store that peddles the company's first-rate line of backpacks, sleeping bags and other outdoor gear at full retail prices. You can also buy maps, books and doodads. See the N Michigan Ave & Oak St Shopping map in this chapter.

Photography

See the Photography & Video section of the Facts for the Visitor chapter for details on film and camera purchases.

Souvenirs

Cultural Trinkets The following stores sell souvenirs cuts above the generic T-shirt, ashtray, or refrigerator magnet standard.

Chicago Architecture Foundation (☎ 312-922-3432, 224 S Michigan Ave; Map 3) This is heaven for anyone with an edifice complex. Books, posters, post cards and more celebrate local architecture. The Frank Lloyd Wright section alone contains enough material to research a doctoral thesis. But for a good look at what literally lies under today's buildings, peruse David Lowe's *Lost Chicago*. At $16, it chronicles the many architectural gems lost to developers hell-bent on new erections. You'll find another, smaller CAF store in the John Hancock Center (see the N Michigan Ave & Oak St Shopping map in this chapter).

The Symphony Store (☎ 312-294-3345, 220 S Michigan Ave; Map 3) In this store in Symphony Center the Chicago Symphony Orchestra sells a large selection of CDs, tapes and albums of their performances all over the world. The shop even carries T-shirts – highly tasteful ones, of course.

Art Institute Store (☎ 312-443-3535, 111 S Michigan Ave; Map 3) This hugely popular store sells poster ($18 and up) and postcard ($1) versions of popular works from the Art Institute's collection. There's another branch of the store in the 900 N Michigan mall *(☎ 312-482-8275, level 5; Map 5)*.

Edible Treats If you want something easy and inexpensive, bless your lucky gift recipients with Tootsie Rolls. They're cheap, they're made in Chicago and you can get them everywhere. If you're feeling more generous, the 1lb Colonial assortment of locally made *Fanny May Candy* is $11.95. The sweet-smelling white outlets blanket the city.

Garrett Popcorn (☎ 312-944-2630, 670 N Michigan Ave; Map 3) Like lemmings drawn to a cliff, people line up by the mob at this

kernel-size store on the Mag Mile. Granted, the caramel corn is heavenly and the cheese popcorn decadent, but is it worth waiting in the rain for a chance to buy some? Actually, yes. But rather than suffering the lines here, try the Loop location *(☎ 312-630-0127, 26 E Randolph St; Map 3)* across from Field's. It's usually line-free.

Local Lore *Chicago Tribune Store (☎ 312-222-3080, Tribune Tower, 435 N Michigan Ave; Map 3)* This company store sells six water glasses emblazoned with famous front pages for $19.95. Included is the memorable 'Dewey Defeats Truman' edition.

City of Chicago Store (☎ 312-742-8811, Chicago Visitor Center, 163 E Pearson St at Michigan Ave; Map 5) This city-run store is a mecca for those wise enough not to try to steal their own 'official' souvenirs. The cheerful city workers will sell you anything from an old voting machine ($55) to a manhole cover emblazoned with the words 'Chicago Sewers' ($100). Street signs for famous local streets are $50. Bargain hunters may want to opt for the Spanish-language alley-rat warning placards ($4).

Sports Memorabilia *Sports World (☎ 312-472-7701, 3555 N Clark St; Map 7)* This store across from Wrigley Field is crammed with authentic Chicago sports duds. All-wool Cubs and White Sox caps just like those worn by the players are $22. All-synthetic baseball caps just like those worn by nerds are $6.

Yesterday (☎ 773-248-8087, 1143 W Addison St; Map 7) If you've ever actually lived through the old classic tale about discovering that your mom has thrown out all of your baseball cards, you can come here to find out what fortune you've lost. Old sports memorabilia is the specialty of this shop, which is older than some of the goods on sale. In fact, some of the stuff dates from those distant years when the Cubs were good.

WHERE TO SHOP

N Michigan Ave has become the premier shopping street, eclipsing the Loop area in the last two decades. But those who venture out of the main shopping area on the Magnificent Mile will find plenty of unique shopping opportunities in the smaller neighborhoods, where you can really buy anything.

The Loop (Map 3)

Shopping in the Loop was a legendary experience through the 1970s. Then the rise of suburban shopping malls and the proliferation of stores on N Michigan Ave brought devastation: four of six Loop department stores closed, and scores of smaller stores left. Recently the area has undergone a rebirth, and although it hasn't yet come close to its former glory, numerous national retailers have moved in to serve the huge population of office workers who need to squeeze shopping into their lunch hours. Note that many of these stores are closed on Sunday.

State St A city initiative has spruced up the State St sidewalks, installed vintage light fixtures and built elegant subway entrances. After so much rejuvenation this strip has managed to lure back one of its famous retailers: Sears, which dealt a major blow to the area's retail life when it closed its flagship State St store in the early 1980s. At press time Sears was constructing a five-floor store in a renovated 17-story building on a site stretching west of State St along the north side of W Madison St, with the project scheduled to be completed in 2001. While State St won't ever again challenge N Michigan Ave, the return of Sears proves that the Loop has become a healthy shopping area in its own right.

Marshall Field's (☎ 312-781-1000, 111 N State St) The grandest old department store in the country, Field's is the best reason not to confine your shopping to N Michigan Ave. It's a full block in size, taking up the area between Randolph St, Wabash Ave, Washington St and State St, with 10 floors of designer clothes, furnishings, gifts, housewares, fine china and crystal and more. A 1990s renovation created a new central atrium and escalators that show off the scope of the store. Dining under the soaring Christmas tree in the 7th-floor Walnut Room is a local family tradition, but

beware: 10 million people in the region all have the same idea. The basement gourmet food court is a good place for quick snacks. The bottom level also features a wealth of smaller-merchandise areas selling household items, gourmet food, stationery and more. You can buy the popular minty chocolate Frango mints throughout the store. Field's also contains a visitor's center in the basement near the Pedway (a subterranean link between various downtown buildings); staff there make reservations at restaurants and shows and offer other services to tourists and visitors.

Carson Pirie Scott & Co (☎ 312-641-7000, 1 S State St) This store has lived in the shadow of Marshall Field's since it opened in 1899. Architecturally, it's a gem. And shopping-wise it's pretty good, too, with

Merry Memories

No matter their background, people who grew up in the Chicago area are brought together by their memories of the city at Christmastime: the bustling crowds laden with bags, the tinkling of the Salvation Army bells, the holiday music playing from the stores, and red noses and cold cheeks – good excuses for a warm and sugary treat. Here are some of the seasonal highlights.

Around Thanksgiving the city puts up its huge **official Christmas Tree** on Daley Plaza in the Loop (Map 3).

Also in the Loop Marshall Field's builds elaborate **Christmas windows** with a theme that changes every few years. The many windows all around the building allow for complex stories to be told. Carson Pirie Scott, one block south, also does a commendable job.

The Sunday before Thanksgiving brings the **Magnificent Mile Festival of Lights**: zillions of little lights are strung in the trees lining N Michigan Ave, and the effect is magical. The lights stay on until Jan 31. Recently, a parade and other hoopla have been added to the tradition.

moderately priced goods and a varied selection spread over six floors. Carson's has attracted a very loyal following of lunchtime shoppers.

The many chain stores that are transforming State St include **Toys 'R' Us** (☎ 312-857-0669, 10 S State St), which is one of the busiest stores in the whole chain. Discount clothiers **TJ Maxx** (☎ 312-553-0515) and **Filene's Basement** (☎ 312-553-1055) are among the stores at 1 N State St.

Wabash Ave Several longtime local retailers that thrive under the roar of the El have been joined by national chains, making this a vibrant shopping street.

Howard Frum (☎ 312-332-5999, 8th floor, 5 S Wabash Ave) A minor celebrity known locally for his nutty TV ads, the namesake of this colorful jewelry store offers his customers free shoe shines and the chance to join running conversations that once were the focus of a feature on National Public Radio.

Jeweler's Building (19 S Wabash Ave) Built in 1882, this is the center of Chicago's family jeweler trade. Hundreds of shops in this building – along with those at **5 S Wabash Ave**, **21 N Wabash Ave** and **55 E Washington St** – sell every kind of watch, ring, ornament and gemstone imaginable. Most are quick to say, 'I can get it for you wholesale!'

Otto Pomper (☎ 312-372-0881, Mid-America Building, 135 S Wabash Ave) Get your Swiss Army knife reconditioned here. You also can buy a new one or pick up some travel binoculars.

Some of the chains here include **Eddie Bauer Outlet** (☎ 312-263-6005, 123 N Wabash Ave) and **The Gap** (☎ 312-853-0243, 133 N Wabash Ave), both good counterparts to Marshall Field's, just across the street.

Near North (Map 3)

Galleries, boutiques, antique malls, chain superstores and more populate the blocks north of the river and west of N Michigan Ave.

Harley Davidson Store (☎ 312-442-7539, 66 E Ohio St) In keeping with the theme park atmosphere of the North Bridge development (see the Shops at North Bridge section, later), Harley Davidson has opened

RICK GERHARTER

Carson Pirie Scott's ornate entrance

a huge store where you can get anything associated with the company's motorcycles except the actual machines. T-shirts, leather jackets, key rings, navel rings and anything else that can be emblazoned with the company's logo are on sale. A few vintage hogs gleam on the sales floor, but the only people getting taken for a ride are the customers.

CompUSA *(☎ 312-787-6776, 101 E Chicago Ave)* This is the place to go if you need something while you're on the road with your laptop. (Perhaps a new game for surreptitious joy during dull meetings?) Visitors from abroad will both laugh and weep at the comparatively cheap prices on hardware and software.

Merchandise Mart *(☎ 312-527-4141)* Touch Camelot at this huge riverside edifice bounded by Wells, Kinzie and Orleans Sts. In 1945 Marshall Field sold what is still the world's largest commercial structure for a song to Joseph P Kennedy, patriarch of the noted politicians. Beautifully restored in the early 1990s, the Mart contains a modest collection of chain stores on its lower floors, which service the lunchtime shopping needs of the thousands of people who work in the behemoth. But the real allure lies on the many floors devoted to distributor showrooms for home furnishings and other interior fittings. As you prowl the halls, you can find next year's hot trends on display today. Technically, only retailers and buyers can shop on these floors, but the displays are simply an elevator ride away for anyone. Don't try to buy anything, though, because you're not allowed. (But think of the savings!)

Paper Source *(☎ 312-337-0798, 232 W Chicago Ave)* Every kind of paper produced is here, with the lightweight merchandise ranging from delicate Japanese handmade creations to iridescent, neon-hued numbers. The store also carries a great selection of rubber stamps.

Pearl *(☎ 312-915-0200, 225 W Chicago Ave)* This chain art-supply store sells discounted art supplies you can use on the paper you bought from Paper Source, above.

Sportmart *(☎ 312-337-6151, 620 N LaSalle St)* In a classic rags-to-riches story,

Morrie Mages got his start in his family's store in the old Maxwell St Jewish ghetto, where some of the city's leading retailers launched their careers by selling clothes between WWI and WWII. Mages built the place into the world's largest sporting goods store, eventually moving it from Maxwell St into its own renovated eight-story warehouse here. A couple of years ago the Chicago-based national chain Sportmart bought Morrie out for a fortune. Now renamed, the store continues his discounting philosophy, albeit without his inveterate promoter's spirit. Check out Mages' *Chicago Sports Hall of Fame*, on the Ontario St exterior wall.

Chinatown (Map 4)

Like Chinatowns the world over, Chicago's version features a myriad of little interesting shops, including the following:

Woks N Things *(☎ 312-842-0787, 2234 S Wentworth Ave)* This busy store carries every kind of utensil and cookware you could want.

Hoi Poloi *(☎ 312-842-7259, 2235 S Wentworth Ave)* Once upon a time, my friend John lived in a place that was decorated, shall we say, in a style best called 'dorm baroque.' Now he shops at this neat store filled with Asian artwork and other funky interior items. Obviously, times do change.

Sun Sun Tong *(☎ 312-842-6398, 2260 S Wentworth Ave)* Hundreds of varieties of tea and herbs make for great aromas here.

N Michigan Ave

The Greater North Michigan Avenue Association likes to claim that the 'Magnificent Mile,' or 'Mag Mile' as it's widely known, is one of the top five shopping streets in the world. It's hard to argue with that. Even the formerly retail-poor south end of N Michigan Ave, near the river, now boasts a number of shopping options, thanks to the 2000 opening of the huge Shops at North Bridge/Nordstrom complex.

See the N Michigan Ave & Oak St Shopping map to find the stores listed here and to see a full listing of the rest of the stores on the street. The crowds peak at lunchtime during

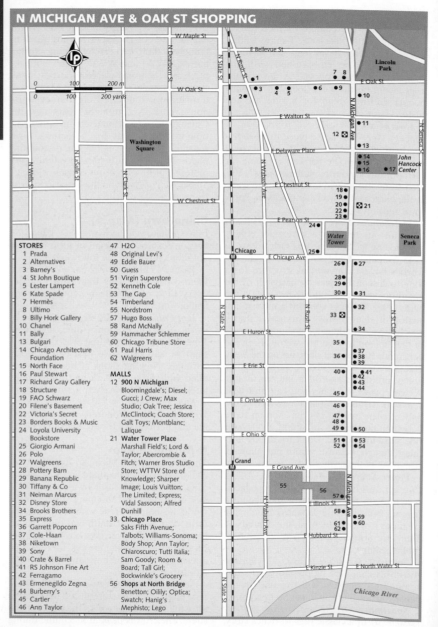

N MICHIGAN AVE & OAK ST SHOPPING

STORES
1 Prada
2 Alternatives
3 Barney's
4 St John Boutique
5 Lester Lampert
6 Kate Spade
7 Hermès
8 Ultimo
9 Billy Hork Gallery
10 Chanel
11 Bally
13 Bulgari
14 Chicago Architecture
   Foundation
15 North Face
16 Paul Stewart
17 Richard Gray Gallery
18 Structure
19 FAO Schwarz
20 Filene's Basement
22 Victoria's Secret
23 Borders Books & Music
24 Loyola University
   Bookstore
25 Giorgio Armani
26 Polo
27 Walgreens
28 Pottery Barn
29 Banana Republic
30 Tiffany & Co
31 Neiman Marcus
32 Disney Store
34 Brooks Brothers
35 Express
36 Garrett Popcorn
37 Cole-Haan
38 Niketown
39 Sony
40 Crate & Barrel
41 RS Johnson Fine Art
42 Ferragamo
43 Ermenegildo Zegna
44 Burberry's
45 Cartier
46 Ann Taylor

47 H2O
48 Original Levi's
49 Eddie Bauer
50 Guess
51 Virgin Superstore
52 Kenneth Cole
53 The Gap
54 Timberland
55 Nordstrom
57 Hugo Boss
58 Rand McNally
59 Hammacher Schlemmer
60 Chicago Tribune Store
61 Paul Harris
62 Walgreens

MALLS
12 **900 N Michigan**
   Bloomingdale's; Diesel;
   Gucci; J Crew; Max
   Studio; Oak Tree; Jessica
   McClintock; Coach Store;
   Galt Toys; Montblanc;
   Lalique
21 **Water Tower Place**
   Marshall Field's; Lord &
   Taylor; Abercrombie &
   Fitch; Warner Bros Studio
   Store; WTTW Store of
   Knowledge; Sharper
   Image; Louis Vuitton;
   The Limited; Express;
   Vidal Sassoon; Alfred
   Dunhill
33 **Chicago Place**
   Saks Fifth Avenue;
   Talbots; Williams-Sonoma;
   Body Shop; Ann Taylor;
   Chiaroscuro; Tutti Italia;
   Sam Goody; Room &
   Board; Tall Girl;
   Bockwinkle's Grocery
56 **Shops at North Bridge**
   Benetton; Oilily; Optica;
   Swatch; Hanig's
   Mephisto; Lego

the week and all day on weekends. Most of these stores are open Sunday afternoon.

Shops at North Bridge This new complex was years in the making. And complex is a good name, since it aptly describes the process of constructing the place. The main buildings of the Shops at North Bridge (*☎ 312-327-2300, 520 N Michigan Ave*) extend over two blocks west from Michigan Ave. A large atrium on the Mag Mile sits next to the shell of what was once the 1929 McGraw-Hill Building. This old veteran, considered an art deco gem by architecture critics, was slated to be demolished to make way for the project. Only a last-minute outcry from the public saved the facade of the building, which was tacked on to the multilevel mall within. A long and strange curved uphill walk leads from the atrium to the actual Nordstrom department store. This was another compromise, as there was simply no way to get Michigan Ave frontage for the store. Nordstrom can only hope that shoppers will be lured down the garden – or, in this case, atrium – path.

The overall North Bridge complex extends for several blocks along Illinois St and Grand Ave west of Michigan Ave. The main shopping complex covers four floors and includes a large, upscale food court that serves food on china 'to make customers feel more at home,' although cynics might suggest that the real purpose is 'to make customers pay more.'

Benetton (*☎ 312-494-9156, level 1*) The European-based clothing chain that specializes in over-the-top ads has opened a large store here.

Lego Store (*☎ 312-494-0760, level 3*) The much-beloved children's building-block company sells just about everything it makes here, including items normally sold only in Europe.

Nordstrom (*☎ 312-464-1515*) This is one of the biggest branches of the Seattle-based department store, which is known for its lavish customer service. The Chicago store plans an active schedule of events featuring appearances by designers.

RICHARD CUMMINS

Tiffany & Co on the Mag Mile

Oilily *(☎ 312-822-9616, level 2)* This women's apparel store features lots of bright colors to counteract gray Chicago days.

Chicago Place This mall *(☎ 312-642-4811, 700 N Michigan Ave)* is a boondoggle. And that's too bad, because it's an attractive building inside and out, with a clever ornamentation theme derived from the wild onions that might have given Chicago its name (see the History section in the Facts about Chicago chapter). But as the third vertical mall to arrive on N Michigan Ave, Chicago Place debuted in an early 1990s market that was barely supporting the first two. A decreasing number of stores populate the floors, until you get to the 7th floor, which has no stores to call its own.

Filled with plants and fountains, the food court on level 8 illustrates how the building itself could blossom if it could just draw a critical mass of tenants.

Ann Taylor *(☎ 312-335-0117, level 2)* This upscale chain sells mainstream women's wear.

Body Shop *(☎ 312-482-8301, level 1)* Here you can buy cosmetics and potions from the British retailer that wears its corporate conscience on its organic sleeve.

Saks Fifth Avenue *(☎ 312-944-6500)* This large department store holds its own as the mall's anchor. Customers seek out its seven floors of designer men's and women's wear.

Talbots *(☎ 312-944-6059, level 1)* Looking for some office duds? Choose among the conservative women's wear here.

Williams-Sonoma *(☎ 312-787-8991, level 2)* As at all its other locations, Williams-Sonoma offers expensive kitchen doodads for people who refuse to pay half as much.

Water Tower Place In 1977 this building *(☎ 312-440-3166, 835 N Michigan Ave)* brought the concept of vertical shopping malls to Chicago, driving a stake through the heart of State St retail and forever changing the character of N Michigan Ave. Retail business on the street has grown exponentially since then.

The mall, which features 100 stores on seven levels, is in many respects an anomaly. Its popularity with out-of-towners and tourists is inexplicable, since its collection of stores can be found at any mainstream mall in the nation. But nonetheless it's an unbeatable draw that offers a safely familiar shopping experience within the larger urban milieu. Urban dwellers heavily patronize Water Tower for its practical assortment of useful stores. On holidays the crowds can become unbearable.

Foodlife, on the mezzanine, is a good place for a break or a meal. See the Places to Eat chapter for details.

Alfred Dunhill *(☎ 312-467-4455, level 2)* Here's your chance to buy expensive British tobacco and other Limey products.

Lord & Taylor *(☎ 312-787-7400)* This busy department store contains a large main floor plus six more floors that snake up through the building. The men's department offers continual sales on excellent-quality men's wear.

Marshall Field's *(☎ 312-335-7700)* In every respect this is a smaller version of the State St flagship store.

WTTW Store of Knowledge *(☎ 312-642-6826, level 7)* Chicago's PBS station operates a store filled with a items related to PBS shows.

Warner Bros Studio Store *(☎ 312-664-9440, levels 2 & 3)* This large store cheerfully capitalizes on that 'wascally wabbit' and the rest of the Looney Tunes gang.

900 N Michigan This huge mall *(☎ 312-915-3916, 900 N Michigan Ave)* got off to a rocky start in 1989. But it has found its niche as a home to an upscale collection of boutiques, thanks to the fact that the same people manage both this mall and Water Tower Place, and they simply moved all the expensive places over here.

The most visually appealing mall on the inside, 900 N Michigan suffers from an irritating escalator arrangement that forces you to traipse around each floor as you climb. But that feature, coupled with the exclusivity of the shops, means that you won't find crowds here, even at peak times.

Bloomingdale's *(☎ 312-440-4460)* This large department store anchors the mall.

Unlike its New York parent in every respect, this Bloomingdale's has developed a personality more reflective of the Midwest's supposedly no-nonsense values. However, that doesn't mean it doesn't boast a hip and stylish collection of merchandise, which even extends to the kitchen department.

Coach Store (☎ *312-440-1777, level 2)* Come here for expensive leather goods.

Galt Toys (☎ *312-440-9550, level 6)* Here you'll find exquisite stuffed animals at exquisite prices.

J Crew (☎ *312-751-2739, level 2)* This national chain carries smug and sporty clothes for people who want to look smug and sporty.

Individual Stores The highlights among the individual stores along N Michigan Ave include the following:

Crate & Barrel *(312-787-5900, 646 N Michigan Ave)* Within this stunning, almost transparent, white store you'll find modestly priced functional and stylish kitchen goods, along with sleek and comfortable furniture. The place is always mobbed, and with good reason: if you bought everything in your house here, you wouldn't go broke and people would rave about your taste. The Chicago-based owners deserve praise, because they could have put up any monstrosity they wished on this blue-chip site, and they opted for classy. There is another location near Lincoln Park *(☎ 312-573-9800, 854 W North Ave; Map 6)*.

The Gap (☎ *312-335-1896, 555 N Michigan Ave)* Like the world needs another Gap? The buzz on this new huge new store is that is just that: huge. It contains sections for babyGap, GapKids, GapBody, but not apparently anything yet for GapDog. It also features various fashion displays from the entire line.

Neiman Marcus (☎ *312-642-5900, 737 N Michigan Ave)* The prices are predictably

RICHARD CUMMINS

The historic Water Tower stands near the modern heights of the 900 N Michigan mall.

high at the local outpost of this Dallas-based department store, but that's part of the Neiman's cachet. Now in its second decade, it has settled into the Mag Mile quite nicely, thank you, with its selection of designer clothes and accessories and gourmet foods. The café is renowned for its popovers.

Niketown (☎ *312-642-6363, 669 N Michigan Ave)* Why buy your shoes at a discount when you can get them here for full price? More noise than substance, this huge, three-level place sells everything in its corporate parent's catalog. It made a splash when it opened in 1992 because it contains some Michael Jordan memorabilia (not *that* much), but by now many imitators have borrowed its strategy of placing merchandise in a high-concept setting, and this trendsetter seems not so interesting anymore.

Gold Coast (Map 5)

Designer boutiques pop up like mushrooms on the tony blocks just west of Michigan Ave, particularly in the single block of Oak St between Michigan Ave and Rush St. Lots of little boutiques line Oak St, and the names read like the advertiser's index in *Harper's Bazaar*. This about as exclusive as shopping gets. See the N Michigan Ave & Oak St Shopping map for a full list of shops and locations.

Alternatives (☎ *312-266-1545, 942 N Rush St near Oak St)* The kinds of shoes that delight the eye and appall the feet are the specialty here. Alternatives features one of the most cutting-edge collections of shoes in town, at prices that gladden the hearts of budding Imelda Marcoses everywhere.

Barney's (☎ *312-587-1700, 25 E Oak St at Rush St)* An anchor at the west end of the street, this branch of the legendary New York men's store went up during an ill-conceived overexpansion in the 1990s (its debt went through the roof, and Barney's barely avoided liquidation). It has never made the splash the original made in New York, but it does carry a nice selection of its own designer wear and lots of trendy shoes.

Prada (☎ *312-951-1113, 30 E Oak St)* This large store carries the designer's full line.

St John Boutique (☎ *312-943-1941, 51 E Oak St)* Shop for classic women's clothing.

Lester Lampert (☎ *312-944-6888, 57 E Oak St)* Custom-made jewelry is the specialty.

Kate Spade (☎ *312-604-0808, 101 E Oak St)* Dozens of the designer's clean-lined handbags are on display.

Hermés (☎ *312-787-8175, 110 E Oak St)* The Parisian retailer operates a Chicago fashion base here.

Ultimo (☎ *312-787-1171, 114 E Oak St)* This is the place to go for trendy high fashion.

Lincoln Park (Map 6)

Clark St, the main thoroughfare for shopping in Lincoln Park, contains shops of every description. Halsted St in the blocks north and south of Armitage Ave features

some interesting places that cater to women and children.

Raymond Hudd (☎ 773-477-1159, 2545 N Clark St) Custom-made, creative hats have perched on stands throughout this store and on the heads of satisfied customers for almost 50 years. Given the long tradition, the store deserves special credit for its witty contemporary designs.

Kangaroo Connection (☎ 773-248-5499, 1113 W Webster Ave) Native Australians drop their jaws when they see all the familiar treats from down under crammed into this small store. Owner Kathy Schubert's best-seller by far is Vegemite, the gooey Australian yeast concoction.

Saturday's Child (☎ 773-525-8697, 2146 N Halsted St) Remember the episode of the Brady Bunch wherein Peter constructed a working volcano that covered the whole clan in poop? Your own kid can get the makings of his own mess here. However, the vast majority of the toys and games for sale are a blast creatively and intellectually, rather than literally. If you're looking for some movie tie-in toy, don't come here.

Lake View & Wrigleyville (Map 7)

Stuff that's never worn – let alone sold – on Michigan Ave is de rigueur on Halsted and Clark Sts in Lake View. Even if you're not buying, the browsing is entertainment in itself.

Halsted St North of Belmont Ave you'll find the kind of colorful, irreverent, wild and kinky shops you'd expect in a gay neighborhood.

Silver Moon (☎ 773-883-0222, 3337 N Halsted St) The weird and, well, wooly inventory here includes stuffed animal heads.

Gallimaufry Gallery (☎ 773-348-8090, 3345 N Halsted St) Though this may be the most staid store on the street, it still merits extensive browsing – and it does sell some 'essential oils,' plus handmade artworks, toys, crafts and incense.

99th Floor (☎ 773-348-7781, 3406 N Halsted St) You can still buy 'Dead Elvis Masks' ($34.50) here. For more formal occa-

sions, the store carries black pumps with 8-inch heels in men's sizes.

Evil Clown (☎ 773-472-4761, 3418 N Halsted St) This small store sells used CDs acquired from people liquidating their collections ahead of the creditors. The staff know where to find the good stuff. If you want to check out some local bands live, take a look at all the fliers advertising performances.

Batteries Not Included (☎ 773-935-9900, 3420 N Halsted St) You think kids cry when the batteries in their toys run out? You oughta see the frustrated looks on the faces of the adult customers of this place when their toys run out of juice. Some of the vibrating items for sale might have been nuclear missiles in a former life.

We're Everywhere (☎ 773-404-0590, 3434 N Halsted St) The 'package' underwear at this gift shop comes in gift packages. The messages on the many T-shirts range from subtle to in-your-face, with George W Bush being a prime target.

Gay Mart (☎ 773-929-4272, 3457 N Halsted St) The Woolworth of the strip sells toys, novelties, calendars, souvenirs, you name it (although luckily Gay Mart doesn't have one of those smelly parakeet sections). One of the top sellers is Billy, the heroically endowed 'world's first out and proud gay doll.' Ken would just wilt in Billy's presence – that is, if Ken had anything to wilt.

Cupid's Treasure (☎ 773 348 3884, 3519 N Halsted St) Here's the place to buy all those things you wondered if your neighbors owned. Spread through three large rooms, the adult toys on display leave adult browsers giggling like children. The goods – frilly, aromatic, battery-powered, leathery and more – should satisfy even the most imaginative of consenting adults. If you're having trouble deciding, ask the friendly staff, who are always eager to help and earnest in their advice. Consider the following guidance given to one couple: 'The whip requires more skill. With the paddle, it's easy – you just spank.'

Flashy Trash (☎ 773-327-6900, 3524 N Halsted St) From the great logo to the vintage clothes themselves, Flashy Trash is out-and-out hip. Such is the store's premier reputation in town that it's branched out into trendy new clothing.

Brown Elephant (☎ 773-549-5943, 3651 N Halsted St) Everything from furs to studs lines the simple pipe coat racks at this resale shop, which helps to raise funds for the Howard Brown Health Center, an acclaimed clinic serving the gay, lesbian and bisexual community. Among last year's satin dresses you can find some gems, price- and style-wise.

Clark St Near Belmont Ave several stores serve the rebellious needs of full-on punks and teens. On weekend days the sidewalks attract a throng of characters: rich teens from the North Shore, black-clad punks with blond roots, the rest of Lake View's diverse tribes and people selling socialist newspapers. ('Are you tired of working for the rich man?' begins their populist refrain.)

Rocket 69 (☎ 773-472-7878, 3180 N Clark St) Once a really cutting-edge place, Rocket 69 is aging with its customers. The genitalia-covered greeting cards have now given way to a range of rather artistic cards utterly lacking in body parts. However, all is not lost – you can still get nipple rings.

The Alley (☎ 773-525-3180, 3218 N Clark St) This huge place has taken over a large chunk of the block north of the infamous Dunkin' Donuts. A vast emporium based on counterculture and pop trends, the Alley offers everything from head-shop gear to band posters to human-size dog collars. The supply of *Spinal Tap* T-shirts is, thankfully, better than the supply of puppet T-shirts. Among the labyrinth of rooms is one devoted to the Alley's 'Architectural Revolution' store, which sells plaster reproductions of gargoyles, Ionic pillars and other items that have found a mainstream market with non-dog-collar-wearing interior designers. The Alley's adjoining store, **Taboo-Tabou** (☎ 773-548-2266, 858 W Belmont Ave) sells condoms in more flavors than Baskin-Robbins sells ice cream.

Secrets (☎ 773-755-0179, 3229 N Clark St) For folks of a certain persuasion, Secrets offers one-stop shopping: body-piercing, battery-powered novelties and even cigars (non-battery-powered). Some of the lingerie

here is so skimpy that you'll need a body ring just to have something to anchor it to.

Air Wair (☎ 773-244-0099, 3240 N Clark St) This shop features perennial sales on huge, heavy boots of minimal practical value outside of a steel mill (read: Doc Martens). Celebrate your third piercing with a pair.

Chicago Comics (☎ 773-528-1983, 3244 N Clark St) Jazz plays softly on the sound system at this serious store. Inside the big, clean and orderly space, you'll find treasured first issues of Howard the Duck, plus a huge number of alternative comics and 'zines from around the world.

Medusa's Circle (☎ 773-935-5950, 3268 N Clark St) Not sweating enough? Medusa's carries everything for raven-haired folks who like to wear dark velvet clothes on hot days.

Windward Sports (☎ 773-472-6868, 3317 N Clark St) These folks do their best to bring surfing to Lake Michigan. No, they don't even try to ride the 12-inch-high surf – they use the wind. Now *that* they've got, and lots of it. They're a friendly bunch, and they sell all sorts of windsurfing gear. Ask at the store about various beach rentals of windsurfing equipment during the summer.

Disgraceland (☎ 773-281-5875, 3338 N Clark St) The name alone is reason to love this place, although the high-end used clothing is pretty nifty as well. Are those bacon and peanut butter stains I see?

Strange Cargo (☎ 773-327-8090, 3448 N Clark St) Maybe this store should really be called 'Retro Cargo.' Vinyl jackets from dead bowling alleys share space with bell-bottoms and polychromatic shades (you know: sunglasses). It's a good place to get a leather cop jacket, too.

Southport Ave Whimsy (☎ 773-665-1760, 3234 N Southport Ave) If you need a cool little gift, try this fun place where the shelves are lined with stylish candle holders, little reading lamps, tiny frames and other inexpensive items that don't take up a lot of room in a bag.

Wisteria (☎ 773-880-5868, 3715 N Southport Ave) Here you can find classic, vintage Hawaiian shirts ($65) and other bits of clothing.

POSH *(☎ 773-529-7674, 3729 N Southport Ave)* This gem of a store carries vintage china, much of which once graced the tables of old ocean liners and passenger trains.

Belmont Ave *Chicago Tattooing (☎ 773-528-6969, 922 W Belmont Ave)* Choose from thousands of examples or custom-design your own. If you prefer getting poked with a bigger needle, the shop also does piercings.

Something Old Something New *(☎ 773-271-1300, 1056 W Belmont Ave)* It looks like a laundromat exploded at this chaotic store. But amid the racks and racks of cheap clothing lurk some really cheap items, such as good jeans for $5.

Andersonville (Map 8)

Studio 90 *(☎ 773-878-0097, 5239 N Clark St)* My friend Janice praises the clothes here for being 'comfortable but not stretchy.' Designed by women who work in the store, the many pieces for sale are both eclectic and cute.

Wikstrom's Deli *(☎ 773-275-6100, 5243 N Clark St)* Scandinavians from all over Illinois flock here for homemade *limpa* bread, herring and lutefisk. Caviar in a tube also seems to be a big seller.

The Landmark *(☎ 773-728-5301, 5301 N Clark St)* This collection of shops is a neighborhood…well, you get it. Anyway, the many boutiques sell lots of neat little things. I'm always enamored of the Pooh Store, which stocks all kinds of items relating to the honey-loving British bear.

Erickson Jewelers *(☎ 773-275-2010, 5304 N Clark St)* Many people know this place not for the jewels but for the jewel-like exterior. The classic facade has been carefully maintained since its renovation in the early 1940s. Once inside, you'll find an assortment of watches, baubles and the like.

Paper Trail *(☎ 773-275-2191, 5307 N Clark St)* Here's where you find the cards the designers at Hallmark probably want to create, if only such creativity wouldn't cost them their jobs.

The store's Chihuahua card collection is matched in scope only by the fat women's butt series.

Alamo Shoes *(☎ 773-784-8936, 5321 N Clark St)* This throwback to the 1960s sells everything from Birkenstocks to hiking boots for men and women, all at really good prices. The enthusiastic staffers hop off to the backroom and emerge with stacks of boxes until you find what you want or you're entirely walled in by the possibilities.

Wicker Park & Bucktown (Map 9)

Shops on Milwaukee Ave are a mix of the really cheap and the really expensive. You

Bucktown, home to eclectic shops

can buy inexpensive Mexican CDs and high-priced objets d'art in adjoining stores. North on Damen Ave, the scene becomes much more solidly gentrified.

***Una Mae's Freak Boutique** (☎ 773-276-7002, 1422 N Milwaukee Ave)* It's unlikely that the solid suburban women who once wore the pillbox hats and fine Republican cloth coats on sale here would ever have thought of themselves as freaks. And their pierced grandkids who buy up this vintage stuff probably don't think of themselves as freaks either.

***Meble** (☎ 773-772-8200, 1462 N Milwaukee Ave)* It's worth just browsing here to see the weird and wonderful mix of pricey props, antiques and conceptual art pieces. If you're thinking of buying, beware: much of the stuff is made of metal and probably won't work as carry-on baggage.

***Botanica** (☎ 773-486-5894, 1524 N Milwaukee Ave)* This old storefront sells devotional art and paraphernalia without an ounce of irony. What you do with your sacred candle once out of the store is your business.

***Le Garage** (☎ 773-278-2234, 1649 N Damen Ave)* The sign above the door here advertises 'work clothes' – which may make sense if your job requires you to wear black lace and velvet tops, leather pants or pastel-colored jeans.

***Climate** (☎ 773-862-7075, 1702 N Damen Ave)* 'Eclectic' doesn't do justice to the array of cute little items packed into this small store. The huge range of candles for sale includes a large brown number called 'chocolate volcano.'

***Red Balloon Co** (☎ 773-489-9800, 2060 N Damen Ave)* The trendy set who once wore black and hung out in divey Bucktown clubs now have trendy kids who don't wear black and get their adorable kiddie wear here.

***Saffron** (☎ 773-486-7753, 2064 N Damen Ave)* Custom clothing with a lacey Victorian look is the specialty here. A few daring numbers actually reveal ankles and wrists!

New Maxwell St Market (Map 10)

Much changed from the original, the new market has moved from Maxwell St to a stretch of S Canal St between Taylor St and the equivalent of 15th St, near the river. This relocation was supposedly sparked by the University of Illinois' insatiable need to expand southward (which is partly true), but mostly it was caused by the city's desire to reclaim the original market's area, which had become Chicago's own wild bazaar, with drug dealers and vendors of stolen hubcaps openly competing for customers. One whole block had even seceded from the US and declared itself an anarchist state. In a postscript, years after the market was snuffed out at its old Maxwell St location, the battered VW buses of the anarchist state remain.

The city bureaucracy closely monitors the new location, but the rough edges remain. Nonetheless, every Sunday morning hundreds of vendors set up stalls that sell everything from Cubs jerseys in the wrong colors to tacos for $1. You can still buy hubcaps, but the odds that they're fresh from your own car are somewhat diminished.

The market is a scenic 15-minute walk over the river from the Roosevelt El Station. From the Clinton Station, on the Blue Line, the walk passes through boring blocks.

Excursions

The rich prairie responsible for much of Chicago's original wealth is, by its very grain-growing nature, not the most dynamic of destinations. In fact, one of the biggest complaints of people living in Chicago is the dearth of exciting weekend getaways.

Still, the following destinations can provide a good counterpoint to your time in Chicago; they're good places to stop if you are motoring off someplace else. Frank Lloyd Wright and Ernest Hemingway fans in particular will enjoy Oak Park, while outdoor types can find some surprisingly good rural hikes within an hour's drive of the Loop.

NORTH OF CHICAGO
Evanston
population 74,000

A clean, pleasant place 14 miles north of the Loop, Evanston combines sprawling old houses with a compact and walkable downtown shopping district. Much of the town is dominated by Northwestern University.

The Methodists who founded the town in 1850 would be happy to see that today it is still hard to buy a beer here; the scarcity of spirits is a lingering effect of both the Methodist ethos and a rule once passed by Northwestern that forbade the sale of alcohol within 4 miles of campus.

During rush hour you can ride the CTA Purple Line Evanston Express to and from the Loop. At other times, ride the Red Line to Howard and transfer to a Purple Line local. The Davis Station is in the heart of town. Alternately, you can take the Metra/Union Pacific North Line from the Richard B Ogilvie Transportation Center in the West Loop ($2.75 one-way) to the Davis St stop. The drive north from Chicago on Sheridan Rd is especially scenic.

Northwestern University Lacking the grand vision of its rival, the University of Chicago, the campus of Northwestern University (☎ 847-491-7271) holds more interest for its faculty and students than for visitors.

Founded in 1851, the university has grown to more than 10,000 students. The undergraduate arts and sciences programs are especially strong. Music and drama students apply their talents throughout the Chicago creative community, which means that NU itself doesn't have the same sort of lively campus cultural scene you find at, for example, Indiana University.

The less said on the topic of college sports at Northwestern, the better. The Wildcats football squad experienced a brief moment of glory in the 1990s. But it soon returned to its traditional spot as doormat for the Big 10, laboring under the pejorative 'Mildcats' moniker, among others. During the 2000 season the players looked sort of good again, but then came the Alamo Bowl, where they relived every Mildcat nightmare against Nebraska. No one here talks about a 'winning tradition.' NU fans have also never developed the pre- and postgame traditions that make games at other Big 10 schools such fun. In fact, the festivities here are more reminiscent of a big high school game. Tickets are usually available for the fall home games at **Ryan Stadium** (☎ 847-491-2287, 1501 Central Ave), a short walk from the CTA Central El stop on the appropriately shaded Purple Line.

Other Northwestern athletic pursuits are not much grander – these men and women are truly here for their brains – although the fencing squad is said to be pretty good.

The main Northwestern campus is just north of Evanston's center and is east of Sheridan Rd. NU's medical, legal and business graduate programs – all among the top five of their kind in the nation – are located in Chicago's Streeterville neighborhood.

Mitchell Museum of the American Indian This large regional museum (☎ 847-475-1030, Kendall College, 2600 Central Park Ave at Central Ave; admission $3/2 for adults/children; open 10am-5pm Tues-Sat, until 8pm Thur, noon-4pm Sun) documents the lives of

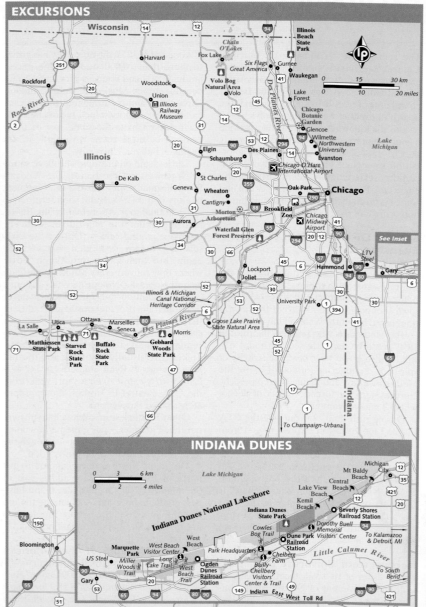

Native Americans in the Midwest, both past and present. The artwork that is on display – including pottery, textiles, clothing, baskets and quilts – illustrates aspects of the Indians' daily existence. Special exhibits let visitors handle traditional everyday objects, such as the stone tools used to make cornmeal. You'll never eat a corn tortilla so nonchalantly again – making one is wrist-killing work. Many Native Americans who live in the area take an active role in the displays, temporary exhibitions and lectures that the museum hosts.

North Shore

Chicago's northern suburbs on the lake are pleasant and gracious places that are worth every dollar the residents pay in property taxes. Quiet yet urbane, they became popular in the late 19th century, when the carriage set had had enough of Chicago's fires, riots, tainted water and other big city excitement and beat an eager retreat to the bucolic shores of Lake Michigan.

If you have a car, a drive through the North Shore communities provides a glimpse of the beautiful homes and stately gardens. Head north from Chicago on Lake Shore Dr. When it ends, turn right on Sheridan Rd, drive north through Rogers Park to Evanston and you're on your way. The classic 30-mile drive follows Sheridan through towns that include Kenilworth, Wilmette, Winnetka, Glencoe, Highland Park and the apex of the drive and of social standing: Lake Forest. Just be sure to watch the signs, as Sheridan twists and turns. Return via the Edens Expressway (I-94).

Baha'i House of Worship This Baha'i establishment (*☎ 847-853-2300, 100 Linden Ave in Wilmette; free; open 10am-10pm daily Apr-Sept, until 5pm other times*), a glistening white showpiece surrounded by lovely

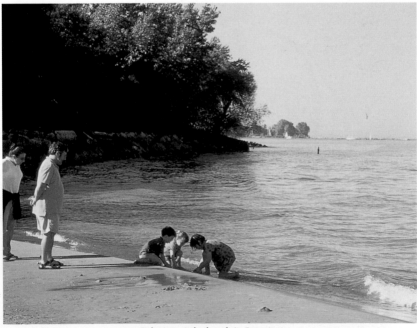

Relaxing at the beach in Evanston

RICK GERHARTER

gardens, enjoys a dramatic location on the lake. You might have seen this huge white-domed edifice as you flew over Wilmette on the way into Chicago. Completed in 1953 by members of the Baha'i faith, a Persian sect, the temple is one of seven major Baha'i houses of worship worldwide. In summer the abundance of blooming flowers provides a colorful contrast to the white cement.

Wilmette is the last stop on the CTA Purple Line. Catch an express in the Loop during rush hours, or take the Red Line to Howard and transfer to the Purple. The temple is a short walk east from the Linden Station.

Chicago Botanic Garden This elaborate garden (☎ *847-835-5440, 1000 Lake-Cook Rd; free; open 8am-dusk daily*) is in tony Glencoe, a half-mile east of the Edens Expressway (I-94). The Chicago Horticultural Society runs the facility, which features thousands of plants in 20 distinctive settings on 385 acres. There is a tram tour of the site, but come on, it's not that big and what better way to explore gardens than on foot? Among the leafy sights you'll see are a prairie garden, an herb garden, a Japanese garden and a rose garden. Frequent demonstrations show you how to try to replicate the gardens at home. For fun, assign each member of the group a letter and see who can find the most plants beginning with that letter. For instance, the letter G will garner geraniums, grapes, ginkgo trees, gourds and of course, grass.

Although admission is free, the garden still collects plenty of dough by charging $7 for parking, since the only people likely to walk here are those out of gas. Public transportation is not an easy option.

Wilmette's Baha'i House of Worship

Lake Forest The toniest of the status suburbs is also the farthest north. Built in 1916, the gracious downtown area owes its inspiration to English market towns, plus other European designs. Many consider this to be the first suburban shopping area, but its influences are hard to detect in your average strip mall.

The rewarding destination of a Sheridan Rd drive, Lake Forest is about 45 minutes to an hour north of the city, depending on traffic. The Metra/Union Pacific North Line offers frequent service right to the heart of downtown ($3.90 one-way).

Illinois Beach State Park Just north of Waukegan, Illinois Beach State Park *(☎ 847-662-4811, Lake Front, Zion; free; open dawn-8pm daily)* features 6 miles of the remaining lake dunes in Illinois. It's a good alternative to the crowded sands of the Indiana dunes, although some will be put off by the Zion nuclear power plant that bisects the beach. Public transportation is bad, so you're better off driving north from the city for about 40 miles along Sheridan Rd.

Gurnee Hold on to your stomach at **Six Flags Great America** *(☎ 847-249-1776, off I-94 at Grand Ave; admission and unlimited rides $39/19.50 for adults/children)*, a 300-acre amusement park that's part of the national chain. The names of the rides – such as Shock Wave and Viper – should tell you what to expect. There's no gold ring for those who guess the theme of the Giant Drop. Anyone less than 54 inches tall is kept away from the wild rides and sent packing to the marketing-driven Camp Cartoon Network and Looney Tunes. The park opens at 10am and closes, according to a complex schedule, between 5pm and 10pm. During some months it's open daily, but at either end of the season (which runs from mid-April to October 31) it's only open on weekends.

Marathon runners will feel at home at **Gurnee Mills** *(☎ 847-263-7500, west of I-94 at the Grand Ave exit)*, an endless outlet mall in Gurnee, 40 minutes north of the city. Everything is cheap, cheap, cheap at the outlet stores run by national chains such as Ann Taylor, The Gap, Panasonic, Maidenform and about 200 others. But before your bargain hormones go into overdrive, consider the ugly secret of many of these places: no longer do they sell their own top-notch merchandise or T-shirts that inexplicably ended up with three sleeves. Instead, to protect their own retail stores and resellers, these 'outlet' stores often sell lower quality merchandise produced specifically for the bargain-hunting masses. A final note: if you weary of the chase and sit down in one of the rest areas, a TV will urge you to get back up and shop.

Gurnee lies on I-94, inland from the scenic North Shore communities.

NORTHWEST OF CHICAGO
Des Plaines
population 53,000

This is where it all began, billions and billions of burgers ago. The **McDonald's Museum** *(☎ 847-297-5022, 400 N Lee St)* occupies the very first outlet that fast-food magnate Ray Kroc built back in 1955. Still based in the Chicago area (Oak Brook), the McDonald's corporation displays its corporate pride at this site, where you'll see a video presentation and lots of mementos and original equipment. However, the museum's hours are somewhat less predictable than the cooking time of your french fries; it's best to call first to confirm.

Des Plaines lies 17 miles northwest of the Loop, off I-294.

Schaumburg
population 69,000

Schaumburg has long been the butt of jokes made by smug city dwellers. And why not? Completely given over to unfettered development, it is home to soulless subdivisions and strings of chain stores – the only national chains you won't find here are those that have gone bankrupt.

The heart of this supposed city is **Woodfield Mall** *(☎ 847-330-1537; open 9am-9pm daily)*, where the cheery motto is 'Shop Happily Ever After.' Boasting that it contains the largest amount of retail space in the world (the Mall of America nightmare, in suburban Minneapolis, is bigger but much of its space is devoted to a Peanuts amusement park), Woodfield includes more than 300 stores, scores of restaurants, big department stores and an ocean of a parking lot. In fact, the latter is often crowded with idling charter buses that bring in legions of shoppers from all over the Midwest, often passing mall after mall with the same stores in order to reach Woodfield. Don't come here unless you're doing a sociological study on the wonders of a Brobdingnagian retail monster.

Schaumburg and Woodfield Mall lie at the junction of the Northwest Tollway (I-90) and I-290.

Volo Bog Natural Area

You'll find one of the most unusual habitats in Illinois at the Volo Bog Natural Area (☎ 815-344-1294, 28478 W Brandenburg Rd; free admission; open dawn-dusk). Insatiable, creeping moss is slowly filling in a large lake, left behind from the last ice age 12,000 years ago. This geologic horror movie is the only one in the Midwest and is home to a number of rare plant and animal species. A short nature trail winds through the area, and on weekends experts stand by to make sense of the whole mossy mess. Volunteer naturalists lead one-hour public tours at 11am and 1pm Saturday and Sunday. To get there from Volo (which is 32 miles northwest of the Loop), go north on Hwy 12/Hwy 59 to Sullivan Lake Rd and turn west, following signs to the parking lot.

Illinois Railway Museum

One of the best museums of its kind in the US, the Illinois Railway Museum (☎ 815-923-4000) boasts more than 200 acres full of historic trains that date from the mid-1800s to the present. Models on display include steam, diesel and electric locomotives, plus passenger and freight cars, many of which are protected by large sheds. As you walk around, you'll see many of the hundreds of volunteers who keep the place going. With little provocation they'll happily relate story after story about the equipment. (They'll also tell you their great fear: that soon, unfettered

development will bring the first subdivisions to this location, 60 miles from Chicago.)

Admission times vary widely, but the grounds generally are open at least 10am to 4pm daily from April 1 to October 30; call to confirm. Steam trains run over 9 miles of track on weekends from May to September. When the trains are running, admission is $8/6 for adults/children. At other times admission is cheaper, and on weekdays in April and May and from mid-September to October 31, the museum is free.

To get there, take the exit for US Hwy 20 and Marengo off the Northwest Tollway (I-90), then drive north for 4½ miles to Union and follow signs.

WEST OF CHICAGO
Oak Park
population 54,000

Oak Park is the place to go if you admire the designs of Frank Lloyd Wright. For 10 years – from 1889 until 1908, when he took a surprise trip to Europe (see the boxed text 'He Was Not Morally Up to Snuff') – Wright worked and lived in a studio in Oak Park. Strolling the streets of this pleasant old town is like stepping back into one of those 1950s TV sitcoms, with all its bland bucolic charm. Native son Ernest Hemingway was unmoved, though – he called Oak Park a 'village of wide lawns and narrow minds.'

To see some examples of Wright's work, which dots the town, ask for the architectural walking-tour map at the **Oak Park Visitors Center** (☎ 708-848-1500, 158 N Forest Ave at Lake St; open 10am-5pm daily). The helpful, plain-talking volunteers provide a wide variety of information.

Staff at the **Frank Lloyd Wright Home & Studio** (☎ 708-848-1976, 951 Chicago Ave; admission $8/6 for adults/children; tours 11am, 1pm & 3pm daily) offer tours of the complex, the neighborhood and some other Wright-designed homes. Self-guided walking tours, including audio tours, are also available.

The studio is a fascinating place, filled with the details that made Wright's style distinctive. Note how he molded plaster to look like bronze and stained cheap pine to look like rare hardwood. Always in financial trouble,

RICK GERHARTER

Frank Lloyd Wright Home & Studio, Oak Park

spendthrift Wright was adept at making the ordinary seem extraordinary. The studio's bookstore sells mountains of Wright-related paraphernalia. Unfortunately, all the books seem to have been written by supplicants, sycophants and adoring relatives.

One block away, the **Moore House** *(333 N Forest Ave)* is Wright's bizarre interpretation of an English manor house that was first built in 1895. In later years of his life, Wright called the house 'repugnant' and said he had only taken the commission originally because he needed the money. He claimed that he walked out of his way to avoid passing it. Check to see if the Oak Park Visitors Center is offering tours.

Oak Park honors another famous local – despite the crack about the lawns – at the **Ernest Hemingway Museum** *(☎ 708-848-* *2222, 200 N Oak Park Ave; admission $6/free for adults/children; open 1pm-5pm Thur-Sun; 10am-5pm Sat)*. The exhibits begin with his middle-class Oak Park background and his innocent years before he went off to find adventure. Other displays follow the rest of his life, focusing on his writings in Spain and during WWII. Admission includes admittance to **Hemingway's Birthplace** *(339 N Oak Park Ave)*, where you can see his first room. 'Papa' was born here in 1899 in the home of his maternal grandparents.

The CTA Green Line and the Metra/ Union Pacific West Line serve Oak Park from Chicago with frequent and fast service. The CTA offers the more interesting ride. On either line, exit at the Oak Park stop, walk north one block on Oak Park Ave to Lake St, turn left and walk west on Lake to

EXCURSIONS

'He Was Not Morally Up to Snuff'

Oak Park might boast a good portion of Frank Lloyd Wright's legacy, but you can't accuse locals of glossing over his checkered reputation. That Wright was 'not morally up to snuff' was an observation made by a woman who worked in Oak Park's official visitor information center. She made a variety of cutting comments about the acerbic and philandering Wright, who once ran off to Europe with Mamah Borthwick Cheney, the wife of a client, instead of going home to his wife and six kids at his Oak Park studio.

Born in Wisconsin in 1867 and always a prodigy, Wright went to Chicago in 1887 to work for Louis Sullivan as a drafter. But in 1893 that relationship ended when Sullivan found out that Wright was moonlighting and not cutting the firm in on his profits.

After his European escapade in 1908, Wright worked from studios on a Wisconsin farm, where he lived with Cheney although he was still married to his first wife. Public condemnation was harsh. On Christmas Day in 1911, Wright held a press conference to explain his infidelity, proclaiming that he, as a 'thinking man,' did not have to follow the rules of 'the ordinary man.'

In 1914, a deranged servant murdered Cheney. Wright found consolation with Miriam Noel, who had sent him a letter of sympathy. They married in 1923 and divorced in 1927. In 1928 Wright married his third and final wife, Olga Ivanovna, with whom he had had a child in 1925.

Wright spent most of his later years working at his home in the Arizona desert, where he died in 1959 at the age of 90. His personal life notwithstanding, Wright was already rightfully recognized as the most original of all American architects when he died.

On the same day that the visitor center staffer passed moral judgment, a touring architect outside the Moore House offered the following anecdote about his own run-in with the tart-tongued Wright: 'I was 19 and going to a small architecture school back east. Wright came and spoke. Afterwards I tried to speak to him because I admired him. He looked at me and said, "You'll never be an architect, because you go to school in a shoe factory." Then he hit me with his cane and drove away.'

---

the visitor center, which is five minutes from the Oak Park stop.

By car, take I-290 west, exiting north on Harlem Ave; take Harlem north to Lake St and turn right. Oak Park is 8 miles from the Loop.

Brookfield Zoo

With 2700 animals and 215 acres, Brookfield Zoo (☎ 708-485-0263, www.brookfieldzoo .org, 8400 W 31st St in Brookfield; admission $6/3 for adults/children, free Tue & Thur Oct-Mar; parking $4; open 9:30am-6pm daily May-Sept, until 5pm other times) can easily gobble up an entire day. Much more commercially oriented than Chicago's Lincoln Park Zoo, it boasts several special attractions, some of which cost extra.

Because most visitors use the North Gate and tend to stop at the nearby attractions first, you can avoid some of the crowds by starting in the southern part of the zoo and working back north. You'll soon find that the exhibits have names invented by the marketing department. Some highlights follow.

Really three exhibits, the **Fragile Kingdom** includes an indoor African desert scene, an indoor Asian rain forest scene and an outdoor collection of big cats. The desert scene achieves the feel of an Indiana Jones movie set and includes jackals, monitor lizards and naked mole rats.

The largest indoor exhibit at the zoo is **Tropic World: A Primate's Journey**, with three areas that represent rain forests in South America, Asia and Africa. Frequent showers douse the animals but spare the visitors. Check out Ramar, a male gorilla who was brought here in 1998 to improve the zoo's flaccid breeding program. Sadly, Ramar has been a major letdown, ignoring the simian charms of a succession of potential mates.

If walking with bats is your idea of a nightmare, skip the **Australia House**. Otherwise, the exhibit is well worth a stop. Couch potatoes and other critters with low metabolic rates will identify with the perpetually snoozing wombats.

Upstairs at the **Seven Seas Panorama** you can sit in the 2000-seat amphitheater and see trainers putting dolphins through their paces. Downstairs, visitors can behold the dolphins for free through the underwater viewing windows. Watch the dolphins looking through windows into the kitchen where their meals are prepared.

Built on 5 acres and set in a mythical African game reserve called Makundi National Park, **Habitat Africa!** features impressive details, especially in the kopje area, which represents a rocky outcrop rising from the African savanna.

The **Living Coast** imitates a portion of the coast of Chile and Peru, where the world's driest desert meets one of the ocean's richest breeding grounds. Sharks, turtles, penguins and 60 other species live in and around the huge tank of water.

The Hollywood train station is near the zoo's main entrance and is served by frequent Metra/BNSF trains from Chicago's Union Station ($2.75 one-way). If you're driving to the zoo, which is 14 miles from the Loop, go west on the Eisenhower Expressway (I-290) to the 1st Ave exit, then south to 31st. Follow signs to the zoo.

Morton Arboretum

A private nature preserve on more than 1700 acres, the Morton Arboretum *(☎ 630-719-2400, admission $7 per car, $3 on Wed; open 7am-5pm daily, until 7pm Apr-Oct)* combines a wide variety of terrain and trees. The sights range from manicured shrubs, to special plantings of trees not native to the area, to long stretches of local forest and

prairie. Many trees are marked with small informational signs.

Twenty-five miles of trails wind through the arboretum, but a realistic circular path covering most of the preserve runs for 6 to 7 miles. Plan your course using the map you receive at the entrance. Parts of the arboretum are quite hilly, with paths that feel pleasantly rural. However, large sections of the park seem to have been designed with drivers, rather than walkers, in mind. Many people tour the entire location without once leaving their car, a situation befitting the park's suburban location. If you find your way to the middle of the arboretum, you'll enjoy the relative quiet there, but toward the edges you'll hear noise from I-88 and other busy roads. And then there are those constantly touring automobiles...

The arboretum is 25 miles west of Chicago on Route 53, just north of I-88. This is a car-only trip.

Cantigny

Colonel Robert R McCormick was one of America's best screwball millionaires. A newspaper publisher along the lines of William Randolph Hearst, he was editor of the *Chicago Tribune* from 1914 until he died in 1955. Under his leadership the *Tribune* became a powerful and idiosyncratic newspaper, the apex of an empire that included radio stations, ships, real estate and more.

A staunch conservative, McCormick used his newspaper to trumpet his political beliefs. He vilified President Franklin Delano Roosevelt during the 1930s and apologized for Adolf Hitler right up until the Nazi dictator declared war on the US. He also tirelessly promoted his idea for a huge convention center on the city's unspoiled lakefront. His newspaper continued the campaign after McCormick's death and steamrolled politicians into supporting the project by threatening to publish unfavorable articles about them. The resulting McCormick Place has been dubbed 'The Mistake on the Lake,' since there were vast tracts of city land elsewhere that could have been used for the center.

EXCURSIONS

For insight into the colonel, you can't miss a visit to Cantigny (☎ *630-668-5161, 1 S 151 Winfield Rd, Wheaton; admission free, parking $5; grounds open 9am-dusk Tues-Sun, mansion & museum open 10am-4pm*). Cantigny includes a large herb garden; the colonel's mansion, filled with artwork provided by his two wives; and a rather large and complex museum devoted to the exploits of the US Army's First Division, the force that gave McCormick his title.

To get to Cantigny, which lies 25 miles west of the Loop, follow Hwy 38 for 5 miles west from I-355.

Geneva & St Charles

These two towns on the Fox River are major weekend destinations. Both Geneva and St Charles feature nicely restored downtowns with a plethora of antique shops. Geneva enjoys the advantage of being accessible via the Metra/Union Pacific West Line from Chicago ($4.65 one-way, 70-minute trip). Everything else out here is along Hwy 31.

Both towns are very walkable; you can stroll from antique shop to antique shop, stopping in emporiums devoted to fudge, potpourri, aromatherapy goop, fragile straw-flower arrangements and all the other goodies that make your trip to a cute town so profitable for the local merchants. Oh, and did we say fudge?

The **Geneva Chamber of Commerce** (☎ *630-232-6060, PO Box 481, 60134*) and the **St Charles Convention & Visitors' Bureau** (☎ *630-377-6161, 311 N 2nd St, 60174*) can provide lists of the ever-growing number of B&Bs.

One of the major attractions is the **Kane County Flea Market** (☎ *630-377-2252; open noon-5pm Sat, 7am-5pm Sun on the first weekend every month*), which draws hundreds of dealers selling everything from junk to rare curios. The market is in the fairgrounds off Randall Rd, between Geneva and St Charles.

SOUTHWEST OF CHICAGO

The 2200-acre **Waterfall Glen Forest Preserve** (*open dawn-dusk daily*) completely surrounds the **Argonne National Laboratory**, where research is done on nuclear bombs. The setting features some of the most diverse scenery in the area, including a waterfall, a deep limestone ravine, prairie, woods, marsh and a pond.

In the past the site supplied the limestone used for Chicago's Water Tower and contained a nursery where trees were grown for Lincoln Park. Although the lab is in the middle, it's almost impossible to see. It doesn't even glow. On the south side of the preserve is a large field popular with people flying radio-controlled planes.

The main hiking trail is one of the area's most beautiful walks; the 9-mile loop is also – by local standards – hilly and strenuous. Maps are usually not available, so study the large one posted at the parking lot. The main trail is marked by brown plastic posts with orange circles. Follow them carefully, because it's easy to miss a turn and end up amid apartments or houses. The best way to proceed from the parking lot is counterclockwise, so that you'll get through the less interesting terrain first, saving the lake for the end. About 4 miles into the hike, the trail follows some old limestone walls under a thick canopy of trees.

The park is 19 miles southwest of Chicago, off Cass Ave, 1½ miles south of the Cass Ave exit off I-55. The trailhead is at the large map adjacent to the main parking lot.

Illinois & Michigan Canal Corridor

Dubbed a National Heritage Corridor, this linear park run by the National Park Service encompasses 41 towns, 11 state parks and scores of historic sites.

The I&M Canal resulted from merchants' desire for a waterway that linked the Mississippi River basin with the Great Lakes and made it possible to ship goods by boat from the eastern US to New Orleans and on to the Caribbean. In 1836 the first shovelful of dirt was turned, and during the next 12 years, thousands of immigrants, primarily Irish, were lured to Chicago to work on the 96-mile course.

After the canal opened in 1848, the constant flow of goods through Chicago propelled the city's economic development. In

1900 the I&M Canal was supplemented by the much deeper Chicago Sanitary & Ship Canal, a much more navigable waterway that, sadly, became Chicago's de facto drainpipe.

Competition from railroads and other waterways caused the I&M Canal to molder for most of the 20th century. The establishment of the park in 1984 has spurred restoration and development of the I&M Canal's remaining sites and of some of the historic towns along the route.

The I&M Canal and related sights are a car-only trip. Most are easily accessible from Chicago off I-55 and I-80.

Orientation & Information The Heritage Corridor driving route can be hard to follow, and the sites are greatly dispersed. It's a good idea to get some of the available free maps in advance so you can plan your itinerary – the trip can easily fill a day. One bonus: most sites are free.

The **Heritage Corridor Visitors' Bureau** (☎ *815-727-2323, 800-926-2262, 81 N Chicago St, Joliet, 60431)* offers information on the parks as well as food and lodging details for the region.

The **Illinois & Michigan Canal Heritage Corridor Commission** (☎ *815-740-2047, 200 W Eighth St, Lockport, 60441; open 10am-5pm Wed-Sun)* is the source for all the excellent National Park Service brochures and maps of the corridor. The one devoted to archaeology is especially good. The staff here also know when various information centers along the canal are open.

I&M Canal State Trail Already 61 miles in length (and slowly growing), the Illinois & Michigan Canal State Trail runs from I-55 in the east to La Salle in the west. The path follows the canal and makes an ideal route for biking, hiking and snowmobiling. You can also wilderness camp along the length of the canal. For many activities, such as snowmobiling and camping, advance registration is required at one of three information centers: Gebhard Woods State Park (☎ 815-942-0796), Channahon Access (☎ 815-467-4271) and Buffalo Rock State Park (☎ 815-433-2224). The centers

also have information about the portions of the canal suitable for canoeing. Call for details.

Lockport A good place to start the tour is the town of Lockport, 33 miles southwest of Chicago on Hwy 171, a historic place that's been bypassed by most of the development that has afflicted much-larger Joliet, to its south. The center of Lockport, which is on the National Register of Historic Places, includes the **I&M Canal Museum** (☎ *815-838-5080, 803 S State St; admission free; open 1pm-4:30pm daily)*, housed in the original 1837 home of the canal commissioners. It contains all the maps and brochures you didn't get in advance, as well as displays about life along the waterway when more flowed by than just the odd fallen leaf.

The surviving Lock No 1 is the highlight of the 2½-mile **Gaylord Donnelley Canal Trail**, which follows the canal through town and passes several exhibits along the way.

Morris The Kankakee and Des Plaines Rivers join near Morris, home to the **Goose Lake Prairie State Natural Area** (☎ *815-942-2899; open dawn-dusk daily)*, which contains the largest surviving portion of tall-grass prairie in Illinois. The plants, which early pioneers likened to an ocean of color, grew up to 10 or more feet in height and blossomed in waves through the growing season; what little survives is still worth seeing. A visitor center explains the unique ecology of the prairie, and on weekends a naturalist is usually around to answer questions. The area is on Jugtown Rd, which is off Lorenzo Rd (accessible from I-55 in the east and Hwy 47 in the west).

Seneca This small town is home to the **Seneca Grain Elevator**, a fascinating affair that towers over the canal, which is little more than a muddy ditch here. Completed in 1862, the 65-foot building is one of the oldest survivors from the early grain industry. Check with the Heritage Corridor Commission for hours, and be sure to get a copy of the heavily illustrated Park Service

EXCURSIONS

brochure that explains the workings of the place. Seneca is 65 miles from Chicago, on Route 6 off I-80.

On Hwy 6 about 4 miles west of Seneca, **Marseilles** has become known for two reasons: it's the site of the National Weather Service tornado warning radar and it boasts a quaint downtown with a cluster of antique stores and cute cafés.

Ottawa The **Illinois Waterway Visitors' Center** (☎ 815-667-4054; admission free; open 9am-8pm daily June-Sept, 8am-5pm other times) overlooks the Starved Rock

Lock, a major point on the waterway that replaced the I&M Canal. The lock is the focus of the center's several exhibits and observation deck. It's located some 88 miles from Chicago, off Dee Bennett Rd and Hwy 178.

Utica A charming small town, Utica has found itself a profitable place near the end of the I&M Canal zone and across the river from Starved Rock State Park. It's a good place to stroll or to stay if you're planning a visit to either Starved Rock or Matthiessen State Park.

EXCURSIONS

Gambling

Riverboat gambling began in Illinois in 1991. In the years since then, the entire motif has turned out to be a sham: the boats stopped leaving port in 1999, which makes them nothing more than small, somewhat cramped casinos. Meanwhile, state legislators are cutting deals to allow regular casino gambling on land. This would save casino-hungry yet landlocked Rosemont the effort of digging a big moat.

There's no mistaking riverboat gambling in Illinois for the gambling found in the mega-casinos of Nevada. Still, during an average month gamblers drop almost $1.25 billion into slot machines statewide and wager another $200 million at tables. Many of the customers are retirees lured to the 'boats' by cheap bus rides. But there's no question about who really wins: the average visitor to a riverboat casino leaves about $50 poorer.

The following casinos all lie within an hour of Chicago. Unless you get a bus ride, expect to drive. The floating casinos stay open almost 24 hours a day (usually 8:30am to 6:30am) and you can enter and exit as you wish; no longer do you have to wait for 'sailings.'

Empress Casino Joliet (☎ 815-744-9400, Empress Dr) Obelisks flank the entrance of the Empress, on the Des Plaines River near the confluence of I-55 and I-80 in Joliet. The building, a North African spectacle, looks like an extremely loose approximation of an Egyptian palace. The Empress I and Empress II are nearly identical sleek, modern-looking vessels, both simply decorated and almost devoid of windows.

Harrah's Joliet Casino (☎ 800-427-7247, 151 N Joliet St) Harrah's two boats are quite different from each other. The Northern Star is a modern yachtlike craft. The Southern Star II resembles an old riverboat complete with a big, working paddle wheel on the rear. To get there from Chicago, follow I-55 to Joliet.

Hollywood Casino Aurora (☎ 800-888-7777, 1 New York St) The Hollywood Casino's boats, City of Lights I and City of Lights II, look like riverboats without the paddle wheels. Inside, the rather opulent gaming areas feature brightly colored decor that reflects the Hollywood theme. To get there from Chicago, take I-290 west to I-88.

Grand Victoria Casino (☎ 847-888-1000, 250 S Grove Ave) Operated by Circus Circus Enterprises – one of the largest casino operators in Las Vegas – the Grand Victoria, on the Fox River in downtown Elgin, is a floating behemoth. Almost all of the 1200 gambling positions are on

The **LaSalle County Historical Society** (☎ 815-667-4861, Mill St at Canal St; admission $1/50¢ for adults/children; open noon-4pm Fri-Sun, also Wed & Thur June-Sept) features displays of items used by the people who lived and worked near the I&M Canal.

If you'd like to stay here, try the ***Starved Rock Inn*** (☎ 815-667-4238, at Hwys 6 and 178), where rustic cabins cost $49 to $60.

Starved Rock State Park One of the most popular parks in Illinois, Starved Rock State Park (☎ 815-667-4906, PO Box 509; admission free; open dawn-dusk daily) features more than 2600 acres of wooded bluffs, with 18 canyons that were carved through the limestone during the last ice age. After heavy rains a waterfall cascades down the head of each canyon.

According to legend, a band of Illinois Native Americans got trapped atop the park's 130-foot sandstone butte during a battle with the Ottawa and starved to death – hence the park name. Today the highest bluff here offers spectacular views. Some 15 miles of hiking trails wander through the park, and the Illinois River and

Gambling

one deck, giving the casino a spacious feel that approaches the roominess of some Las Vegas casinos. Reach the casino via I-90 west from Chicago.

Harrah's East Chicago (☎ 219-378-3000, Pastrick Marina) Another boat on a voyage to nowhere, the Harrah's barge is a huge four-level affair. It's 30 minutes from downtown Chicago on Hwy 912 (Cline Ave) in East Chicago. Plans call for a big hotel to be added in late 2001.

The following two casinos in northwest Indiana still have to abide by that state's rules requiring them to weigh anchor. They also close by 3am every night.

Trump Casino (☎ 888-218-7867) High-volume New York developer and self-promoter Donald Trump has found tough odds with his big-ticket casino, which lies in a remote part of Gary, Indiana, reachable by I-90 (take the Cline Ave/Hwy 912 exit and go north 3 miles). He's imperiously renamed the location 'Buffington Harbor' to camouflage the Gary connection, but gamblers seem to prefer the looser rules in Illinois.

Empress III (☎ 888-436-7737, 825 Empress Dr) Developers dug a big hole, filled it with water and plopped a boat into it. Voilà! Riverboat gambling in Hammond! Just off Hwy 41, the Empress operation seems to be biding its time until the Indiana legislature can be swayed to allow it to build a huge casino on land.

canyon waterways provide opportunities for paddled canoe jaunts. You can also take guided nature tours. The park rents canoes, horses, bikes and skis on a seasonal basis.

The **park visitor center** *(open 9am-5pm daily June-Sept & 1pm-4pm daily, 10am-4pm weekends at other times)* offers full information on the many rental opportunities, as well as the hiking trails and other park features. Although the park gets very crowded on summer weekends, you can always leave the throngs behind by hiking beyond Wildcat Canyon, which is less than a mile east of the main parking area. Less than a mile from this point is La Salle Canyon, where a waterfall turns into a glistening ice fall in the winter.

The park has become a popular spot for *camping*, with 133 electrified sites ($11). The *Starved Rock Lodge (☎ 815-667-4211, 800-868-7625, fax 815-667-4455)*, right in the park, manages to be rustic and modern at the same time. The 70-plus comfortable rooms start at $75 for doubles; cabins start at $65.

The park is off Hwy 178, a mile south of Utica, which lies across the river.

Matthiessen State Park A companion to Starved Rock, Matthiessen State Park *(☎ 815-667-4868)* is just across Hwy 178 but often attracts fewer crowds. It features dramatic limestone cliffs and chasms formed by water runoff to the river. Hiking, skiing and equestrian trails meander through the park.

NORTHWESTERN INDIANA

Most visitors think of this area as little more than a gray-and-brown blur outside the car as they whiz along I-80 or the Indiana Toll Road. The center of steel production in the US, northwestern Indiana suffers from the predictable side effects of heavy industry. Towns such as Hammond, Whiting and East Chicago bear all the environmental scars. Most Chicagoans only know of Whiting through the local news, which periodically updates them on the town's chemical plant explosions.

Gary is the most blighted of all. A company town built in the early 20th century by US Steel, it has degenerated into a center of poverty, decay and desolation, to say nothing of crime. It's not really a place to visit unless you're a sociology student. Even Gary native, pop star and oxygen fanatic Michael Jackson doesn't come back to his childhood home at 2300 Jackson St (the street was named for President Andrew Jackson long before Michael was born). His family has long since moved to sunnier (read: California) climes since the Jackson Five gave their first performance at Gary's Roosevelt High School in 1965.

Gary has tried to gamble its way to prosperity by giving out casino licenses, but so far the results have yielded little more than freshly paved roads; see the boxed text 'Gambling.'

The steel mills that line the Lake Michigan shore are enormous temples of industry. Raw materials from the Iron Range in Minnesota arrive in boats and feed huge blast furnaces, whose fiery output gives them a primordial quality. Unfortunately, typical American liability fears – coupled with little regard for public relations – means that the mills are mostly off limits to the public. The closest you can come to experiencing some of their awe is on an Amtrak or South Shore train that travels on tracks bisecting some of the plants.

LTV Steel does offer occasional **industrial tours** *(☎ 219-391-2226)* that give you the chance to see the entire steel-making process from the raw taconite pellets through the final roll of galvanized sheet metal. Call for details.

Indiana Dunes

Despite the dearth of natural attractions in northern Indiana, the Indiana Dunes are easily the most scenic part of the state. The prevailing winds of Lake Michigan have created more than 20 miles of sandy beaches and dunes here. On a windy day you can place an obstacle on the beach and watch a dune form behind it. Behind the sands, large areas of woods and wetlands have become major wildlife habitats.

Preserving the dunes, which today stretch about 21 miles east from Gary to Michigan City, has always been a struggle. The occasional vast and stinky steel mill amid the bucolic beauty shows which way the struggle has frequently gone. Initial attempts to designate the area as a national park in 1913 flopped under pressure from industry. The state of Indiana did manage to wrest some territory away from hungry industrialists in 1923, with the creation of Indiana Dunes State Park near Chesterton. In the 1950s Bethlehem Steel's construction of what was then the world's largest steel mill, on prime dunes at Burns Harbor, solidified public pressure to save the remaining stretches. Activist Dorothy Buell and Illinois Senator Paul Douglas led the fight, which resulted in the creation of the Indiana Dunes National Lakeshore in 1966. In the decades since, the designation has also effectively saved the dunes from full-scale real estate development. The areas where such development occurred in the 1950s and early '60s give some idea of the horrors that could have spread.

Today the entire area attracts huge crowds in summer months, when people from Chicago to South Bend flock to the shores for good swimming and general frivolity. Most don't take the time to explore the area's diverse natural wonders, but hikes offer escape from the crowds. Other times of year, the lake winds and pervasive desolation make the dunes a moody and memorable experience. You may well hear the low hum of the 'singing sands,' an unusual sound caused by the zillions of grains of sand hitting each other in the wind.

From Chicago, the frequent trains on the South Shore Line make a day trip to the dunes an excellent option (see the Getting There & Away section, later).

Indiana Dunes National Lakeshore

Administered by the National Park Service, this area encompasses much of the surviving dunes east and west of the state park. It also preserves large areas of wetlands and woods up to 2 miles behind the shoreline.

The **Dorothy Buell Memorial Visitors' Center** (☎ *219-926-7561, www.nps.gov/indu, Kemil Rd; open 9am-5pm daily*) features a section on the park's flora and fauna. The free, official map is up to the usual excellent park service standards. The center is just off Hwy 12, near the Beverly Shores rail station.

EXCURSIONS

MARK E GIBSON

Relaxing in the sun at Indiana Dunes State Park on Lake Michigan

The main attractions here are the beaches. Obviously, anywhere there are dunes there's beach, but only certain areas are developed. Swimming is allowed anywhere along the national lakeshore. On busy days, a short hike away from the folks clogging up a developed beach will yield an almost deserted strand. Developed beaches with lifeguards in summer, restrooms and concessions include the following:

Central Beach is a good place to escape the crowds. **Kemil Beach** lies right in the middle of a 10-mile stretch of beach. You can get away from the crowds by walking a mile or two east.

Mt Baldy Beach boasts the highest dunes, with namesake Mt Baldy offering the best views all the way to Chicago from its 120-foot peak. Don't look east or you'll see the environmental travesty of downtown Michigan City's coal-powered electric plant and huge cooling tower. The closest beach to Michigan City, this is by far the busiest of the lot.

West Beach is one of the best beaches because it draws fewer crowds than the others and features a number of nature hikes and trails.

If you'd rather be on your feet than flat on your back on the sand, the park service has done a good job of developing hiking trails through a range of terrain and environments.

A scenic **nature trail** begins at the Bailly-Chellberg Visitors' Center, a major site that's some distance from the beaches. The trail winds through the forest, whose diversity continues to astound botanists. Among the plants growing here are dogwood, Arctic berries and even cactus. The 1¾-mile trail passes restored log cabins from the 1820s and a farm built by Swedes in the 1870s.

The nicely varied 4-mile walk at **Cowles Bog Trail** combines marsh and dunes. The **Miller Woods Trail** passes dunes, woods and ponds, plus the Paul H Douglas Center for Environmental Education (☎ 219-926-7561), which offers day programs. At West Beach the **Long Lake Trail** is a classic wetlands walk around an inland lake.

Much of the national park area is good for **cycling**, although the traffic and the narrow shoulders on Hwy 12 can make that road dangerous. However, the Calumet Bike Trail runs west from near Michigan City almost to the Chelberg Farm, in the middle of the national lakeshore. **Cross-country skiing** is popular in the inland areas, especially along the trails described above.

Indiana Dunes State Park On summer days Indiana Dunes State Park (☎ 219-926-1952, 1600 North 25 E in Chesterton; admission $2-5 per person depending on day and season; beaches open daily, usually 9am-sunset, park open 7am-11pm daily Apr-Sept & 8am-10pm other times) is jammed with people hitting the beach. Several tall dunes attract those who like to climb to the top, roll all the way down and then say hello to their lunch.

During the summer you'll find hot dog stands and other amenities of varying merit. Unlike the neighboring national lakeshore, the state park regulates where you can swim and where you can't. Some of the other regulations have made it impossible for you to bring Fido or Bud: dogs and alcohol are strictly verboten.

Away from the mobbed beaches, the park features many secluded natural areas. In winter **cross-country skiing** is very popular; a ski rental facility operates near Wilson shelter. In summer the **hiking** can be excellent. Some highlights among the numbered trails include the following:

2 – good for spring flowers and ferns and popular with cross-country skiers

4 – passes through dunes that are in the process of being colonized by black oak trees

8 – surmounts three of the highest dunes and offers great views as a reward

Getting There & Away Trains on the South Shore Line (☎ 800-356-2079) depart frequently from Randolph St Station in Chicago and offer access to both the national lakeshore and the state park. The three key stops for the parks and beaches are Ogden Dunes ($6 one-way, 70 minutes), Dune Park ($6 one-way, 79 minutes) and Beverly Shores ($7 one-way, 85 minutes). Trains also come west from South Bend, which is 55 minutes from Beverly Shores.

To get to Lake View and Kemil Beaches and the Dorothy Buell Visitors' Center, exit at the Beverly Shores Station. For Indiana Dunes State Park and Cowles Bog Trail, get off at Dune Park. For West Beach, use the Ogden Dunes stop. All of the sights listed lie within a 2-mile walk of their respective stations.

If you're traveling by car, you'll do a lot of your driving along Hwy 12, a two-lane road that passes virtually all of the major sites at Indiana Dunes; it follows an old pioneer trail that linked Forts Dearborn and Wayne, which became Chicago and Fort Wayne, respectively. Quite scenic in parts, it carries the name Dunes Hwy for much of its length in the national park. I-94 links Chicago with Detroit and passes just south, and a few miles farther south is the Indiana Toll Rd (I-80/90); you can exit at either Portage (No 31) or Chesterton (No 39). The entrance to the state park lies at the end of Hwy 49, which connects to Hwy 12, Hwy 20, I-94 and the Indiana Toll Road (I-80/90).

You can park at all the beaches, trails and sights listed above. But on a warm weekend, the parking lots – just like the patches of sand closest to the lots – are stuffed to capacity, and the access roads are as coagulated as the hideous cheese on those snack bar nachos.

EXCURSIONS

Thanks

Many thanks to the travelers who used the last edition and wrote to us with helpful hints, useful advice and interesting anecdotes:

Susan Bidwell, EK Buckley, Geoff Caflisch, Joanna Clifton, Wendy Coe, Brenda Cooke, Miss Dorf, Laura Grego, Johannes Heinecke, Julia Hinde, Ingrid Hubbard, Teresa Johnston, John Kemp-Gee, Adrian Knight, David Lay, Cameron Lewis, Richard Tay, Steve Taylor

LONELY PLANET

You already know that Lonely Planet produces more than this one guidebook, but you might not be aware of the other products we have on this region. Here is a selection of titles which you may want to check out as well:

USA
ISBN 1 86450 308 4
US$24.99 • UK£14.99 • 179FF

Great Lakes
ISBN 1 86450 139 1
US$19.99 • UK£13.99 • 159FF

Hiking in the USA
ISBN 0 86442 600 3
US$24.99 • UK£14.99 • 179FF

USA Phrasebook
ISBN 0 86450 182 0
US$6.99 • UK£4.50 • 49FF

New York City
ISBN 1 86450 180 4
US$16.99 • UK£10.99 • 129FF

Toronto
ISBN 1 86450 217 7
US$15.99 • UK£9.99 • 119FF

Available wherever books are sold.

Index

Text

Places to Stay

Places to Eat

Bold indicates maps.

Boxed Text

MAP 1 CHICAGO

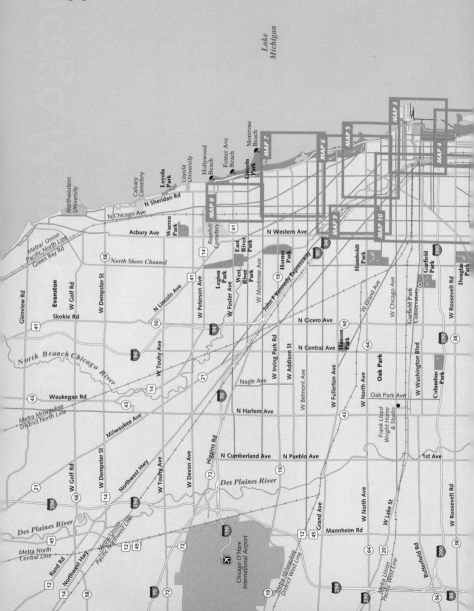

Calumet Ave

Wolf Lake

Calumet Park

Calumet River

Calumet Ave

Lake Calumet

Little Calumet River

130th St

Pullman

Jackson Park Beach

67th St Beach

South Shore Country Club Park

Rainbow Park

Jackson Park Golf Course

W 79th St

Jackson Park

S Lake Shore Drive

S Stony Island Ave

S 95th St

Metra Electric/South Shore Line

S Martin Luther King Jr Drive

S State St

Chicago State University

Metra Rock Island District Line

S Vincennes Ave

S Halsted St

MAP 11

MAP 12

Sherman Park

McKinley Park

E 51st St

S Ashland Ave

S Damen Ave

S Ashland Ave

S Western Ave

Marquette Park

Calumet Sag Channel

Sanitary Drainage and Ship Canal

S Kedzie Ave

W 55th St

S Archer Ave

W 59th St

W 63rd St

W Marquette Rd

Southwest Hwy

111th St

Burr Oak Ave

S Cicero Ave

Sportsman's Park Race Track

Hawthorne Race Track

S Cicero Ave

Chicago Midway Airport

Southwest Service Line

S Cicero Ave

Calumet Sag Rd

127th St

W Cermak Rd

Cicero

W Ogden Ave

W Pershing Rd

Adlai Stevenson Expressway

W 79th St

W 95th St

Metra SouthWest Service Line

S Harlem Ave

S Harlem Ave

Brookfield Zoo

S Archer Ave

Metra Heritage Corridor Line

96th Ave

Southwest Hwy

W Cermak Rd

W 31st St

W Ogden Ave

Plainfield Rd

Joliet Rd

143rd St

Salt Creek

W 55th St

Metra Burlington Northern Santa Fe Line

S Archer Ave

Des Plaines River

Garfield Ave

MAP 2 CHICAGO TRANSIT

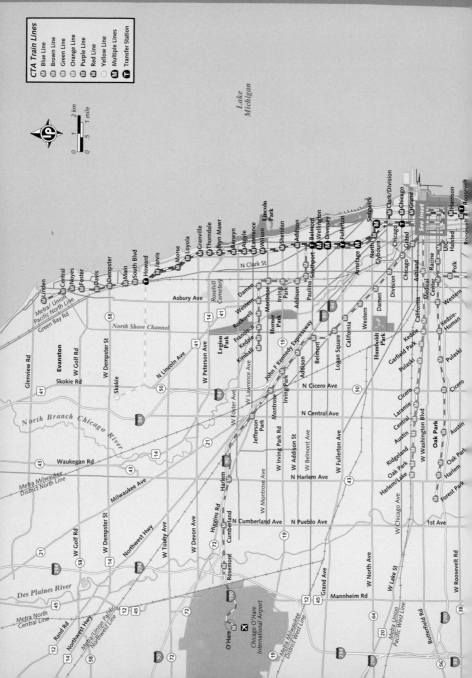

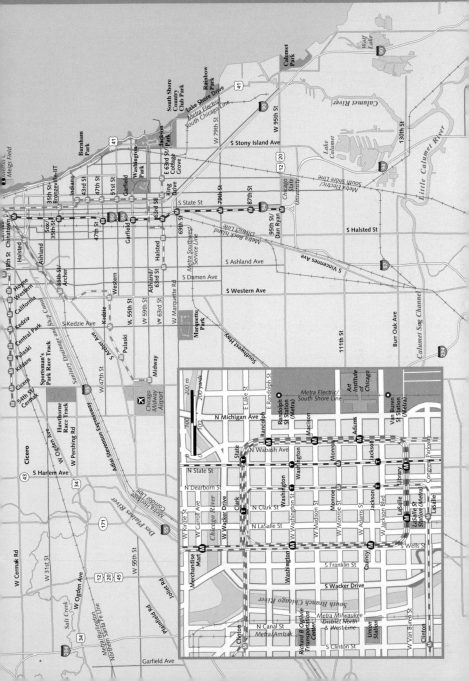

MAP 3 NEAR NORTH & LOOP

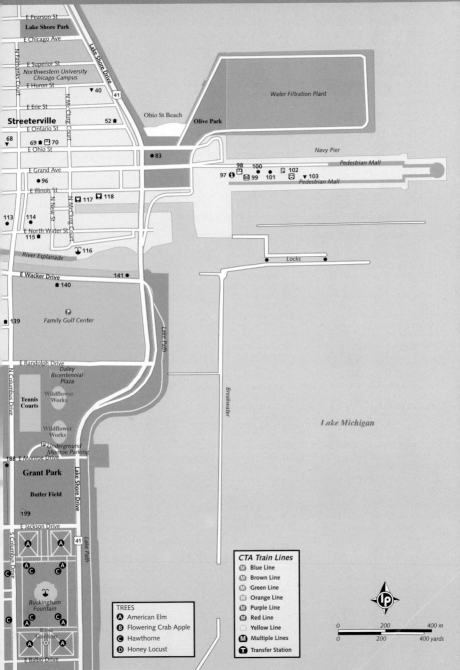

E Pearson St
Lake Shore Park
E Chicago Ave

E Superior St
Northwestern University
Chicago Campus
E Huron St
▼ 40
41

Streeterville
52 ▪
Ohio St Beach
Olive Park

68
▼
69 ▪ 70
E Ontario St
E Ohio St
● 83

Navy Pier

E Grand Ave
● 96
E Illinois St
157 117
118

113
●
114
●
115 ▪
E North Water St Court

River Esplanade
116

E Wacker Drive
141 ●
▪ 140

▪ 139
Family Golf Center

98 100
97 ⓘ 99 101
102
▼ 103
Pedestrian Mall
Pedestrian Mall

Water Filtration Plant

Locks

Lake Path

E Randolph Drive
Daley
Bicentennial
Plaza
**Tennis
Courts**
Wildflower
Works
Wildflower
Works
Underground
Monroe Parking
188
E Monroe Drive

Grant Park

Butler Field

199

E Jackson Drive
41

Ⓐ
Ⓐ
Ⓒ
Ⓒ
Ⓐ
Ⓒ
Ⓐ
Buckingham
Fountain
Ⓒ
Ⓐ
Ⓒ
Ⓐ
Ⓒ
Rose
Gardens
Ⓐ

E Balbo Drive

Breakwater

Lake Michigan

CTA Train Lines
Ⓜ Blue Line
Ⓜ Brown Line
Ⓜ Green Line
Ⓜ Orange Line
Ⓜ Purple Line
Ⓜ Red Line
Ⓜ Yellow Line
Ⓜ Multiple Lines
Ⓣ Transfer Station

TREES
Ⓐ American Elm
Ⓑ Flowering Crab Apple
Ⓒ Hawthorne
Ⓓ Honey Locust

0   200   400 m
0   200   400 yards

N Fairbanks Court
N McClurg Court
Lake Shore Drive
N New St
N McClurg Court
N Columbus Drive
N Columbus Drive
S Columbus Drive
Lake Shore Drive
Lake Path

MAP 3 NEAR NORTH & LOOP

PLACES TO STAY
- 15 The Peninsula
- 20 Howard Johnson Inn
- 26 Radisson Hotel & Suites
- 33 Hotel Wacker
- 35 Omni Chicago Hotel
- 47 Cass Hotel
- 50 Motel 6
- 52 W Chicago-Lakeshore
- 55 Ohio House Motel
- 59 Embassy Suites Chicago-Downtown; Papagus
- 64 Lenox Suites
- 67 Best Western Inn of Chicago
- 69 Holiday Inn-Chicago City Centre
- 76 Hilton Garden Inn
- 81 Chicago Marriott Hotel
- 95 Hotel Inter-Continental Chicago
- 106 Hampton Inn & Suites-Chicago River North
- 108 Courtyard by Marriott Chicago Downtown
- 115 Sheraton Chicago Hotel and Towers; Spectators
- 126 House of Blues Hotel
- 127 Westin River North
- 135 Renaissance Chicago Hotel
- 138 Hyatt Regency Chicago
- 139 Fairmont
- 140 Swissôtel Chicago; Palm
- 153 Hotel Allegro
- 165 Hotel Burnham
- 176 Silversmith
- 179 W Chicago City Center
- 182 Palmer House Hilton
- 211 Hostelling International-Chicago

PLACES TO EAT
- 8 Cafe Iberico
- 13 Pockets
- 14 Giordano's
- 21 Mike's Rainbow Restaurant
- 22 Whole Foods
- 23 Blackhawk Lodge
- 24 Rosebud on Rush
- 28 Erie Cafe
- 30 Green Door Tavern
- 31 Mr Beef
- 32 Leona's
- 34 Thai Star
- 38 Tru
- 40 Treasure Island
- 42 Ed Debevic's
- 43 Gino's East
- 44 Big Bowl; Wildfire
- 45 Pasha
- 48 O'Neil's Bar & Grill
- 49 Bice
- 51 Hatsuhana
- 53 Carson's-The Place for Ribs
- 56 Rock & Roll McDonald's
- 57 Rainforest Cafe
- 58 Hard Rock Cafe
- 62 Big Bowl
- 65 Heaven on Seven; 600 N Michigan Theaters
- 66 Bandera
- 68 Dao
- 72 Cyrano's Bistrot
- 77 Pizzeria Uno
- 80 Joe's Steak & Stone Crab
- 82 Boston Blackies
- 84 Gene and Georgetti
- 85 Hudson Club
- 89 Zinfandel
- 90 Spago
- 91 Ben Pao
- 103 Riva
- 105 Frontera Grill; Topolobampo
- 122 Brasserie Jo
- 123 Trattoria Parma
- 124 Gold Coast Dogs
- 125 Harry Caray's
- 130 Shaw's Crab House; Blue Crab Lounge
- 144 Corner Bakery; Peterino's
- 158 Heaven on Seven
- 164 Sopraffina
- 168 Boudin Bakery
- 170 Heartwise Express
- 180 Italian Village
- 181 The Grillroom
- 183 Miller's Pub
- 191 Berghoff; Stand Up Bar
- 194 Russian Tea Time
- 200 European Sunny Cafe
- 201 Pockets
- 202 Burrito Buggy
- 208 Everest
- 214 Artist's Snack Shop

THEATERS
- 102 Chicago Shakespeare Theater
- 142 Goodman Theatre
- 145 Ford Center/Oriental Theater
- 146 Noble Fool Theatre Company
- 149 Chicago Theater
- 154 Cadillac Palace Theater
- 173 Shubert Theater
- 213 Auditorium Theater

BARS & CLUBS
- 7 Brehon Pub
- 10 Clark St Ale House
- 11 Blue Chicago
- 12 Celtic Crossing
- 46 Excalibur
- 73 Voyeur
- 74 Blue Chicago on Clark
- 78 ESPNZone
- 88 Jazz Showcase
- 104 The Baton
- 107 Gentry
- 111 Billy Goat Tavern (lower level)
- 117 Dick's Last Resort; River East Plaza
- 118 Tavern on the Pier
- 128 House of Blues; Marina City
- 129 Andy's

OTHER
- 1 Orca Aart
- 2 Paper Source
- 3 Water Tower
- 4 Abraham Lincoln Book Shop
- 5 Carol Ehlers Gallery
- 6 Pearl
- 9 Police Station
- 16 CompUSA
- 17 Douglas Dawson Gallery
- 18 Jean Albano Gallery
- 19 Robert Henry Adams Fine Art
- 25 Chicago Place
- 27 Rora
- 29 Zolla-Lieberman Gallery
- 36 Terra Museum of American Art
- 37 Garrett Popcorn
- 39 Northwestern Memorial Hospital
- 41 Akainyah
- 54 Sportmart
- 60 Tree Studios
- 61 Medinah Temple
- 63 Harley Davidson Store
- 70 McClurg Court Theaters
- 71 Being Born
- 75 Fort Dearborn Post Office
- 79 DisneyQuest
- 83 Lake Point Tower
- 86 Rita Bucheit Ltd
- 87 Anti-Cruelty Society
- 92 American Medical Association
- 93 Nordstrom
- 94 Shops at North Bridge
- 96 River East Center
- 97 Illinois Marketplace Visitor Information Center
- 98 IMAX Theater
- 99 Chicago Children's Museum
- 100 Ferris Wheel
- 101 Skyline Stage
- 109 Jazz Record Mart
- 110 Lakeshore Athletic Club
- 112 Tribune Tower
- 113 NBC Tower
- 114 Floor Clock
- 116 Centennial Fountain
- 119 Antiques Centre at Kinzie Square
- 120 Antiquarians Building
- 121 Jay Robert's Antique Warehouse
- 131 Wrigley Building

MAP 3 NEAR NORTH & LOOP

Chicagoans make the best of a long winter.

RAY HILLSTROM JR

MAP 4 SOUTH LOOP & NEAR SOUTH SIDE

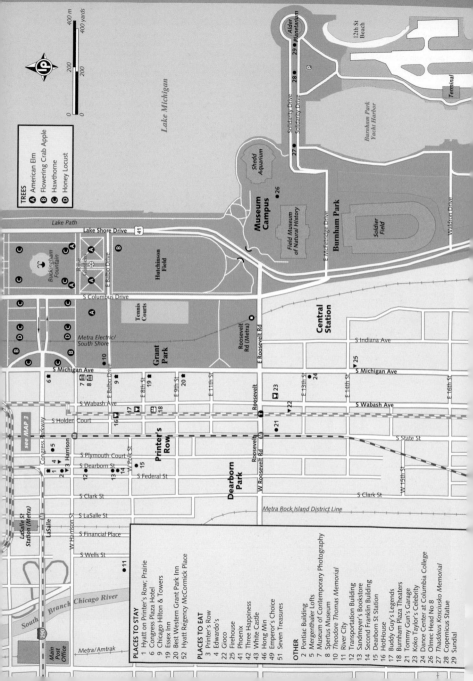

TREES
- A American Elm
- B Flowering Crab Apple
- C Hawthorne
- D Honey Locust

Lake Michigan

400 m
200
0

400 yards
200
0

12th St Beach

Adler Planetarium

Solidarity Drive

Burnham Park Yacht Harbor

Terminal

Waldron Drive

Shedd Aquarium

Museum Campus

Field Museum of Natural History

Burnham Park

Soldier Field

E McFetridge Drive

Lake Path

Lake Shore Drive

Buckingham Fountain

Rose Garden

E Balbo Drive

Hutchinson Field

S Columbus Drive

Tennis Courts

Grant Park

Metra Electric/ South Shore

S Michigan Ave

S Wabash Ave

S Holden Court

Congress Parkway

S Plymouth Court

S Dearborn St

S Federal St

S Clark St

S LaSalle St

S Financial Place

S Wells St

W Harrison St

LaSalle

LaSalle St Station (Metra)

Printer's Row

Dearborn Park

Central Station

Roosevelt Rd (Metra)

E Roosevelt Rd

S Indiana Ave

S Michigan Ave

S Wabash Ave

S State St

S Clark St

W 15th St

E 8th St

E 9th St

E 11th St

E 13th St

E 11th St

E 16th St

E Balbo Drive

E Harrison St

W Polk St

W Roosevelt Rd

Metra Rock Island District Line

see MAP 3

Chicago River

South Branch

Main Post Office

Metra/Amtrak

PLACES TO STAY
1 Hyatt on Printer's Row; Prairie
6 Congress Plaza Hotel
9 Chicago Hilton & Towers
19 Essex Inn
20 Best Western Grant Park Inn
52 Hyatt Regency McCormick Place

PLACES TO EAT
3 Printer's Row
4 Edwardo's
22 Gioco
25 Firehouse
41 Phoenix
42 Three Happiness
43 White Castle
46 Hong Min
49 Emperor's Choice
51 Seven Treasures

OTHER
2 Pontiac Building
5 Mergenthaler Lofts
7 Museum of Contemporary Photography
8 Spertus Museum
10 Theodore Thomas Memorial
11 River City
12 Transportation Building
13 Sandmeyer's Bookstore
14 Second Franklin Building
15 Dearborn St Station
16 HotHouse
17 Buddy Guy's Legends
18 Burnham Plaza Theaters
21 Tommy Gun's Garage
23 Koko Taylor's Celebrity
24 Dance Center at Columbia College
26 Olmec Head No 8
27 Thaddeus Kosciusko Memorial
28 Copernicus Statue
29 Sundial

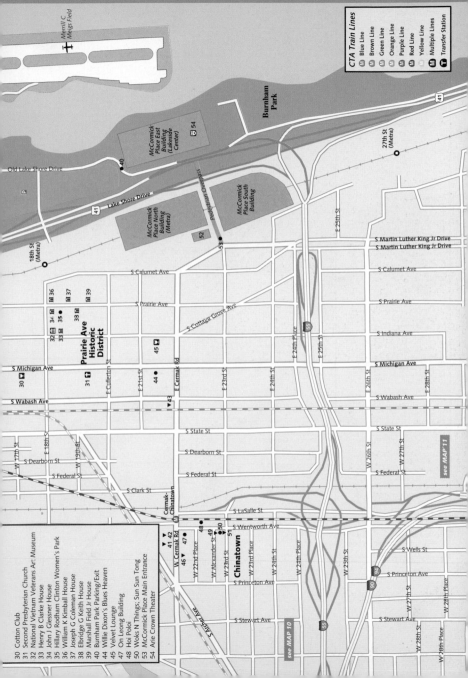

CTA Train Lines

- **Bl** Blue Line
- **Br** Brown Line
- **G** Green Line
- **O** Orange Line
- **P** Purple Line
- **R** Red Line
- **Y** Yellow Line
- **M** Multiple Lines
- **T** Transfer Station

Merrill C
Meigs Field

Burnham Park

Old Lake Shore Drive

McCormick Place East Building (Lakeside Center)

54

41 Lake Shore Drive

McCormick Place North Building (Metra)

McCormick Place South Building

Pedestrian Overpass

52

53

18th St (Metra)

27th St (Metra)

S Martin Luther King Jr Drive
S Martin Luther King Jr Drive

S Calumet Ave

S Calumet Ave

36
37
39

S Prairie Ave

S Prairie Ave

32
33 34 35
33

33

S Cottage Grove Ave

S Indiana Ave

E 24th Place

E 25th St

Prairie Ave Historic District

45

S Michigan Ave

S Michigan Ave

30

31

44

E Culterton St

E 21st St

S Cermak Rd

E Cermak St

E 23rd St

E 24th St

E 26th St

E 28th St

43

S Wabash Ave

S Wabash Ave

S State St

S State St

S Dearborn St

W 26th St

W 27th St

W 17th St

E 18th St

S Dearborn St

W 19th St

S Federal St

S Federal St

S Clark St

Cermak-Chinatown

S LaSalle St

S Wentworth Ave

S Wells St

41 42
46 47
48
49
50
51

W Cermak Rd

W 22nd Place

S Alexander St

W 23rd Place

W 24th Place

S Princeton Ave

W 25th Place

W 27th St

Chinatown

S Princeton Ave

S Stewart Ave

S Stewart Ave

W 28th Place

W 28th Place

30 Cotton Club
31 Second Presbyterian Church
32 National Vietnam Veterans Art Museum
33 Henry B Clarke House
34 John J Glessner House
35 Hillary Rodham Clinton Women's Park
36 William K Kimball House
37 Joseph G Coleman House
38 Elbridge G Keith House
39 Marshall Field Jr House
40 Burnham Park Parking/Exit
44 Willie Dixon's Blues Heaven
45 Velvet Lounge
47 On Leong Building
48 Hoi Poloi
50 Woks N Things; Sun Sun Tong
53 McCormick Place Main Entrance
54 Arie Crown Theater

see MAP 11

see MAP 10

MAP 5 GOLD COAST

CTA Train Lines
Ⓜ Blue Line
Ⓜ Brown Line
Ⓜ Green Line
Ⓜ Orange Line
Ⓜ Purple Line
Ⓜ Red Line
Ⓜ Yellow Line
Ⓜ Multiple Lines
Ⓣ Transfer Station

Lincoln
Park Zoo

South
Pond

Lincoln Park

North Ave
Beach

North Ave
Beach
House

Lake Michigan

LaSalle Drive

see MAP 6

W Menomonee St
W Willow St
W St Paul Ave
W Eugenie St

W North Ave

N Lincoln Park West
N Clark St
N Stockton Drive
N Cannon Drive
Lake Shore Drive

N Orleans St
N North Park Ave
N Wieland St
N Wells St
N LaSalle St
N Clark St
N Dearborn St
N State St
N Astor St

W Burton Pl

W Schiller St

W Evergreen Ave

Gold Coast

W Goethe St

W Scott St

Clark/Division

E Banks St

E Scott St

E Division St

E Elm St

E Cedar St

W Maple St

W Oak St

Washington
Square

W Chestnut St

W Institute Place

Chicago

Oak St
Beach

E Bellevue Place

E Walton St

E Delaware Place

John
Hancock
Center

E Chestnut St

E Pearson St

Seneca
Park

Lake Shore Park

E Chicago Ave

Northwestern University
Chicago Campus

see MAP 3

N Franklin St
N Orleans St
N Wells St
N LaSalle St
N Clark St
N Dearborn St
N State St
N Wabash Ave
N Rush St
N Michigan Ave
N Seneca St
N DeWitt Place
Lake Shore Drive

MAP 6 OLD TOWN & LINCOLN PARK

see MAP 7

see MAP 9

see MAP 10

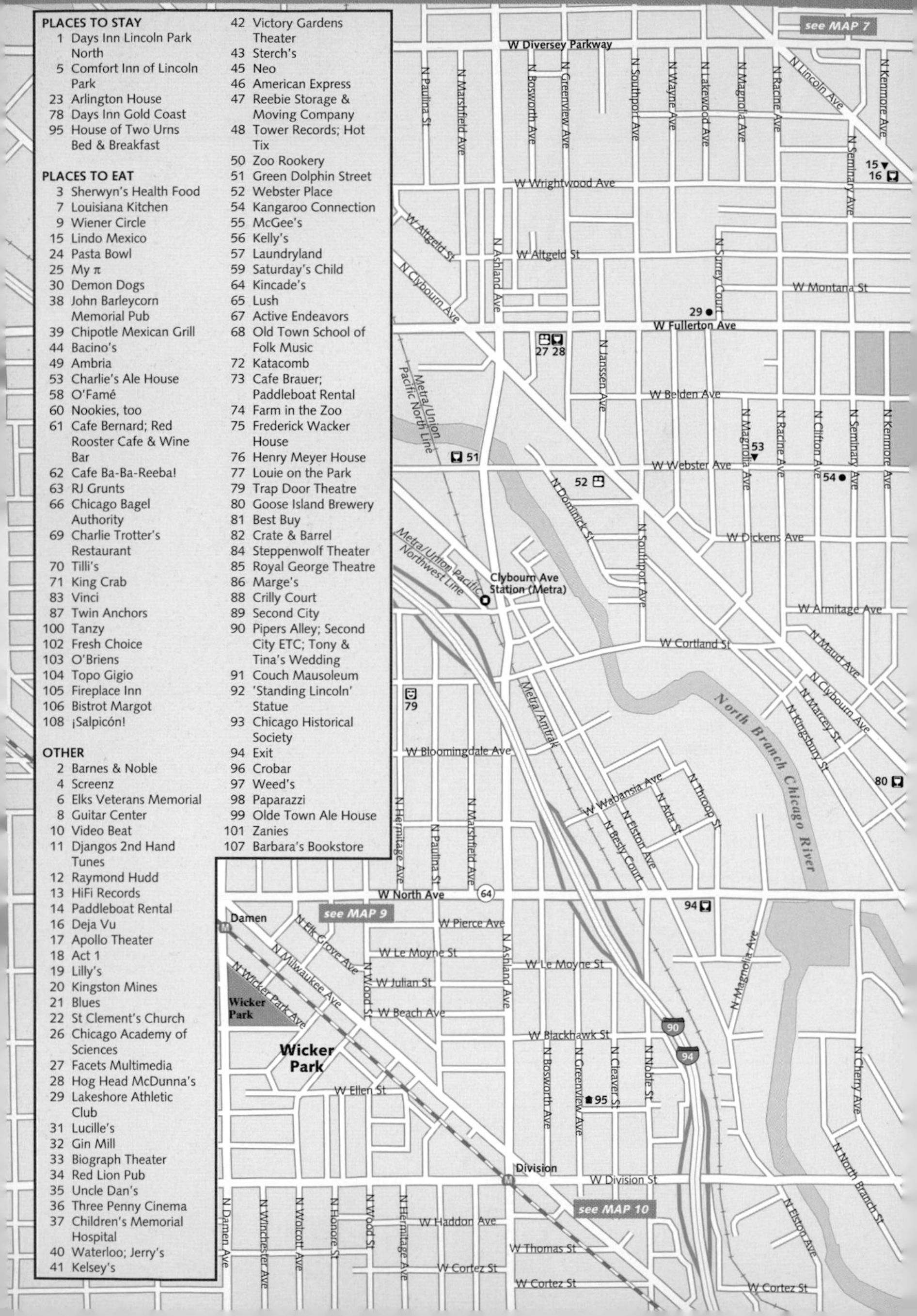

M Diversey

W Diversey Parkway
W Diversey Pkwy

Diversey Harbor

Fullerton Beach

N Sheffield Ave
N Wilton Ave
N Mildred St
N Dayton St

7

8

1
2 3
5
4 N Clark St
6

W Schubert Ave

N Burling St
N Orchard St

N Hampden Court

N Lakeview Ave

9
10
11
12
13

W Wrightwood Ave

N Cannon Drive

14

North Pond

20
17 19
18
31
32 33
34
35
36
30

W Lill Ave
W Altgeld St

21
22

23
24 25

W Deming Place
W St James Pl
W Arlington Place
W Arlington Place

26

M Fullerton
T Fullerton

De Paul University

37

Lincoln Park

38

39
40
43
44
41
42

45
46
47
48
49

W Fullerton Ave

50

N Stockton Drive

Lincoln Park Conservatory

N Lincoln Ave

W Belden Ave

55
56

57
59
60
61
62

58

69

W Webster Ave

N Geneva Terrace

Oz Park

W Dickens Ave

63

N Lincoln Ave
N Mohawk St
N Cleveland Ave
N Hudson Ave
N Sedgwick St
N Orleans St

W Dickens Ave

Lincoln Park

N Stockton Drive

Lincoln Park Zoo

Lake Michigan

64 65
66 67
68
70
71

M Armitage

W Armitage Ave

N Dayton St
N Halsted St
N Burling St
N Orchard St
N Howe St

W Wisconsin St

72
73
74

South Pond

North Ave Beach

W Wisconsin St
W Menomonee St

N Sheffield Ave
N Bissell St
N Fremont St

83

84 85

81

82

M North/Clybourn

97

96

98

71

W Willow St

86
87
88

N Park Court

W Menomonee St
W Willow St
W St Paul Ave

75
76
77 78
89
90

Old Town

W Eugenie St
W Eugenie St

64

N LaSalle Drive

91 92
93

North Ave Beach House

64 W North Ave

99 100 101
102
103
104
105
106

M Sedgwick

N Sedgwick St
N North Park Ave
N Orleans St
N Wieland St
N North Park Ave
N LaSalle St
N Clark St
N Dearborn St
N State Parkway
N Astor St

W Blackhawk St

107

108

W Schiller St

W Evergreen Ave

W Goethe St

W Scott St

Gold Coast

see MAP 5

E Banks St

E Scott St

N Clybourn Ave
N Ogden Ave

W Blackhawk St

Stanton Schiller Park

W Evergreen Ave

W Sullivan St

W Scott St

Goose Island

North Branch Chicago River

N Kingsbury St
N Dayton St
N Halsted St

W Division St

M Clark/Division

E Division St
E Elm St
E Cedar St
E Bellevue St

N Cherry Ave
N Hickory Ave
N Crosby St
N Larrabee St
N Cambridge Ave
N Cleveland Ave

N Hooker St

W Elm St

Cabrini-Green

W Maple St

N Orleans St
N Wells St
N LaSalle St
N Clark St
N Dearborn St

to MAP 3

N Lake Shore Drive
N Lake Shore Drive

41

41

M

IP

0   200   400 m
0   200   400 yards

CTA Train Lines

M Blue Line
M Brown Line
M Green Line
M Orange Line
M Purple Line
M Red Line
M Yellow Line
M Multiple Lines
T Transfer Station

MAP 7 LAKE VIEW & WRIGLEYVILLE

to MAP 8

W Cuttom Ave

Graceland Cemetery

W Buena Ave

W Berteau Ave

0 200 400 m
0 200 400 yards

W Belle Plaine Ave

● 1

W Irving Park Rd ⑲

W Irving Park Rd ⑲

Sheridan Ⓜ

W Dakin St

2 ▼   3 ▣

Hebrew Cemetery

5 ▼

W Sheridan Rd

W Byron St

Wunders Cemetery

W Grace St

● 6

W Grace St

▣ 7

▼ 4

8 ●   ▼ 9
      ▼ 10
      ▣ 11
      ▼ 12

Wrigleyville

W Bradley Place

13 ▼   ▣ 14
       ● 15
       ● 16

17 ▼
18 ▼
19 ▼
20 ▼
21 ▣

W Waveland Ave

W Waveland Ave

▼ 24
▼ 25

Wrigley Field

● 22

26 ▣

29 ●
30 ▼

Addison Ⓜ

W Addison St

W Addison St

● 27   28 ▣

31 ▼
33 ▼
35 ▼
37 ▼
38 ▼

46 ●

▼ 47

32 ▣

W Eddy St

34 ▼
36 ▼

39 ▼
41 ▼
43 ▼

W Cornelia Ave

48 ▼

▼ 49
▼ 50

W Cornelia Ave

40 ▼
42 ▼
44 ▼
45 ▼

51 ▼

▣ 52
▼ 53

▼ 55
▼ 56
▼ 57

W Newport Ave

59 ▼
60 ▼

61 ▼
62 ▼
63 ▼

65 ▼

Paulina Ⓜ

Southport Ⓜ

58 ▼

W Roscoe St

64 ▼

W Roscoe St

66 ▼
67 ▼
68 ▼

72 ▼
73 ▼

69 ▼

71 ▼

74 ▼

W Buckingham Pl

76 ▼
77 ▼

79 ▼

75 ▼

78 ▼

80 ▼

W School St

W Henderson St

W School St

▼ 81

89 ▼
90 ▼
91 ▼
92 ▼

93 ▼

▣ 83

82 ●

W Melrose St

86 ▼

94 ▼
95 ▼

▣ 96
▼ 97

84 ● 85 ●

87 ▼
88 ▼

Belmont Ⓣ

W Belmont Ave

W Belmont Ave

106 ▼ 107 ●

▣ 100

▣ 101 ▣ 102

103 ▼

108 ▼

▣ 109

W Fletcher St

105 ▼

W Fletcher St

104 ▼

99 ●

W Barry Ave

W Barry Ave

W Nelson St

112 ▼

Wellington Ⓜ

110 ▣

W Wellington Ave

W Wellington Ave

111 ▣

W Oakdale Ave

W Oakdale Ave

114 ▼

▼ 115

W George St

W George St

● 116

113 ●

to MAP 6

Lincoln Park

W Wolfram St

W Wolfram St

Diversey Ⓜ

W Diversey Parkway

CTA Train Lines

Ⓜ Blue Line
Ⓜ Brown Line
Ⓜ Green Line
Ⓜ Orange Line
Ⓜ Purple Line
Ⓜ Red Line
Ⓜ Yellow Line
Ⓜ Multiple Lines
Ⓣ Transfer Station

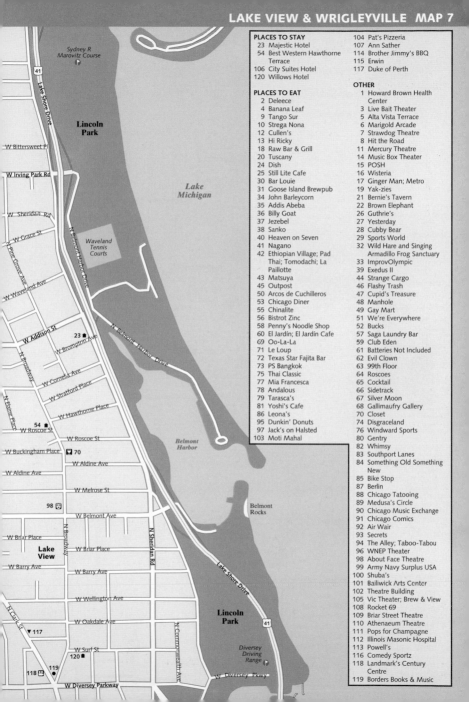

PLACES TO STAY
23 Majestic Hotel
54 Best Western Hawthorne Terrace
106 City Suites Hotel
120 Willows Hotel

PLACES TO EAT
2 Deleece
4 Banana Leaf
9 Tango Sur
10 Strega Nona
12 Cullen's
13 Hi Ricky
18 Raw Bar & Grill
20 Tuscany
24 Dish
25 Still Lite Cafe
30 Bar Louie
31 Goose Island Brewpub
34 John Barleycorn
35 Addis Abeba
36 Billy Goat
37 Jezebel
38 Sanko
40 Heaven on Seven
41 Nagano
42 Ethiopian Village; Pad Thai; Tomodachi; La Paillotte
43 Matsuya
45 Outpost
50 Arcos de Cuchilleros
53 Chicago Diner
55 Chinalite
56 Bistrot Zinc
58 Penny's Noodle Shop
60 El Jardín; El Jardín Cafe
69 Oo-La-La
71 Le Loup
72 Texas Star Fajita Bar
73 PS Bangkok
75 Thai Classic
77 Mia Francesca
78 Andalous
79 Tarasca's
81 Yoshi's Cafe
86 Leona's
95 Dunkin' Donuts
97 Jack's on Halsted
103 Moti Mahal

104 Pat's Pizzeria
107 Ann Sather
114 Brother Jimmy's BBQ
115 Erwin
117 Duke of Perth

OTHER
1 Howard Brown Health Center
3 Live Bait Theater
5 Alta Vista Terrace
6 Marigold Arcade
7 Strawdog Theatre
8 Hit the Road
11 Mercury Theatre
14 Music Box Theater
15 POSH
16 Wisteria
17 Ginger Man; Metro
19 Yak-zies
21 Bernie's Tavern
22 Brown Elephant
26 Guthrie's
27 Yesterday
28 Cubby Bear
29 Sports World
32 Wild Hare and Singing Armadillo Frog Sanctuary
33 ImprovOlympic
39 Exedus II
44 Strange Cargo
46 Flashy Trash
47 Cupid's Treasure
48 Manhole
49 Gay Mart
51 We're Everywhere
52 Bucks
57 Saga Laundry Bar
59 Club Eden
61 Batteries Not Included
62 Evil Clown
63 99th Floor
64 Roscoes
65 Cocktail
66 Sidetrack
67 Silver Moon
68 Gallimaufry Gallery
70 Closet
74 Disgraceland
76 Windward Sports
80 Gentry
82 Whimsy
83 Southport Lanes
84 Something Old Something New
85 Bike Stop
87 Berlin
88 Chicago Tatooing
89 Medusa's Circle
90 Chicago Music Exchange
91 Chicago Comics
92 Air Wair
93 Secrets
94 The Alley; Taboo-Tabou
96 WNEP Theater
98 About Face Theatre
99 Army Navy Surplus USA
100 Shuba's
101 Bailiwick Arts Center
102 Theatre Building
105 Vic Theater; Brew & View
108 Rocket 69
109 Briar Street Theatre
110 Athenaeum Theatre
111 Pops for Champagne
112 Illinois Masonic Hospital
113 Powell's
116 Comedy Sportz
118 Landmark's Century Centre
119 Borders Books & Music

MAP 8 ANDERSONVILLE

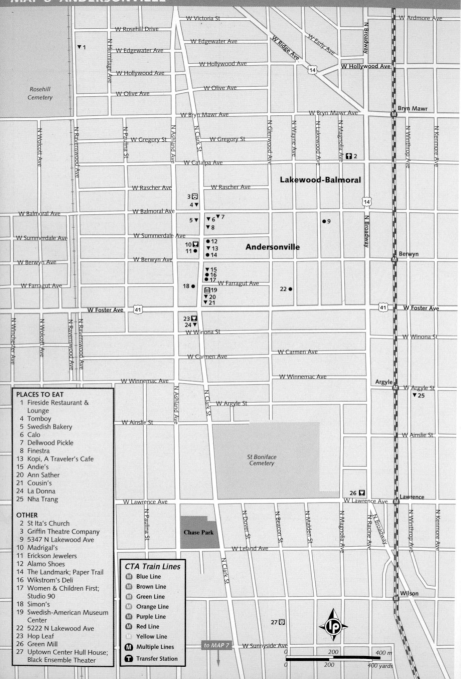

Rosehill Cemetery

▼1

W Rosehill Drive
W Victoria St
W Edgewater Ave
W Edgewater Ave
W Hollywood Ave
W Hollywood Ave
W Olive Ave
W Olive Ave
W Bryn Mawr Ave
W Gregory St
W Gregory St
W Catalpa Ave
W Rascher Ave
W Rascher Ave
W Balmoral Ave
W Balmoral Ave
W Summerdale Ave
W Summerdale Ave
W Berwyn Ave
W Berwyn Ave
W Farragut Ave
W Farragut Ave
W Foster Ave
W Winona St
W Carmen Ave
W Carmen Ave
W Winnemac Ave
W Winnemac Ave
W Argyle St
W Argyle St
W Ainslie St
W Ainslie St
W Lawrence Ave
W Lawrence Ave
W Leland Ave
W Sunnyside Ave

W Ardmore Ave
W Early Ave
W Ridge Ave
W Hollywood Ave
Bryn Mawr
Lakewood-Balmoral
Andersonville
Berwyn
Argyle
Lawrence
Wilson
St Boniface Cemetery
Chase Park
St Ita's Church

N Hermitage Ave
N Ravenswood Ave
N Paulina St
N Ashland Ave
N Clark St
N Glenwood Ave
N Wayne Ave
N Lakewood Ave
N Magnolia Ave
N Broadway
N Winthrop Ave
N Kenmore Ave
N Wolcott Ave
N Winchester Ave
N Wolcott Ave
N Ravenswood Ave
N Dover St
N Beacon St
N Malden St
N Magnolia Ave
N Racine Ave
N Broadway
N Winthrop Ave
N Kenmore Ave

14
14
14
41
41

2

3 ⬚
4 ▼
5 ▼
▼6 ▼7
▼8
• 9
10 ⬚
11 •
• 12
▼ 13
• 14
18 •
▼ 15
• 16
• 17
🏛19
▼ 20
▼ 21
22 •
23 ⬚
24 ▼
25 ▼
26 ⬚
27 ⬚

to MAP 7

200   400 m
200   400 yards

PLACES TO EAT
1 Fireside Restaurant & Lounge
4 Tomboy
5 Swedish Bakery
6 Calo
7 Dellwood Pickle
8 Finestra
13 Kopi, A Traveler's Cafe
15 Andie's
20 Ann Sather
21 Cousin's
24 La Donna
25 Nha Trang

OTHER
2 St Ita's Church
3 Griffin Theatre Company
9 5347 N Lakewood Ave
10 Madrigal's
11 Erickson Jewelers
12 Alamo Shoes
14 The Landmark; Paper Trail
16 Wikstrom's Deli
17 Women & Children First; Studio 90
18 Simon's
19 Swedish-American Museum Center
22 5222 N Lakewood Ave
23 Hop Leaf
26 Green Mill
27 Uptown Center Hull House; Black Ensemble Theater

CTA Train Lines
Ⓜ Blue Line
Ⓜ Brown Line
Ⓜ Green Line
Ⓜ Orange Line
Ⓜ Purple Line
Ⓜ Red Line
Ⓜ Yellow Line
Ⓜ Multiple Lines
Ⓣ Transfer Station